The Pursuit of Peace

The Pursuit of Peace

Leonard W. Doob

GREENWOOD PRESS

WESTPORT, CONNECTICUT • LONDON, ENGLAND

Library of Congress Cataloging in Publication Data

Doob, Leonard William, 1909-
  The pursuit of peace.

  Bibliography: p.
  Includes index.
  1.   Peace.   2.   Peace—Research.   I.   Title.
JX1952.D66   327.1'72   80–1201
ISBN 0–313–22630–X (lib. bdg.)

Library of Congress Catalog Card Number: 80–1201
ISBN: 0–313–22630–X

First published in 1981

Greenwood Press
A division of Congressional Information Service, Inc.
88 Post Road West
Westport, Connecticut 06881

Printed in the United States of America

10 9 8 7 6 5 4 3 2 1

To Three Other Pursuers
Chris, Tony, Nick

Contents

The Pursuit
of Peace

1.
Prologue

Let us peacefully begin to pursue peace by proclaiming five propositions probably not evoking dissent, at least at first glance, but requiring studied reflection. First, no matter how the terms are defined, peace is considered desirable, war undesirable. The horrors of war and the joys of peace are proclaimed in many languages: *quelle terrible chose que la guerre;*[1] *schon immer war die Sehnsucht nach Frieden eine der stärksten Triebkräfte im Denken der Menschheit;*[2] "for as long as men and women have talked about war, they have talked about it in terms of right and wrong."[3] But wars persist, and there are societies in which they are truly valued: some human beings, perhaps all human beings at some time, obviously find them more attractive or necessary than peace. These positive features of war, however, are ordinarily justified reluctantly or deceptively.

Secondly, "the power to destroy the entire world, which never existed before, now unites the world."[4] Unquestionably the first part of the assertion is valid, but the second part is little more than an unsubstantiated prayer. Nobody, except a paranoid idiot, wishes to unleash the deadly weapons of our time, unless some compelling excuse—self-defense?—is at hand or can be fabricated. Are we only paying lip service when we agree that, because of the deadly weapons, the pursuit of peace is a "collective obligation" no longer to be ignored? Can we afford to await some prior reform—a change in child-rearing practices?—before international conflicts can be controlled? At this point in time wars may occur less frequently than in the Middle Ages, but their scope and the damage they cause is much, much greater.[5]

Thirdly, statesmen, biologists, social scientists, and ordinary individuals are sharply divided as to whether peace can ever be attained. Optimistic hopes that wars can be prevented compete with pessimistic forebodings that they are inevitable.[6] A middle position suggests that armed violence can never be eliminated, but possibly—probably?—"the ritual organization of violence" which leads to the slaughtering of millions can be made to disappear.[7]

We are, fourthly, literally engulfed in ideas, devices, plans, and proposals that purport to be sound prescriptions for peace. They range from the reformation of man or his philosophy to strengthening developing countries or the United Nations,[8] but they are less detailed and precise than the war plans of military staffs.

Fifthly and finally, peace and war have preoccupied many of mankind's most profound thinkers since classical times.[9] Recently they have been the objects of intensive research. The consequences of all this thought and scholarly endeavor are unclear. Some modern sages are convinced that for the first time in history there exists "a reasonably accurate, comprehensive, scientifically-based picture" of human destiny[10] that can be enlisted in behalf of peace. The contrary view is also vehemently expressed that "knowledge necessary for effective peace action" simply does not exist.[11] (See Chapter Appendix 1.1: Propositions Concerning Peace.)*

The peace research mentioned in the fifth proposition above and in Chapter Appendix 1.1 as well as relevant knowledge from modern social science, psychology, psychiatry, and history will be *sampled* throughout this book. *Sampled* is set in italics to emphasize my own fallibility and the vast resources (not all of them significant) at our disposal; inevitably the choice must be somewhat biased. The aim, however, is to offer representative research.

Another unoriginal bias must be expressed in this prologue. Like most peace researchers, I believe I am on the side of the angels. I favor peace, not war. Conceivably, I think, peace is possible, or at least some wars are avoidable. But I am cynical. As has been cogently argued, when the world's population growth and indeed also the arms race are contemplated, I am convinced that no technical solution to the problem of war-peace is close by or even probable. Wars occur; for all the reasons suggested in Chapter Appendix 1.1, they are evil. End of preaching.

Without being properly defined, the words *peace* and *war* slip by in ordinary speech and also so far in this account: a very impolite and confusing procedure, any right-thinking woman or man must agree. Having struggled with the concept of evil[12]—surely one of war's progenitors and descendants—I am fully aware of the futility of forcing a definition of

---

*Chapter appendixes provide additional, hopefully not unimportant, information and and documentation when necessary. They are segregated at the end of each chapter in order to simplify the exposition.

cosmic categories upon myself or anyone else. Consulting the wise men or common usage is of no great assistance. (See Chapter Appendix 1.2: Defining War and Peace.) Under these somewhat bewildering circumstances all that can be done, in my opinion, is to assemble the most cogent and potentially useful connotations of the two terms:

1. War and peace are at the ends of a continuum, at one extreme of which is the worst possible holocaust, at the other the most alluring utopia. Any specific action by a government must fall some place along this continuum; thus, as is obvious, preparing for battle or carrying out a bombing raid leans toward the war end, disarmament or negotiation toward the peace end; in between is economic warfare (scarce goods are given or sold to, or bought from countries that actually are, or hopefully might become, friendly; they are withheld or not bought from unfriendly countries).[13] The reference to a continuum is in line with the view that "the transition between war and peace" in recent years has become "very fluid."[14] The expression *war-peace* hereafter shall signal the continuum.

2. War-peace refers not to a single event but a series of events in time. For peace is not attained by a treaty or a conference when one side surrenders and fighting ceases.[15] Closer scrutiny reveals that the end of hostilities means only that one aspect of the situation has changed, namely, the formal fighting; that individuals' attitudes on both sides probably remain relatively fixed; and that the armistice or cease-fire is only the first in a series of events that will occur, doubtless, during the succeeding years.

3. War-peace refers also both to overt actions and to covert feelings, attitudes, and impulses of many individuals living in one or more societies. Overtly, there may or may not be fighting, a large or a small budget for armaments, an aggressive or a mild foreign policy. Covertly, the citizens of a country may or may not feel secure, anxious, or exploited. An individual at peace with himself behaves in a particular manner and does not suffer from internal conflicts—but ordinarily war-peace includes "a social system,"[16] which means that many individuals are interacting now and in the future.

The referents of war-peace are ordinarily three in number: the individuals who experience war-peace; the countries or ethnic groups which are at peace or at war; and the relations between those countries or groups. The trinity is often reduced to a duality: the individual and his society. For example, a contrast can be drawn between the "inborn biological traits of the human species" and the "imperfection in human institutions."[17] War-peace, it must be emphasized, always involves human beings even when they are never or not immediately either observable or identifiable; this self-evident proposition is one of the central features emphasized in the present analysis. Since such an approach is admittedly vulnerable, however, the criticism directed against it must be examined at some length. (See Chapter Appendix 1.3: Individuals, Countries, and International Relations.) What should be done, in my opinion, is to push the approach via persons as far as possible, knowing full well that in many instances the quest may turn out to be futile.

To explore the implications of this approach, let me be concrete: no one can deny that Germany invaded Poland on 1 September 1939 and that World War II then began. Here is a historical fact, and for purposes of the historical record the statement as it stands is sufficient. When the question is asked concerning the reasons for the invasion, however, references must be made principally to particular leaders in Germany, Poland, and other countries. We are thus on the level of individuals. Why did Hitler make the decision to launch the invasion? The explanation is to be found in his personality, in the German people, and in previous events which had an impact upon him and them. The Germans who supported Hitler fully, partially, or not at all cannot be adequately specified, although Hitler's close associates are reasonably well known. The events in the past can be named, such as the Treaty of Versailles, the inflation in Germany after World War I, and the depression of the 1930s. These events conceal the names of individuals but describe the outcome of interactions between innumerable persons inside and outside Germany. A knowledge of the interactions, if it can be acquired—and only bits and pieces can be—would provide additional insight into the outbreak of the war. Tracing each interaction, however, requires such a tremendous effort that in a finite world it becomes necessary at some point to say *halt*: reduce Hitler's personal decision to invade Poland to the acts of individuals, but deal with prior events as impersonal occurrences without attempting a similar reduction. Such a search for persons becomes necessary when an attempt is made, as at the Nuremberg trials after World War II, to punish those leaders who, according to some criteria, are criminally responsible for beginning a war or for inhuman actions during the conflict; but entire "nations" are punished when they are occupied by victors or when their governments are forced to pay reparations. Similarly it might be possible to locate and analyze at least some of the persons who have promoted the traditional friendship between the United States and Canada. For the war-peace analysis such a search would be a waste of time *if* only the present policies of the Canadian and American governments are being discussed but not when deviations from the policies occur.

There is no escape, therefore, from collective, individual-dodging terms such as *nation*, *government*, and *foreign office*, but they will be used as sparingly as possible. Occasionally, when the additional phrase does not sound too awkward, these terms will be preceded by *leaders in*, *persons in*, or *individuals in*, even when those leaders, persons, or individuals cannot be identified or located. Also, less frequently, the word *nation* will be enclosed in quotation marks to indicate that it is functioning as a metaphor. Preference, whenever possible, will be given to the word *country* since countries at least from one standpoint are not metaphors: they are fixed pieces of land observable on maps and from planes.

A wisp of poetry suggests a way of referring to these persons or individuals: each man in his time plays many parts, and time refers not only, as Shakespeare stated, to the progression and changes throughout his life but also to the interrelated orientations and roles he assumes from day to day, even from moment to moment. Three roles may be distinguished on the basis of their referents:

1. *Individual*: the persons's feelings and actions regarding himself and his goals and regarding his primary groups (family, associations, school, church). He reads a report in the local newspaper and wonders how the event will affect him or his community.

2. *National*: the persons's feelings and actions regarding the country in which he lives and with which he identifies himself. He reads another report in the paper and wonders how the event will affect his country's economy or its defense program.

3. *International*: the persons's feelings and actions regarding other countries, the relation of his own country to one or more other countries, or to the international community. He reads yet another report in the paper and wonders how the event will affect the foreign policy of a particular country.

Since the same person can be oriented in each of these three ways, no sharp lines can or should be drawn to separate them: some consistency is to be anticipated in his feelings and behavior, no matter how he is oriented in a given situation. He may be stubborn or relaxed regarding his own ambitions, his fellow employees, his patriotism, and a neighboring country. Complete consistency is seldom attained: the negotiator who relaxes at home may be a very stern diplomat abroad. Thus arises the problem of personality and personality traits.

OVERVIEW: A MODEL FOR ROUTES

Whether we who would pursue the study of war-peace are like the blind men whose reports differ because they are touching different parts of the elephant is doubtful for two reasons. We are not blind, and we know we are having contact with different parts of the beast. Also the word *elephant* does not quite convey the magnitude of the pursuit; some kind of prehistoric dinosaur would seem more appropriate. But unquestionably the problem is gigantic, and existing analyses largely depend upon the kind of question raised and the data examined. A particular war or wars in general may be attributed to human nature, to a tradition of nationalism within a society, or to the failure of diplomacy. What is needed is an overview which neglects none of the details and which somehow places all or almost all of them in perspective: "like all human problems, that of war and peace can only be studied and thought about piecemeal and in compartments, and there is no danger in doing this provided we cling like limpets to the fact that each piece is a piece and not the whole meal, that each compartment is a single compartment and not the whole train."[18] Let us, therefore, cling.

On page 9 is a single, staggering diagram: an elephant—or dinosaur. Peering at the monster without warning is like looking directly into the sun: not one's eyes but one's intellect can be severely damaged. To avoid damage observe only the numbered sections, one at a time. Those sections will be called *routes*. In the exposition which follows as well as throughout the subheadings and the headings of the chapter appendixes of this book, the appropriate arabic numbers, with or without letters in lowercase, will be enclosed in parentheses.

Route 1: Personality

The beginning—and also perhaps the end—is the personality of the individual, whether he be a diplomat or a soldier, an entrepreneur or a workman, an adult or a child. He plays some active or passive role in war-peace. To comprehend him, four concepts are arbitrarily selected which subsume alternative nomenclature: *motives* or drives, impulses, goals; *beliefs* or knowledge, cognitions, opinions, stereotypes, ideologies; *attitudes* or feelings, emotions, affect; and *skill* or intelligence, ability, aptitude. The four concepts are explained and operationalized in the next chapter. The double arrows in the diagram suggest the constant interactions between and among the four variables. It may not be possible to identify the ideal combination of attributes that incline an individual to peace or the contrary combination that tips him toward war, but the ideal and its opposite can at least be designated by a reference, respectively, to *homo pacificus* and *homo maleficus*. Like the economic man postulated by economists, the political man postulated by political scientists, and the theologic man postulated by anyone seeking to comprehend evil, the *homines pacifici* and *malefici* are types never or seldom perfectly realized but useful perhaps as heuristic models.

Route 2: Behavior

The next route indicates the behavior of the individual. It begins with his *personality*, for almost everything he does is affected by the motives, beliefs, attitudes, and skills he brings to a situation. He perceives some kind of change within or outside himself; except for some intense stimulus like a loud noise or a piercing pain, that *perception* depends in part on his personality. Next he passes *judgment* upon what he is perceiving or has perceived;

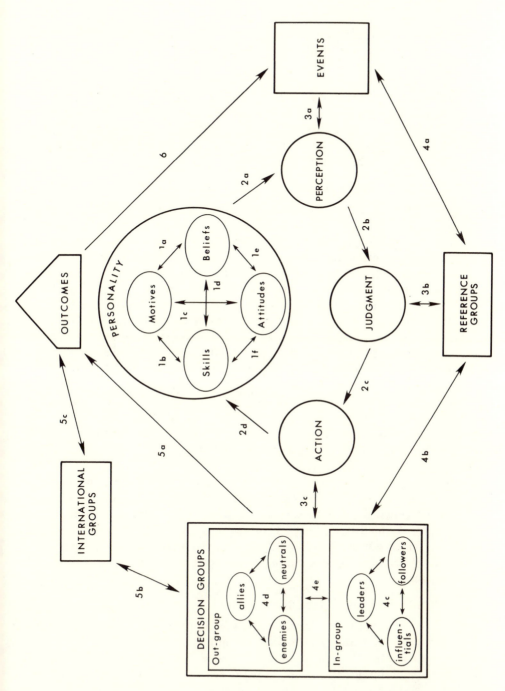

in the jargon of our times, this aspect of behavior is often referred to as decision-making. The judgment may be a fleeting impression or the outcome of a long train of thought; it may be fully or partially conscious, or quite unconscious. A distinction between judgment and *action* is necessary because a judgment is internal, solipsistically encased, and hence covert; whereas action obviously is public, overt, and hence potentially influential. The arrows in the diagram indicate the flow of behavior from personality to action; and the arrow between action and personality suggests that experiences in the past are likely to have an effect upon the individual and his behavior in the present and the future.

Route 3: Determinants

Up to this point the two routes being examined lead to an understanding of the individual and his behavior. From most standpoints these routes are sufficient to comprehend a dictator or a conscientious objector, but they are obviously inadequate for two reasons: they do not indicate the external influences that affect the individual and they fail to suggest the complexity which appears when many persons or groups are the focus of attention when analyzing countries or international relations. *Events* represent a way of referring to a complicated constellation of stimuli to which other names can be given, such as conflicts, natural resources, crowds, education, propaganda. The events may reach the individual directly through his sense organs or through a communication via one of the mass media, an official, a peer, a friend, or a relative. As the individual passes judgment, he may be affected by one of the many *reference groups* which he finds significant or which exercise power over him: his family, social class, ethnic group, and "nation," all of which can be subsumed under the concepts of society and culture. *Decision groups* are those relating directly to actions affecting war-peace, and include governments. They consist of an *in-group* (the individual's own nation or government) and *out-groups* (foreign countries). The double-winged arrows signify that the perception, judgment, and action of the individual may be affected by these groups and he may also affect them.[19] A small but perhaps helpful point: in the diagram all groups are represented not by circles or ellipses, which are reserved for the individual, but by rectangles and a pentagon to indicate that their analysis is of a different order.

Route 4: Group Interactions

Route 4 consists of a detailed analysis, in their own right, of the groups potentially or actually affecting the individual. It includes much of the subject matter of what is ordinarily called international relations in academic and diplomatic circles; thus the relation between the home government and a foreign government is Route 4e. The groups themselves can be the subject of a separate inquiry, as when it is determined that the long-range goal of a government is territorial expansion; such a goal is perceived by the individual indirectly, for example, by reading a paragraph in a school textbook or watching a televised speech by a prime minister. In the in-group are *leaders* (statesmen, politicians, diplomats), *influential persons* (ranging from those dominating mass media to an attractive or powerful individual in a tiny neighborhood), and *followers* (who may or may not have a voice in the decisions). Out-groups include other "nations" which are *allies*, *enemies*, or *neutrals*.

Route 5: War-Peace

This route leads to war or peace—or to some sort of compromise. The basic decision concerning war-peace is almost always achieved through the interaction between in- and out-groups (#4e). The decision may be carried out directly and the *outcome* then emerges without modification (#5a). Another route is possible: the conflict or the decision is submitted to some international agency such as the International Court of Justice, the United Nations, established or unconventional diplomatic channels, or the good offices of neutral governments (#5b). The problem may be referred back to the governments and so Route 5b is double-arrowed; or the outcome may be exclusively determined (#5c). By now the individual is likely to be totally submerged, but not always. An identifiable person, such as the secretary-general of the United Nations, may attempt to prevent a disagreement between two governments from developing into a full-scale war: after perceiving the conflict (#3a) he decides to take action (#s 2b, 2c), asks the governments to send representatives to appear before the Security Council (#s 4e, 5b), and so forth.

Route 6: Outcomes

The final consequence is some variant of war-peace which itself is an event and undoubtedly has impact upon one or more persons (#3a) as well as upon groups within the society (#4a) and governments (#4b). The impact includes the casualties and costs of war as well as the benefits of peace.

Hopefully the elephant or the dinosaur now seems less formidable. In the chapters that follow the insertion of route numbers after each sub-heading and chapter appendix may enable the reader to comprehend systematically the part of the beast being explored in a given section. Other numbers could be added in the text since the routes continually interact, but they have been omitted to avoid cluttering the exposition with too many pedantic reminders. Additional odds and ends which further explain and justify the diagram are mercifully relegated to Chapter Appendix 1.4: The Analysis of War and Peace.

LEITMOTIVS

Five leitmotivs will become apparent: they are guides to understanding the recurrent problems encountered along the six routes. In another sense they are the generalizations, observations, guesses, and summaries which can be salvaged and then appraised or challenged as the complicated subject of war-peace is displayed. Some, hopefully not all, will sound like platitudes, yet it seems necessary to call attention to the most useful bits of substantiated wisdom. At the risk of burdening the reader with too many preliminary concepts, I list their headings:

P. *Proposition*: an especially promising generalization or hypothesis relevant to war-peace; most of the propositions reflect what is thought to be current knowledge in the social sciences, and all of them relate two or more factors to each other or to one another.

V. *Variability-Uniqueness*: fluctuations or deviations from person to person or group to group (societies, associations, countries) usually indicating that a person or group differs from the norm or a generalization. The two are paired because variability usually results from unique instances. In each case, the proposition being implied is: "A proposition concerning X must take variability or uniqueness or both into account."

E. *Extrapolation*: derivation of a future occurrence or event from a similar occurrence or event or from a trend in the present or past. In each case, the proposition being implied is: "A proposition concerning X is based upon an inference concerning the future on the basis of the present or the past."

I. *Ignorance*: absence of information relevant to the problem at hand. In each case, the proposition being implied is: "Any proposition concerning X may not be valid since adequate information is lacking."

M. *Multivariance*: the numerous causes or factors associated with a problem, trend, event, activity. In each case, the proposition being implied is: "An analysis or explanation of X must be based on numerous factors."

As with the recurring routes, discreet references will be made to these leitmotivs by placing the hopefully mnemonically helpful letters listed above, preceded by cf., in parentheses. These cf.s, which would remind the reader of the leitmotivs, may be ignored without suffering intellectual damnation. All the leitmotivs are listed in appendixes at the end of the volume.

REALITY, PERFECTION, REALIZATION

The war-peace problem must be analyzed like any other policy question facing decision makers. What is the situation as it now exists? What is the desirable situation which conceivably would eliminate or at least mitigate whatever defects are discerned in the present situation? What measures should be taken in order to achieve that desirable situation or at least an approximation thereof? From these questions the three parts of this book are derived:

1. *Reality*: relevant knowledge concerning individuals and their society; an analysis is made of the status quo, hopefully from a scientific or scholarly standpoint. If there be something rotten in the state of the world as demonstrated by the presence of war, the rot must be located before trying to extirpate it.

2. *Perfection*: the plans and dreams of men concerning the kinds of persons they would be as well as the kinds of societies and the relations between countries they would foster in order to pursue peace and other desirable goals; delineated are utopias never to be attained but ever to function as inspirations.

3. *Realization*: the actions that have actually been or could be taken by individuals and their leaders to move slightly closer to perfection; the focus is upon the practical sphere of change or reform. To be anticipated is not a glib manual, a how-to-achieve-peace-now-and-forever-after set of proposals, but a patient, aggravatingly cautious, yes-but-maybe-perhaps analysis of possibilities.

Like almost every aspect of war-peace, the three divisions interact and are closely related. What the individuals, the leaders and followers of the country, or those responsible for "international relations" do at a given moment (reality) may depend in part on what he or they would achieve (perfection) and what he or they know is, or can be rendered, practical (realization). Beliefs about perfection may be affected by the limitations of reality and practical problems appearing in connection with realization. Realization is guided by some conception of perfection and of the reality at hand. "Locked within our present frame of reference," a political scientist has dismally observed, "we seem incapable of visualizing plausible routes" away from the hazards and imperfections of our present world.[20] Perhaps the combination of reality, perfection, and realization can locate slightly more fruitful routes. Let us try.

For now we are equipped with concepts, routes on a diagram, and didactic leitmotivs. With this intellectual baggage a journey in pursuit of peace can begin. The goal is to have men and women, whoever they are, pass judgments and take appropriate action. If they are *homines pacifici*, they will lean toward peace whether passing judgment alone or in groups and regardless of their position in the milieu or in the process of war-peace. The challenge is to try to determine how such a state of affairs can be facilitated.

CHAPTER APPENDIXES

1.1 PROPOSITIONS CONCERNING PEACE

Undesirability of war. Evidence that good men abhor war is easy to find among classical Greek[21] and Chinese[22] philosophers, popes and European leaders in the sixteenth century,[23] psychologists,[24] psychiatrists,[25] lawyers,[26] and of course pacifists.[27] The arguments against war are self-evident and are symbolized by the words destruction, death, innocence, waste, suffering, cruelty, atrocity, hate. A war-engendered proclivity to kill may carry over into civilian life, with the result that violence can be more easily committed or tolerated. Even resentment may be felt toward those who have liberated a country from a harsh enemy: it is humiliating to have been dependent on others to gain freedom. Contrary views concerning the desirability of war, however, also exist. According to Theodore Roosevelt, "a just war is in the long run far better for a nation's soul than the most prosperous peace obtained by acquiescence in wrong or in injustice."[28] A few philosophers and many generals believe that wars contribute to "the higher development of mankind."[29] Other reasons for praising wars have been advanced. Without war, many of the manly virtues, such as valor and discipline, would disappear, a possibility—as explained in Chapter 7—that worried William James: perhaps war is able "to redeem life from flat degeneration."[30] The sacrifices demanded by war, Hegel believed, bind citizens to their state; in a peaceful society nothing would be unplanned or unexpected; life would grow dull; citizens would not be motivated to change their society.[31] As a result of wars, tyrants have been overthrown, internal crises have been settled.[32] According to the admission of an advocate of nonviolence, war is "the ultimate sanction" both in international negotiation and in preserving a country's values or existence.[33] There is said to be an "underlying wish for war" leading to an immediate confrontation with an enemy instead of a patient hope for means to avert the conflict.[34]

Attainment of peace. Perhaps the very thought of attaining peace is foolish. Although the number—not the intensity— of wars did not increase between 1816 and 1965, during only 24 of those 150 years was there a period in which 144 countries with a population of at least half a million were not fighting a war.[35] Also throughout the first two and a half decades following World War II, on the average per year over twenty domestic, regional, and international "rivalries and quarrels" between small states or between a small state and a middle- or superpower have been noted. The annual average number of disturbances involving exclusively the middle- or superpowers was 1.3.[36]

Peace research. The volume of current research, if not its quality or relevance, is staggering. In addition to an International Peace Research Association,[37] at least one hundred institutes in the United States alone are devoted to the study of peace and disarmament. Similar European groups are situated largely in the northern countries,[38] and some are in communist lands.[39] The number increases every year.[40] As is to be anticipated, these scholarly centers generally publish books and journals summarizing the research which almost always has an antiwar bias, whether the research is methodological, historical, sociological, psychological, anthropological, or survey-oriented. One bibliography has listed 149 journals and 3,369 books and articles having peace as a theme.[41] Investigated have been the causes of war, the problems of disarmament and control, the risks involved in various foreign policies, the patterns tending toward a world state, and the devising of a peace curriculum.[42] Methodologies include case histories of wars, cross-national and cross-cultural comparisons of war, simulations of wars and negotiations, laboratory experiments, surveys of public opinion, utilization of facts and theories from the social and other sciences, and the construction of mathematical models.[43] The latter is illustrated by an attempt to express in equations the vital statistics (battle strength, casualties, and deaths) of the United States beginning with the Civil War and ending with the start of the Vietnam disaster.[44] American researchers have been accused of concentrating upon topics within the so-called establishment, such as the decision-making processes of the elite or the construction of "utopian models," and hence are said to neglect "the social forces" needed to effect significant changes.[45] Peace researchers, according to one scholar, ought to be able to discharge three roles: providing policymakers with advice based on their findings; conducting investigations and theorizing, regardless of whether their papers or books become influential; or opposing the regime in power if their research gives rise to such a political stance.[46]

1.2 DEFINING WAR AND PEACE

Whether, in attempting to define the two terms, assistance is sought in a standard dictionary ("a state of usually open and declared armed hostile conflict between political units")[47] or from a scholar ("the art of organizing and employing armed forces to accomplish the purposes of a group")[48], it becomes clear that the definitions contain other concepts crying aloud to be defined in their own right. The term cold war, for example, suggests a condition somewhere between what is ordinarily called war and peace: there is no fighting but preparations for warfare continue. But what does, what should one say about "subversive propaganda; infiltration of government agencies, of political parties, or of organizations to control their policy; espionage to obtain forbidden information; dispatch of volunteers, guerrillas, or filibustering to initiate or participate in civil strife, by or on behalf of a government or from its territory with its acquiescence"? If all these actions constitute "intervention,"[49] then intervention so defined either is one of the forms of warfare or it may lead toward or away from overt hostilities.

Likewise, although always interesting, etymology may be of no immediate assistance in clarifying current or desirable usage. Thus the term for peace in Greek is *irene* which perhaps is related to the verb meaning "I conjugate, I order." Possibly this word originally referred to "the opposite of war" and did not include the "the complex set of promises, pledges, and commitments" necessary for peace to be attained.[50] We know, therefore, that peace or its equivalent has acquired different meanings over time within Western society. After defining peace as the "more or less lasting suspension of violent modes of rivalry between political units," one writer then notes that this rivalry can be suspended in at least three ways: the units are "in balance," one unit dominates another, or one unit absorbs the other, for example, in an empire. Should all three of these suspensions be referred to as peace?[51] The problem of definition becomes even more difficult when a non-Western culture is contemplated. In Japanese, for example, there is "a high degree of correlation between the words 'heiwa' (peace) and 'chowa' (harmony)"; and in Chinese classics, "the term ho p'ing (peace) corresponded to a well-ordered state of mind."[52] A formal definition of the *science of peace*, a neologism for which is *irenology*, utilizes the word *peace* without clarifying the concept.[53] A group of professional officers interested in peacekeeping calls peace "a condition that exists in the relations between groups, classes, or states when there is an absence of violence (direct or indirect) or the threat of violence."[54]

1.3 INDIVIDUALS, COUNTRIES, AND INTERNATIONAL RELATIONS

Peace research[55] and peace plans[56] very frequently place emphasis on all three referents of this appendix. In ancient China, a classical treatise by a disciple of Confucius stresses at the outset the need to develop "man's personality and virtues" by cultivating "humane and social relations" and it ends by specifying "the prerequisites for government" in order to attain "the final achievement of an ideal world commonwealth."[57] Plato's approach has a similar implication: war, he thought, was "derived from causes which are also the causes of almost all the evils in states, private as well as public."[58] In the talmudic and midrashic literature of classical Judaism, *shalom* designates "well-being, wholeness, a friendly attitude" as well as "harmony between members of a community and between nations."[59] A psychoanalyst recognizes in effect the same three categories as he writes in behalf of peace.[60]

The duality—the individual versus the nation—is also profusely employed. A Japanese writer believes that peace "in different cultures" (ancient Judaism, Greece, Rome, China and Japan, India) refers to an individual factor, "tranquility of mind," as well as to two social ones, "realization of justice" and "maintenance of good order."[61] An influential economist, writing on the economic costs of war before 1914, approvingly cites the cliché, "You cannot leave human nature out of the account."[62] The platitudinous consensus seems to be that the reply to the oft-posed question of whether "man in society [can] be best understood by studying man or by studying society"[63] is to say emphatically that neither can be neglected. Noteworthy if not thrilling is the fact that sweeping statements seemingly concerned with one of the factors ("the only cause of war is anarchy") eventually smuggle in the other factor ("anarchy occurs wherever men or nations try to live together without each surrendering their sovereignty").[64] Or the somewhat glib statement that "usually the psychological factors and human traits can be classified as conditions of war more correctly than as causes"[65] does not bear close scrutiny, since it is not clouds in the sky or apples on trees that cause war but individuals, whether leaders or followers, all of whom have "human traits" and within whom "psychological factors" are located.

The relation between persons and countries is often made explicit. According to one political scientist a "nation" is really a "shorthand expression" that "does not refer to any organism but . . . to those making decisions on behalf of the people, those influencing those decisions, or all the citizens."[66] Before employing the expression, a historian defines the same concept as "a body of men, inhabiting a definite territory, who normally are drawn from different races, but possess a common stock of thoughts and feelings acquired and transmitted during the course of a common history."[67] Often, however, it is contended that the emphasis should be placed upon some collective entity such as the "nation" rather than its citizens, but eventually reference is made to the latter. An anthropologist states that warfare "is a struggle between social organisms, not individuals" and "its explanation is therefore social or cultural, not psychological"; but then he admits that "to be sure, there would be no wars if there were no people."[68] But the emphasis may also be reversed. According to a psychiatrist, "to understand tensions between nations, one must first understand tensions between individuals."[69] When it is said that "traditionally nations have attempted to control or manipulate the behavior of other nations by the use of punishment or the threat of punishment,"[70] it should be evident that it is leaders who are being punished or threatened and that their reactions can best be understood in terms applicable to any learning situation:[71] will rewards or punishments be more effective, not in general terms, but for this particular set of human beings? "It goes without saying," any persons or any civil servant will say, that the implementation of a formal regulation, such as that between the civilian staff of the secretary-general of the United Nations and the military commanders of its peacekeeping forces, may depend in large part upon the personal relations existing among the individuals concerned with the problem. If the aim is to improve the relation between staff and forces, it is essential to peer behind the abstractions symbolized by the two groups and to locate the persons actually having contact with one another.

When conventionally notable thinkers like Hobbes, Kant, and Marx agree that wars result from defects in states and that they can be reduced or eliminated only through the reform of states, doubts arise: can defects or reforms of states be reduced to actions of individuals? Perhaps not completely, yet it is extremely useful not to overlook the fact that some persons or groups of persons initiate the reforms, even when—again—they are not identifiable. Whenever identification is possible we can perhaps come closer to understanding or even resolving the war-peace problems.

But do we? A psychologist has declared that "the psychological and psychiatric emphasis" may validly account for "immediate" tendencies supporting aggressive wars; but those tendencies are "the result of hunger, exploitation, tradition, and social structure" and therefore "for 'long-run' causation, social, historical, and economic influences are often decisive."[72] Again, such "influences" are not and have not been ripples in the sky; they have come from human beings whose interaction, however, may have been so complex that they as individuals never can be specified. On a "super-organic" level, they can be called "influences," but only because adequate causal information is lacking or because we cannot program computers to provide insight into the complicated interactions that perforce receive the convenient tag.

1.4 THE ANALYSIS OF WAR AND PEACE

The diagram on page 9 does not have the elegance and simplicity characterizing the model of DNA. Is it necessary to work with such a complicated diagram? I think it is. Without it, one of the factors related to war-peace might be overlooked. In addition, to subsume some of the factors under a less cumbersome model might damage some aspect of research, analysis, or point of view. Even a glance at the diagram suggests the kind of overall generalization that must emerge in the pursuit of peace: since each of the numerous factors can be variously weighted, any proposition is likely to have limited applicability, validity, or utility. Thus the variable of leaders who make decisions concerning a country's war-peace plans must be weighted more heavily under an authoritarian than under a democratic regime.

In keeping with the approach described in the text, the diagram concentrates upon the individual; for this reason Route 1 tries to lead to an understanding of his personality. But war-peace, I have also said, is frequently considered to be not an individual but a group phenomenon. The diagram merely suggests a way of analyzing separately each of the individuals composing the group (for example, #3b) when and if it seems important to do so and the relevant data are available; thus it emphasizes the desirability of doing just that to gain insight into war-peace. I am not arguing that the other routes are useless: no, they are necessary to comprehend not only war-peace but also the individual himself since he may be affected by their decisions (as in #3c). In addition, even if virtually all information were available concerning every person within a group (a cabinet discussing whether to declare war, for instance), there is no guarantee that complete understanding of their decision would be attained. What emerges may very well depend on the dynamics of their discussion or interaction and cannot easily be related to them as personalities (#4c).

Routes 1 and 2 are followed only when attention is concentrated upon identifiable persons. Admittedly, as indicated in Chapter Appendix 1.3, adequate data are seldom available. An additional difficulty arises because each individual is unique, more or less, and hence both the components of his personality (#1) and his reaction to what he perceives in his milieu (#3a) may be similarly unique. For present purposes there is a satisfactory solution to this problem. Without neglecting uniqueness, it is possible also to think in terms of modal tendencies likely to have consequences for war-peace. If it is known, for example, that all or most persons in a given country have an unfriendly attitude toward another country, that would be a fact probably inclining them to be hostile. Then if they affect war-peace decisions either indirectly as citizens or directly as political leaders (#s 3c, 4c), those attitudes become highly relevant. An unfriendly attitude may also be more salient or compelling in some persons than in others. Among psychopaths it may be overpowering, among normal persons lukewarm. In short, an understanding of war-peace requires that we know not only the referent of an attitude but also its role in the decision process of those who possess it.

NOTES

1. Czar Alexander I, ascription by Leo Tolstoy, *War and Peace*. New York: Penguin Books, 1957. Vol. 1, p. 295.

2. Daniel Frei, *Kriegsverhütung und Friedenssicherung*. Frauenfeld: Huber, 1970. P. 11.

3. Michael Walzer, *Just and Unjust Wars*. New York: Basic Books, 1977. P. 3.

4. John Somerville, *The Peace Revolution*. Westport: Greenwood, 1975. P. 217.

5. Arnold Simoni, *Beyond Repair*. New York: Macmillan, 1972. P. 37.

6. Mortimer J. Adler, *How to Think About War and Peace*. New York: Simon and Schuster, 1944. P. 8.

7. Walter Millis and James Real, *The Abolition of War*. New York: Macmillan, 1963. P. 142.

8. Andrew W. Cordier and Kenneth Maxwell (eds.), *Paths to World Order*. New York: Columbia University Press, 1967.

9. Franz Christ, *Gestalt und Geschichte des europäischen Friedengedankens*. Ronco-Ascona, Tessin: Verlag des Andragogiums, 1968.

10. Julian Huxley, Foreward in Theo F. Lentz, *Towards a Science of Peace*. New York: Bookman Associates, 1955. P. vi.

11. Lentz, ibid., p. 56.

12. Leonard W. Doob, *Panorama of Evil*. Westport: Greenwood, 1978.

13. Peter Wallensteen, Scarce goods as political weapons. *Journal of Peace Research*, 1976, 13, 277-98.

14. Bert V. A. Röling, *Einführung in die Wissenschaft von Krieg und Frieden*. Neukirchen-Vluyn: Neukirchener Verlag, 1970. P. 7.

15. George B. de Huszar, *New Perspectives on Peace*. Chicago: University of Chicago, 1944. Pp. 1-2.

16. Kenneth E. Boulding, Toward a theory of peace. In Roger Fisher (ed.), *International Conflict and Behavioral Science*. New York: Basic Books, 1964. Pp. 70-87.

17. David Brook, *Search for Peace*. New York: Dodd, Mead, 1970. P. 1. Also Irving Louis Horowitz, *The Idea of War and Peace in Contemporary Philosophy*. New York: Paine-Whitman, 1957. Pp. 30-31.

18. Leonard S. Woolf, *The Framework of a Lasting Peace*. New York: Garland, 1971. P. 9.

19. Cf. Norman S. Endler and David Magnusson, Toward an interactional psychology of personality. *Psychological Bulletin*, 1976, 83, 956-74.

20. Richard A. Falk, *A Study of Future Worlds*. New York: Free Press, 1975. P. 493.

21. Helmut Berve, *Friedensordunungen in der griechischen Geschichte*. Munich: Bayerische Akademie der Wissenschaften, 1967.

22. Helmut G. Callis, History and the idea of mankind. In W. Warren Wagar, *History and the Idea of Mankind*. Albuquerque: University of New Mexico Press, 1971. Pp. 27-46.

23. S. Strauz-Hupé and S. T. Possony, *International Relations*. New York: McGraw-Hill, 1950. P. 812.

24. Gordon W. Allport et al., The psychologists' manifesto. In Theodore M. Newcomb and Eugene L. Hartley (eds.), *Readings in Social Psychology*, first edition. New York: Holt, 1947. Pp. 655-57.

25. Jerome D. Frank, *Sanity and Survival*. New York: Random House, 1968.

26. William C. Brewer, *Permanent Peace*. Philadelphia: Dorrance, 1940.

27. Mercedes M. Randall (ed.), *Beyond Nationalism*. New York: Twayne, 1972.

28. Quoted by William McDougall, *Janus: The Conquest of War*. New York: Dutton, 1927. P. 5.

29. Rainer Kabel, *Mobilmachung zum Frieden*. Tübingen: Katzmann, 1971. P. 40.

30. William James, The moral equivalent of war. In William James, *Memories and Studies*. New York: Longmans, Green, 1924. Pp. 267-96.

31. Paraphrased from George Kateb, *Utopia and its Enemies*. Glencoe: Free Press, 1963. Pp. 114-25.

32. R. G. Bell, *Alternative to War*. London: James Clarke, 1959. P. 33.

33. Gene Sharp, The political equivalent of war. *International Conciliation*, 1965, no. 555.

34. Maurice L. Farber, The Armageddon complex. *Public Opinion Quarterly*, 1951, 15, 217-24.

35. J. David Singer and Melvin Small, *The Wages of War, 1816-1965*. New York: Wiley, 1972. Pp. 201, 379.

36. Edward E. Azar, *Probe for Peace*. Minneapolis: Burgess, 1973. P. 3.

37. International Peace Research Association Proceedings, *Third General Conference*. Assen: Van Gorcum, 1970.

38. Herman Schmid, Peace research and politics. *Journal of Peace Research*, 1968, no. 3, 217-32.

39. Mari Holmboe Ruge, Present trends in peace research. *International Peace Research Association*, 1966, 293-331.

40. Kabel, op. cit., p. 110.

41. Gerta Scharffenorth and Wolfgang Huber, *Neue Bibliographie zur Friedensforschung*. Munich: Kösel-Verlag, 1973.

42. Paul Noack, *Friedensforschung*. Freudenstadt: Eurobuch Verlag, 1970. P. 34.

43. Dean G. Pruitt and Richard C. Snyder (eds.), *Theory and Research on the Causes of War*. Englewood Cliffs: Prentice-Hall, 1969.

44. John Voevodsky, Quantitative behavior of warring nations. *Journal of Psychology*, 1969, 72, 269-92.

45. Martin Oppenheimer, The peace research game. In Elisabeth T. Crawford and Albert T. Biderman, *Social Scientists and International Affairs*. New York: Wiley, 1969. Pp. 170-73.

46. Juergen Dedring, *Recent Advances in Peace and Conflict Research*. Beverly Hills: Sage, 1976. P. 211.

47. Philip Babcock Gove (ed.), *Webster's Third New International Dictionary*. Springfield: Merriam, 1963. P. 2,575.

48. Quincy Wright, *The Study of International Relations*. New York: Appleton-Century-Crofts, 1955. P. 148.

49. Quincy Wright, Intervention and civil strife. *Proceedings of the International Peace Research Association*, 1968, no. 2, 370-72.

50. Gerado Zampaglione, *The Idea of Peace in Antiquity*. Notre Dame: University of Notre Dame Press, 1973. Pp. 26-27.

51. Raymond Aron, *Peace and War*. Garden City: Anchor, 1966. P. 134.

52. Takeshi Ishida, Beyond the traditional concepts of peace in different cultures. *Journal of Peace Research*, 1969, 6, 133-45.

53. J. C. Starke, *An Introduction to the Science of Peace (Irenology)*. Leyden: A. W. Sitjthoff, 1968. P. 16.

54. International Peace Academy, *Peacekeeper's Handbook*. New York: International Peace Academy, 1978. P. I/6.

55. Frei, op. cit.

56. John Galtung, Peace. *International Encyclopedia of the Social Sciences*, 1968, 11, 487-96.

57. Callis, op. cit., pp. 28-32.

58. Quoted by Zampaglione, op. cit., p. 56.

59. Nahum Glatzer, The concept of peace in classical Judaism. In Erich Fromm and Hans Herzfeld (eds.), *Der Friede*. Heidelberg: Lamber Schneider, 1961. Pp. 27-38.

60. J. C. Flugel, Some neglected aspects of world integration. In T. H. Pear (ed.), *Psychological Factors of Peace and War*. New York: Philosophical Library, 1950. Pp. 111-38.

61. Ishida, op. cit., p. 139.

62. Norman Angell, *The Great Illusion*. New York: Putnam's, 1912. P. 149.

63. Kenneth N. Waltz, *Man, the State and War*. New York: Columbia University Press, 1954. P. 5. Cf. Sondra Herman, *Eleven against War*. Stanford: Hoover Institution, 1969. Pp. 220-21.

64. Adler, op. cit., p. 69.

65. John Lewis, On human rights. In UNESCO (ed.), *Human Rights*. New York: Columbia University Press, 1949. Pp. 54-77.

66. Werner Levi, On the causes of war and the conditions of peace. *Journal of Conflict Resolution*, 1960, 4, 411-20.

67. Louis L. Snyder, *The Meaning of Nationalism*. New Brunswick: Rutgers University Press, 1954. P. 32. Cf. Carlton J. H. Hayes, *Essays on Nationalism*. New York: Macmillan, 1937. P. 6.

68. Leslie A. White, *The Science of Culture*. New York: Farrar, Strauss, 1949. Pp. 132-33.

69. Hjalmar Helweg, Denmark. In George W. Kisker (ed.), *World Tension*. New York: Prentice-Hall, 1951. Pp. 40-51.

70. John R. Raser, Learning and affect in international politics. *Journal of Peace Research*, 1965, 2, 216-27.

71. Knud Larsen, Development and maintenance of hostile international images. *Peace Research Review*, 1973, 6, no. 1, 77-104.

72. Hadley Cantril (ed.), *Tensions that Cause Wars*. Urbana: University of Illinois Press, 1950. P. 136.

Part 1:
REALITY

2.
Individual Reality

We begin with the reality of Route 1, the personality who may be a *homo pacificus* or a *homo maleficus* and whose orientation at a given moment may be on an individual, national, or international level. Reality out there—events, the reference groups of the society, and the decision groups—must first be perceived before, in some metaphysical sense, it exists psychologically. Language usually intervenes or mediates the judgment: words or concepts are needed to comprehend, express, or utilize reality.

The ancient, persistent, and honorable question concerning the nature of human nature is unavoidable (cf. I).* For wars, as is so obvious, would not persist "were human nature not what it is, but neither would Sunday schools and brothels, philanthropic organizations and criminal gangs."[1] From this standpoint, therefore, human nature is sufficiently plastic to give rise to the noble or ignoble behavior associated with *homo pacificus* or *maleficus* (cf. P). Discussions as to whether war or peace is the normal condition of mankind seem futile even when it is tempting to believe that wars are abnormal because they are frustrating and prevent human beings from attaining "the normal condition" of peace toward which they allegedly strive.[2] I prefer to ditch the issue entirely and to agree that it is really a *problème quasi-métaphysique*,[3] although I am not entirely clear as to what that fully means. A belief in the normality or abnormality of war or peace, however, is important if and when it affects judgments and actions. The truly challenging problem is to determine the conditions which make individuals prone to go in one direction rather than another, to promote Sunday schools rather than brothels, philanthropic organizations rather than criminal gangs, peace rather than war.

---

*See pages 11-12 for an explanation of the cross-referencing system.

MOTIVES (#s 1a, b, c)

Hurting or wishing to hurt other persons literally or figuratively is a critical component of war; in more or less conventional terms, the motive is designated by the term *aggression*. And so, instead of asking whether war or peace is normal, a similar query can be focused upon aggression: is aggression an inevitable component of personality? The reply is also similar: human beings have a "latent" potential for violence or aggression,[4] they may engage in hurt-inflicting conflict for "social and psychological reasons,"[5] but—in the broad perspective of anthropology—they can learn to become "virtually unaggressive."[6] (See Chapter Appendix 2.1: Basis for Aggression.)

Aggressive impulses and behavior arise in large part, perhaps exclusively (though this is sometimes denied), as a result of prior frustrations, that is, the inability to attain or retain a goal that is prized (cf. P). At first glance the fact that it seems easy to evoke an individual's hostility against his fellows[7] would account not only for wars but also for conflicts in general, and particularly for the ability of leaders to induce their followers to participate in war. For it is true that a frustrated person often expresses anger and hostility; and he may seek scapegoats, whether they be close at hand or whether they are, like potential enemies or the inhabitants of another country, only symbolically present. A number of caveats and reservations, however, must be quickly added to such a psychological, reductionist explanation (cf. M).

First of all, susceptibility to aggression—regardless of the frustration—varies somewhat idiosyncratically from person to person (cf. V). Possibly male sex hormones incline males to be more aggressive than females;[8] thus as ever a genetic factor may play some role at least with respect to the strength of the motive. Then, like any other human action, aggressiveness in specific forms has learned components. In fact, many soldiers in battle are reluctant to engage in the ultimate of aggressive actions—the killing of the enemy. They may have been taught throughout their lives that human beings are not to be murdered and they are suddenly reminded that their opponents are human; or they may follow a moral or religious principle which places a taboo on murder. Many, therefore, are able or willing to kill only after overcoming "the fear of killing"[9] for reasons to be found in their concurrent beliefs and attitudes regarding the enemy. According to an authority, soldiers in battle seek to help the men next to them and "a company fights to keep pace with its flanks."[10] Similarly, the best American soldiers in World War II and the Korean War came from "well-integrated small groups, squads, and companies" whose prime value was "loyalty and respect" for one another.[11] Manifest aggression, therefore, may be powered by a social, nonaggressive drive; ever strong is the individual orientation to conform, in this instance to conform by killing. Often, moreover, what appears to be aggression may not be aggressive at all (cf. I). Just as a hawk swooping down on a small bird is not aggressive but predatory,[12] so the warrior may fight not to express or displace aggression but to defend himself or to obey orders. (See Chapter Appendix 2.2: Killing.)

Modern warfare requires enormous logistical support so that the most effective soldier "seems to have been replaced by the strategist, the scientist, and the technician"[13] who are not necessarily motivated by aggression and who delegate the killing to others. The majority of men and women assisting a war effort, therefore, are in occupations not appreciably different psychologically from those of peacetime. They are remote from the battlefield. The routine to which they adhere in manufacturing and distributing war matériel is very similar to the one they follow in processing shoes or ice cream. They are assisting killing but—unlike the Nazi officials who ordered Jews, gypsies, and others to be liquidated[14]—they can overlook the link between their actions and the end result.

In summary, it would appear that a frustration-sequence provides a clue only to limited aspects of war-peace (cf. P). Within any society some persons are inevitably frustrated if only because their goals cannot be achieved: basic ones as a result of real scarcity (the compelling trio of food, clothing, and shelter), less basic or derived ones as a result of artificial scarcity (titles, status, prestige, for example). War taps many motives, always in conjunction with other aspects of the personality (cf. M).

The other very strong motives evoked by war do not necessarily have aggressive components. Years ago a distinguished psychoanalyst pointed to "the moral paradox" of war: on the one hand, war is completely contrary to "all the recognized canons of morality," but on the other hand it evokes qualities "of the highest moral value" and induces "a sort of moral fervor" difficult to attain in any other way.[15] That fervor includes excitement, pride in one's country, symbolic displacement upon a common enemy, increase in self-esteem, "an end to uncertainty," an opportunity to commit suicide respectably, and of course satisfaction accorded a variety of unconscious mechanisms.[16] Individually oriented ingredients, such as those just listed, even if derived from undocumented, intuitive extrapolations from neurotic patients (cf. E) may have a face validity to which enemies of wars (including William James whose "moral equivalent of war" will be examined more closely in Chapter 7) are likely to give grudging consent. A bit of wisdom was once obtained from a schizophrenic patient who, when asked about his occupation, replied, "Soldier by instinct, and a man of peace by design."[17] In addition, wars may be gratifying to some persons because they remove "the obligation of conscious selection."[18] Men, sometimes women are drafted into the armed services, compelled to curtail their existence, and so forth, all in the interest of a cause securing their nationally oriented assent.

The goals which would be achieved or protected by war are legion (cf. V). Laymen and social scientists are not the least bit shy in listing their own pet designations. For war-peace, however, one terms leads all others: *security*. The context usually includes the "nation"; for example, it has been proclaimed that "each political unit aspires to survive" and hence "makes security a primary objective."[19] Security, however, is a somewhat careless cliché, its implicit meaning is complicated. A limited number of persons, usually leaders, affirm that they wish to retain the present political apparatus, the economic system, or some aspect of their culture which they believe to be threatened by an out-group. They are worried about their own power, or they believe that existing institutions and privileges can be retained only by some change such as territorial expansion. They may then try to persuade their followers that their security is also threatened and, if they are successful, their propaganda in behalf of war is likely to be effective. Thus the subjective reality of the Turkish Cypriotes before the arrival of Turkish troops in 1974 involved, they thought, the danger that the Greek Cypriotes who constituted a majority of about four to one would conquer them. And so they were convinced that their existence could be preserved only with the help of the Turkish army from the mainland.

A conclusion emerges: the motivational potential for war and peace exists. Both depend upon learning[20] certain beliefs fostered by tradition, leaders, groups, and the media of communication. Like religion and the arts—or, again, Sunday schools and brothels—war is another institution which can be encouraged or discouraged.[21] Within every society the usual individual differences appear: some persons are more aggression- and war-prone than others (cf. V). According to modern social science, the partial explanation for such proneness is to be sought in early childhood experiences. The undeniable connection between socialization practices and adult personality, however, as will be frequently admitted in these pages, is difficult to specify in detail (cf. I). Psychoanalytically, the bond between parent and child is believed to be the culprit or the paragon more frequently than any other factor. Does the parent encourage a love relationship to develop and then punish the child by threatening to withdraw that love?[22] Does the young male first identify with his mother and then later develop "compulsive masculinity" as a defense against such identification?[23] As a result of early experiences—according to one line of speculation—does the male child unconsciously identify with an aggressor (who originally may have been his father) as a self-imposed punishment for actually hating the aggressor?[24] Is it of critical importance to provide adequate gratification for the child's "instincts" as they are evoked?[25] In different words perhaps, do children whose parents follow so-called modern, Freudian, or neo-Freudian child psychology really grow up to be less aggressive and hence less likely to commit violent acts? Even though the replies are uncertain, the questions are important, for they point vaguely to the problem of realizing peace which will be Part 3 of this book.

BELIEFS (#s 1a, d, e)

In the previous section on motives frequent references have been made to beliefs. Motives relating to war-peace are not likely to be expressed or to be strong unless they are accompanied by appropriate beliefs. The variables characterizing the personality continually interact, so that usually the complex has to be simultaneously considered (cf. M). Beliefs refer to the way individuals perceive and conceptualize reality. They include the tendency to stereotype the perception of one's own and other "nations." An equivalent term, fashionable at the moment, is image—sometimes national image or international image.[26] When the question of the truth or falsity of a system of related beliefs arises, the concept of ideology is invoked; it has come to refer to a state of affairs which "may guide future action or merely rationalize past events."[27] Sometimes opinion is used as a very closely related synonym. Values represent a combination of beliefs and attitudes.

Perhaps the most important beliefs for present purposes are ones already mentioned: the linking of security and the self with one's "nation." Being subject to the authority exercised by the state and its officials is not necessarily pleasant—think of the imposition of taxes or speed limits—but the restriction can be happily accepted if it is believed, in slightly flamboyant language, that the authority in question "obeys truth, guarantees men's rights, and recommends itself to free men by its respect for liberty."[28] In more prosaic words: citizens support governments which in their opinion help them satisfy basic and derived needs. Belligerency or aggressiveness increases when it is believed that failing to arm, to capture or regain a territory, or to win a war means that important values "might not prevail or survive"[29] (cf. P). Patriots have definite beliefs about their own country: for them reality includes the nature of their land, the personalities of their compatriots, in short their entire culture.[30] The psychoanalysts (cited in Chapter Appendix 2.2) who interviewed Palestinian Arabs and Israelis emphasize land in this context, particularly those features which "have become incorporated in the extended self of individuals."[31] When the frustration results from the threat of war or from protracted hostilities as in the Middle East—or even during a harmless laboratory exercise that would simulate war[32]— the beliefs in the form of stereotypes or extensions of self become salient, are likely to be simplified and polarized, and influence behavior[33] (cf. P). Patriotic beliefs, moreover, tend to be so strong that, according to a psychoanalyst, even a discussion about disarmament is phrased in terms of the possible rather than the probable, a way of thinking he asserts—vividly if misleadingly from a sociological standpoint—to be "paranoid" rather than "sane."[34]

The individual probably has beliefs about war-peace itself. Specifically, he may point with some confidence to the "causes" of war or the "cause" of at least one particular war. These notions of reality may spring out of more general views of human behavior: are persons puppets manipulated by outside forces or do they manage their own destiny; is their behavior determined by the roles they are forced to play or by their own character traits? Wars thus may be considered independent of human will, like floods and earthquakes, or dependent on the exercise of free choice. Tolstoy, as will be indicated later, subscribed to the former view, but it is intriguing also to note that in his philosophic writings and in the way of life he eventually evolved for himself he seemed to be proclaiming that good men could avoid war. A belief in the inevitability of war may exist because mankind has endured so many wars in the past and hence the future must resemble the past (cf. E). Anticipating and preparing for war under "war-minded" leaders may in fact be "the indispensable condition of war,"[35] an instance par excellence of a self-fulfilling prophecy: followers expect something to happen and, inadvertently or deliberately, they validate the prophecy by facilitating the turn of events in the direction they have foreseen. Belief in war's inevitability may be related to other aspects of war-peace. In one study, employing samples of American high school, college, and graduate students as well as sociologists and psychologists, such a belief during the American excursion into Vietnam was accompanied by a negative view of human nature which was considered to be responsible for war; by a belief that wars could be effectively prevented through deterrence; and by generally belligerent attitudes regarding that particular war.[36]

The source of most persons' beliefs concerning war is likely to be very indirect. According to one surmise, about ten years afterwards events no longer seem real even to those who participated in them, and a decade later they "shade off into fond memories." The first generation has experienced the events, the second receives a direct account about them from participants, but the third views them only as "history."[37] In retrospect veterans of a war try to forget the horrors and to stress the heroism and camaraderie. Eventually the ways in which past wars are portrayed in tradition by observers and historians give rise to expectations concerning the nature of future wars (cf. E).

Studies of children testify to the slow but steady growth of war-peace beliefs. (See Chapter Appendix 2.3: Learning of Beliefs.) Not only because they are transmitted during early and late childhood, but also because, being so "deeply rooted in our language and traditions,"[38] they are constantly reinforced by the mass media and ceremonies, such beliefs tend to resist change[39]—unless they are contradicted by a forceful event (cf. P). Whether or not an event is forceful depends upon the perceiver and the way in which that event is communicated to him. Evidence for change comes from real life (regarding the possibility of atomic warfare)[40] and the laboratory (regarding the Vietnam War).[41] Whether such changes promote war or peace, however, is partially a function of the variable about to be considered, that of attitudes.

ATTITUDES (#s 1c, e, f)

For a pragmatic reason the term *attitude* is being used here to include all affective processes associated with war-peace because it is a concept which has given rise to many fairly impressive studies. In addition, an attitude, though a private affair for the individual, implies a referent or set of referents in objective reality toward which or whom the feelings are directed. To try to classify attitudes by means of those referents is pointless since literally a thesaurus would be necessary. Individuals have attitudes toward everything in the universe. They seldom if ever react completely neutrally to what they perceive.

It is almost impossible not to be ethnocentric and to feel that one's own in-group (the community, "nation," state) is "virtuous and superior" and that some out-group is "contemptible, immoral, and inferior."[42] Patriotic attitudes or a love of some area with a distinctive culture has deep psychological roots and therefore a national orientation is likely to be both strong and salient in most persons, at least from time to time (cf. P). A psychoanalyst, true to one of the older traditions of his craft, asserts that "belonging to a nation means the successful mastery of the Oedipus complex,"[43] which for a Freudian like him is the acme of good mental health. The committee of psychoanalysts already mentioned in this chapter assembled evidence indicating, they think, that for many Jews everywhere establishing Israel as a nation "led almost immediately to a very personal and fundamental expansion of the extended self to the State," a condition they call "a narcissistic hypercathexis of the State."[44] Among all peoples, a parallel and more parsimonious explanation of patriotism points to the fact that, since basic and derived drives (ranging from food and drink to sociability and language) are evoked and satisfied in the region where one lives, every individual tends to be motivated to perpetuate this source of gratification. Patriotism, however, can exist without nationalism; in theory at least ethnocentric love of country does not require ethnocentric hatred of other lands.[45]

Attitudes, including ethnocentrism and patriotism, are learned either directly or indirectly (cf. V). They may result from a series of experiences with other persons or objects, from a single traumatic experience, or from a process of differentiation in which the person gradually focuses upon one component or an all-embracing pleasant or unpleasant reaction. In theory, at any rate, the individual comes to dislike another country because he has had a series of unpleasant contacts with its citizens, because he has had a single extremely unpleasant contact with a particular out-grouper, or because at first his contacts with all strangers were unpleasant and then later he has focused the resulting feelings upon the individuals of the particular country. In all three instances he assumes or intuits that the past unpleasantness will be repeated in the future (cf. E). The most common method of acquiring an attitude, and the one most relevant to patriotism, however, is indirect: the individual adopts the attitudes of persons whom he respects or must respect (his parents, peers, teachers). He learns in the absence of direct or continuous experience with the referent because he would not or cannot deviate from those persons.[46] The attitude is then stored within him as a vague feeling or a succinct verbal expression.

Some attitudes change over time, but it is not always possible to locate the causes (cf. I). Others remain relatively stable, perhaps when they are embodied in a consistent, simple cognitive structure.[47] Very clear is the fact that attitudes do not exist in isolation, but are related to other attitudes, to beliefs, and to personality traits within the individual. (See Chapter Appendix 2.4: Correlates of Attitudes.) In addition, although they may remain private and unexpressed, attitudes are not useless, detached predispositions: they have some effect, however seemingly removed, upon overt behavior. (See Chapter Appendix 2.5: Attitudes and Actions.)

SKILLS (#s 1b, d, f)

Every person has certain disserviceable and serviceable skills enabling him less or more successfully to cope with his environment. The skills include a very general proclivity like intelligence as well as specific capabilities, agility, and sensitivity. Whether or not he can control his impulses, acquire various beliefs, and change some or many of his attitudes depends in part upon an ability to learn new ways of behavior which in turn can be affected by diverse factors such as his genetic or innate constitution, hormonal secretions, and personality traits.

The ability to judge other persons accurately is clearly related to experience.[48] Individuals in various European countries tended to use nationality in judging others more frequently than occupation.[49] Their stereotypes about foreign nationals may well have decreased judgmental skill, but it might also be argued that, since nationality implies culture and since personality and behavior are related to culture, the utilization of that clue may indeed have been helpful.

Some leaders are more skillful than others in responding to and influencing their followers, but we are uncertain concerning the components of that skill (cf. I, V) because, among many complications, "different people want different things of leadership" and hence "leadership is an interactional phenomenon."[50] Even more elusive are the skills required to negotiate with the representatives of other governments. From the consequences of diplomatic and similar activity it can only be deduced that the skills of the particular individuals occupying positions of power affect the policy of a country, whether concerning the allies the leaders choose, the treaties they negotiate, or the preparations for war they undertake in the short or long run. (See Chapter Appendix 2.6: Avoiding World War II.)

As indicated earlier in this chapter during the discussion of motives, skill in hurting others physically, which reaches its zenith for most individuals in wars, is patiently acquired (cf. P). For this reason governments have war academies and training camps. Part of the skill may result from natural endowment; for example, precise muscular coordination is required in piloting a plane. Another part, no doubt a larger part, is derived from experience. Can this experience begin in the nursery or the home when children are given an opportunity to enjoy toys such as tanks, planes, and guns? According to one psychoanalyst, the skill factor here is less important than the motive or attitude; the use of popguns will not eventually harm the mature adult if the child has been fortunate enough to have parents who discharge their parental roles "adequately,"[51] a term not easy to operationalize. Psychologists and psychiatrists in modern countries continue to try to discover the attributes of a man which will make him a good soldier, especially under the stress of combat conditions; and they have succeeded in developing elaborate screening and testing procedures to assess the skills and personality traits likely to be associated with fighting efficiency.[52] It is perhaps doubtful whether the skillful soldier ipso facto should be called a *homo maleficus* because of this training, especially if he has been drafted. Some of the skills and possibly also the traits that make him a good soldier may be useful in civilian life.

The skill tapped in responding to, or resisting a communication or a series of communications concerning any aspect of war-peace at first glance seems to be a variant of intelligence. Highly intelligent persons, in comparison with the less intelligent, may be able more easily to learn the content of a communication and hence to be influenced by it, or they may be able to perceive falsehoods in a communication and so remain unaffected. Measured intelligence, however, is confounded with education and hence, again, experience is significant.[53] Personality traits may also play a role: some encourage persuasibility (responsiveness to symbols, low self-esteem, orientation toward other persons' values rather than toward one's own), others discourage it (hostility, withdrawal tendencies).[54]

SALIENCE AND PERSONALITY (#1, 2a)

Whatever motives, beliefs, attitudes, and skills comprise an individual's personality are of little or no great significance to war-peace unless or until they become salient. A devout person may well be acquainted with the tenets of his faith that have, or should have, implications for his attitude toward war. But if those principles are only weakly established within his personality, if there is nothing in the immediate environment to remind him that he has them, or if he is not referring his own values or actions to some group in which such principles apply, they will not be salient and hence will exert little or no influence upon him. Doubtless different issues have been salient for American leaders during the international crises in the 1960s concerning Berlin, Cuba, and Taiwan;[55] in the 1970s concerning Vietnam, China, Namibia, Zimbabwe, Somalia, Ethiopia, South Africa; and always concerning the Soviet Union. All leaders may assert that deep down they follow a consistent foreign policy, but on the surface they usually seek fluctuating goals and hopefully avoid different frustrations from situation to situation. An intriguing question to ask is whether attitudes toward war-peace are salient during peacetime. (See Chapter Appendix 2.7: Surprises.)

There is constant interaction among an individual's motives, beliefs, attitudes, and skills as well as between his personality and his inclination to act. The interaction over time usually results in some consistency and justifies the postulation of a *personality trait* as the individual's characteristic way of thinking, judging, or acting in a variety of situations (cf. V). Personality in turn is a way of describing the consistency among the traits themselves and plays a major role in affecting what the person perceives, what he finds salient. Like traits and personality, the interaction can be and has been variously expressed. According to one account, for example, both Confucian and Maoist psychologies emphasize "clustering" among "three mental phenomena: knowing, feeling, and promptings to act,"[56] a trio not unlike three of the four variables employed here to designate the bases of personality. No variable, in short, ordinarily operates in isolation (cf. P), for its effect is likely to be dependent upon one or more of the other variables, upon a trait, or upon the personality. Reactions which seem surprising can usually be explained, in whole or in part, by considering the interaction of more than a single variable within the personality. (See again Chapter Appendix 2.4.)

CHAPTER APPENDIXES

2.1 BASIS FOR AGGRESSION (#s, 1, 2, 3)

The popular view that aggression must be innate stems largely from ethologists, especially from one ingenious investigator.[57] The value of animal data for human societies, in spite of the recent claims of so-called sociobiologists, is uncertain (cf. E). Besides, when the potential for aggression is conceded, it matters very little whether its basis is genetic or not; the cultural overlay is so thick that analogies from animal behavior are not very compelling. A contrary view, expressed in a book with the modest title of "Man into Wolf," suggests that "an original peaceful life among the fruit-bearing trees of some terrestial paradise" was disrupted when men began eating meat rather than only fruits and vegetables.[58] In any case, an examination of how aggression is cultivated or not cultivated in a particular society conclusively indicates the role of social factors, which means the individual's long-range groups. No single society can serve as a convincing prototype; yet, at least to illustrate the process, arbitrary reference is made to the Fulani in northern Nigeria. The value males there seek to embody is that of "aggressive dominance." As young boys they beat their highly valued cattle so thoroughly that the animals never graze onto unfenced fields. They are taught they must launch a physical attack against another person when they themselves have been attacked; not to counterattack subjects them to the dishonor of being called a coward. They fight each other with sticks; when hit by opponents from other clans, they show no emotion in spite of the pain. They are proud of the scars they consequently receive.[59] The Fulani thus do not inherit but acquire the aggressive virtue they seek, first by dominating cattle and then by responding belligerently and eagerly to the attack of their peers.

The absence of aggression, moreover, cannot be used as evidence against an aggressive proclivity. An anthropologist once reported that he had never seen a Balinese "annoyed because he was interrupted in the course of some series of acts."[60] Somehow, if that were so, the Balinese must not have interpreted the interruption as a frustration and hence there was no aggression; or else these people successfully concealed their anger from the foreign observer.

2.2 KILLING (#s 1, 2)

Five telling, moving episodes have been collected which indicate that individual soldiers have had "a great reluctance to shoot" even when a member of the enemy forces is being held in their gunsight:

1. English soldiers in World War I: "a solitary German . . . with his head down and his arms stretched in front of him, as if he were going to take a high dive through the earth . . . looked too funny" to shoot.
2. A British officer in World War I seeing a German soldier taking a bath—"I disliked the idea of shooting a naked man."
3. A British volunteer on the Loyalist side in the Spanish Civil War observing an enemy soldier "half-dressed and . . . holding up his trousers with both hands"—"I did not shoot partly because of that detail about his trousers. . . . a man who is

holding up his trousers isn't a 'Fascist,' he is visibly a fellow-creature, similar to yourself, and you don't feel like shooting him."

4. A British soldier in World War II watching a German soldier, during "a wonderfully vulgar sunrise," wandering "like a sleep-walker across our line of fire. . . . for the moment he had forgotten war and—as we had been doing—was reveling in the promise of warmth and spring." When asked whether the German should be shot, the reply was, "No, just scare him off."

5. An Italian officer and corporal in World War I watching Austrian soldiers drinking their morning coffee and seeing one of them light a cigarette—"they were showing themselves to us as they really were, men and soldiers like us"; also the "cigarette formed an invisible link between us" since "no sooner did I see its smoke than I wanted a cigarette myself."[61]

Even though the incidents are not quite as idyllic as they may sound (in the first case, the funny soldier was no threat and was soon captured; in the second, the officer handed his rifle to a sergeant who killed the man), it seems clear that the initial reluctance to shoot resulted in large part from the fact that each of the five enemies, in the words of the British soldier, was perceived as "a fellow-creature, similar to yourself."

In addition, combatants may have principles against killing. The same author reminds us that during the My Lai massacre by American soldiers during the Vietnam War—they killed over 400 civilians in a small village—"there were a few who refused to fire their guns and others had to be ordered to fire two or three times before they could bring themselves to do so."[62] A vivid incident is also recalled from World War II:

In the Netherlands, the Dutch tell of a German soldier who was a member of an execution squad ordered to shoot innocent hostages. Suddenly he stepped out of rank and refused to participate in the execution. On the spot he was charged with treason by the officer in charge and was placed with the hostages, where he was promptly executed by his comrades.[63]

According to a reliable source in the *Infantry Journal* published by the United States Army:

A commander of infantry will be well advised to believe that when he engages the enemy not more than one quarter of his men will ever strike a real blow unless they are compelled by almost overpowering circumstances or unless all junior leaders constantly "ride herd" on troops with the specific mission of increasing fire.

The 25 percent estimate stands even for well-trained and campaign-seasoned troops.[64] The same writer reports that:

Studies by Medical Corp psychiatrists of the combat fatigue cases in the European Theater . . . found that fear of killing, rather than fear of being killed, was the most common cause of battle fatigue in the individual, and that fear of failure ran a strong second.

It may be true that by and large "our common life is sustained by a strong moral and legal presumption against the use of force"[65] and hence killing for most persons is abhorrent or impossible. But some soldiers kill, and killing is facilitated by other tendencies within the personality. During the Korean War the percentage of American soldiers willing or able to fire on the enemy is reported to have risen to 50 percent and in some defensive situations every man discharged his gun.[66] In the Vietnam War men in the following categories were more likely to commit atrocities than those not embraced by the category: the young, those from rural backgrounds, volunteers, those with older brothers who had been killed in combat, and those devoted to sports with a clear-cut team of opponents such as football (cf. V).[67]

Some or perhaps most killing must be accompanied by beliefs concerning the victim. The killer may believe, correctly or incorrectly, that he is killing in self-defense. Or else he dehumanizes the victim and hence his sensibility can be suspended.[68] The bombadier in a plane knows and hopes his bombs will destroy the enemy, since that is the purpose of his mission, but from his vantage point aloft he cannot see the persons he will kill. Killing is also easier when responsibility, direct or indirect, can be placed upon another person or at least removed from the self. Members of a firing squad never know whose bullet has slain the convicted person, or at least they can believe that their own bullet was only one of many. For those in actual combat, however, the sight of death, whether of the enemy or one's forces, may remain traumatic:

"Oh! Oh!" moaned Nesvitsky, as if in excruciating pain, clutching at the staff-officer's arm. "Look, a man has fallen! One is down, one fallen!"
"Two, I think?"
"If I were Tsar I would never make war," said Nesvitsky, turning away.[69]

The threat to what the individual considers to be his own important goals (for example, security) is frustrating, so frustrating that he is likely to react violently—and then he is able to kill in cold blood. The value embodying one of these goals is especially precious when it involves persons or objects believed to be an extension of the self; hence fighting ruthlessly in behalf of one's "nation" or shooting one's enemy almost gleefully becomes an act of self-defense. On the basis of clinical evidence from their patients and from interviewing Palestine Arabs and Israelis, a group of psychoanalytically inclined psychiatrists call this extension of the self "narcissism"; they believe that "what characterizes narcissistic rage in the spectrum of human aggressive responses is that it expresses the need to right a wrong and undo a hurt," so that those suffering the frustration of this "narcissistic injury" have "an unrelenting compulsion in the pursuit of this vengeful 'justice.' "[70]

2.3 LEARNING OF BELIEFS (#s 1; 2a, b; 3a, b)

One summary of the literature on the learning of beliefs suggests that between the ages of five and eleven the child in Western societies begins to comprehend "the conception of nation and of its place in the world"; similarly his feelings develop "in a parallel fashion, extending outward from himself, his family, and his immediate environment, to his country."[71] Illustrative of such research, all based on samples of children either interviewed or badgered with questionnaires in the indicated countries, are the following:

Britain: between the ages of eight and ten more was known concerning liked than disliked countries.[72]

Britain and Japan: the concept of nuclear war appeared "late on the scene."[73]

Canada: by the age of eight there was awareness of the international system and of the United Nations which varied with social class, intelligence, and, above all, age.[74]

U.S.A.: between grades two and eight more children believed that the United Nations rather than the United States "does most to keep peace in the world."[75]

U.S.A.: between the ages of nine and twelve belief in "the nonaggressiveness of war" and its legality increased.[76]

Attitudes are gradually buttressed by beliefs. American children, for example, were generally able to give reasons for their ratings of different nations.[77] Perhaps most significant of all—though not the least bit surprising—are data from the mid-1960s demonstrating not only very little disagreement between American twelfth-grade children and their parents regarding political party affiliation but also varying degrees of disagreement with respect to political and social questions.[78] This nonremarkable discovery suggests that one of the important sources for beliefs, the home, is supplemented by influential teachers in school, peers, and the mass media.

2.4 CORRELATES OF ATTITUDES (#s 1c, e, f)

Source of change: Unless a controlled experiment is conducted, it is usually impossible to pinpoint the reason for a change in attitude—or in any kind of belief or action for that matter. Ideally there must be two equivalent groups, an experimental and a control group; a measurement before and after the alleged cause of change, such as an event or a communication; and an opportunity for the experimental but not for the control group to be exposed to that source of change. In realistic situations the ideal can be seldom if ever approximated, one illustration of which may suffice. Between 1924 and 1977 the upperclassmen in the high schools of Middletown (a pseudonym for a midwestern community which in the original study was thought to be more or less typical of some American communities) were found to have become, from one standpoint, less patriotic: fewer of them believed that "the United States is unquestionably the best country in the world" (92 versus 78 percent) and fewer subscribed to the platitude, "my country, right or wrong" (61 versus 49 percent).[79] One can only guess at the explanation: World War II as well as the Korean and Vietnam wars; development of the mass media; changes in the curriculum, including greater emphasis on social studies; the prevailing opinion of the times. Without a control group and without being able to manipulate one factor at a time or in combination, the precise sources of the change remain unknowable.

Overall correlates: In my opinion, it is impossible to provide a definitive résumé of the scattered research on the correlates of attitudes because so many different questionnaires, scales, and interviews have been employed. As good a summary of the questionnaire section of that literature as any has suggested that, at least up to 1968, Americans favoring military deterrence by the United States tended to be anticommunist, antiwelfare, pro-laissez-faire capitalism, politically conservative, antidemocratic, authoritarian, anti-intellectual, nationalistic, patriotic, and orthodoxly religious.[80] Another summary points in similar directions when American research with reference to the contemporary "dove decision maker" is semiseriously delineated. Such a person might be seen:

As a middle-aged Jewish Negress who has received a college education to attain the status of a physician or English professor, who resides outside a big city but not too far from the nation's capital. She is nonauthoritarian, nonethnocentric, flexible, achievement oriented, neither cynical nor alienated, optimistic, and an intellectual with much tolerance of ambiguity. Her political views are neither conservative nor nationalist. She participates actively in politics, does not anticipate war, does not expect her country to survive or be victorious in war, and takes few risks. Her decisions are peaceful when the information inputs are neither perceptually complex nor cognitively simple and made when mutual trust, friendliness, and communications are maintained at high levels (though short of communications overload). Peace is more likely to emerge if the prototypic decisionmaker is in possession of accurate information and advisers are in initial disagreement over alternatives so that stereotypic decoding of inputs and provocative encoding of outputs is absent; there is concern for long-range implications and longer time for making a decision and drawing up contingency plans.[81]

Each of the above designations, believe it or not, springs from some paper-and-pencil or interviewing schedule. Why female, for example? Surveys often suggest, such as ones interviewing samples in the United States during the 1960s, that more women than men expressed less-belligerent attitudes.[82]

Correlates between attitudes: I will quickly throw together representative findings which may be skipped over lightly but which are recommended if the reader is to appreciate, laboriously, the difficulties encountered when generalizations in this area are sought (cf. V). For the indicated samples significantly positive relations—but with exceptions—have been established betweeen or among the specified attitudes:

Australian adults: holding warlike attitudes *and* favoring capital punishment.[83]

Members of American peace organizations: joining *and* being liberal and internationally minded.[84]

American college students: favoring military preparedness *and* also favoring firmer approaches to the problem of delinquency.[85]

Canadian and American children and college students: nationality *and* attitude toward the other's and one's own country—Canadians more favorably disposed toward Canada than Americans toward America; and Americans more favorably disposed toward Canadians than Canadians toward Americans, presumably because Canadians were worried about American influence upon their country and Americans were not worried about Canadian influence.[86]

Young Norwegian males while applying to enter, or while studying in, a military or naval academy: attitudes toward foreign affairs *and* patriotism in a nationalistic sense as well as way of coping with individual and social conflicts.[87]

American and British students and adults: with notable exceptions, having militarist attitudes *and* being religiously devout and orthodox.[88]

American undergraduates: demonstrating against the Vietnam War *and* being less authoritarian.[89]

In many of the above studies, it has doubtless been noted, the correlates involve not only attitudes but also beliefs and aspects of action; attitudes cannot easily be ripped out of their context within the personality.

Correlates with personality traits: the last study cited above illustrates the correlation between attitude and the personality as a whole. For authoritarianism is often thought to be not a belief but a personality trait, a distinction that happily need not detain us. Other studies, as the previously mentioned 1968 summary suggests, confirm the association.[90] In addition, in the same format as above:

American college students: becoming more "pro-world-minded" after being in a European center for ten weeks *and* "sociability, original thinking, benevolence, and esthetic values."[91]

Canadian undergraduates and adults: "punitiveness" that included ideologies related to militarism, religiosity, conservatism, and nationalism *and* personality with respect to extraversion, misanthropy, and recollection of strict discipline as a child as well as less knowledge of foreign affairs.[92]

German, Flemish, French, Dutch, and Belgian (Walloon) adolescents: approval of their political institutions and various judgments concerning American and Soviet foreign policy *and* dogmatism and authoritarianism.[93]

American adolescents, college, and graduate students: militarism and religiosity *and* neuroticism and extraversion.[94]

American college students: propensity to retaliate in a laboratory game *and* tendency toward authoritarianism.[95]

A large variety of English and Americans: radical political beliefs *and* being "tenderminded" or theoretical rather than practical as well as favoring various beliefs (pacificism, abolition of death penalty, incompatibility of patriotism and peace, ability to cure criminals, inclination to abandon national sovereignty, abolition of a double standard of morals).[96]

American college students: tendency toward political aggression *and* "anality" crudely measured (for example, "In general I spend my money very carefully and give few gifts").[97]

Sometimes it seems fruitful to speculate concerning the relation between personality traits and attitudes. In 1976, for example, samples of Americans tended to have favorable attitudes toward those countries which were similar to their own country with respect to race, language, religion, political system, and level of economic activity and also those in which the United States had economic or military interest.[98] Presumably the tendency was to find foreigners attractive who resembled oneself or who had complementary goals.

Correlates with demographic factors: Like the prototype of the "Jewish Negress" who has received a college education, war-peace attitudes may be related to demographic factors:

American undergraduates: years spent in college.[99]

Persons in general (presumably Westerners) and American adults: age, and hence world conditions when born, and the resulting expectations during socialization.[100]

Japanese adults: participation in the community, reading of newspapers.[101]

American adults: education, occupational status, income, attention devoted to newspapers and magazines, and age.[102]

Unspecified French and Germans: prejudices regarding each other and the passing of time (that is, 1914 or 1939 versus ca. 1965).[103]

Middle-aged, white Americans: greater stability of seven attitudes over a period of less than a year (three of which seem related to war-peace: gun control, amnesty for draft dodgers, reduction of the Defense Department budget) among college graduates than those without a college education.[104]

Individual differences: Both in the cited research and clearly in real life, attitudes vary considerably from individual to individual, and deviations from the norm of a group or from the majority are inevitable. On a cultural level, for example, varying percentages of elites, nonelites, and students in Ceylon, Nepal, and India completed the incomplete statement, "If you want peace, be prepared for . . . . . " Most of the projections were "consistent" with a policy of nonviolence. There was also, however, considerable variability within each national sample among adherents to the different religions.[105] Case histories of Americans resisting the draft during the Vietnam War reveal that each individual had somewhat different attitudinal reasons behind his stance: they ranged from a combination of Marxism and an emphasis upon "privacy, independence, and responsibility" to aesthetic values acquired from one's wife.[106]

Fallibility of measurements: It is difficult to avoid reckless, undocumented statements concerning the nature of attitudes associated with war-peace (cf. I). Psychiatrists, for example, according to a historian, are said to find "three of the major characteristics" of neurosis in nationalism, namely, "anxiety, sense of inferiority, and instability."[107] Even though quantitative research on attitudes is probably an improvement over such a provocative, unsubstantiated guess, several warnings must be issued concerning the findings. The variety of measuring instruments has already been mentioned. Most of the samples are relatively small and not necessarily representative even of the general universe from which they have been drawn. Attitudes in general, particularly those concerned with war-peace problems, cannot be speedily or easily ascertained, inasmuch as patriotism can be variously expressed. Once more, reactions of Americans to the Vietnam War may serve as a dramatic illustration. Then, as almost always, the wording of the question in surveys could affect the expression of attitudes. In 1966, 70 percent of a sample approved the United States bombing of oil storage dumps in North Vietnam (a favorable attitude toward extending the war) and two months later 51 percent of another sample claimed to subscribe to the proposal that their country submit the Vietnam problem to the United Nations (a favorable attitude toward limiting the war).[108] Right before the invasion of Cambodia by American troops, 7 percent of a sample favored that action; immediately after the invasion, although only 12 percent believed the action would shorten the war, 50 percent believed that the president had made the right decision. Such data, it has been pointed out, suggest how malleable the opinions of Amercans are and how the president's prestige rises when he takes positive action.[109] Probing, moreover, may reveal subtle relations and the deeper meaning of an attitude than the direct response to a straightforward question (cf. V). Again the Vietnam War: at first glance it may have appeared that the majority of Americans were on the side of peace, since they believed it had been a mistake for their country to become enmeshed in that war. Closer questioning of the same individuals, however, revealed that almost as many favored escalating, rather than withdrawing from, the conflict. Get it over with, they were saying in effect. Opposition to the war, moreover, sometimes stemmed not from pacifist or ethical values but from the conviction that the war was intruding upon their lives, thereby affecting their economic well-being and "quality of life."[110] Beware, in short, of surveys that reveal a favorable attitude toward peace, for Americans at any rate are as ready to pay lip service to this value as they are to their own desire, as phrased by a French writer for all peoples, "to be rich, happy, or famous."[111]

Absence of Correlates: The numerous relations between attitudes and other variables related to war-peace mentioned briefly in the text and at length in this chapter appendix should not obscure one very important fact:

again and again negative results have been reported. No or no significant relation has been found, for example, between attitudes or actions regarding aspects of war-peace and each of the following: (a) nationalism,[112] (b) a personality trait involving the person's conviction concerning forces controlling his destiny,[113] (c) age and sex,[114] and (d) miscellaneous factors such as marital status, job satisfaction, and interest in international affairs.[115] Some of these findings reflect differences within individuals which may be either idiosyncratic or cultural in nature. Here is one of the many reasons why peace can be only pursued and not realized: the components of *homo pacificus* to be cultivated or facilitated are so elusive. We must rest content with the flabby generalization that there is likely to exist some but not a perfect relation between war-peace attitudes and other variables—though not always.

2.5 ATTITUDES AND ACTION (#s 1, 2)

In the late 1960s a schedule of questions was administered to 5,000 university students in 60 universities located in 19 different developed and developing countries. The respondents were asked whether or not they had engaged in political demonstrations. Demonstrators in the West tended to be opposed to war, to private property, to explanations of war and aggression based on hereditary theories, to the traditional family structure, and to inequality. In South Africa, however, this form of action was related to different attitudes: the European demonstrators tended to lean toward the right, to be optimistic concerning their country's progress, and to favor the acquiring of nuclear weapons; and the highly selected group of Africans was opposed to the use of drugs.[116] American students active against the war in Vietnam, according to one summary of the research, tended to be above average with respect to humanitarian attitudes and a variety of democratic values.[117] In all instances, then, the action of demonstrating was linked to predispositions within the activists.

Rather than summarize similar studies, the older ones of which discovered discrepancies between attitude and action[118] because they failed to take other attitudes and beliefs into account,[119] it seems more useful to mention an elaborate theoretical model in which attitudes play a key role. The model ambitiously seeks to predict behavior from verbal utterances—but the variables have usually also been ascertained through paper-and-pencil questionnaires given to Westerners who are accustomed to having pins stuck into them by investigators (cf. E). Action, it is postulated, depends upon the individual's intention to perform an act; the intention depends upon his attitude toward the act in question (which in turn depends upon his belief concerning the consequences of the act and his attitude toward those consequences) as well as upon his subjective norms concerning the act (which depend upon his belief as to whether other persons who are important to him in *their* turn believe he should or should not perform the act, and that belief of his depends upon the normative beliefs existing within the society and his own motivation to comply with the norm and the wishes of others)[120] (cf. M). Here is not the place to quibble as to whether the correct number of angels are dancing on the heads of the pins—what about unconsciously motivated, reflexive, abnormal acts? It is sufficient to note that the model has inspired American investigators to collect relevant data, most of which verifies the fact that attitudes provide one of the many useful clues to action.

2.6 AVOIDING WORLD WAR II (#s 1, 2, 3c)

Six smaller European countries—Sweden, Spain, Finland, Norway, Switzerland, and Turkey—sought to avoid being drawn into World War II. Sweden and Spain succeeded. Finland and Norway, in spite of skillful efforts by their leaders, eventually were invaded and compelled to fight. Switzerland remained and still remains "unique." Its neutrality has been known and respected for many years; its mountains are physical barriers and "in the twentieth century no one has doubted that Switzerland would defend itself if attacked."[121] The Germans, if they had been able to stage a successful invasion, could have profitably used the Swiss railways to transport additional troops into Italy, but the Swiss revealed their plan to repel such an attack and to render the transportation system useless by dynamiting strategic tunnels. As a neutral, Switzerland was important to both sides; for example, intelligence concerning the enemy could be gathered by the belligerents from travellers, spies, and others. The three principal ethnic groups of the country—the French-, German-, and Italian-speaking sections—would have created internal difficulties for an invader. Switzerland has hesitated even to join the United Nations, so aloof is the posture of neutrality its leaders would maintain.

All the powers could have found Turkey a valuable ally for a variety of reasons, including its geographical position and its chrome that was badly needed for the German war machine:

Thanks to the competition among three great powers to influence Turkey, the Turks' skill in bargaining, their immunity to propaganda, their understanding of the military and economic position of the parties involved at each stage, and their lack of sentiment, Turkey stayed out of the war. Thus it escaped both possible annihilation by the Germans and occupation by the Russians. Meanwhile, the Turks suffered relatively little economic deprivation. Despite some temporary lapses, they succeeded in retaining the good will of the Western Allies, who never seriously doubted that they favored the Allied side.[122]

And so at the very last moment Turkish leaders declared war on the Axis powers when it was to their advantage to do so.

Presumably the leaders of the four countries that avoided the war possessed the ability to weigh carefully the various pressures being exerted upon them. They estimated the effects a policy would have, they made their decisions, and then they convinced other leaders in the threatening countries that neutrality would be advantageous to both sides. Very sensitive skill was needed to weigh the alternatives. Perhaps the decision was easiest for the Swiss; they had only to decide not to enter the war and then to indicate by words and actions their ability to repel an invasion and render their country useless to the Germans.

2.7 SURPRISES (#s 1, 2, 3a)

The somewhat surprising data that emerge when the salience of war-peace is investigated can be illustrated by one study that was conducted in the early 1960s and focused upon interviews with representative samples in fourteen countries. Respondents were approached with completely unstructured questions, first concerning "what really matters in your own life," and then concerning "your fears and worries about the future." After rating these hopes and fears, they were asked the same open-ended questions about their own country. Although of course there were large individual differences within and between the samples (cf. V), three generalizations can be extracted from the voluminous data. First, with some exceptions, few persons spontaneously listed peace among their personal hopes or war among their fears. The exceptions were the fear of war for the German, Polish, and kibbutz samples. Then, with only a single exception (again the kibbutz respondents), war as a fear was mentioned more frequently than peace as a hope. Thirdly, with no exceptions, both peace and war appeared as the responses more frequently when the referent was the "nation" rather than the "self."[123] By and large, therefore, as measured in this particular way and with the indicated exceptions, war-peace was not salient among many persons in spite of what must be called the nonpeaceful state of the world at the time. War, however, was more salient than peace, and war-peace was more salient in connection with "nation" than with the "self." The explanation for some of the fluctuations is elusive. Clearly 62 percent of the Poles personally feared war since their country had recently been ravaged by the Germans, and 47 percent of the German sample perhaps could not forget the devastation of World War II. But why was the corresponding figure for the Israelis, whose country was at the time surrounded by unfriendly neighbors, only 26 percent? Also, why would 73 percent of the kibbutz sample and only 16 percent of the nonkibbutz Israeli sample have mentioned peace as a hope for their "nation"? Separate investigations of each situation would have been necessary to try to understand the last surprise.

Illustrations of reactions that seem surprising only because attention is concentrated on a single variable are numerous. Anxiety concerning the consequences of modern warfare may not weaken attitudes favoring war, but may lead to "bellicose intransigency at the national level," to an increase in "ethnocentric solidarity," yet not to the growth of "international conciliatoriness."[124] Possibly also those who have not experienced war may have "less fear of it."[125] Or it might seem reasonable to believe that anxiety is likely to be experienced in primitive form when the enemy's planes are visible in the sky or when bombs burst nearby. In Belfast during the 1970s, however, the mental health of persons living in fringe neighborhoods which had not experienced violence (though there were signs of conflict, such as barricades, boarded-up windows, as well as information about violence elsewhere in the city) tended to be worse than it was in those neighborhoods where there had been violence.[126] In this instance, as is generally true in war-torn areas, anticipation or belief was worse than reality. Also, the arousal of one motive may repress another: individuals may protect themselves against anxiety by believing that the unpleasant—such as the nightmare of "deliberate thermonuclear war and Hitler-type challenges"—is "unreal and improbable."[127]

Even a trivial incident in a Canadian laboratory contains a surprise which disappears when it is known what beliefs are made salient, in this instance by the investigator. Ordinarily, it would be anticipated, an insult by a peer would be frustrating and hence give rise to aggression against him. In a setting contrived by the experimenter, each subject was told, under different circumstances, to shock a fellow student. Presumably being insulted by that fellow student (who was actually a confederate of the investigator) would be frustrating and hence give rise to more aggression, in the form of a stronger shock, than would not being insulted by him. Actually, these subjects tended to administer a stronger shock *but* only after being told that the shock would hurt the victim. Other subjects were informed that the shock would help the insult-giver perform the task at hand; they tended to deliver not a stronger but a weaker shock than those who had not been insulted.[128] A belief, in short, intervened: in both instances the insulted subjects had been frustrated but, whether they expressed aggression by shocking or not shocking depended on whether they believed the shock, respectively, would hurt or help the source of their frustration.

Almost inevitably, as a result of the well-established and constantly observed variability between individuals and societies, individual and cultural differences are expected to appear. It comes as no surprise, however, to be reminded that human beings everywhere have similar basic drives and hence seek similar goals. What may transcend common sense, perhaps, is that similarities exist in connection with phenomena that represent interactions in different societies. Everywhere, for example, the criteria for judging some actions to be evil can be considered very similar, at least on an abstract level.[129] Rumors, which are symptoms of anxiety, during the Biafran conflict in Nigeria could be analyzed by means of the same categories as those employed to classify rumors in the United States during World War II,[130] even though the two countries and the media transmitting the rumors differed so markedly.

NOTES

1. Kenneth N. Waltz, *Man, the State and War*. New York: Columbia University Press, 1954. P. 80.

2. Mortimer J. Adler, *How to Think About War and Peace*. New York: Simon and Schuster, 1944. P. 40. Cf. Matthew Melko, *52 Peaceful Societies*. Oakville: CPRI Press, 1973. P. 188.

3. Gaston Bouthoul, *A voir la Paix*. Paris: Bernard Grasset, 1967. P. 230.

4. Jerome D. Frank, *Sanity and Survival*. New York: Random House, 1968. P. 288.

5. Stephen D. Nelson, Nature/nurture revisited. *Journal of Conflict Resolution*, 1974, 18, 285-335.

6. Ashley Montagu, *Learning Non-Aggression*. New York: Oxford University Press, 1978. P. 6.

7. Alexander Mitscherlich, On hostility and man-made stupidity. *Journal of the American Psychoanalytic Association*, 1971, 19, 819-34.

8. Frank, op. cit., pp. 47-49.

9. S. L. A. Marshall, *Men against Fire*. New York: Infantry Journal, 1947. P. 78.

10. Ibid. p. 161.

11. H. L. Nieburg, *Political Violence*. New York: St. Martin's Press, 1969. P. 107.

12. Anatol Rapoport, Is warmaking a characteristic of human beings or of culture? *Scientific American*, 1965, 213, no. 4, 115-18.

13. Ibid.

14. Erich Kahler, *The Tower and the Abyss*. New York: George Braziller, 1957. Pp. 72-74.

15. J. C. Flugel, *The Moral Paradox of Peace and War*. London: Watts, 1941. Pp. 33-34.

16. Franco Fornari, *The Psychoanalysis of War*. New York: Doubleday, 1974. Pp. xv, 69-93. Edward Glover, *War, Sadism and Pacificism*. London: Allen & Unwin, 1933. P. 75. Margaret Mead, The psychology of warless man. In Arthur Larson (ed.), *A Warless World*. New York: McGraw-Hill, 1962. Pp. 131-42.

17. Julius Laffal, *A Source Document in Schizophrenia*. Hope Valley, R.I.: Gallery Press, 1979. P. 38.

18. Santiago Genovés, *Is Peace Inevitable?* New York: Walker, 1970. P. 38.

19. Raymond Aron, *Peace and War*. Garden City: Anchor, 1966. P. 64, italics deleted.

20. Mark A. May, *A Social Psychology of War and Peace*. New Haven: Yale University Press, 1943. P. 20.

21. Margaret Mead, War is only an invention— not a biological necessity. In David Brook (ed.), *Search for Peace*. New York: Dodd, Mead, 1970. Pp. 402-5.

22. John W. M. Whiting and Irvin L. Child, *Child Training and Personality*. New Haven: Yale University Press, 1953. P. 261.

23. Robert A. LeVine and Donald T. Campbell, *Ethnocentrism*. New York: Wiley, 1972. P. 150.

24. William Eckhart, Psychology of war and peace. *Journal of Human Relations*, 1968, 16, 239-49.

25. Alix Strachey, *The Unconscious Motives of War*. New York: International Universities Press, n.d. P. 228.

26. William A. Scott, Psychological and social correlates of international images. In Herbert C. Kelman (ed.), *International Behavior*. New York: Holt, Rinehart and Winston, 1965. Pp. 45-69. Also Milton J. Rosenberg, Images in relation to the policy process. In Kelman (ed.), op. cit., pp. 278-334.

27. Leo Kuper, *The Pity of It All*. Minneapolis: University of Minnesota Press, 1977. P. 111.

28. Thomas Merton, *On Peace*. New York: McCall, 1971, P. 54.

29. Arthur Larson, The struggle of ideas. In Larson (ed.), op. cit., pp. 98-116.

30. Leonard W. Doob, *Patriotism and Nationalism*. New Haven: Yale University Press, 1964. Pp. 22-23.

31. Committee on International Relations, *Self-Involvement in the Middle East Conflict*. New York: Group for the Advancement of Psychiatry, 1978. P. 575.

32. Michael J. Driver, *Conceptual Structure and Group Processes in an Inter-nation Simulation*. Princeton: Educational Testing Service, 1962.

33. Robin Jenkins, Perception in Crises. *Proceedings of the International Peace Research Association, Second Conference*, 1, 155-75.

34. Erich Fromm, The case for unilateral disarmament. In Quincy Wright et al. (eds.), *Preventing World War III*. New York: Simon and Schuster, 1962. Pp. 178-91.

35. Gordon W. Allport, The role of expectancy. In Hadley Cantril (ed.), *Tensions that Cause Wars*. Urbana: University of Illinois Press, 1950. Pp. 43-78.

36. Donald Granberg, War expectancy. *International Journal of Group Tensions*, 1975, 5, nos. 1 & 2, 8-25.

37. Bouthoul, op. cit., p. 243.

38. Judd Marmor, Psychological problems of warlessness. In Larson (ed.), op. cit., p. 124.

39. Frank, op. cit., pp. 124-29.

40. Cf. Leonard Beaton, *The Struggle for Peace*. London: Allen & Unwin, 1966. P. 113.

41. Richard D. Sherman, Dimensional salience in the perception of nations as a function of attitudes toward war and anticipated social interaction. *Journal of Personality and Social Psychology*, 1973, 27, 65-73.

42. LeVine and Campbell, op. cit., p. 12.

43. Géza Róheim, The psychology of patriotism. *American Imago*, 1950, 7, 3-19.

44. Committee on International Relations, op. cit., p. 503.

45. Doob, op. cit., pp. 266-77.

46. Gordon W. Allport, Attitudes. In Carl Murchison (ed.), *A Handbook of Social Psychology*. Worcester: Clark University Press, 1935. Pp. 798-844.

47. Victoria Steinitz, Cognitive imbalance. *Human Relations*, 1969, 22, 287-308.

48. Leonard W. Doob, *Pathways to People*. New Haven: Yale University Press, 1975. Pp. 185-94.

49. Renate Mayntz and Howard V. Perlmutter, Einige Versuchsergebnisse zum Problem der Vorstellungsbildung und Interpretation von Kommunikationen. *Kölner Zeitschrift für Soziologie und Sozialpsychologie*, 1956, 8, 292-330.

50. Cecil A. Gibb, Leadership. In Gardner Lindzey and Elliot Aronson (eds.), *The Handbook of Social Psychology*. Reading: Addison-Wesley, 1969. Vol. 4, pp. 205-82.

51. Glover, op. cit., pp. 86-95.

52. Peter Watson, *War on the Mind*. New York: Basic Books, 1978. Pp. 193-223.

53. Carl I. Hovland, Arthur A. Lumsdaine, and Fred D. Sheffield, *Experiments on Mass Communication*. Princeton: Princeton University Press, 1949. Pp. 147-75.

54. Irving L. Janis, Personality as a factor in susceptibility to persuasion. In Wilbur Schramm (ed.), *The Science of Human Communication*. New York: Basic Books, 1963. Pp. 54-64.

55. Cf. Oran R. Young, *The Politics of Force*. Princeton: Princeton University Press, 1968. P. 266.

56. Donald J. Munro, *The Concept of Man in Contemporary China*. Ann Arbor: University of Michigan Press, 1977. P. 26.

57. Konrad Lorenz, *On Aggression*. New York: Harcourt, Brace, 1966. Especially Ch. 4.

58. Robert Eisler, *Man into Wolf*. London: Spring Books, [1951?].

59. Dale F. Lott and Benjamin L. Hart, Aggressive domination of cattle by Fulani herdsmen and its relation to aggression in Fulani culture and personality. *Ethos*, 1977, 5, 174-86.

60. Gregory Bateson, The frustration-aggression hypothesis and culture. *Psychological Review*, 1941, 48, 350-55.

61. Cited in Michael Walzer, *Just and Unjust Wars*. New York: Basic Books, 1977. Pp. 139-41.

62. Ibid., pp. 309-10.

63. J. Glenn Gray, quoted by Walzer, op. cit., p. 314.

64. Marshall, op. cit., p. 50.

65. Ralph B. Potter, Jr., The moral logic of war. In Charles R. Beitz and Theodore Herman (eds.), *Peace and War*. San Francisco: Freeman, 1973. Pp. 5-16.

66. S. L. A. Marshall cited by Watson, op. cit., p. 46.

67. Summarized by Watson, op. cit., pp. 244-45.

68. Viola W. Bernard, Perry Ottenberg, and Fritz Redl, Dehumanization. In Milton Schwebel (ed.), *Behavioral Science and Human Survival*. Palo Alto: Science and Behavior Books, 1965. Pp. 64-82.

69. Leo Tolstoy, *War and Peace*. New York: Penguin Books, 1957. P. 168.

70. Committee on International Relations, op. cit., p. 421.

71. David Statt, The influence of national power on the child's view of the world. *Journal of Peace Research*, 1974, 11, 245-47.

72. Nicholas Johnson, Development of English children's concept of Germany. *Journal of Social Psychology*, 1973, 90, 259-67.

73. Peter Cooper, The development of the concept of war. *Journal of Peace Research*, 1965, 2, 1-17.

74. Ela T. Zurick, The child's orientation to international conflict and the United Nations. *Proceedings of the International Peace Research Association*, 1970, 3, 170-89.

75. Robert D. Hess and Judith V. Torney, *The Development of Political Attitudes in Children*. Garden City: Doubleday, 1968. P. 36.

76. Harry R. Targ, Children's developing orientations to international politics. *Journal of Peace Research*, 1970, 7, 79-98.

77. H. Meltzer, Children's thinking about nations and races. *Journal of Genetic Psychology*, 1941, 58, 181-99.

78. M. Kent Jennings and Richard G. Niemi, The transmission of political values from parents to child. *American Political Science Review*, 1968, 62, 169-84.

79. Theodore Caplow and Howard M. Bahr, Half a century of change in adolescent attitudes. *Public Opinion Quarterly*, 1973, 43, no. 1, 1-17.

80. Eckhardt, op. cit.

81. Michael Haas, International socialization. In Michael Haas (ed.), *International Systems*. New York: Chandler, 1974. Pp. 52-75.

82. Ibid.

83. David G. Beswick, Attitudes to taking human life. *Australian and New Zealand Journal of Sociology*, 1970, 6, 120-30.

84. Jerome D. Frank and Earl N. Nash, Commitment to peace work. *American Journal of Orthopsychiatry*, 1965, 35, 106-21; 1967, 37, 112-19.

85. Vernon Jones, Attitudes of college students and their changes. *Genetic Psychology Monograph*, 1970, 81, 3-80.

86. Bernie I. Silverman and Shelly Battram, Canadians' and Americans' national impressions. *Sociology and Social Research*, 1975, 59, 163-70.

87. Bjorn Christiansen, *Attitudes towards Foreign Affairs as a Function of Personality*. Oslo: Oslo University Press, 1959. P. 232.

88. Elbert W. Russell, Christianity and militarism. *Peace Research Reviews*, 1971, 4, no. 3, 1-77.

89. Richard R. Izzett, Authoritarianism and attitudes toward the Vietnam war as reflected in behavioral and self-report. *Journal of Personality and Social Psychology*, 1971, 17, 145-48.

90. For example: Daniel J. Levinson, Authoritarian personality and foreign policy. *Journal of Conflict Resolution*, 1957, 1, 37-47.

91. Erich Prien, Personality correlates and changes in proworldminded and antiworldmindedness following an intercultural experience. *Journal of Social Psychology*, 1966, 68, 243-47.

92. William Eckhardt and Norman Z. Alcock, Ideology and personality in war/peace attitudes. *Journal of Social Psychology*, 1970, 81, 105-16.

93. W. Doise, Autoritarisme, dogmatisme, et mode d'approche des relations internationalités. *Journal de Psychologie Normale et Pathologique*, 1969, 66, 35-53.

94. William Eckhardt, Ideology and personality in social attitudes. *Peace Research Reviews*, 1969, 3, no. 2, 1-106.

95. Morris F. Friedell, A laboratory experiment in retaliation. *Journal of Conflict Resolution*, 1968, 12, 355-73.

96. H. J. Eysenck, War and aggressiveness. In T. H. Pear (ed.), *Psychological Factors of Peace and War*. New York: Philosophical Library, 1950. Pp. 49-81.

97. Maurice L. Farber, Psychoanalytic hypotheses in the study of war. *Journal of Social Issues*, 1955, 11, no. 1, 29-35.

98. Miroslav Nincic and Bruce Russett, The effect of similarity and interest on attitudes toward foreign countries. *Public Opinion Quarterly*, 1979, 43, 68-78.

99. Jones, op. cit.

100. Marvin S. Soroas, Adding an intergenerational dimension to conceptions of peace. *Journal of Peace Research*, 1976, 13, no. 3, 173-83. Also Vincent Jeffries, Political generations and the acceptance or rejection of nuclear warfare. *Journal of Social Issues*, 1974, 30, 119-36.

101. Yasumasa Kuroda, Peace-war orientation in a Japanese community. *Journal of Peace Research*, 1966, no. 3, 380-88.

102. Richard F. Hamilton, A research note on the mass support for "tough" military initiatives. *American Sociological Review*, 1968, 33, 439-45.

103. Walter Millis and James Real, *The Abolition of War*. New York: Macmillan, 1963. P. 117.

104. George D. Bishop, David L. Hamilton, and John B. McConahay, Attitudes and nonattitudes in the belief systems of mass publics. *Journal of Social Psychology*, 1980, 110, 53-64.

105. T. K. Unnithan and Yogendra Singh, *Sociology of Nonviolence and Peace*. New Delhi: Indian International Centre, 1969. Pp. 36-38.

106. Lewis Merklin Jr., *They Chose Honor*. New York: Harper and Row, 1974.

107. Louis L. Snyder, *The Meaning of Nationalism*. New Brunswick: Rutgers University Press, 1954. P. 96.

108. Milton J. Rosenberg, Sidney Verba, and Philip E. Converse, *Vietnam and the Silent Majority*. New York: Harper and Row, 1970. P. 22.

109. Ibid., p. 27.

110. Ibid., pp. 38-41.

111. Julien Freund, *Le Nouvel Age*. Paris: Marcel Rivière, 1970. P. 145.

112. Kenneth Terhune, Nationalistic aspiration, loyalty, and internationalism. *Journal of Peace Research*, 1965, 2, 277-87.

113. Mary P. Lowther, The decline of public concern. *Kansas Journal of Sociology*, 1973, 9, 77-88.

114. Eckhardt, op. cit.

115. Mari Holmboe Ruge, "Are you a member of a peace organization?" *Journal of Peace Research*, 1966, 3, 389-94.

116. D. Finlay, C. Iversen, and J. Raser, *Handbook for Multi-National Student Survey*. Cited by William Eckhardt and Christopher Young, *Governments under Fire*. New Haven: HRAF Press, 1977. Pp. 15-18.

117. Eckhardt and Young, op. cit., pp. 25-26.

118. For example, the influential study by Richard La Piere, Attitudes and actions. *Social Forces*, 1934, 13, 230-37.

119. For example, Douglas W. Bray, The prediction of behavior from two attitude scales. *Journal of Abnormal and Social Psychology*, 1950, 45, 64-84.

120. Icek Ajzen and Martin Fishbein, Attitude-behavior relations. *Psychological Bulletin*, 1977, 84, 888-918.

121. Aron, op. cit., p. 165.

122. Annette Baker Fox, *The Power of Small States*. Chicago: University of Chicago Press, 1959. Pp. 541-42.

123. Hadley Cantril, *The Pattern of Human Concerns*. New Brunswick: Rutgers University Press, 1965. Pp. 1-23.

124. LeVine and Campbell, op. cit., p. 32.

125. Matthew Melko, *52 Peaceful Societies*. Oakville: CPRI Press, 1973. P. 182.

126. Morris Fraser, *Children in Conflict*. New York: Basic Books, 1973. Pp. 50-59.

127. Martin Niemöller, Comments. In Edward Reed (ed.), *Beyond Coexistence*. New York: Grossman, 1968. Pp. 115-17.

128. Brendan Gail Rule and Andrew R. Nesdale, Differing functions of aggression. *Journal of Personality*, 1974, 42, 467-81.

129. Leonard W. Doob, *Panorama of Evil*. Westport: Greenwood, 1978. Pp. 25-38.

130. Nwokocha K. U. Nkpa, Rumor mongering in war time. *Journal of Social Psychology*, 1975, 96, 27-35.

3.
National Reality

If "wars begin in the minds of men," as the oft-quoted sentence of UNESCO's preamble maintains, it is necessary to attempt to discover the circumstances under which nationally oriented individuals choose war rather than peace. In this role some of them come to believe, however hesitatingly, that "the tribe or the state is the unit within which killing is murder and outside of which killing is proof of manhood and bravery."[1] What beliefs and attitudes must they have, what kinds of persons must they be, to subscribe to that doctrine; and what aspects of a society in turn encourage such beliefs and such persons?

SOVEREIGNTY AND NATIONAL HONOR
(#s 1a, d, e; 3; 4c*)

As indicated in the last chapter while introducing the concept of attitude, all persons, or almost all, quickly or eventually acquire a love of family, of neighborhood, of region, and probably also of "nation." Freud once bluntly wrote Einstein that "a community is held together by . . . the compelling force of violence and emotional ties (identification is the technical name) between its members."[2] Identification occurs when the individual believes his own welfare and that of the significant group to which he belongs is linked to some other person or group; and it is facilitated by subjectively real similarity between himself and the others. The factual basis for similarity is not so important as the belief in its existence. While it may be true, according to one set of conservative criteria, that "less than 10 percent of the world's nations are essentially homogeneous,"[3] nationals

*See pages 11-12 for an explanation of the cross-referencing system.

themselves are likely to believe that they and their fellows share a common cultural and historical background as well as many cultural traits, especially when those within the boundaries of the "nation" use the same language (cf. P).

In-groupers are also convinced that they differ significantly in many respects from peoples in other countries and that in some sense they themselves are desirably distinctive. In effect they think of themselves as "the chosen people" or "the human beings," as if other nations have not been so selected or are subhuman. They have a strong tendency, consequently, to exaggerate "the virtues and grandeur" of their country and thus to justify the war-peace actions taken by leaders in their behalf.[4] Patriotic nationals consider government to be the ultimate authority commanding conformity, obedience, and "supreme loyalty."[5] In their international role they feel gratified or frustrated as the status and prestige of their country's name in other lands changes.[6]

During a pause in a workshop once organized by a few Americans who tried to help unofficial representatives from Somalia, Ethiopia, and Kenya search for a solution to their boundary disputes,[7] I gently asked a Somali why he showed concern for his Somali "brothers" in one of the disrupted areas when—from the standpoint of reality—he knew none of them and when they actually were not his brothers even in the sense of a very extended family. He literally gasped and looked at me in amazement. Surely, he said in effect, these people are of the same flesh and culture as I; when they are subjected to the tyranny of a foreign state, I cannot remain unmoved. This gifted man was no mere follower in his land; at the time, he was influential in government and subsequently his prestige and power increased. His judgment as a follower and his war-peace actions as a leader were affected by this belief in the unity of Somalis everywhere. On another occasion in Africa before a sophisticated, all-African audience I followed the precedent of previous African lecturers in the same seminar and began my remarks with "Mr. Chairman, dear brothers." What I believe to have been amazement or hostility rippled through my listeners. My skin pigmentation evidently disqualified me from claiming common ties with them although—as I then stressed for pedagogical purposes—they and I probably shared more beliefs and attitudes than they themselves had in common with the other African societies I was about to mention.

It is, however, not necessary to step outside the West to find similar illustrations of strong emotions associated with strangers who are compatriots. Hitler was able to use the alleged attack upon unknown Germans as the reason to invade Poland at the outset of World War II and many of his followers responded enthusiastically to this strategem. During the seizure of the American embassy in Teheran in 1979-1981, Americans expressed their indignation and their sympathy with the fifty-two hostages in various ways: by more or less uniting behind their president at first, by demanding some kind of action (including even military retaliation), and by sending Christmas cards and gifts to the prisoners. Ulterior motives may also function to reinforce identification with fellow countrymen, but the point to be emphasized here is the ease with which such identification and kinship emotions can be evoked.

Patriotism varies from individual to individual, from country to country, and from time to time within a country (cf. V). Nationals may lose some confidence in their government after a scandal such as Watergate, but they retain loyalty to some group with which they consider their welfare and interests to be linked. (See Chapter Appendix 3.1: Variability in Patriotism.) In areas where competition for loyalty exists, such as Northern Ireland during the 1970s, the individual can quickly specify the group to which he and also his parents belong.[8] And of course patriotism is strengthened whenever there appears to be a threat from outsiders, especially during a war. In well-established countries, identification with the aims and symbols of the "nation" is taught from the outset of a child's conscious existence and is constantly reinforced by events and interactions with others. A patriotic predisposition, therefore, is likely to play a role when the individual is under stress or whenever he is reminded of his own heritage and of his "nation"-linked security.

Just as peoples in all societies enjoy certain privileges, so nationals judge that "nations" merit similar status. A country's "right and power freely to take her own decisions in such matters as she considers vital to her destiny" is the operational meaning of national sovereignty.[9] The "nation" is thus personified: "it" pursues goals and takes offense when those goals are frustrated; "it" is supposed to react aggressively when "it" is insulted. This metaphor may be, as ever, a necessary shorthand device in the absence of adequate information concerning those responsible for making the decision (cf. I) when such psychologizing is employed (for instance, to describe certain aspects of the conflict between the Soviet Union and the United States during the five months of the Cuban crisis in 1963).[10] The term as a vocal vibration or a written symbol can then evoke powerful reactions since its literary character is not likely to be consciously recognized. Overlooked are the facts concerning the actions and interactions of the leaders on both sides who threaten, yet negotiate with one another.

The existence of a belief in national sovereignty is typified by the banal assertion, "My country, right or wrong." According to a Freudian, exercising the usual restraint and modesty of many psychoanalysts, no one but "a thoroughly antisocial adult would assert, "Myself, right or wrong." If he had such an egocentric thought, he probably would not express it: "only a madman says, 'I am always right' "[11] The individual's judgments are beclouded by his group and by pressures from other persons in his society.

Even upon reflection, as he passes judgment, he may continue to believe in the righteousness of his country.

A major hindrance to the pursuit of peace is the fact that the leaders of every sovereign government believe they have the right to declare war under circumstances they themselves have the privilege of specifying (cf. P). Nowhere in the Charter of the United Nations is this right denied explicitly. War is not outlawed; in fact, defensive war is declared to be legal in Article 51 ("Nothing in the present Charter shall impair the inherent right of individual or collective self-defence if an armed attack occurs against a member of the United Nations, until the Security Council has taken measures necessary to maintaining international peace and security"). Sovereignty also includes the opposite right, that of remaining neutral, even when a risk exists, even when the country does or will benefit from the sacrifices of one of the belligerents, and even when its leaders and many of its followers subscribe to the values for which that belligerent is fighting.[12]

"National honor," like sovereignty, also has a mystical connotation: "something transcending concrete national interests and pecuniary rights, something intangible and immaterial, something ethereal and spiritual, something beyond price."[13] The symbol, however, has been accorded a semblance of reality in a report of the second Hague conference in 1907 which stated that an "international commission of inquiry" should mediate disputes between countries provided they involve "neither honor nor vital interest" and only when they arise "from a difference of opinion on points of fact."[14] The metaphor of "honor" is obviously similar to an individual's honor which in earlier times could be avenged, if sullied, by combat in the form of a duel. Just as a slur on one's mother or paternity may be considered "fighting" words, so lack of respect shown a country's leaders or flag by individuals from another country usually requires an apology or may produce the threat of armed conflict.

Issues phrased in terms of sovereignty or honor are likely to evoke patriotic attitudes and, in the face of a "real" or alleged threat from the outside, to strengthen bonds among whoever perceives the offense.[15] As symbols, moreover, national sovereignty and honor may be meaningful to nationals who worry about their own security or the territory which they themselves would like to occupy and which is now denied them by a hostile country. When a leader, such as the president of the United States, argues in behalf of human rights and directly or indirectly declares that leaders in countries he specifies should protect and not violate those rights, he may be expressing his own view and that of many of his followers, but the leaders to whom his attack is directed immediately consider that he is infringing upon their sovereignty by asking them to accept his scale of values. What right has an outsider, they think, to tell us how to run our country in any respect?

PREDISPOSING CAUSES OF WAR-PEACE (#s 3, 4)

The title of a somewhat scholarly, polemical article written by an extremely gifted and influential anthropologist during World War II epitomizes the challenge before us: "war is only an invention, not a biological necessity."[16] With what kinds of societies are war-peace outcomes associated? Certainly there must be conditions among men as well as traditional or novel events during their lives that produce, as it were, *homines pacifici* and hence peaceful personalities, judgments, and action. The problem can be phrased as a search for the predisposing, the long enduring causes of war-peace in the milieu as well as the precipitating, the more immediate causes. Americans like to believe, for example, that their country has no appreciable military tradition and no desire for additional territory: predisposing causes for going to war are believed to be absent. Their government, however, allegedly declares war as a result of precipitating causes such as the sinking of the Lusitania and Germany's declaration of unrestricted warfare before World War I and Pearl Harbor before World War II. The distinction between the two types of causes, like most distinctions, is not absolute but simply a useful, attention-focusing device.

As the search for predisposing causes begins in this chapter and resumes for precipitating causes in the next chapter, any sane or impartial person— including me—must be of two minds. On the one hand, modern warfare is such a "complicated social institution"[17] that abstract generalizations, even with exceptions, are likely to be elusive (cf. M). On the other hand, the contrary hypothesis leaps out of the conviction that the Swiss milieu with no wars and the German with too many wars during the past century or so must be different in specifiable ways. There is no a priori way to select one hypothesis rather than the other (cf. I).

Instead, since a choice must be made, let it be the second alternative and let it be based only on the optimistic hope that a set of environmental or societal conditions can be discerned that at least make war unlikely.[18] Stray bits of observations by anthropologists bolster the hope. A member of that guild once asserted that there have been societies in which war is "completely unknown," as evidence for which he cited an early British anthropologist who claimed that the aboriginal Australians, Eskimos, Ceylonese, Veda, and Hottentots had been warless. He thought too that war, not having existed allegedly before the Neolithic Age, must be "less than ten thousand years old."[19] Another anthropologist also indicates that members of her discipline "have come across cultures where neither violence, nor aggression, nor competition play a significant role" and that such societies have existed when their natural resources have been either abundant or scarce.[20]

One approach to the problem of discovering the predisposing causes of war-peace is, as it were, to leave the solution to a computer after a number of assumptions have been made and after selected data have been fed into the machine (cf. E). What emerges, as can be seen in Chapter Appendix 3.2 (Correlates of War-Peace), is a set of suggestive categories requiring further exploration. That exploration is attempted by considering slightly more sophisticated studies, details of which also can be found, if the reader is patient, in the same Chapter Appendix. The relevant research can be grouped under six headings which, in my opinion, are the best approximations of predisposing causes that can be located. In order to avoid repetition, two points applicable to all the headings are made in advance:

a. The propositions attain a degree of validity only after one or more of the key concepts has been carefully defined; the definitions are also offered in Chapter Appendix 3.2.
b. Deviant instances always appear (cf. V).

1. *"Primitivity"*: the more "primitive" the society, the less inclined toward war its inhabitants are likely to be (cf. P). Possibly the explanation for the negative association stems from the fact that so-called primitive societies tend to be isolated. An isolated group is not likely to have any, or very frequent contact with other groups and will not compete for land, women, or whatever produces conflicts for scarce resources. An examination of one component of primitivity, however, suggests that personality traits perhaps favorable to war-proneness may possibly be linked with the primitive *or* the nonprimitive. A nomadic existence, requiring hunting in addition to gathering, tends to emphasize the traits of "self-reliance and achievement," whereas agricultural and pastoral societies tend to develop individuals with the traits of "obedience and responsibility."[21] The first set would be desirable for individual warriors, the second for members of an armed force. In addition, the evidence suggests that all is not peace and love in non-Western societies: some that might be called "primitive" are also war-prone.

2. *Political centralization*: the greater the political centralization, the higher the degree of military sophistication (cf. P)—and military sophistication tends to be associated with military success.[22] It would follow that centralization, being related to sophistication, in turn must be related to success. Probably centralized governments encourage the skills needed for military success because their organization enables them to provide the necessary training and tools, because they may be less isolated and hence more vulnerable than those without such an organization, or because for some unknowable reasons they are more highly motivated to defend their way of life. In addition to the usual exceptions, mild surprises arise in connection with the investigation from which the proposition emerges. No relation exists between political centralization and either particular tactical systems or the use of shock weapons. Military sophistication is *not* associated either with casualty rates (at least when one statistical method is employed)

or—which is more important—with the likelihood of being attacked by an enemy.[23] The development of military skills, consequently, may not be a reaction to a real threat of losses; and sophisticated military skills apparently do not act as deterrents against attack.

3. *Military expenditures*: the greater a country's military expenditures, the greater the probability it will go to war (cf. P). Correlations of this kind are difficult to interpret (cf. I). The leaders of a country may increase military expenditures because the threat of war exists, and the threat of war may be perceived initially or later by its opponents because of the increase in those expenditures. Also, massive military expenditures (for example, by North Vietnam, Laos, and Israel in the mid-1960s, documented in Chapter Appendix 3.2) may result in large part from being engaged in warfare; without the expenditures the countries could be more successfully attacked. In addition, these reviews of past conflicts provoke the trite questions to which attention must eventually be addressed as the more general problem of deterrence is discussed: must the future repeat the past, is the past a guide to the future (cf. E)?

4. *Internal conditions*: conditions within a society have a greater effect on foreign policy and war-peace than relations between states (cf. P). Among those conditions are the presence or absence of violence within the society. Internal violence might thus be negatively correlated with external warfare: the greater the internal violence, the weaker the war-proclivity; or the greater the tendency to release aggression through war, the weaker the tendency toward internal violence. The reference to aggression raises difficult problems, for the expression of agression through crime (an internal condition) is different from that released by war (an external condition). A crime like murder can be perpetrated by an individual acting alone, but war is a cooperative effort for those who kill and for those offering logistical support to the killers. Leaders and some "rigidly organized struggle groups" may not be releasing their own aggression through warfare but may actually hunt down enemies (scapegoats) in order deliberately or unwittingly to retain their own positions by increasing in-group unity or to maintain their own unity or social cohesion.[24] In any case, some relation between internal conditions and wars seems to exist, a relation that will be examined again in connection with the issue of "the moral equivalent of war." Even the elimination of poverty in order to reduce internal frustration and hence aggression is not a surefire panacea, as the oft-cited Chapter Appendix 3.2 seeks to suggest.

5. *Early and later gratifications*: the greater the modal gratification or nonfrustration during socialization, the less the tendency to be war-prone (cf. P). This proposition is merely the repeated challenge to try to locate the conditions in early and late childhood which promote gratification rather than frustration (cf. I). It is difficult to meet the challenge as illustrated in a

volume titled "Learning Non-Aggression"[25] whose contents are too stimulating and important to be relegated to Chapter Appendix 3.2. The nonaggression depicted there is learned in seven "nonliterate" societies ranging in geographical location from New Guinea to Zaire. For each ethnic group the analysis is made by an anthropologist who has lived among the people, learned their language, won their confidence, and carefully observed their behavior. The first and most lasting impression to be gained from such praiseworthy studies is that nonviolence results not from one or more societal values or modes of rearing children but from, in the phrase of one of the investigators, "a particular pattern of controls"[26] which tends to be more or less unique in each society (cf. V). One cannot, one should not, rip a given social-psychological factor out of the context, as a computer approach must, and associate it cross-culturally with nonviolence. For each of the seven societies, my impression is, one factor is mentioned—along with others—which plays a contributory role in that society but not in the other six: "young infants remained in almost continual bodily contact with their mother, her housemates, or her gardening associates" (Fore of New Guinea); "the 'wrong-doer' withdraws and turns the frustration and anger against the self" (the !Kung of what was then South-West Africa); "one wants to see oneself as a good person" (the Qipisamiut in the eastern Arctic); "flight seems always preferred to fight" (Semai of West Malaysia); "everyone was enmeshed in a network of close relationships with some people, shading into more distant relationships with others" (Aborigines in Australia); "how else could that child as a child or as an adult face the world with such invincible faith in its ultimate goodness?" (Mbuti of Zaire); "if one does not strive and force things, then reality will inevitably take care of the individual" (Tahiti). One of the reasons, but not the only one, for such variability is the different environments in which the peoples of these societies live; hence it is not surprising that the !Kung, living in the harsh, inhospitable Kalahari Desert, produce nonaggression in different ways and for different reasons than do the Tahitians in surroundings providing "a varied and bounteous supply of food and other needs"[27] (cf. V).

What other generalizations concerning the promotion of nonaggression can be squeezed out of these seven case histories other than the influence of the environment? Only two, I think, but they are very important. First, as the title of the book suggests and as already emphasized in the previous chapter, nonaggression must be learned: it is learned in early childhood, and it results from loving and consistent treatment of the child during those years, however much the expression of that love may vary from society to society. Secondly, the members of the society must place a high value on nonaggression and on modes of action that gently punish aggressive behavior. No generalization, however, seems capable, in turn, of indicating more or less exactly why nonviolence rather than violence is highly valued in a particular society. At the outset of the present section reference was made to the view of an anthropologist that the natural resources in apparently peaceful societies can be either abundant or scarce.[28] Probably, therefore, the norm and the behavior in each instance must be traced to a unique set of circumstances, including the interaction between the environment and a host of factors such as the location with respect to other societies, contacts with those societies, historical development, and so on—maybe what is irreverently called "chance" or "good luck" also must be invoked (cf. I).

6. *Multivariance and uniqueness*: war-peace in any society fluctuates with a multitude of unique factors (cf. M). Should we rest content with such a flabby proposition? Yes, it seems necessary to do so. Each of the five propositions just considered has some validity but must also tolerate exceptions. We thus possess no single key to war-peace, but a collection of keys. Even when an attempt is made to consider a number of factors simultaneously, as indicated in Chapter Appendix 3.2, relatively little variance is accounted for. Similarly, analyses of particular conflicts point to the uniqueness of each war; much depends upon the variables subject to scrutiny as well as upon the particular country or culture that is examined. Reducing the war-peace problem to uniqueness, however, is not equivalent to succumbing to despair. The variables that have been isolated in any one study, though unique to that situation, provide useful guides to the future. They can be incorporated into a checklist, for there is always the possibility, maybe even the probability, that one or more of them will prove to be decisive in the societies being examined or generally in the pursuit of peace. In addition, the search for a generalization is made more difficult as a result of the interaction between all the predisposing causes which have been considered and the precipitating causes. In fact, "conventional explanations of wars," at least concerning those in Europe during the last few centuries, have highlighted the decisions of particular leaders and hence are attributed to "strategic reasoning."[29] Let us now turn to those precipitating causes as well as the decision makers themselves.

CHAPTER APPENDIXES

3.1 VARIABILITY OF PATRIOTISM (#s 1, 4c)

It is obvious that many nationals, especially in democratic societies, do not consider their leaders' decisions infallible; they do not hesitate, except perhaps in time of war, to speak up and criticize their government. They do not believe they are unpatriotic, no matter what their opponents think. Their criticism, they hope, will improve their country or prevent it from declining with respect to the issues that stir their ire.

At the beginning of the 1960s, more or less representative samples in five countries were asked, "what are the things about this country you are most proud of?" For better or worse, the replies revealed, as might have been anticipated, fluctuations from country to country. Americans, for example, predominantly referred to their governmental and political institutions and their economic system; West Germans to characteristics of their people and also to their economic system.[30]

Similarly, national sovereignty, like any other value, may on occasion be considered less important, at least nominally, than some other belief. In the early days of independence after World War II there was a tendency for those African leaders who favored modernizing their countries in the Western sense and centralizing their governments to pay lip service to Pan-Africanism, which meant limiting national sovereignty.[31] This proposed sacrifice soon gave way to assertions of nationalism and the inviolate, sacred character of the old colonial boundaries. Now the limitations upon sovereignty imposed by the Organization of African Unity are as scanty or nonexistent as those to which members of the United Nations pledge themselves.

On less lofty levels nationals are likely to agree not with specific details of their country's foreign policy but with its more general outlines. Most Americans, for example, favor the Monroe Doctrine, and their leaders would probably not dare depart from its principle. The sharp division of opinion over the Panama Canal treaties in 1978 did not reflect contrary tendencies; evoked were traditional attitudes and beliefs regarding the canal as well as relations with other Latin American countries besides Panama. Even in a harmless simulation exercise concerned with hypothetical countries, students of political science in Norway paid more attention to the multilateral institutions in the make-believe system and by and large utilized them more fully than did roughly comparable American students. Perhaps this finding reflects a different emphasis placed upon multilateral activity in the two countries. A less wealthy country like Norway cannot afford the more "expensive" form of bilateral negotiation preferred by the United States.[32]

3.2 CORRELATES OF WAR-PEACE (# 3)

When the responsibility for finding the correlates is assigned, as it were, to a computer, four steps must be taken. First, societies are dichotomized in one of four ways in terms of war-peace: warfare prevalent versus not prevalent; military glory strongly or moderately versus negligibly emphasized; considerable versus limited or negligible threat from armed attack; and commonly chronic versus rare or infrequent warfare.[33] These four divisions, not surprisingly, are related to one another even when the same societies or tribes are not compared.[34] The next step is to select various attributes of the societies that have been investigated and then to program the computer to determine which of those attributes are related to the four war-peace dichotomies. A conventional criterion is invoked: an association between the war-peace criterion and a given attribute could occur by chance only five times in a hundred (p.$<$.05). In addition, it is assumed that conditions in each society have not been influenced by any other society in the sample ("Galton's problem"). Under the conditions specified, the computer printout reveals seventeen significant associations between the first dichotomy and other attributes of societies for which data are available; thirty for the second; and zero for the third and fourth. The two zero sets of associations should serve as a warning that whatever emerges from statistical analyses via computers depends upon the criterion of war-peace that is selected and the attributes of the societies in question.

Consider the first dichotomy and the seventeen emerging associations. Of the forty-three societies—the only ones with adequate information for this particular study—thirty-four fall into the category of warfare "prevalent," nine "not prevalent." The seventeen associations, in my opinion, are too diffuse to be meaningful; hence not the investigator but I have classified them into half-a-dozen categories. Wars, then, tend to be associated with:

a. habitation patterns: fixed settlements; cities or towns
b. occupations: animal husbandry; metal working; weaving
c. political and social structures: a large or at least a minimal state; complex social hierarchies; stratification along class lines; slavery
d. recreation: games of chance; games not limited to skill
e. a socialization practice: high inferred anxiety among children
f. personality traits: emphasis on military glory; extreme bellicosity; high narcissism; extreme boastfulness

A seventeenth association, that between war and the presence of a post-partum taboo, may have some connection with socialization practices since the sexual behavior of the parents is thus regulated as the socialization of the newborn child begins. The first two categories resemble somewhat those characteristics of "primitivity" mentioned in the text of the present chapter and below; the third that of "political centralization"; the fourth that of "internal conditions"; and the last two those of "early and later gratifications." By squeezing the printout, in brief, some guidance has been obtained, although it is impossible to know how the factors interact and how each should be weighted in any combination.

Other studies, without or with assistance from computers, will now be considered under the rubrics outlined in the text.

1. *"Primitivity"*: an "index of primitivity" has been devised on the basis of data from 652, yes 652, societies. The criteria include the economy (whether hunting, pastoral, or agricultural), the political organization (whether clan, village, tribe, or state), and the basis for social organization (whether sex and age, professional, or caste). The index is negatively correlated

with belligerence, defined as engaging "in aggressive warfare for economic or political purposes." None of the most primitive societies engaged in such warfare, 95 percent of the least primitive did. The relations become even more impressive when another variable, "degree of contact with other societies," is simultaneously considered. Again, none of those societies that were most "primitive" and isolated could be characterized as belligerent, and all those classified as the least "primitive" and the least isolated could be called belligerent.[35] Another analysis, based upon other societies, replicates the generalization: less warlike societies tend to be nomadic, hence they have no fixed agriculture or animal husbandry, little or no private property, and of course no cities or towns.[36]

Whether or not the factor of isolation accounts for the negative relation between "primitivity" and warfare, however, may be an artifact of the way war is defined. According to one writer, a war should be called a "true war" only when it satisfies the following conditions: the ability of the belligerents to engage in tactical operations and to carry on after being defeated in the first battle; and the existence of a command, logistical supplies, and clear objectives. After examining some of the available anthropological evidence, especially in Africa, the conclusion is drawn that "the noncivilized fighter is no soldier, his warfare is not war, his butchering is futile and primitive because his operations lack organization and because he has developed the functions of leadership and command so poorly."[37] The "primitive" groups, therefore, tend to lack the organizational skill and machinery to wage war in a sophisticated sense.

The same writer, however, concedes that "many carefully planned actions" have occurred in Africa. He thus admits at least a partial exception to his generalization (cf. V). The Masai in eastern Africa, a nomadic tribe if ever there was one, certainly have been one of the most successful warriors in that part of the world. The Jibaro Indians of eastern Equador, who might be considered "primitive" because they have "no tribal organization" and do not recognize "any common political authority"[38] (hence they have been classified as "nonprofessional" and "uncentralized"),[39] apparently are not pacifists:

The wars, the blood feuds within the tribes, and the wars of extermination between the different tribes are continuous, being nourished by their superstitious belief in witchcraft. These wars are the greatest curse of the Jibaros and are felt to be so even by themselves, at least so far as the feuds within the tribes are concerned. On the other hand, the wars are to such a degree one with their whole life and essence that only powerful pressure from outside or a radical change of their whole character and moral views could make them abstain from them. This one may judge even from the fact that from a victory over his enemies the Jibaro warrior not only expects honors and fame in the ordinary sense of the word but also certain material benefits.[40]

Obviously their so-called primitivity did not prevent the Jibaro from fighting even if the author cited above would not consider the bloodshed an instance of "true war."

2. *Political centralization*: the proposition is derived from a study of a carefully selected sample of fifty traditional societies concerning which information on three variables has been chosen.[41] "Warfare" here is defined as armed combat between political communities; "political central-ization" as uncentralized bands and tribes versus centralized chiefdoms and states (anthropological classifications and similar to the political structures mentioned above); and "military sophistication" as an index derived from eleven military practices (a professional military organization, shock rather than projectile weapons, field fortifications, fortified villages, and so forth). The statistical generalization emerges when the societies are dichotomized with respect to both political centralization and military sophistication. Of course military sophistication tends to be associated with military success. The deviants from the association are impressive: three societies (Monarchi, Marshallese, and Aymara) have centralized political systems but are low in military sophistication;[42] and the bloody feuds of the "uncentralized" Jibaro have already been pointed out.

3. *Military expenditures*: the proposition receives somewhat impressive support. Two studies by anthropologists suggest that military expenditures do not act as deterrents, though they may have other functions. The first examined a variety of traditional societies, the second was based on a thorough statistical analysis (though modestly called "a pilot study") of a carefully drawn sample of twenty cases from two thousand years of history starting with the Han Dynasty against the Huns in 125-116 B.C. and ending with the conflict between France and England in 1776-1789. The conclusion of the first investigation, "to prepare for war is more likely to provoke war than to prevent it,"[43] is echoed by the second: "the search for peace and security through armed force is in vain."[44] The latter investigation found "a little support" for the common view that military preparations contribute to victory and that both "the quality and mobility of armed forces" dimin-ish the chances of losing territory:

It is often said that God is on the side of the largest battalions. If God takes sides, it is not the side of the largest battalions, nor that of the best fortified battalions, nor that of the most renowned. Rather God, if he takes sides at all, seems to stand at the side of the well-trained battalions.[45]

A similar nonassociation between war and the deterrent of preparing for war emerges in the twentieth century. In the mid-1960s, 121 nations were ranked with respect to the percentage of their gross national income devoted to defense expenditures. Heading the list were war-prone nations, North

Vietnam (19.7 percent) followed by Laos (15.6) and with Israel number 5 (12.2), the Soviet Union number 9 (9.0), China number 13 (7.9), and the United States number 15 (7.6). Toward the bottom and tied for 116th place were peaceful Jamaica and Malawi (0.6) and at the very bottom Iceland (0.0).[46] Among 96 international disputes between 1816 and 1965 those provoking arms races tended decidedly to escalate into wars.[47]

4. *Internal conditions*: a tour de force that would provide a résumé of "recent research," necessarily of a restricted kind, concludes that "the attributes of states are more significant determinants of their external behavior than are attributes of the external interrelationship patterns of which they are parties."[48] The domestic problems refer to the actions of citizens, particularly violent or aggressive ones, and could well include the factor of recreation appearing on the computer printout mentioned above. The inverse relation between the release of internal and external aggresssion is postulated by one anthropologist who "looks at the world" and then offers intuitive evidence suggesting that the blocking of "a tribe's customary outlet for aggression in war" ought to lead to "an increase in intratribal hostility (perhaps in the form of witchcraft) or in pathological states of melancholy resultant upon anger being turned inward against the self."[49] The asserted relation is tenuously confirmed in an analysis of fifty societies, all traditional or nonliterate except for Egypt and Japan, but only when the level of "political centralization" is high and only when the measure of internal aggression is "feuding" and not "internal war" (defined as "warfare between culturally similar political communities").[50] External conflicts, furthermore, may lead to internal disintegration if the group's social system lacks "solidarity" or if unity is not "despotically enforced."[51] In addition, the internal security may be of concern to leaders rather than to the mass of followers. An investigation of European countries starting in the eighteenth century indicates that often but not always there has been "a correlation between international instability and the domestic insecurity of elites."[52] As ever, there is contradictory evidence: cross-culturally, according to an anthropological study, the "channeling of aggression into war does not appear to be of great importance in reducing the level of crime and theft."[53]

One internal condition, poverty, might be expected to lead to frustration, some of the aggression from which could be displaced upon an enemy outside the country. It has been claimed, however—on the basis of not completely convincing evidence—that, at least among developing countries, poverty as such can be "a stabilizing factor" and hence, perhaps, domestic and international disputes are likely to appear only when the standard of living and educational level are rising.[54] Thus increasing expectations and not poverty per se incline nationals toward unrest, and the unrest may or may not result in warfare (cf. I). Other complications intrude. After World

War II, for example, many developed countries began distributing foreign aid not only to strengthen or establish ties of friendship, but also presumably to relieve or help banish poverty. But foreign aid of this kind does not appear to be the solution to the problem of aggression or war. First, if anything, the gaps between developed and developing countries seem at the moment to be widening and not diminishing,[55] except in the case of the oil-producing countries. Unrest frequently accompanies the distribution of such aid; corruption occurs, and people's rising expectations after receiving some benefits make them feel frustrated in other spheres. The educated elite who often have benefited from the aid and who remain unemployed after attending a university find aggressive outlets in protests and other disturbances having some relation to warlike activities. Thus the action taken to relieve poverty may lead to frustration and aggressive actions.

5. *Early and later gratifications*: ever since Freud, modern social scientists and others have turned to the socialization of children to explain modal behavior within a society. One study of traditional societies seems encouraging at first glance. It revealed an association between the presence of warfare in a society and two practices: (a) nonindulgence in infancy or childhood and (b) relatively heavy restrictions upon sexual activity either early or later in life, or both.[56] The analysis of the seven nonaggressive societies discussed in the body of this chapter, however, suggests that the matter is not that simple. In addition, there remains the chicken-and-the-egg problem of accounting for the modal socialization practices of a society (cf. I).

6. *Multivariance and uniqueness*: one investigator has surveyed the anthropological literature and believes that militarism can be explained by isolating not a single but "three basic variables" of significance "in primitive societies"—and, he adds, "as well as modern societies"—which are clearly related to some of the propositions propounded in this section's discussion of predisposing causes: private property, "frustrated personality," and "egoistic morality."[57] The three were most frequently associated with militarism and war, but none of the relationships approaches unity or perfection. Another attempt to summarize current knowledge resulted in the statistically based conclusion that "peaceful states are minor powers which seldom participate in foreign affairs," and therefore they engage in "little foreign conflict" and have "little domestic violence"; they are also "economically underdeveloped." Furthermore, the same summary indicates, nations prone to avoid war have "homogeneous populations" and "more homicides than either suicides or alcoholics."[58] Noteworthy in the above generalization is the host of qualifiers: "seldom," "little," and "more."

When attention is concentrated not upon postulated variables but upon particular countries, only approximate generalizations and unique instances emerge. A detailed, informal analysis has been made of fifty-two societies which have enjoyed internal and external peace for a century or more. They range from the Old Kingdom in the Nile Valley (2650-2350 B.C.) to the relations between Canada and the United States (starting in 1866). The most general conclusion turns out to be equivocal: "Peace can be achieved within a considerable variety of circumstances, and . . . such circumstances occur frequently, or can be created when they do not exist." Among the Chinese, in addition to other factors, for example, "a highly developed code of ethics and conduct" was associated with peace; among the Swiss, unsurprisingly, "a policy of strict neutrality," "a willingness to make things very difficult for any attacker," and "making themselves useful to great powers as a center of diplomatic exchange." Very scattered and mostly miscellaneous hints, however, pop out of these data. There seems to have been some association between peace and the following: relative isolation and prosperity; the presence of a large elite; a provision for provincial autonomy for the citizens of the country; an emphasis on defensive rather than offensive military techniques; a government not overreaching itself "in external commitments." Peace under a conqueror could be "born of satiation with war." On the other hand, some factors seem to have played no role in the pursuit of peace: religious unity; a system of succession in the political hierarchy; population ratio; international courts; or—perhaps most surprising of all—any particular type of political, social, or economic system. Cultural homogeneity or the avoidance of international cooperation may or may not have been influential. Little wonder, in short, that the author of this bit of intriguing scholarship courageously admits that "good luck" must be included as one of the factors determining peace.[59]

Accounting for any of the predisposing causes of war-peace also runs into the problem of uniqueness. A single illustration may be sufficient. When an anthropologist examined sixty societies—carefully selected so that reliable data were available and presumptive evidence existed that their development had been independent of one another—an additional factor not heretofore mentioned is postulated: there is a marked tendency for external warfare to be associated with matrilocal residence and internal conflicts with patrilocal. Why? In patrilocal societies, the writer reasons, brothers and uncles live side by side; rivalries develop within the face-to-face groups. When societies migrate from one locality to another, they must close ranks in order to survive. Adopting the matrilocal form of residence separates brothers and uncles and thus diminishes or eliminates their conflicts, and warfare can be more effectively carried on against other societies which may resent the intruder.[60] If this theory is correct, then the form in which hostility and warfare are expressed, but only among traditional societies, results from a series of historical circumstances, each of which is somewhat rare and yet reflects similar social or psychological processes. The fine theory has been challenged: perhaps external warfare may be a cause rather than a consequence of migration and type of residence, and the latter in turn may be affected by the contributions women make to the society's subsistence.[61] Perhaps professional military organizations tend to exist in small, matrilocal and in large, patrilocal societies.[62]

NOTES

1. H. L. Nieburg, *Political Violence*. New York: St. Martin's Press, 1969. P. 115.

2. Sigmund Freud, Why War? In Joan Riviere (trans.), *Collected Papers of Sigmund Freud*. New York: Basic Books, 1959. Vol. 5, pp. 273-87.

3. Walker Connor, The politics of ethnonationalism. *Journal of International Affairs*, 1973, 27, 1-21.

4. Ross Stagner, *Psychological Aspects of International Conflict*. Belmont: Wadsworth, 1967. P. 51.

5. Hans Kohn, *Nationalism*. Princeton: Nostrand, 1955. P. 9. Cf. also Bryant Wedge, Psychiatry and international affairs. *Science*, 1967, 157, 281-85.

6. Amitai Etzioni, International prestige and peaceful competition. In Quincy Wright, William E. Evan, and Morton Deutsch (eds.), *Preventing World War III*. New York: Simon and Schuster, 1962. Pp. 226-45.

7. Leonard W. Doob (ed.), *Resolving Conflict in Africa*. New Haven: Yale University Press, 1970.

8. Richard Rose, *Governing without Consensus*. London: Faber and Faber, 1971. P. 507.

9. Salvador de Madariaga, Blueprint for a world commonwealth. In Carnegie Endowment for International Peace, *Perspectives on Peace 1910-1960*. New York: Praeger, 1960. Pp. 47-64.

10. Amitai Etzioni, The Kennedy experiment. *Western Political Quarterly*, 1967, 20, 361-80.

11. Alix Strachey, *The Unconscious Motives of War*. New York: International Universities Press, n.d. P. 202.

12. Michael Walzer, *Just and Unjust Wars*. New York: Basic Books, 1977. Pp. 234-38.

13. Carlton J. H. Hayes, *Essays on Nationalism*. New York: Macmillan, 1937. P. 183.

14. Leo Perla, *What is "National Honor"?* New York: Macmillan, 1918. Pp. 24-25.

15. Cf. Robert A. LeVine, Socialization, social structure, and intersocietal images. In Herbert C. Kelman (ed.), *International Behavior*. New York: Holt, Rinehart and Winston, 1965. P. 45-69.

16. Margaret Mead, War is only an invention—not a biological necessity. In David Brook (ed.), *Search for Peace*. New York: Dodd, Mead, 1970. Pp. 12-16.

17. Judd Marmor, Psychological problems of warlessness. In Arthur Larson (ed.), *A Warless World*. New York: McGraw-Hill, 1952. Pp. 117-30.

18. Emil Obermann, *Gesellschaft und Verteidigung*. Stuttgart: Stuttgarter Verlagskontor, 1971. P. 31.

19. Santiago Genovés, *Is Peace Inevitable?* New York: Alker, Pp. 19-21.

20. Ruth H. Landman, Not every society eats the enemy. *AAUW Journal*, 1970, 63, 157-59.

21. Herbert Barry, Irvin L. Child, and Margaret K. Bacon, Relation of child training to subsistence economy. *American Anthropologist*, 1959, 61, 51-63.

22. Keith F. Otterbein, *The Evolution of War*. New Haven: HRAF Press, 1970. Pp. 105-6.

23. Ibid., pp. 41, 46, 82, 90.

24. Lewis Coser, *The Functions of Social Conflict*. Glencoe: Free Press, 1956. P. 110.

25. Ashley Montagu, *Learning Non-Aggression*. New York: Oxford University Press, 1978.

26. Ibid., p. 231.

27. Ibid., pp. 16, 43, 65, 97, 148, 171, 225, 226.

28. Landman, op. cit.

29. Anatol Rapoport, Two views on conflict. In International Peace Research Association, *Proceedings of the International Peace Research Association Inaugural Conference*. Assen: Van Gorcum, 1966. Pp. 78-99.

30. Gabriel A. Almond and Sydney Verba, *The Civic Culture*. Princton: Princton University Press, 1963. P. 102.

31. Immanuel Wallerstein, *Nationalism*. New York: Vintage Books, 1961. P. 106.

32. Mari Holmboe Ruge, Small-power vs. big-power perspective on foreign policy. *Proceedings of the International Peace Research Association*, 1970, 3, 293-331.

33. Robert D. Textor, *A Cross-Cultural Summary*. New Haven: HRAF Press, 1967. Codings 416-19.

34. Elbert Russell, Factors of human aggression. *Behavior Science Notes*, 1972, 7, 275-312.

35. Tom Broch and Johan Galtung, Belligerence among the primitives. *Journal of Peace Research*, 1966, 3, no. 1, 33-45.

36. William Eckhardt, Primitve militarism. *Journal of Peace Research*, 1975, 12, 55-62.

37. Harry Holbert Turney-High, *Primitive War*. Columbia: University of South Carolina Press, 1949. P. 227.

38. Rafael Karsten, Blood revenge and war among the Jibaro Indians of eastern Equador. In Paul Bohannan (ed.), *Law and Warfare*. Garden City: Natural History Press, 1967. Pp. 303-25.

39. Otterbein, op. cit., p. 8.

40. Karsten, op. cit.

41. Otterbein, op. cit., p. 3.

42. Ibid., pp. 19, 72-73, 74, 105-6.

43. Eckhardt, op. cit.

44. Raoul Naroll, Vern L. Bullough, and Frada Naroll, *Military Deterrence in History*. Albany: State University of New York Press, 1974. P. 343.

45. Ibid., pp. 328, 337.

46. Charles L. Taylor and Michael C. Hudson, *World Handbook of Political and Social Indicators*. New Haven: Yale University Press, 1971. Pp. 34-36.

47. Michael D. Wallace, Arms races and escalation. *Journal of Conflict Resolution*, 1979, 23, 3-16.

48. Juergen Dedring, *Recent Advances in Peace and Conflict Research*. Beverly Hills: Sage Publications, 1976. P. 83.

49. Clyde Kluckhohn, *Mirror for Man*. New York: McGraw-Hill, 1949. P. 267.

50. Keith F. Otterbein, Internal war. *American Anthropologist*, 1968, 70, 277-89.

51. Coser, op. cit., p. 95.

52. Richard N. Rosecrance, *Action and Reaction in World Politics*. Boston: Little, Brown, 1963. P. 304.

53. Russell, op. cit.

54. Marion Mushkat, The small states and research into aspects of war and peace. *International Journal of Group Tensions*, 1971, 1, 124-53.

55. Bert V. A. Röling, An introduction to the problem of poverty, development, and peace. *Proceedings of the International Peace Research Association*, 1968, 22, 1-18.

56. Russell, op. cit.

57. Eckhardt, op. cit.

58. Michael Haas, International socialization. In Michael Haas (ed.), *International Systems.* New York: Chandler, 1974. Pp. 51-75.

59. Matthew Melko, *52 Peaceful Societies.* Oakville: CPRI Press, 1973. Pp. 170, 178-88.

60. William Tulio Divale, Migration, external warfare, and matrilocal residence. *Behavior Science Research*, 1974, 9, 75-133.

61. Carol R. Ember, An evaluation of alternative theories of matrilocal versus patrilocal residence. *Behavior Science Research*, 1974, 9, 135-49.

62. Harold Carter, Jr., Military organization as a response to residence and size of population. *Behavior Science Research*, 1977, 12, 271-90.

4.

International Reality

The war-peace problems of this chapter ordinarily fall under conventional, prosaic headings such as international relations, international politics, diplomacy, and history. An effort to refer, whenever possible, to specific individuals in their international roles and orientations is especially difficult in such a context because conflicts between countries include so many different persons. The routes from personality to decision groups and war-peace outcomes, nevertheless, must be heavily traversed.

PRECIPITATING CAUSES OF WAR-PEACE (#s 3, 4*)

The struggle in the last chapter to determine the predisposing causes of war-peace has been conducted broadly and somewhat vainly: what kinds of societies are more or less war-prone as a result of conditions in their milieu, including their socialization practices? A related but more immediate question is now raised: what induces any society, whether war-prone or not, to abandon peace and go to war? The deadly lightning of war may come from, or strike any country. When? Why?

The number of opinions concerning the precipitating causes of war is truly staggering. Descriptively I think there is agreement on only one point: wars, whatever their underlying dynamics,[1] involve conflict of some sort, conflict between tribes or states, which means that some persons on either side have or think they have goals that cannot be shared or simultaneously attained. When the problem is approached in terms of the motives, beliefs, attitudes, and skills of the participants, the first question to be answered is: who are the participants? Certainly the leaders, secondarily also their followers.

*See pages 11-12 for an explanation of the cross-referencing system.

Almost without exception it is the leaders of modern nations who abandon peace and declare war, but influentials and followers generally must or do accept their decisions since, they are usually told, it is the enemy who is responsible for the conflict.

Leaders, influentials, and followers are more or less distinctive and certainly their interactions with one another and with their counterparts in other countries are equally distinctive. For this reason, the search for a singular, immediate cause of war, however praiseworthy, is likely to be futile. Indeed, competent scholars, in spite of their good intentions and their ambitions to emit transcending generalizations, often consider each war to be sui generis (cf. V), and hence generalizations "must be modified and adjusted to fit the distinctive circumstances of particular wars."[2] Historians who concentrate upon those circumstances then conclude their analyses with such a multiplicity of theories that, in my opinion, they emerge with no coherent or useful generalizations. Statistical analyses fare no better (see Chapter Appendix 4.1: Historical Theories). The problem of precipitating causes, nevertheless, is so important that the topic must be reviewed at some length.

Perhaps the most frequently mentioned theory concerning war is some version of an economic thesis, whether non-Marxian or Marxian. By and large, the conclusion must be, such a theory is valuable in proposing a setting for war-peace, but it merits criticism on two grounds: it fails to distinguish between predisposing and precipitating causes (cf. P); and it may even be ultimately incorrect. The need for raw materials and for foreign markets undoubtedly played a role as European powers acquired colonies during the last two centuries and hence contributed to many wars in the past. Both historical surveys and at least one statistical analysis indicate a very strong relation between imperialism (whose goal is largely, though not exclusively, economic) and both civil and international wars.[3] Similarly the energy crisis in the West has affected Western policies regarding the oil-producing countries and hence may have increased the danger of war. But the motive behind economic development or the need for oil reflects general cultural and political currents within the countries seeking expansion or fuel. If Americans used and wasted less energy, for example, their partial dependence on Arab countries would be less. Their actions in this respect reflect a whole set of values involving comfort, prestige, competitiveness, and so on, no one of which can be called strictly economic. Likewise no simple relation exists between the economic status of a group and its desire for more material and nonmaterial goods, a desire that is not necessarily associated with war. Slaves or workers may or may not rebel; and perhaps—as suggested in Chapter Appendix 3.2—only after their expectations have risen following some improvement in their status quo do they begin to pass judgment and to voice demands leading to violence or war.

As was suggested decades ago, for the "nation" as a whole the economic gains from victory—however alluring they seem in prospect—are an "illusion";[4] the sheer costs of waging war and recovering from it are staggering. A motive, however, that effectively produces action must be considered significant even when those so motivated fail to achieve their goals. Another false but motivating illusion is fear concerning the economic effects of disarming. While it is true that immediate disarmament may have severe economic repercussions and dislocations,[5] the billions spent on armaments could eventually be used for productive, peaceful purposes. In addition, disarmament also entails costly expenditures since in the modern world it is accompanied by inspection, monitoring, and international armies and organizations; hence it "may require as much investment as the arms race"[6] and soften the economic dislocations.

One clever writer, in part with tongue in cheek, has punctured the economic argument by advancing a case for "the white flag principle": it is better to surrender than to win a battle or a war. He maintains, quite convincingly at times, that throughout history the loser and not the winner of war has profited from the conflict in many ways, including the economic. The victors assume the responsibility for governing and caring for the vanquished so that in the long run theirs is an economic loss. They are likely to endure disillusionment and corruption. Their casualty rates, he suggests by selecting his evidence, tend to be higher. In contrast, those who surrender seize the initiative to end the war; usually prisoners of war lead a better and certainly a safer existence than soldiers on the battlefield; and most important of all the losers after defeat experience an economic miracle and a brilliant recovery. It makes no economic sense to wage a war.[7] (See Chapter Appendix 4.2: Economic Determinism.)

A reasonable conclusion from the historical, statistical, and economic (including the Marxian) analysis of war is that the precipitating causes are numerous and are weighted differently in each conflict (cf. P). If one says, for example, that wars break out when leaders and followers are motivated to fight and when they possess appropriate beliefs and attitudes—certainly not a brilliant statement—then each of these three factors may vary in importance from 1 to 99 percent, yet most certainly no one of them can be reduced to zero or be as high as 100 percent. In some epochs or for some wars, the economic factors may be most significant, in others much less so. During a five-year period starting in 1955, for example, there seemed to be little relation between war, belligerency short of war, and hostile diplomacy among seventy-five neighboring countries on the one hand and the following factors ordinarily thought to be promising candidates for precipitating causes of war on the other hand: those countries' political systems, their languages, their religions, and the number of countries with which they had geographical contact. The association did not improve when the size and economic development of the countries were simultaneously taken into account.[8]

The moment an eclectic approach to the problem of war's precipitating causes is adopted, a Pandora's box of factors is opened and out pop exotic hypotheses. Ordinarily, for example, science fiction is not included among those causes, but a brilliant survey of how future wars have been imagined by novelists, poets, dramatists, and journalists reveals the influence this type of fiction has had in the West during the last two centuries (cf. V).[9] Such a "cause" seems farfetched until it is pointed out that literary works of this sort reflect the hopes and fears of the authors and also of the era in which they are written. They are read by leaders and followers and hence may affect judgments and decisions. (See Chapter Appendix 4.3: Science Fiction.)

Another approach is to abandon the attempt to find causes of war-peace and to employ simple, straightforward actuarial reasoning: what is known specifically about the past can be utilized to predict what will happen in the future (cf. E). What happens when past-to-future reasoning is employed? A study of alignments between countries in modern times suggests that the crucial determining factor is not their proximity, similarity, economic capabilities, or trade, but whether they have "cooperated in the past." Yet "it is not possible to determine whether previous attempts at cooperation were in any way successful and thereby became the basis for future cooperation, or whether aligning nations shared similar problems and cooperated regardless of past successes."[10] Yes, Britain and the United States have not been at war since 1815 and hence will not fight in the future. Japan and the United States opposed each other during World War II and will, therefore, in the future? With reference to the present, it might be said that these latter two countries in a sense were aligned ever since the penetration of Commodore Perry and until relations began to deteriorate prior to Pearl Harbor in 1941. Since 1945 relations have been relatively smooth again. The reasoning thus seems tenuous and becomes even more so when applied to the Western and also the Soviet bloc of nations. "The realm of conjecture based on history," therefore, is of "limited pragmatic value":

Suppose, for instance, that I had been asked by the French government of the 1920s to advise them, on the basis of [the author's own study of 52 peaceful societies] how they might maintain peace for the next hundred years. I might have advised them to build a wall of powerful forts along their unprotected eastern border, since barriers of this kind had been effective in maintaining peace for other countries. Then I should have advised them to support stable, neutral, border countries like Belgium, since my study had shown that such countries will protect your flank, inasmuch as they won't collapse quickly and you will be able to go to their support if anyone else attacks them, and fight the war in their territory.

Such conclusions, of course, are exactly those the French came to for themselves, with utterly disastrous results.[11]

More extensive actuarial approaches are statistical in nature and have been considered in Chapter Appendix 4.1.

Perhaps the stress on multivariance, accompanied by the attempt to deflate every straightforward theory concerning the causes of war, is beginning to sound monotonous and exaggerated (cf. M). For certainly some wars seem relatively simple to explain—at least on the surface, I add immediately and skeptically. In the modern era, for example, time and time again native peoples have waged war on their colonial rulers in order to achieve independence. Guerrillas have sometimes had limited objectives, such as publicizing their cause or existence if need be through acts of terror; or they have sought to demonstrate their strength by capturing and retaining one or more villages in the country they would liberate. Here there seem to be no problems, until the question is raised as to why colonial peoples have wished independence so devoutly that they have been willing to make the sacrifices associated with war to obtain it. And then we find ourselves again in the whirlpool of multiple causes, unless it be blandly asserted that the desire for independence is self-evident and requires no further analysis.

I take refuge from the irate reader by daring to join hands with Tolstoy whose views on the precipitating causes of war have been echoed in this presentation. (See Chapter Appendix 4.4: Tolstoy.)

LEADERS AND OFFICIALS (# 4)

So much has been written about leaders and about specific heroes and villains that the title of this section is deservedly yawn-producing. Erasmus in "The Education of a Christian Prince," however, has issued the challenge:

Although a prince ought nowhere to be precipitate in his plans, there is no place for him to be more deliberate and circumspect than in the matter of going to war. Some evils come from one source and others from another, but from war comes the shipwreck of all that is good and from it the sea of all calamities pours out.[12]

Yawn or no yawn, therefore, the roles of leaders and officials in war-peace dare not be tossed aside as a result of boredom or banality. They are too important to be ignored.

On an abstract, a priori level it seems evident that the role of leaders is a function of three interrelated factors: their own personalities and hence capabilities; interaction with their followers and influential persons in their society; and also their relations with out-groups that are allies, neutrals, and potential or actual enemies (cf. P). Similarly the conduct of diplomats, that is, leaders in international affairs, depends upon the government they represent, the tradition of their country, the power they command, and their opponents.[13] The role of leaders and diplomats more often than not is concealed behind metaphors which refer to "the government," "the nation," "the foreign office," so that the identity and precise actions of the decision makers may remain unknown (cf. I). (See Chapter Appendix 4.5: Metaphors.) The weight to be given the factor of leadership and that of influentials and followers varies from society to society and within a given society from time to time (cf. V). Only one point is beyond doubt: for leaders to lead they must have a "mandate to rule" whether they base their authority or legitimization on deities, as kings and aristocrats have in the past; on a military or police force loyal to them; or—particularly in the Western world since the French Revolution—on the will of their followers, however that will is expressed.[14] Otherwise it is evident that many factors are involved in decision making, unless the leader is truly a supreme dictator (cf. M). Usually information about the dynamics of real-life decisions is lacking, so that ambitious academic investigators must resort to the make-believe antics of simulation in order to gain at least preliminary insight into the parameters of the problem.

Neologisms or semineologisms have been devised to call attention to aspects of the decision-making process of leaders. A colorful and provocative one is that of "groupthink" (yes, one word) to indicate the tendency for dissenters belonging to the leader's in-group consciously or unconsciously to suppress their dissent in order to retain rapport between themselves and their superiors as they interact and thus to contribute to the latter's confidence.[15] The one appealing factor so often considered crucial by biographers and the mass media is the leader's personality. It is, however, quite hopeless to speculate concerning leaders' motives because too much needs to be said and too much remains unknown (cf. I). One can assume, I suppose, that each leader has various identifications—"ethnic, regional, caste or class, racial, and national"[16]—which may or may not be salient and which may or may not determine his behavior during a crisis. In one of his orientations, almost every leader must to some extent abhor the idea of war, but he must also realize, as William James observed while offering his conception of war's equivalent, that "so far, war has been the only force that can discipline a whole community" and hence can easily be used as an expedient to achieve unity among his followers.[17] Typologies of leaders likewise are numerous without necessarily serving a useful purpose. A distinction has been made, for example, between leaders who are "person-minded" since they are "mindful" of their constituents and those who are "object-minded" since they ruthlessly love power and believe that individuals are "things to be manipulated in the service of a cause."[18] Intuitively the distinction is appealing, although overlapping between the two types must be considerable. I would guess that most leaders have more than a touch of object-mindedness, since power brings gratification and therefore the desire to retain control is likely to be strong.

Obviously the personalities of leaders and officials are diverse (cf. V). It is clear that each of them undoubtedly has his own philosophy or "conception du monde."[19] That conception must be related to early childhood experiences as well as to other aspects of their personalities. An indignant psychoanalyst asserts that leaders "frequently" have an "abnormal makeup" and he avers that "a common circumstance" in the background of Hitler, Mussolini, and Stalin was a childhood in which they were dominated and then released "from repression by their fathers' deaths" around the age of puberty.[20] Such a view is undoubtedly too simple; not all leaders have such backgrounds and not all persons with such backgrounds become leaders. Possibly, however, leaders with certain repressions or compulsions originating in the past are not likely to become *homines pacifici*. Although, according to one summary, "the influence of personality on decision outcome [in international politics] is largely unexplored"[21] and although in fact investigators who have attempted to assess the effect of personality conclude that the personal characteristics of diplomats account for relatively little of their activity[22] or at most are said to have only a contributory but not a major influence upon their actions,[23] nevertheless, some aspect of an official's attitude toward foreign affairs may be related to his personality. (See Chapter Appendix 4.6: Leadership Research.)

In short, the multivariant nature of the decision-making process precludes easy generalizations about the role of leaders' personalities in that process. According to an historical analysis of "all" wars since 1700, also cited in Chapter Appendix 4.1, "at least seven factors" appear to have "strongly influenced" the relevant leaders. Two refer to predispositions: their "personality and experience" and also the prevailing "nationalism and ideology" in the various states. Four involve perception or predictions concerning the international situation at hand: the country's own "military strength and the ability to apply that strength efficiently in the likely theater of war"; "the state of the economy" and the country's "ability to sustain the war envisioned"; the existence of "internal unity or discord" at home and in the enemy's domain; and "estimates of how outside nations will behave if war should occur." The seventh is simply "knowledge or forgetfulness of the realities and sufferings of war." Each of these factors sounds sensible, and it can well be imagined that leaders in the past functioned according to the model. The same investigator, however, believes that, like the predisposing and precipitating causes of war, the factors he himself has isolated "varied so much from one mind to another, and from one nation to another, that the same evidence could support different conclusions,'' with the result that a given factor has turned out to facilitate either war or peace.[24] Conceivably decision makers could function rationally by assessing all relevant data and by transcending the "personality and experience" factor; then, with the help of a computer, they could conclude whether their side would win or lose (cf. E). But, as a German sociologist is quoted as saying, exact knowledge of this kind "is very often attainable only by the actual fighting out of the conflict";[25] and a modern, learned negotiator discusses decision-making factors in a chapter he calls "The Fog of Military Estimates."[26]

And so there is no solid basis for thinking that war-peace judgments and decisions are made rationally, almost no matter how rationality is defined (cf. P). The conclusion is true even though leaders may try to sit back and pierce the fog: they may feel uninvolved because "in general those who plan do not kill and those who kill do not plan."[27] A refreshing survey of models based on documents concerning decisions and simulations concludes that in their national roles leaders are constrained by the "situational forces" of their milieu and of the countries they represent; and in their individual roles they seek solutions consistent with their own private images, they distort what they perceive since they are subject to stress, and they try to view the world and especially their opponents as more certain and orderly than the facts warrant.[28] The "overwhelming" evidence of history, according to one social scientist, indicates that leaders have based their decisions primarily upon what they thought must be done to preserve their nations' "interests" and only secondarily upon moral considerations,[29] a generalization that sheds very little light on how the decisions were actually made. Nonrationality, it may or may not be comforting to know, is not confined to war-peace decisions: one theorist argues that decisions in general involving complex issues are never likely to be "rational-comprehensive" but result from "muddling through" as best one can on the basis of necessarily limited information.[30]

An additional complication reducing the rational component of war-peace decisions stems from the fact that in this modern age judgments often must be quickly passed. Leaders must guess, and some may have to guess at virtually a moment's notice, whether inflicting nuclear damage upon an enemy is worthwhile on the basis of "a virtually untested tradeoff calculation."[31] In the meantime those in powerful nations realize full well they are forever faced with what has been called the "delicate balance of terror" provoked by the possibility of nuclear warfare.[32] That terror, which began immediately after American planes dropped atomic bombs on Hiroshima and Nagasaki, in the view of General Smuts "should put war out of court for good and all."[33] According to the optimistic hope of a political scientist writing a few years after World War II, the two World Wars and the new weapons have "conspired to force a broadening out of attention to include the world of human beings in most calculations of international action."[34] Officials as well as followers, nevertheless, have gradually become more or less inured to the possibility of the destruction the deadly weapons can cause.[35] Only when a new kind of bomb or plane or negotiations such as the SALT talks throughout the 1960s and 1970s are publicly mentioned is anxiety aroused and the awesome prospects become salient. Will the "hot lines" connecting the leaders of powerful countries prevent their leaders from having to make last-minute, less rational decisions? I think the question is unanswerable.

To a greater or less degree, leadership skills may have some effect upon war-peace judgments. As indicated in Chapter Appendix 2.6, some European leaders but not others managed to keep their countries neutral in World War II. Virtually all modern statesmen have only a lay knowledge of the sciences that guide the construction and use of the new deadly weapons; hence somehow they must skillfully evaluate the views of consultants who seldom are in complete agreement with one another. After an election in which an opposing political party comes into power, the newly enthroned leaders may not comprehend the background or the policies they inherit and may thus be dependent, in British terminology, upon the permanent secretaries of the departments they head. Responsibility for international judgments, moreover, may be given to individuals who are experts on domestic policy or other subjects.[36] In the West and sometimes elsewhere many officials have been trained in the study of law, and their permanent secretaries or civil servants also subscribe to the view that decisions should be, or should appear to be lawful.

When they initiate a war, whether or not they truly believe what they say, leaders must have both the skill and the facilities to communicate the decision to influentials and other followers in acceptable terms. The "conflict of interests," they must maintain, is "so deep that it cannot be resolved either by unilateral retreat or by mutual compromise and therefore can only be resolved by war."[37] Generally the responsibility is placed upon the enemy: "they" were going to attack "us," or they have in fact attacked us; we must intervene to protect our fellow countrymen or to prevent other countries from continuing to be or from being overrun by the forces of evil.[38] We are, therefore, fighting a just war. The notion of a just war, just for whatever reasons, is one of the most powerful tools in the kit of leaders (cf. P). It stems from a tradition reaching back to classical Greece[39] and is clearly part of the Christian heritage. A modern Luthern minister, for example, believes that "Christian realism" rejects both militarism and pacifism and argues that a "permissible war" to achieve "peace with honor" should have six attributes which range from having the war "declared by a legitimate authority" and a belief that the war is the "lesser of two evils" to the "real probability of success through military means" and the exhaustion of "all other efforts to gain a morally just solution to a conflict."[40]

Behind the just war is a cornucopia of legal, moral, and emotional principles ready to be tapped. They may be called absolutistic or personificative. The former include appeals to determinism (divine sanction, destiny, nature, and humanitarian responsibility); to the transcendental values of peace and freedom; to legality and semilegality (sovereignty, justice, contract, the rights of the majority, and the alleged superiority of one nation or ethnic group). The latter refer to appeals based upon the extension of family symbols (birthright, consanguinity, similarity of culture); upon temporal factors ("we" were there first, "we" have been there the longest, the status quo must be maintained); upon human justifications (needs, achievement, demands of public opinion, and revenge).[41] The war cry is not likely to be phrased exclusively in economic terms, although the possibility or promise of economic gain may lurk in the background. Little wonder that officials can easily find the proper text to justify whatever decision they would make regarding war-peace.

Just as leaders provide noble-sounding and ostensibly ethical reasons to engage in a just war, so they and their generals are able to discover equally compelling reasons for violating the rules of war or for committing atrocities against prisoners of war and civilians. If the conviction exists that one is fighting for freedom, freedom now or in the future, freedom for one's own group or for mankind, it is too easy to believe that some principles must be sacrificed to achieve the postulated goal. The so-called rules of war, whether embodied in treaties or the moral codes of mankind, may therefore be suspended. Deadly actions like the indiscriminate bombing of whole cities as occurred on both sides during World War II are justified in terms of the "supreme emergency" which leaders assert confronts their country; or inhuman blows against the enemy are phrased, correctly or not, as reprisals.[42]

Yet another kind of skill is needed for those leaders in power who judge whether and how to end a war, regardless of whether they themselves have been its initiator: when should one concede defeat, what terms should the apparent victor offer to induce surrender? According to one analysis, wars begin when the antagonists have dissimilar judgments concerning "their ability or inability to impose their will by force rather than by some other means on the rival nation"; they usually end when they "agree on their relative strength."[43] Somehow leaders must weigh the advantages and disadvantages of agreeing to a cease-fire, taking into account such factors as casualties, the chances for victory or defeat, domestic and international public opinion, and the gains and losses from a possible peace treaty. Events may suggest that further resistance is futile. In World War II Hitler never made a formal decision concerning surrender; instead he sought to pull down the temple of his country before he himself committed suicide.

Leaders are judged by what they accomplish or fail to accomplish. Sometimes the judgment is easy to make: Caesar conquered Gaul; Napoleon and Hitler did not subdue the Soviet Union; Wilson did not keep the United States out of war; Churchill and Roosevelt (or at least their armies) drove the Germans out of North Africa, France, the Low Countries, and some of the Balkans. In these instances, the goals have been stated by the leaders themselves and there is objective evidence concerning their failure or successes. And yet it can be argued that their decisions had many origins in addition to their own beliefs and attitudes, such as the spirit of the time in which they lived or the demands of their followers. The ultimate consequences of the decisions may be elusive or subject to various interpretations by different judges (cf. I). President Truman in 1945 permitted atomic bombs to be dropped on Japan whose leaders quickly surrendered. Was that a wise or a good decision in view of the American lives thus saved and the Japanese lives thus lost, in view of the subsequent development and proliferation of nuclear weapons, in view of the cold war and its armament races? Was it necessary, as some have suggested after the fact,[44] to drop the bombs, for would it not have been possible to have a group of Japanese scientists and engineers (or a comparable group from neutral Switzerland or Sweden whom the Japanese experts would trust) visit Los Alamos or some laboratory to observe the technical advances about to be completed and then have them communicate to Japanese political leaders the fact that Americans actually had the capability of implementing theory and manufacturing the weapon? Now that the deadliness of these weapons and their newer versions has been demonstrated, so that the question of credibility or feasibility is no longer involved, should foreign policies be predicated on the dangerous assumption of deterrence?

Perhaps, then, it is true in general, if I may again end a section by invoking Tolstoy's analysis of Napoleon's invasion of Russia, that:

All the innumerable individuals who took part in the war acted in accordance with their natural dispositions, habits, circumstances, and aims. They were moved by fear or vanity, they rejoiced or were indignant, they argued and supposed that they knew what they were doing and did it of their own free will, whereas they were all involuntary tools of history, working out a process concealed from them but intelligible to us.[45]

Today Tolstoy's analysis is phenomenologically correct no doubt. The tribute to ''us'' I suppose is a reference to the value of hindsight.

FOLLOWERS (# 4c)

Clearly it has been impossible to approach leaders and officials in the previous section without frequent references to the reciprocal relation existing between them and their followers. In their international role followers have varying influence upon war-peace policies (cf. V), but some always bear the brunt of war and virtually all benefit from peace. The term *public opinion* is used loosely to refer not only to the beliefs but also to the attitudes and motives of these followers.

The precise relation between leaders and followers depends in large part upon the political system in which they are embedded. In a democracy followers are able somewhat effectively to communicate with leaders by voting, as well as through the mass media, informal contacts, and especially influential peers. In contrast, not sharp but evident, leaders of authoritarian regimes probably pay less attention to followers as they make crucial war-peace decisions, although—after the decisions have been made and especially if war is declared—they are compelled to use the media and legal or extra-legal means to induce or strengthen cooperation among military and civilian personnel. Over time, moreover, the relation may shift. In Western society, followers played only a minor role in the wars of antiquity and the early Christian Era. During those centuries "alien dynasties or conquerors" easily appropriated large territories and then imposed their languages, architecture, or religion upon peasants "to whom one conqueror was much the same as another."[46] Only within the first half of the current century have followers emerged "as a serious check on government action,"[47] or at least so it has seemed.

Actually there is little evidence to indicate that followers are all-powerful in the modern era. Generally they are not consulted directly concerning vital policy decisions. Solely as tourists, students, and scholars do they obtain firsthand information about other countries which has not been filtered through the mass media. One explanation for their relatively slight influence is that they are more likely to think and act in their individual or national roles unless an international crisis is at hand. (See Chapter Appendix 4.7: Surveys of Followers.) Modern leaders have at their disposal, if I may distort somewhat the optimism of one writer, "knowledge and techniques" enabling them to influence followers "in desired directions and so exercise a greater control over international events."[48] Obviously sophistication in the social and biological sciences and the technological advances in the mass media are a double-edged sword that can be employed in behalf of peace or war. Leaders are well acquainted with their powers in this respect, as is demonstrated simply by mentioning the words advertising, psychological warfare, political warfare, and public relations, all of which affect the ways in which audiences immediately perceive events and subsequently their judgments and actions. Followers, however, are not completely inactive. They do not react favorably to all the communications that inundate them. They produce communications of their own. When they are anxious or uncertain about their destiny—usually the situation during a war—they spread rumors that may or may not strengthen morale.

The most prominent and significant tool employed by leaders in affecting followers is of course language. Here attention is called to the slippery nature of the vocabulary related to war-peace. The word *war* itself continues to be the label applied to international conflicts "in spite of the qualitative change" that has taken place in modern warfare,[49] thus giving the misleading impression that the similarities between the struggles culminating in the unification of Italy in the nineteenth century and a present or future war are greater than the differences between them. Terms such as *megatons* or *thirty million casualties* become little more than vocal vibrations[50] since the realities they represent, being difficult for most persons to grasp, recede into the background. Glib sentences slip by without really suggesting their true meaning. When an American officer announced in 1968 that it had been necessary to shell a South Vietnam town "regardless of civilian casualties . . . to rout the Vietcong," he was really declaring, according to one interpretation, that "it became necessary to destroy the town in order to save it."[51] Aside from oversimplifying situations and eliciting emotional reactions, the language of leaders may be unintelligible to their opponents, with the result that the "conscious scope of conflict" is diffused and the real issues may be misunderstood;[52] but the jargon and the slogans enlist the loyalty and support of followers.

The reasons for the appeal of the "nation" to most followers have been mentioned many times in these pages. Any form of out-group competition serves a similar function. Regionalism, for example, asserts itself in countries as diverse as the Soviet Union and Great Britain. Patriotism also links together followers in their national and international roles. In addition, ties are strengthened by the semblance at least of a common culture, a common language, and a common belief in the nation's purposes and destiny; by political unity over a period of time; and by leaders who perpetuate their country's history and myths.[53] From another era: "We will arise, we will go to war as one man for our father the Tsar. . . . We are Russians and will not grudge our blood for the defence of our faith, the throne, and the Fatherland!"[54]

For some of the reasons previously cited and for others, on the surface war seems to offer a more powerful, if not more positive, attraction than peace (cf. P). The threat of the enemy, the out-group, whether real or imaginary, whether spontaneously experienced or manipulated from above, provides a strong motive to cooperate with leaders. It is not true, according to a coterie of political scientists who examined the North Atlantic countries, that "modern life, with rapid transportation, mass communication, and literacy tends to be more international than life in past decades or centuries, and hence more conducive to the growth of international or supranational institutions."[55] Legends that strengthen nationalism and encourage revenge, such as the belief among many Germans that they would not have lost World War I had it not been for the stab in the back their fighting armies received from various "traitors" on the front,[56] are likely to persist; as do historically founded enmities, such as that between Greeks and Turks. For scapegoats, real or imagined, are convenient targets for many forms of human misery, and an external enemy can serve that function most effectively. Perhaps it would be well to ponder the following statement not only to note and explode its glibness but also sadly to evaluate its touch of apparent validity: "War is a sizeable component in the educational industry, being itself a form of education."[57]

For persons engaged in battle or subject to bombing war may be hell, but even for them and surely for those far removed from combat war brings gratifications facilitating their obedience. During World War II, according to one observer, most Americans did not suffer but enjoyed "a better way of life." Their earnings were appreciably higher than during the depression years and there was virtually no unemployment. Simple actions, such as carpooling or not hoarding, the Office of Civilian Defense interpreted as significant contributions to winning the war: it proclaimed that "the empty seat is a gift to Hitler" and "hoarders are on the same level as spies."[58]

All leaders, influential persons, and followers certainly do not have war or war-preparedness as their objective. Although peace prophets may be influential among their own followers, so far they have not been noticeably successsful throughout society or among policymakers. It is too easy to assert that their partial failure lies in the fact that peace is *une oeuvre du politique*, "a work of politics,"[59] for most of them have tried valiantly to function politically by exerting pressure upon policymakers and through demonstrations and protests.[60] It is also not true, as romantics and others sometimes proclaim, that "the people will insist that the right policies be adopted if only they know what the right policies are."[61] For it is leaders who try to formulate policies in such a way that they are made to appear "right." Hitler again is a case in point. As supreme decision maker he could not disregard completely those who were his actual or potential followers. Leading industrialists supported him as he rose to political power and thereafter,[62] although they themselves may have wished only to retain their own economic dominance and not necessarily to go to war. He gained, moreover, the support of many German nationals who were in the mood to respond to him as a result of many factors, including especially the severe economic depression, the fear of social democracy and communism, and the indignity of the Treaty of Versailles. In the equation accounting for the success of the Nazis, consequently, the variable of Hitler must be heavily weighted, but that of his followers and most, though not all of the German people had more than a negligible effect.

PREVENTION (# 5)

Obviously, avoiding or preventing war is the crucial way to pursue peace. This section glances at the past and the present: through what organizations has the goal of peace been sought? The glance at existing mechanisms must begin on a pessimistic note: the machinery is far from perfect; wars continually occur; the threat of war looms; new forms of terror crop up. And yet, it must be repeated, the world's situation would probably be even worse in the absence of peacekeeping, peacemaking, and peace-building machinery. Desirable changes and improvements in what we now have are discussed in Part 3.

A continuum of choices confronts national leaders who would avoid war.[63] They can seek to resolve conflicts through negotiation, mediation, or arbitration; or at the other extreme they can go to war. In between they may hope to prevent an attack by strengthening their own war-making potential or by enlisting allies. They may do nothing. Clearly it is beyond the scope of the present treatise to consider all the alternatives in detail. A full account even of the alliances in Europe—including their successes and failures—would require an analysis beginning with the Holy Alliance[64] and ending with the many regional pacts now in existence. In the pages that follow, therefore, passing reference can be made only to the most important peace-pursuing groups.

The most prominent formal organization that would promote peace, settle conflicts, and prevent war is the United Nations to which more than 150 countries belong. Attached are the International Court of Justice, the Trusteeship Council, and the Economic and Social Council; fourteen specialized agencies including the International Labor Organization, the Food and Agriculture Organization, the United Nations Educational, Scientific, and Cultural Organization (UNESCO), the World Health Organization, and so on; various relief and peacekeeping organizations; and numerous groups concerned with special programs. Regional organizations have been formed, as countenanced by the United Nations charter— the Organization of American States, the Organization of African Unity, the Council of Europe, and the League of Arab States—which stand ready to settle disputes among their own members. Special agencies or commissions address themselves to questions concerning navigation, boundaries, fisheries, the flow of economic goods, and others.[65] Ad hoc governmental organizations are established to deal with passing but pressing problems, such as the Five-Power Group in 1978 for facilitating Namibia's independence. There is no hard-and-fast rule concerning the proper organization to consult when disputes arise. It is often presumed that regional or subregional machinery should be utilized before the dispute is brought to the United

Nations or some other international organization since governments within a smaller, perhaps more homogeneous regional body are more likely to be reasonably well-acquainted with each other's problems; but there is "little evidence" to show that regional bodies have been more effective than the international ones in dealing with serious conflicts.[66] The actual record concerning the utilization of peace machinery and their successes, twenty years before and twenty years after World War II, is given in Chapter Appendix 4.8. That record is a spotty one.

But there are grounds for cheer. When power is operationally defined in terms of economic development and population size, during these same periods it was by and large the powerful governments that tended to be involved in serious conflicts; in contrast, the less-powerful countries were more inclined to recognize the International Court of Justice as the body having jurisdiction over their disputes.[67] Then the less serious disputes have often been settled before they could become serious. Countries like Canada and the United States, or England and Iceland, have been temporarily at odds over economic issues. These "minor" disagreements have been resolved through direct negotiation, a special commission, or some form of mediation resulting in accords sufficiently satisfying to both parties. Such disputes were not likely to develop into armed conflict, but at least that possibility was removed before they could escalate. The performance of the United Nations, moreover, has not been unimpressive, even when one recalls the ghastly conflicts that shed blood in the Middle East, the subcontinent of India and Pakistan, Vietnam, Cambodia, and Cyprus. The truly difficult cases have generally been tossed to the United Nations and then the complaint has usually come from the weaker nations. It seems fair to conclude, consequently, that present peacekeeping and peacemaking machinery would perhaps be adequate if—yes, *if*—modern states were to refer their disputes to the appropriate organization and if they were then to abide by its resolutions or decisions (cf. P).[68]

An anthropological study of conflicts in forty-eight traditional societies provides clues to these particular conflicts but not to those among modern societies. (See Chapter Appendix 4.9: Negotiations in Traditional Societies.) Otherwise speculation, a term that here disguises ignorance (cf. I), uniqueness (cf. V), and multivariance, would suggest the reasons why leaders choose one way of resolving conflicts rather than another. Possibly part of the explanation is to be found in the individual leaders themselves who may or may not be motivated to prevent war and whose policy decisions therefore point in one direction rather than another. A decision in favor of a peaceful settlement may seem impossible when a policymaker ascribes to a potential enemy "aggressive designs" that conceivably can be implemented through the use of force.[69] During a war, as phrased at the very end of a

German film depicting the misdeeds of the Nazis, both leaders and followers may resolve that "something like this should never happen again." But afterwards everyone is weary, it is said, and tends "to fall back into patterns of habitual behavior," with the result that the new peace-building organization departs from the dream and resembles the prewar organization.[70]

The unique character of each situation again looms. Why, for example, did the League of Nations fail to prevent World War II? According to one acute analysis, some of the obvious explanations can be discarded or must be considered only contributory: the worldwide depression at the time, bad luck, the foreign policies of France and Britain, the failure of the United States to join the organization, the late appearance of the Soviet Union as a member, or the selection of Lord Curzon rather than Lord Cecil as foreign secretary in England. Experience had shown that the League could not settle disputes through negotiation or "amicable agreement," as a result of which League members felt it was necessary to resort to force to produce change and to go to war in order to maintain peace.[71] To what extent do the leaders of modern nations have a similar attitude regarding the United Nations?

Instances in which the available peacemaking machinery is ignored also require idiosyncratic explanations. Since World War II, some of the serious conflicts have been not between but within nations. The civil wars in Nigeria and Lebanon and guerilla actions in southern Africa are cases in point. The good offices of established organizations have not been utilized to end such bloodshed; instead ad hoc mediators have attempted to intervene. In the conflict between Protestants and Catholics in Northern Ireland, international groups could only stand by because this tragedy was considered a domestic affair within the United Kingdom. Clearly, negotiations between disputing nations are difficult when tangentially but vitally interested leaders do not appear at the negotiating table. The failure to resolve the conflict between the Greek and Turkish communities on Cyprus after the fighting in the summer of 1974 clearly was of concern to Greece and Turkey and, directly or indirectly, to great powers with interests in the area (Great Britain, the Soviet Union, the United States, and perhaps some of the Arab states). They not too coyly tried to exert pressure without actually participating in the negotiations. Although leaders in the Soviet Union and the United States facilitated the war between Ethiopia and Somalia over the Ogaden in 1977-1978, they played only sporadic and inconsistent roles even in encouraging a cease-fire. Under such circumstances what occurs during negotiations may be less important than the diplomatic maneuvers behind the scenes or concurrent actions such as the supplying of armies or arms.

A limited form of prevention, that of avoiding or mitigating some of the cruelties resulting from or related to war, is embodied in various codes and conventions to which Western and other nations have agreed in principle beginning in the nineteenth century.[72] The first Red Cross convention took place in Geneva in 1864, and various protocols have been added before and since World War II. The attempt has thus been made to help civilians, the wounded and sick, and prisoners of war. Except for the banning of gas and bacteria as weapons, however, these attempts to make war more humane "against the imperatives of military necessity" have been "relatively ineffective,"[73] as the civilian casualty figures from Coventry, Dresden, Hamburg, Hiroshima, London, Nagasaki, and so on, violently demonstrate. All nations have subscribed to the Geneva convention regarding the treatment of war prisoners, but among the subscribers subtle devices have been employed from time to time, contrary at least to the spirit of the convention, to elicit information and intelligence from prisoners. In brief, humanitarianism and other goals, however noble in principle, cannot be enforced during a war. At the most, leaders on the losing but not on the winning side can be tried as war criminals, as at the Nuremberg trials after World War II.

If an ounce of prevention is really helpful, then unrealistically it can be argued that steps should be taken to prevent crises from giving rise to war rather than waiting until leaders of one or more of the parties in conflict decide to utilize existing peacekeeping or peacemaking machinery. But then it would be necessary to be able to anticipate the crisis. Do we possess adequate knowledge in this respect? On a very abstract level it is possible to state that crises arise when any one of the possible precipitating causes of war is present or likely to be present. The abstraction, however, is insufficient; specific forecasts are needed. Alas, I must then add, the experts do not appear to agree when they are asked about future wars. (See Chapter Appendix 4.10: Forecasting Wars.) A conclusion is forced upon us: our knowledge is inadequate to forecast the future of war-peace. We are left with guesswork (cf. I).

CHAPTER APPENDIXES

4.1 HISTORICAL THEORIES (# 4)

One historian, following the tradition of his craft, has surveyed "all" the international wars fought since 1700. One by one he has evaluated various theories that, according to one or more scholars or common sense, have sought to "explain" the presence or absence of war. In his own very abbreviated summary of their "flaws," he refers to the following theories: "capitalists, dictators, monarchs or other individuals or pressure groups"; "governments' aims and ambitions"; "an uneven 'balance' of power"; the decision of "rulers facing internal troubles" to begin a war "in the hope that a victory would promote peace at home"; the situation in which "a nation busily making money will have no spare energy or time for the making of war"; "an innate love of fighting"; "war-weariness" and "war-fever"; "increasing contact between nations"; intentions or accidents; and "changes in society, technology, and warfare."[74] I would add to the reigning chaos and confusion by supplying some additional "causes" propounded by other writers: "value clashes";[75] "self-determination and irredentism," "solidarity and prestige," "self-sufficiency and isolation," "mission and expansion";[76] a whole catalogue ranging from "reaction to perceived threats" and "enthusiasm for ideals" to "bipolarization of power through rival alliances" and "inherent difficulty . . . of organizing for peace."[77] On the surface each proposal sounds or can be made to sound reasonable, does it not? The historian heading this paragraph, he who analyzed "all" the wars, nevertheless refutes every single one of the theories he has reviewed by noting one or more unique wars and often by suggesting that the reverse of a proposition is true; in short, he convincingly argues that each theory is at least partially invalid or not applicable to a given conflict. For example: a war may offer followers a scapegoat for their domestic discontents and function as a diversion, but a leader may not be able to wage war effectively unless he has contented followers. Any one of the factors, according to the same scholar, may produce "rivalry and tension" between nations, but not necessarily war. He adds that "one powerful cause of peace is a defensive war, for war provides the most widely accepted measure of power"; and so he is convinced that "perhaps persistent patterns in war and peace have not been found for the simple reason that they do not exist."[78]

At hand also is a monumental, statistically grounded analysis of the ninety-three interstate, imperial, and colonial wars from 1816 to 1965 between countries with a population of over half a million inhabitants. Trends are discernible, the authors believe, not causes:

The onset of these wars was not cyclical, though their "dominant peaks" were periodic: "about 20 years apart."

More wars began in the spring and autumn, particularly in April and October, than in the other two seasons, but there was no association with the day of the week.

The nations "near the top of any hierarchy based on diplomatic status, military-industrial capability, or related indicators" tended to engage in wars: France and England headed the list, closely followed by Turkey, Russia, and Italy.

Relations between nations tended to be inconsistent, on occasion they were friends, on another occasion enemies; but some were consistently enemies (Russia and Turkey; China and Japan; France and Germany), others were "recurring" partners (France, England, and the United States).

Their conclusion, stated at the outset: "no two wars are the same."[79] Other investigators observe very simply that peace during the nineteenth century was associated with power parity between nations, but during the twentieth with "a clear preponderance of power over the challengers" by the leading country or coalition.[80]

The gross national product and military expenditures per capita of 123 countries during the 1960s have been carefully calculated, on the basis of which the conclusion is drawn that nations which "over-arm" are twenty-five times more likely to become embroiled in a war during the following five years than those which "under-arm." The explanation for this statistical relation, however, is elusive and, as mentioned in the last chapter, dialectical: either a nation begins to arm because of various political grievances and then goes to war; or its foreign policy changes as it rearms, as a result of which that policy follows "a harder line" and finally becomes "so bad" that the nation goes to war.[81] Again, an instance not of a causal relation but a complicated correlation between arms and foreign policy.

An effort has been made to understand the outbreak of World War I by examining in detail events both inside and outside the six major countries from 1871 to 1914. Attention is concentrated upon five variables, each measured quantitatively as indicated here in parentheses: expansion (the colonial area); conflict of interest (violence over colonial issues between the major powers); military capability (military budgets); alliances (total number with other countries); and violence-behavior (actions directed toward all other nations).[82] As the history of each nation during that period is reported largely in terms of those variables, any unbiased reader, I think, must be impressed with the unique way in which they are combined country by country. The same impression is conveyed, and largely conceded by the authors, as they make an elaborate statistical analysis of the various factors, quantifiable whenever possible, affecting the five variables. The size of the colonial area, for example, they attempt to link with population density, national income per capita, trade per capita, and military expenditures; and that size in turn affected the military expenditures and the intensity of the conflicts with other nations over colonial matters. In qualitative terms the statistical analysis of one country is summarized as follows:

The case of Britain . . . illustrates the extent to which violence-behavior can be traced to domestic factors of growth and expansion. The population and national-income variables, in various combinations, proved to be important determinants of colonial area (expansion) and military expenditures. Expansion (colonial area) led to increased conflict with other nations over colonial matters (intersections) and thus, at least during the early years of the period studied, to increased military expenditures. These increases contributed to violence-behavior primarily through the intervening link of alliances. This brief sketch leaves out many important relationships in the case of Britain.[83]

That pattern of events, in the form of the above "brief sketch," was not repeated in the other five countries; Germany, for example, is called "a unique case." Uniqueness, uniqueness, there is no escape from this leitmotiv.

As a nonhistorian reviewing historical theories the present writer perforce has wondered how and why members of that discipline select facts or alleged facts from the multiplicity of available events and then seek to explain a particular war or to explain wars in general. Fortunately, in the tradition of the sociology of knowledge, two American historians have provided a brilliant, if tentative analysis of the historiography of wars which merits a summary.[84] Historians, these two writers demonstrate, derive the causes of war from their own ideological approach to the nature of man and his society: "Ideology clearly conditions the writing of history, both through historians' 'common sense' and through the formal theory they imbibe." Members of their discipline, they suggest, fall into three categories, each of which has a distinctive ideology and from which a theory of war is constructed. In broad strokes and generally in their own words and phrases:

1. *Conservative*: "man is a creature of only modest capabilities" and should be dependent upon "the historical community" without "unnecessarily" deviating from past tradition; when leadership is entrusted to an elite with demonstrated abilities "individuals and nations will achieve the freedom to act and live in accord with their own traditions." Wars tend to occur because those individuals and nations are "basically aggressive in behavior" and "when nations lose their internal discipline and order, or when international hierarchies break down" wars are "natural, almost inevitable."

2. *Liberal*: man is "potentially rational and self-reliant" and should be "free" to exercise his "capacities"; undesirable are "all forms of power that might impair or oppose the achievement" of "equality and social mobility"; "freedom and democracy are most fully realized in capitalist societies." Wars tend to occur "wherever a state limits citizens' freedom": individuals then become "discontent," "irrational," or "anxious"; they and their leaders "fall victims to misperceptions and stereotypes"; they experience "tension" when their "needs" are not satisfied and they lack "security." Or, from another standpoint, wars are likely when competing groups within a society are in conflict, pursue their own interests, and seek to reduce their fears and anxieties; wars may result, too, from the exercise of "bureaucratic power" (such as the military). Wars, therefore, are not "an inherent characteristic" of men or their society.

3. *Radical*: man is "fundamentally rational" and can "control" his environment: he is able to have a "program designed to transform" the "existing social order" in "humanitarian and democratic directions" by exercising "political power to overthrow the coercive state"; "private property and capitalism" must be rejected; social class is significant. Wars tend to occur because the "social structures" in which men are embedded are beyond their "immediate control," so that conflicts result from "long-term factors such as economic competition, imperialism, nationalism, racism, and the like"; because the "military-industrial complex" has great influence; and because "a ruling class or ruling groups" make "rational and premeditated (not irrational or accidental) decisions" to wage war. (See also Chapter Appendix 4.2: Economic Determinism.)

From my standpoint, these theories represent a combination of what I have been calling predisposing and precipitating causes of war, with emphasis upon the former. I imagine the authors would call my analysis eclectic, and that is how they label their own conception. Like me, therefore, they produce no overall theory of wars because, in spite of themselves, they recognize the unique character of each war. If anything, they say, their personal ideology is somewhere on "that fuzzy line" between liberal and radical, and so their theory of war is similarly oriented. The only "recurrent elements" they can find in "the historical process" are "long-term cycles in public moods, alternations related loosely to certain specific kinds of events"; such moods "are partly conscious and partly unconscious." They discern, in their own phrasing, six phases: relative satisfaction/confidence; disappointment/anxiety; dissatisfaction/aggression resulting in attempts at domestic reform or the defense of the status quo; dissatisfaction/aggression resulting in war or an aggressive foreign policy; exhaustion/anxiety; and relaxation/adjustment. Clearly, they add, this "sketchy model" seeks to incorporate all three approaches to war and requires validation. For the moment, it appears challengingly descriptive; and, like almost all historians' theories, it assumes that extrapolation from the past into the future is both feasible and fruitful.

4.2 ECONOMIC DETERMINISM (# 4)

In simplest terms, theories of economic determinism assume that wars are fought because those in power—political leaders, businessmen, bankers —believe that military victory will produce economic gains. There are "economic drives behind national policy," it has been suggested. In the United States the interest of corporations is equated with the national interest; critical resources must be safeguarded; markets must be developed; and so forth. These economic drives are hitched to the military which potentially or actually, in the case of a big power like the United States, protects economic interests abroad; or, in a simple phrase, the villain is economic imperialism.[85] This essentially Marxian viewpoint represents an important truth, certainly among modern nations where trade follows the flag and vice versa, but more has to be added. The presumption is that the decision makers—the leaders—are driven only by economic motives in their international role and are relatively unaffected by other motives as they make judgments concerning war-peace. Whether they are or can in fact be so one-sided is doubtful. Even if their motive for provoking war were totally economic, those being attacked may fight back not simply for economic reasons but as the only way, in their judgment, to protect their own mode of life. The losses to victors and victims alike from waging war have been stressed in the text of this chapter.

Since an economic explanation of war is associated with Marxists, attention must be turned to two Soviet writers who have analyzed war-peace from their historic standpoint.[86] First, they believe the approach of what they call "Western science" is to stress as predisposing causes one or more of the following: human nature, social order ("concepts of the state and national sovereignty"), divine will, and various geopolitical and demographic processes. These theories, they say, not only "ignore" the real causes of war but lead also to recommendations to avoid war which are "either fatalistic or utopian and therefore harmful." They concede, however, some merit in aspects of the Western theories and then, after a respectful bow to Lenin and to a congress of the Communist party of the Soviet Union, they present their own conception:

Lying at the base of international conflicts and wars are profound social roots—a sum total of economic, political, ideological, military and other ties and interrelations among classes, nations, states, and systems of states. Therefore, only a concrete historical analysis of the entire system of economic and political mutual relations of states and peoples can provide an answer on the causes and essence of war.[87]

There is nothing especially Marxian in this theory, I think, for the "sum total" appears to include every factor ever associated with the predisposing and precipitating causes of war, including—under the heading of "ideological"—the psychological ones.

4.3 SCIENCE FICTION (#s 1, 2, 3)

Before World War I a number of German authors wrote books and articles emphasizing how the glory of their empire would spread. Some French writers suggested how France would avenge her defeat in the Franco-Prussian War. Assorted British novelists were obsessed with the possibility that their country would be invaded from the continent.[88] Readers of these French and British works probably acquired beliefs eventually tapped by the war itself. Imaginative accounts of how a projected tunnel under the North Sea would enable England to be invaded by French forces were widely disseminated and may have contributed to the abandonment of the idea. As prime minister, Gladstone felt compelled to attack publicly a very popular short story about a possible invasion from the continent and warned his constitutents to "be on your guard against alarmism."[89] The stories served to suggest to policymakers and the general public the consequences of following a particular policy and to expose the possible dangers resulting from inadequate military operation. Since World War II the fiction has emphasized the devastation almost certain to result from a thermonuclear conflict.

Although the earlier writers used whatever data they could muster concerning both the weapons then in existence as well as possible military strategies, with rare exceptions the tales describing the shape of the war that actually began in 1914 failed completely to foresee its form. In this instance their readers must have anticipated events less horrible than they turned out to be. We are not likely ever to know precisely how writing of this sort affects the war-peace anticipation, no more than we can pinpoint the contribution of *Uncle Tom's Cabin* to the American Civil War (cf. I). Science fiction and other forms of fiction may not directly "cause" wars, but they may contribute to the overall constellation that facilitates or inhibits their onset.

4.4 TOLSTOY (# 4)

Tolstoy's view is perhaps best expressed, as might be anticipated, in his *War and Peace*. This transcending novel contains what might be called scholarly research on the Napoleonic wars by a very gifted nonprofessional. Out of context—but no matter—herewith what I think to be his most pungent statements which are as monistically fixated upon historical necessity, broadly defined, as Marx was upon economic necessity, more narrowly defined.

We can understand how it naturally seemed to Napoleon that the war was caused by England's intrigues. . . . We can understand how to the English Parliament Napoleon's ambition seemed to be the cause of the war; to the Duke of Oldenburg it was the outrage done to him; to the merchants the cause of the war was the Continental System, which was ruining Europe. Generals and veterans of the army traced the cause of the war to the necessity of providing them with employment, while to the legitimists of the day it was the vital need for re-establishing *les bons principles*; and the diplomats set it down to the alliance between Russia and Austria in 1809 not having been concealed tactfully enough from Napoleon, and to the awkward wording of Memorandum No. 178. We can understand how these and an incalculable and endless number of other reasons—the number corresponding to the infinite variety of points of view—presented themselves to men of that day; but for us of posterity, contemplating the accomplished fact in all its magnitude, and seeking to fathom its simple and terrible meaning, these explanations appear insufficient. . . . The deeper we delve in search of these causes the more of them do we discover; and each separate cause or whole series of causes appears to us equally valid in itself and equally unsound by its insignificance in comparison with the size of the event, and by its impuissance (without the co-operation of all the other coincident causes) to occasion the event. . . . Had any one of these causes been absent, nothing could have happened. And so all these causes—these myriads of causes—coincided to bring about what happened. And so there was no exclusive reason for that occurrence; the war came about because it was bound to come about. . . .

To elicit the laws of history we must leave aside kings, ministers and generals, and select for study the homogeneous, infinitesimal elements which influence the masses.

It is beyond the power of the human intellect to encompass *all* the causes of any phenomenon. But the impulse to search into causes is inherent in man's very nature. . . . There are laws governing events: some we are ignorant of, others we are groping our way to. The discovery of these laws becomes possible only when we finally give up looking for such causes in the will of any one man. . . .

The higher the human intellect soars in the discovery of possible purposes, the more obvious it becomes that the ultimate purpose is beyond our comprehension.

History has for its subject the life of nations and of humanity. To catch hold of and encompass in words—to describe exactly—the life of a single people, much less of humanity, would appear impossible.[90]

Tolstoy is saying in effect that the precipitating causes of war-peace are too complicated to be grasped by leaders or followers who are the participants or by historians and other scholars who would reconstruct what has happened in the past or will happen in the future. Instead he is emphasizing the supreme importance of predisposing causes without, however, being able to identify them.

4.5 METAPHORS (# 4)

Almost any event concerning war-peace is reported in the mass media by means of some metaphorical reference. Sometimes the motive to conceal is transparent: the "spokesman for the Foreign Office," "from a person in high position," "the Defense Department announces," provides information without indicating precisely who has released the information. Or when it was suggested in the mid-1960s that "the United States has a rather favorable underlying attitude toward the United Nations actions which is in noticeable contrast to the typical Soviet suspicion or hostility toward many United Nations operations,"[91] the crisp assertion must mean that the favorable and unfavorable attitudes possessed, respectively, by unspecified American and Soviet leaders for individual, national, or international reasons (and I truly wonder which!) were inferred from their public declarations and their actions. Or again and again for almost two decades it was said that the "United States" was assisting or fighting for South Vietnam in behalf of freedom, to help prevent the spread of communism, or for some other metaphorical cliché. After studying the so-called Pentagon Papers, which in fact were forty-seven volumes describing how and why the United States became involved in the Vietnam War, a sociologist concluded that the war "was neither a Democratic nor a Republican war, but a war conducted by the political elite, often without regard to basic technical advice and considerations, and for reasons that had far less to do with curbing communism than with the failure of the other arms of government in their responsibility to curb executive egotism."[92] During the war, the decision to initiate large-scale bombing of Vietnam was "planned and decided upon months in advance, without any thought of asking for the authorization or approval of Congress," in fact the planning of the operations was deliberately concealed from Congress and from most citizens.[93] Such an analysis suggests that in this instance or at least until very late in the war, the role of followers was negligible and that of leaders overpowering. Similarly, when it is stated that "a crisis in international politics is a process of interaction occurring at higher levels of perceived intensity than the ordinary flow of events,"[94] presumably the "intensity" is "perceived" by unidentified leaders which may or may not spill over upon some of the followers. As ever, the delicate tool of language, though generally facilitating communication, can also be employed to mislead or confuse an audience.

4.6 LEADERSHIP RESEARCH (# 4c)

Personality: Hopefully typical and illuminating examples of the research include:

1. A questionnaire administered to 126 Foreign Service officers in the United States Department: tendencies for those scoring high in self-esteem to approve of American foreign policy; for those displaying interpersonal hostility to favor the use of force in settling disputes; for those wanting to be more active and personally influential also to favor force.[95]

2. A fairly systematic survey of American presidents and secretaries of state between 1898 and 1968: a tendency for those high in dominance over subordinates to favor the use of force in international relations.[96]

3. Military and diplomatic elites in various Western and non-Western countries: a tendency for such persons to be similar with respect to a need for achievement and for power as well as with respect to rigidity and "paranoia."[97]

4. Thirty-seven country desk and political assistants at the American Department of State: a slight but significant tendency for rigidity and dogmatism to be associated with a hard-line policy regarding communism.[98]

5. A comparison of 387 American Foreign Service officers with other occupational groups on the basis of replies to a questionnaire: a tendency for the officers to analyze information impressionistically and intuitively rather than formally or methodically, and also to prefer to work for themselves within a formal organization rather than through a hierarchy.[99]

6. Ratings of attributes "in terms of importance or usefulness to attaining top ranks of the Foreign Service and possibly becoming an ambassador" by an unspecified number of American Foreign Service officers: a tendency to rate, at the high end of the scale, extensive Washington experience, concentration on political work, managerial experience, winning respect of colleagues, mastering a foreign language, and good political connections.[100]

7. A comparison of ten United States congressmen whose voting records during the Eighty-first Congress in 1949-1950 indicated they strongly favored foreign aid with ten others strongly opposed to such aid by estimating their "personality characteristics" on the basis of what they had said in their speeches on the floor of the House: a tendency for an "interest in international involvement" to be associated with

optimism and "cognitive complexity" (inferred by noting the number of reasons they advanced in favor of their position on an issue, their use of qualifying adjectives which allegedly demonstrated their willingness to believe an issue might be ambiguous, and their flexibility in reacting to "objects and ideas in the environment").[101]

Common sense and experience are also invoked to try to describe decision-making and the traits operating therein. It is thought that "in a mediation effort in which the power of the conflicting parties is not grossly unequal, agreement between them is likely to be achieved at the time when they are both least rigid" and that such a state of affairs may occur "early in the dispute before their public positions have hardened, or it may be at some later time when the disputants are most conscious of the risks inherent in a failure to agree."[102] Such factors are situation-specific, and I suppose the negotiators bring to the conference table idiosyncratic traits such as stubborness, pride, and self-confidence. I doubt whether more has been thus proclaimed other than that decision makers make decisions. Another example of undocumented common sense is the assertion that "states"— presumably the leaders of states, maybe also their followers—"in most cases" are willing "to pay a higher price" to defend the status quo than to change it, the evidence for which is said to be "the pain we feel on losing $5.00 is greater than the pleasure we experience in finding the same amount of money."[103] Maybe yes, maybe no; but certainly there must be some differences between the factors determining the decision to wage defensive and offensive wars.

Weighting: A survey of fifty-two peaceful societies previously mentioned illustrates the differing weights to be assigned leaders and followers in connection with war-peace. "Mediocre leadership" was associated with peace but only after the society had become "a going concern." Leadership of this type, however, also occurred toward the end of a peaceful era, whereas at the outset of such periods leaders usually possessed so-called charisma and were "shrewd, efficient" consolidators.[104] In brief, the old trite truism is confirmed: the leader is a product of his times.

Access to information: The United States has "no uniform policy concerning the publication of the facts and considerations" affecting presidential decisions involving foreign affairs.[105] In general we—you, I, investigators, journalists—are everywhere dependent upon one or more of the following sources of information: interviews on and off the record granted by leaders who usually have an ulterior motive in allowing themselves to be interrogated; the cautious, often money-seeking memoirs of retired leaders; official governmental statements; the not necessarily complete set of documents concerning a decision after they have been officially released, usually years after the actual event; inferences based on public statements and events during particular crises; shrewd guesses stemming from theory and available evidence about one or more events during the decision-making process. Even when documentation is available, it is usually difficult to determine the precise motives of a leader; intentions are always elusive.[106] To our sorrow, we are reasonably certain of only one fact: diplomats from major powers in the modern world always reserve "the right to resort to the *ultima ratio*, that is, to violence."[107]

Simulation: The technique of simulation has become fashionable in so-called sophisticated countries among military leaders and policymakers interested in war-peace problems. The directors of an enterprise, whether academic or policy researchers, assign participants, frequently students, to two or more groups which then are supposed to represent governments or military establishments. At least on one occasion practicing diplomats and scholars role-played "their real-life professional" subcultures.[108] The participants are provided with a description as well as the capabilities of two or more real or imaginary countries that are said to be in conflict over some issue such as the location of a boundary. They then engage in role-playing until they reach some kind of decision before the allotted time runs out. An obvious disadvantage of this technique is the difficulty of applying the emerging generalizations to real-life situations. Even the results from one simulation exercise cannot easily be utilized to forecast the result of another exercise: when the same game is repeated under identical conditions but with different players from the same culture, different outcomes are likely to occur.[109] The simulation research has isolated such fairly obvious factors as the setting, the number of participants, estimates concerning the values and information of the opponents, stresses, and timing.[110] One simulation study suggests that, compared with those in noncrisis situations, participants faced with crises are less likely to search for alternative courses of action and hence they identify fewer alternatives.[111] Aside from the probablity that the exercise could not possibly duplicate all the give-and-take factors present in a real negotiating conference, missing from this particular study is another complication usually appearing in an international setting, namely, the semantic confusion resulting from words like *war, peace, cooperation, imperialism, aggression, democracy*, and *freedom* which, though translatable, have different connotations in each society.[112] A survey of the laboratory literature suggests to one writer that negotiation is "a combination of searching, dividing, game-playing, and fraud,"[113] which may well be true but which helps relatively little in comprehending the process.

Ad hoc models: These are procreated to cope with the multivariance clinging to decisions about war-peace. Since leaders must decide whether to limit or escalate a war, whether to cut their losses after combat begins, or whether the right moment is at hand from the standpoint of domestic morale to seek a negotiated peace, analysts have constructed an "escalation ladder" which contains forty-four steps ranging from the first that is called "Ostensible Crisis" to the twenty-second ("Declaration of Limited Nuclear War") and ending with the forty-fourth ("Spasm or Insensate War" listed under the heading of "Aftermaths"). It is bluntly stated that "the order of the rungs is not sacred"; hence it is not implied that "one must go inexorably *up* the ladders" since "one could go down as well as up, or skip steps."[114] Ascending or descending, then, depends upon all the factors associated with decision-making; hence a model of this sort serves only a descriptive function.

4.7 SURVEYS OF FOLLOWERS (# 4c)

During the Vietnam War many Americans believed the United States should withdraw from the conflict. The fighting continued, although eventually perhaps antiwar sentiment affected the executive, and the withdrawal occurred possibly sooner than it would have without the protests. One scholar argues that "no major policy decision in the United States has ever been made in response to a spontaneous public demand."[115] A learned review of public opinion surveys in the United States from the beginning of polling until the 1960s indicates "no relationship" between "popular attitudes and actual levels of spending," even though the increase in antimilitary feeling since 1968 was "absolutely unprecedented" as inferred from the same polls.[116] Less than two months before the onset of World War II in 1939 only 23 percent of a national sample of Americans believed that a war would break out in Europe (63 percent said no)—but were most leaders any wiser? On the other hand, nine months before Pearl Harbor in 1941, 59 percent of another sample were convinced that their country "should take steps now to keep Japan from becoming more powerful, even if this means risking a war with Japan" (26 percent disagreed); and four months before the attack on Hawaii, 80 percent claimed they "would be willing to defend all" of North America, Hawaii, Greenland, and the Panama defense zone (with the continental United States excluded from this part of the question) "if Germany or her allies tried to take it."[117] Survey data from Canada, I would add, also indicate frequent divergences between the opinion of political or labor leaders and their followers on matters relating to foreign policy.[118]

Evidence for the lack of salience of the war-peace problems is not difficult to come by. "Can you think of anything that you personally can do that would prevent another war?" a cross-section of Americans was asked in 1946. Sixty-four percent said no, and the rest could manage only vague responses.[119] A few years earlier, 65 percent of a sample of workers in Detroit believed they had "very little" or "no" influence on governmental decisions, a finding that is perhaps important because those believing in their own effectiveness were "more alert to national issues" and revealed "more constructive and differentiated thought about them."[120]

4.8 UTILIZATION OF PEACEMAKING AGENCIES (# 5b)

One analysis, from which this paragraph and Table 1 are taken, concentrates not upon "minor" disputes or conflicts but upon 77 international conflicts which are said to constitute "most" of the conflicts during the twenty years before and the twenty years after World War II and in which force was used or threatened to be used.[121] In the earlier period there were 38 such conflicts, of which 27 were formally settled; in the latter period, 39, with 25 being formally settled. Table 1 indicates the procedures formally employed to settle or to try to settle the disagreements. In its first column the procedures are ranked with respect to frequency of usage; in the second, in terms of the overall successes resulting from all attempts that were made during the two periods; and in the third, according to the percentages of successes following the use of the particular procedure. Actual percentages are shown in parentheses. Conclusions from these data are:

1. The most frequently employed procedures were international organizations and formal bilateral negotiations; least frequently used were judicial procedures and outside mediations. When the procedures are grouped with respect to noninstitutionalized procedures (the first three rows in Table 1) and institutionalized ones (the last two), it appears that the former were utilized more frequently than the latter. Evidently, the investigator points out, "parties to a conflict expect to derive more benefit from their own actions than from decisions of third parties."

2. Formal bilateral negotiations and international organizations achieved the greatest number of successes, the remaining procedures relatively few, but the institutionalized and the noninstitutionalized were about equally successful.

3. When a particular procedure was utilized, however, success was achieved approaching 50 percent of the time in the case of bilateral negotiations, judicial procedures, and formal multilateral conferences; about one-third and about one-fifth of the time, respectively, via international organizations and outside mediations.

During the first ten years of the United Nation' existence, 108 disputes were thought to have threatened the peace. Forty-five of these were referred to the United Nations; another 10 both to regional organizations and the United Nations; 26 to the regional organizations exclusively; and the remainder, or 27, were not referred to any international organization. Of the 55 disputes in which the United Nations played an exclusive role or operated in conjunction with a regional organization, hostilities broke out

Table 1
Peacemaking Agencies Used in International Conflicts:
1919-39 and 1945-65*

	Settlement Attempts	Overall Successes	Procedure Successes
Formal bilateral negotiations	2 (36)	1 (17)	1 (47)
Outside mediations	5 (7)	5 (2)	5 (22)
Formal multilateral conferences	3 (12)	3 (6)	3 (44)
International organizations	1 (37)	2 (14)	4 (37)
Judicial procedures**	4 (9)	4 (4)	2 (45)

SOURCE: K. J. Holsti, Resolving international conflicts. *Journal of Conflict Resolution*, 1966, 10, 285, 286, and 289.

*arranged by ranks with percentages in parentheses

**1921-1965

in 32 instances and "were stopped, largely as a result of United Nations action" in 10 instances; eventually 7 were settled on the basis of a United Nations resolution and 11 in part as a result of such a resolution, while 13 settlements were reached outside the United Nations and 24 remained unsettled.[122] This commendable peacemaking record of the United Nations, however, is not revealed exclusively by the figures. Many of the disputes were settled by regional organizations and hence were not submitted to the United Nations.[123] More figures: during the first twenty-six years after World War II, those regional associations "helped to isolate conflicts among their members in 74 percent of the relevant cases, helped contribute to the abatement of conflict in 58 percent of the cases, helped end fighting in 44 percent of the relevant cases, and helped to provide a lasting settlement in 32 percent of the cases." These successes, however, "were restricted primarily to cases of low intensity," and again it was the United Nations that received "the hardest cases."[124]

4.9 NEGOTIATIONS IN TRADITIONAL SOCIETIES (# 4e)

In examining forty-eight traditional societies, a distinction has been drawn between conflicts that are "magico-religious" and those that are "politico-economic" in nature. The former are defined by conflicts involving revenge, headhunting, and alleged cannibalism, for in these instances the body being killed is likely to have significance in a magical or religious sense. The latter include conflicts over sovereignty, property, raw materials, and similar concerns. Among these societies the tendency to negotiate a settlement rather than to go to war is found to be significantly more closely related to magico-religious than to politico-economic objectives: exceptions, yes, but a clear-cut tendency. A possible explanation for this relation, according to the investigators, is the fact that substitute and negotiable symbols can be easily found for objectives involving magic and religion which themselves are symbolic in form. In contrast, political or economic objectives are ends in themselves for which substitute objectives are difficult to find; hence force is employed and war results.[125] Wars between nontraditional nations in the present era, however, have both objectives. The West and the Soviet Union or the People's Republic of China differ markedly with respect to ideologies that are clearly symbolic, but they are also competing on material and economic levels; hence it is uncertain which of their differences is more easily negotiable.

4.10 FORECASTING WARS (# 5)

In 1963 and 1964 a panel of one hundred fifty persons, natural and social scientists as well as engineers and writers, was asked to indicate whether they believed there would be another major war within ten or twenty-five years.[126] Of interest here is not their prediction—they tended to estimate the probability at considerably less than 50 percent—but their estimates concerning "the relative probabilities of the modes of outbreak" if there were to be such a war: "(1) inadvertence, 11 percent; (2) escalation of a political crisis, 45 percent; (3) escalation in the level of violence in an ongoing minor war, 37 percent; (4) surprise attack at a time when there is no ostensible crisis, 7 percent."[127] In their view, then, a war was most likely to result, by and large, from escalation, whether internal or external. Two questions must be immediately raised. First, can these two kinds of escalation be controlled so that in fact they do not occur? No clear-cut answer is evident, inasmuch as the decisions resulting in a policy of escalation or nonescalation, though made by leaders in their national and international orientations, are too complex to foresee, no less to control (cf. I). Secondly, should one have confidence in the experts' predictions? I think not. Perhaps they were given an unfair or impossible task. The monograph reporting their opinions—guesses?—does not indicate the rationale or the bases for their predictions; almost anyone, expert or not, can give some kind of reply to a questionnaire.[128] A few years later another panel of experts, also so-called, largely agreed with one another concerning some trends (such as, denial: "There will be a major military attack on the United States during the 1980s"), varied considerably regarding others (for example, "Nuclear armaments will proliferate"), and reached essentially no agreement concerning still others ("There will be a nuclear war").[129] What, then, should one conclude? A vote of no confidence or a message of condolence?

NOTES

1. Cf. Herman Schmid, Peace research and politics. *Journal of Peace Research*, 1968, 3, 217-32.

2. John P. Lovell, *The Search for Peace*. Pittsburgh: International Studies Association, 1974. P. 22. Cf. Dean G. Pruitt and Richard C. Snyder (eds.), *Theory and Research on the Causes of War*. Englewood Cliffs: Prentice-Hall, 1969. Betty Crump Hanson and Bruce M. Russett, Introduction. In Bruce M. Russett (ed.), *Peace, War, and Numbers*. Beverly Hills: Sage, 1972. Pp. 9-17.

3. William Eckhardt and Christopher Young, *Governments under Fire*. New Haven: HRAF Press, 1977.

4. Norman Angell, *The Great Illusion*. New York: Putnam's, 1912.

5. Juliet Saltman, The economic consequences of disarmament. *Peace Research Review*, 1972, 4, no. 5, 1-84.

6. Kenneth E. Boulding as cited by Amitai Etzioni, *The Hard Way to Peace*. New York: Crowell-Collier, 1962. P. 75.

7. Shimon Tzabar, *The White Flag Principle*. London: Allen Lane, Penguin, 1972.

8. Loipuis Terrell, Attribute differences among neighboring states and their levels of foreign conflict behavior. *International Journal of Group Tensions*, 1977, 7, 89-108.

9. I. F. Clarke, *Voices Prophesizing War 1763-1984*. London: Oxford University Press, 1966.

10. John D. Sullivan, Cooperating to conflict. In Russett (ed.), op. cit., pp. 115-18.

11. Matthew Melko, *52 Peaceful Societies*. Oakville: CPRI Press, 1973. Pp. 111-12.

12. Desiderius Erasmus, *The Education of a Christian Prince*. New York: Columbia University Press, 1936. P. 249.

13. Sidney Verba, Assumptions of rationality and non-rationality in models of the international system. In Klaus Knorr and Sidney Verba (eds.), *The International System*. Princeton: Princeton University Press, 1961. Pp. 93-117.

14. Reinhard Bendix, The mandate to rule. *Social Forces*, 1976, 55, 242-56.

15. Irving L. Janis, *Victims of Groupthink*. Boston: Houghton Mifflin, 1972.

16. Margaret Mead and Rhoda Metraux, The anthropology of human conflict. In Elton B. McNeil (ed.), *The Nature of Human Conflict*. Englewood Cliffs: Prentice-Hall, 1965. Pp. 116-38.

17. William James, The moral equivalent of war. In William James, *Memories and Studies*. New York: Longmans, Green, 1924. Pp. 267-96.

18. Gordon W. Allport, The role of expectancy. In Hadley Cantril (ed.), *Tensions that Cause Wars*. Urbana: University of Illinois Press, 1950. Pp. 43-78.

19. Léo Hamon, Less facteurs de guerre. *Proceedings of the International Peace Research Association, Second Conference*, 1968, 1, 176-85.

20. C. S. Bluemel, *War, Politics, and Insanity*. Denver: World Press, 1948. Pp. 12-14.

21. James A. Robinson and Richard C. Snyder, Decision-making in international politics. In Herbert C. Kelman (ed.), *International Behavior*. New York: Holt, Rinehart and Winston, 1965. Pp. 435-63.

22. Verba, op. cit.

23. Bjorn Christiansen, *Attitudes toward Foreign Affairs as a Function of Personality*. Oslo: Oslo University Press, 1959. P. 89.

24. Geoffrey Blainey, *The Causes of War*. London: Macmillan, 1973. Pp. 122, 270.

25. Georg Simmel, cited in Blainey, op. cit., p. 118.

26. Fred Charles Iklé, *Every War Must End*. New York: Columbia University Press, 1971. Chap. 2.

27. Richard J. Barnet, *Roots of War*. New York: Atheneum, 1972. Pp. 13-14.

28. Donald R. Kinder and Janet A. Weiss, In lieu of rationality. *Journal of Conflict Resolution*, 1978, 22, 707-35.

29. Werner Levi, The relative irrelevance of moral norms in international politics. *Social Forces*, 1965, 44, 226-33.

30. Charles E. Lindblom, The science of "muddling through." *Public Administration Review*, 1959, 19, 79-88.

31. Richard A. Falk, *A Study of Future Worlds*. New York: Free Press, 1975. P. 341.

32. Lincoln P. Bloomfield, Disarmament and arms control. *Foreign Policy Association*, *Headline Series*, 1968, no. 187.

33. Cited by W. K. Hancock, *Four Studies of War and Peace in this Century*. London: Cambridge University Press, 1961. P. 117.

34. Frederick S. Dunn, *War and the Minds of Men*. New York: Harpers, 1950. Pp. 17-18.

35. Ralph Luther Moellering, *Modern War and the Christian*. Minneapolis: Augsburg Publishing House, 1969. P. 13.

36. Leonard Beaton, *The Struggle for Peace*. London: Allen and Unwin, 1966. P. 115.

37. Glenn H. Snyder and Paul Diesing, *Conflict among Nations*. Princeton: Princeton University Press, 1977. P. 502.

38. Michael Walzer, *Just and Unjust Wars*. New York: Basic Books, 1977. Pp. 75, 107.

39. Hannah Arendt, *On Revolution*. New York: Viking, 1963. Pp. 2-3.

40. Moellering, op. cit., pp. 42, 48.

41. Leonard W. Doob, *Patriotism and Nationalism*. New Haven: Yale University Press, 1964. Pp. 161-98.

42. Walzer, op. cit., chaps. 13, 16.

43. Blainey, op. cit., pp. 246-47.

44. Arendt, op. cit., p. 7.

45. Leo Tolstoy, *War and Peace*. New York: Penguin Books, 1957. P. 810.

46. Walter Millis and James Real, *The Abolition of War*. New York: Macmillan, 1963. P. 12.

47. F. H. Hinsley, *Power and the Pursuit of Peace*. London: Cambridge University Press, 1963. P. 284.

48. Frederick S. Dunn, *War and the Minds of Men*. New York: Harpers, 1950. P. 3.

49. John Somerville, *The Peace Revolution*. Westport: Greenwood, 1975. P. 117.

50. Charles E. Osgood, Graduated unilateral initiatives for peace. In Quincy Wright, William E. Evan, and Morton Deutsch (eds.), *Preventing World War III*. New York: Simon and Schuster, 1962. Pp. 161-77.

51. Thomas Merton, *On Peace*. New York: McCall, 1971. P. 238.

52. Zellig S. Harris, A language for international cooperation. In Wright, Evans, and Deutsch (eds.), op. cit., pp. 299-309.

53. Doob, op. cit., pp. 223-48.

54. Tolstoy, op. cit., p. 805.

55. Karl W. Deutsch et al., *Political Community and the North Atlantic Area*. Princeton: Princeton University Press, 1957. P. 22.

56. E. J. Gumbel, Vom Fememord zu Reichskanzlei. In Erich Fromm and Hans Herzfeld (eds.), *Der Friede*. Heidelberg: Verlag Lamber Schneider, 1961. Pp. 205-80.

57. Marshall McLuhan and Quentin Fiore, *War and Peace in the Global Village*. New York: McGraw-Hill, 1968. P. 124.

58. Richard Polenberg, *War and Society*. Philadelphia: Lippincott, 1972. Pp. 131-33.

59. Julien Freund, *Le Nouvel Age*. Paris: Marcel Rivière, 1970. P. 148.

60. Cf. Charles Chatfield (ed.), *Peace Movements in America*. New York: Schocken Books, 1973.

61. Kenneth N. Waltz, *Man, the State and War*. New York: Columbia University Press, 1954. P. 17.

62. Max Horkheimer, The lessons of fascism. In Cantril (ed.), op. cit., pp. 209-42.

63. K. J. Holsti, Resolving international conflicts. *Journal of Conflict Resolution*, 1966, 10, 272-96. Helge Hveem, "Blame" as international behavior. *Journal of Peace Research*, 1970, 7, 49-67.

64. S. Strauz-Hupé and S. T. Possony, *International Relations*. New York: McGraw-Hill, 1950. Pp. 816-19.

65. J. F. McMahon, Settlement of disputes in special fields. In Study Group on the Peaceful Settlement of International Disputes (ed.), *Report*. London: David Davies Memorial Institute, 1966. Pp. 191-289.

66. Oscar Schachter, Mechanisms for multilateral mediation and conciliation. Paper presented at Second Annual Meeting of the North American Council of the International Peace Academy. Quebec, 1978.

67. Ib Martin Jarvad, Power versus equality. *Proceedings of the International Peace Research Association*, 1968, 1, 297-314.

68. Cf. Study Group on the Peaceful Settlement of International Disputes (ed.), op. cit., p. 34. Also Hazel Fox, Arbitration. In ibid., pp. 92-121.

69. J. David Singer, Threat perception and the armament-tension dilemma. *Journal of Conflict Resolution*, 1958, 2, 90-105.

70. Werner Levi, *Fundamentals of World Organization*. Minneapolis: University of Minnesota Press, 1950. P. 202.

71. Hinsley, op. cit., pp. 309-19.

72. Olaf Hasselager, The relevance of international law to civilian defense. *Proceedings of the International Peace Research Association*, 1970, 2, 158-76.

73. Richard Baxter, Human rights in war. *Bulletin of the American Academy of Arts and Sciences*, 1977, 31, no. 2, 4-13.

74. Blainey, op. cit., pp. vii, 272-73.

75. Byron L. Fox, International cultural relations. *American Sociological Review*, 1950, 15, 489-95.

76. Doob, op. cit., pp. 206-7.

77. Quincy Wright, *A Study of War*. Chicago: University of Chicago Press, 1965. Pp. 1512-18.

78. Blainey, op. cit., pp. 35, 74-81, 271.

79. J. David Singer and Melvin Small, *The Wages of War, 1816-1965*. New York: Wiley, 1972. Pp. 5, 215, 253, 275, 286-87, 345, 375.

80. Hanson and Russett, op. cit.

81. Alan G. Newcombe, Gernot Koehler, and James West, The prediction of war using an inter-nation tensionmeter. In M. Khan (ed.), *Proceedings of the International Peace Research Association Fifth General Conference*. Oslo: International Peace Research Association, 1975. Pp. 335-61.

82. Nazli Choucri and Robert C. North, *Nations in Conflict*. San Francisco: W. H. Freeman, 1975. P. 25.

83. Ibid., pp. 245-46.

84. Keith L. Nelson and Spencer C. Olin, Jr., *Why War?* Berkeley: University of California Press, 1979. Chaps. 1-3, pp. 188-89.

85. Barnet, op. cit., pp. 139, 340.

86. Yuri Barsegov and Rustem Khairov, A study of the problem of peace. *Journal of Peace Research*, 1973, 10, 71-80.

87. Ibid.

88. I. F. Clarke, op. cit.

89. Ibid., p. 39.

90. Tolstoy, op. cit., pp. 715-16, 717, 977, 1168, 1350, 1400.

91. Oran R. Young, *The Intermediaries*. Princeton: Princeton University Press, 1967. Pp. 189-90.

92. Irving Louis Horowitz, The Pentagon Papers and social science. In Milton J. Rosenberg (ed.), *Beyond Conflict and Containment*. New Brunswick: Transaction Books, 1972. Pp. 297-322.

93. Somerville, op. cit., p. 41.

94. Oran R. Young, *The Politics of Force*. Princeton: Princeton University Press, 1968. P. 15.

95. Lloyd Stanley Etheredge, *A World of Men*. Ph.D. Thesis: Yale University, 1974. Pp. 232-81.

96. Ibid., pp. 109, 118, 144.

97. John R. Raser, Personal characteristics of political decision-makers. *Peace Research Society, Papers*, 1966, 5, 161-82.

98. Bernard Mennis, *American Foreign Policy Officials*. Columbus: Ohio State University Press, 1971.

99. Regis Walther, *Orientations and Behavioral Styles of Foreign Service Officers*. New York: Carnegie Endowment for International Peace, 1965. P. 43.

100. John Ensor Harr, *The Professional Diplomat*. Princeton: Princeton University Press, 1969. Pp. 210-11.

101. Margaret G. Hermann, Some personal characteristics related to foreign aid voting of Congressmen. In Margaret G. Hermann and Thomas V. Milburn (eds.), *A Psychological Examination of Political Leaders*. New York: Free Press, 1977. Pp. 311-24.

102. Elmore Jackson, *Meeting of Minds*. New York: McGraw-Hill, 1952. P. 137, italics deleted.

103. Robert Jervis, *Perception and Misperception in International Problems*. Princeton: Princeton University Press, 1976. P. 51.

104. Melko, op. cit., pp. 178-79.

105. Arthur N. Holcombe, *A Strategy of Peace in a Changing World*. Cambridge: Harvard University Press, 1967. P. 26.

106. Jervis, op. cit., p. 113.

107. Raymond Aron, *Peace and War*. Garden City: Anchor Press, 1966. P. 14.

108. Lincoln Bloomfield, Bellex—the Bellagio "mini-game." In Maureen R. Berman and Joseph E. Johnson (eds.), *Unofficial Diplomats*. New York: Columbia University Press, 1977, pp. 222-40.

109. Michael H. Banks, A. J. R. Groom, and A. N. Oppenheim, International crisis gaming. *Proceedings of the International Peace Research Association*, 1968, 1, 85-124.

110. Jack Sawyer and Harold Guetzkow, Bargaining and negotiation in international relations. In Kelman (ed.), op. cit., pp. 466-520.

111. James A. Robinson, Charles F. Hermann, and Margaret G. Hermann, Search under crisis in political gaming and simulation. In Pruitt and Snyder (eds.), op. cit., pp. 80-94.

112. William A. Glaser, The semantics of the cold war. *Public Opinion Quarterly*, 1956-57, 20, 691-716.

113. John G. Cross, Negotiation as a learning process. *Journal of Conflict Resolution*, 1977, 21, 581-606.

114. Young, *The Intermediaries*, op. cit., P. 194, Young's italics.

115. Barnet, op. cit., p. 243.

116. Bruce M. Russett, The revolt of the masses. In Russett (ed.), op. cit., pp. 299-319.

117. Hadley Cantril, *Public Opinion 1935-1946*. Princeton: Princeton University Press, 1951. Pp. 781-82.

118. Jerome Laulicht, Public opinion and foreign policy decisions. *Journal of Peace Research*, 1965, 2, 147-60.

119. Theodore F. Lentz, *Towards a Science of Peace*. New York: Bookman Associates, 1955. P. 59.

120. Elizabeth Douvan, The sense of effectiveness and response to public issues. *Journal of Social Psychology*, 1958, 47, 111-26.

121. Holsti, op. cit.

122. Ernst B. Haas, *Collective Security and the Future International System*. Denver: University of Denver, 1968. Pp. 38-44.

123. Study Group on the Peaceful Settlement of International Disputes (ed.), op. cit., pp. 24-30.

124. J. S. Nye, *Peace in Parts*. Boston: Little, Brown, 1971. Pp. 170, 175.

125. Stanton Tefft and Douglas Reinhardt, Warfare regulation. *Behavior Science Research*, 1974, 9, 151-74.

126. Olaf Helmer, *Social Technology*. New York: Basic Books, 1966. P. 48.

127. Ibid., p. 68.

128. Ibid., pp. 68-72.

129. Raul de Brigard and Olaf Helmer, *Some Political Societal Developments*. Middletown Institute for the Future, 1970. Pp. 52-53.

Part 2:
PERFECTION

5.
Individual
Perfection

At first blush it must seem presumptuous even to attempt to discuss the perfectability of mankind and society. For throughout the centuries and especially in religious and semireligious creeds savants and simple men and women everywhere have striven to formulate the ideal of perfection and to attain it—with little success, it must be immediately and sadly added, as the evils and the wars engulfing us demonstrate. Peace, however, cannot be pursued without having a pattern as a guide; and perfectability shall be that pattern.

Even dreams about the future affect the present; according to one social psychologist:

There is evidence—much of it, paradoxically, from both Christian and psychiatric sources—which suggests that man's nature is richer, his capacity for joy, creativity, intellectual effort, altruistic service, spontaneity, courage, and love far greater than we commonly suppose; that he is more complete, more consistent, gayer and stronger.[1]

Planning for the future usually assumes that the lot of someone, the planner or the recipients, will be improved and in this sense at least a microscopic step in the direction of perfection is taken, however haltingly (cf. P).* If a belief in perfectability affects action in the form of a self-fulfilling prophecy, so much the better. Or again: perfection may never be achieved, but the idea of perfectability is an incentive for change. More words? No: immortality has not been attained, yet science and medicine have significantly increased life expectancy. A fair analogy? I can only hope so.

Before embarking on this intellectual venture, a number of important, puzzling quibbles must be expressed. First, can peace be achieved on an individual level when there is no "community of peace-loving men"?[2]

_____

*See pages 11-12 for an explanation of the cross-referencing system.

Perfect persons, saints, arise and flourish under all social conditions, but it is perhaps more likely that an individual will have peace of mind and be a *homo pacificus* in a "favorable" environment, however "favorable" may be defined (cf. P). For this reason an intimate relation between human perfection on the one hand and national and international perfection on the other hand is assumed. We search for perfect persons who will create perfect societies and a perfect international order; and we search for such a society and such an order so that perfect persons can be created. Obviously no one other than a deluded idealist anticipates that all persons will achieve perfection. A modern creator of a dull utopia has declared that in order for human beings to be "happy, informed, skillful, well-behaved, and productive"—the attributes of perfection from his viewpoint—"a different physical or cultural environment" must be offered them,[3] and therefore perfect persons are achieved through improvement in the milieu. An approach which would change many individuals by changing their surroundings, however, cannot avoid observing, analyzing, or changing at least a few individuals, inasmuch as environmental changes are wrought not by ghosts or impersonal forces but by leaders, by influential followers, or even by just plain followers who therefore must first be changed if the environment is to be changed. We have here what seems to be an infinite regress (cf. I).

Secondly, no one should be frightened by the prospect of perfection and believe that the ideal is a host of identical angels living in a monotonous heaven. Just as each society has a modal personality—Zulus tend to differ from Frenchmen, and Frenchmen from their neighbors, the Germans and Czechs—around which individual differences also appear (cf. V), so, realistically, it is to be anticipated that even utopian persons would differ from one another as do utopian countries and perhaps also utopian international organizations. According to Scripture, no two angels are alike, and angels have not always lived together in complete harmony.

Also, even the search for perfection cannot itself be perfect. We—you and I—cannot ascend Mount Sinai and there be told what the attributes of *homo pacificus* and his society must be. We can do the next best thing and review what was revealed on Mount Sinai and elsewhere, but the sources are virtually limitless and the choice must consequently be both ethno- and egocentric (cf. I). We are imperfect human beings and the imperfection becomes painfully apparent as we try to cull from mankind's wisdom what seems best for all three orientations: the individual, the national, and the international. Every society of which we have knowledge postulates and tries to achieve ideal human beings (cf. P). A quick glimpse at the conception of a Golden Age in the past suggests the persistence of a universal pattern which men believe once existed and which, they hope, may return: "a life of brotherhood, equality, joy, leisure, plenty, peace, health, and a life of permanent, unrelieved, universal satisfaction."[4] Are these the attributes of *homines pacifici*?

Finally, it could be argued that the problem of perfection is irrelevant to war-peace. Conceivably a strong leader can dedicate his people to peace rather than war, while they remain quite imperfect, and force them to conform. Eventually, however, they may rebel, particularly when it becomes necessary to choose or accept his successor. Then their imperfections may lead to bloodshed and war. Similarly, it might also be believed, cordial relations between the leaders of two states for whatever reason may produce peace almost regardless of the wishes or conditions of the citizens in each country. Again, though, will those relations long endure?

RELIGION (#s 3b, 4b)

The search for attributes of *homo pacificus* begins with religion because most of the world's greatest religions set forth doctrines praising peace and tranquility and condemning war and violence.[5] Peace as a desirable state appears in the Old Testament along with the warlike attributes of Yahveh; it dominates the New Testament, particularly in connection with the life and ethics of Christ; and it motivated most of the early Fathers of the Church.[6] By and large, religions have "done much to promote the image of a lost and promised paradise where the peace that reigns is not of this world."[7] In the middle 1970s a social scientist wrote, "the persistence of war is not challenged by statesmen or major nations and has been questioned only by . . . the Secretary-General of the United Nations and the Pope"[8]—and that papal tradition has been vigorously espoused by the present Pope.[9] In practice, however, as it will be necessary to observe again and again, noble religious doctrines concerning peace are not implemented or else they are drastically modified. Thus Muhammad at the outset of his life advocated peace through the unity of mankind, but later he turned Islam into a religious order seeking to spread his word through conquest.[10]

Accompanying their pursuit of peace the great religions also specify or imply the personalities, traits, and actions to be encouraged in order to achieve that goal. It is clear, however, that, except for the stress on peace, "no common system of religious values" exists[11] (cf. P). Perhaps, then, an attempt to locate the specific attributes of *homo pacificus* through religion should be branded as a hopeless quest. In addition, the major religions have a vast written literature, often with many commentaries which do not agree with one another; and desirable human attributes are usually ambiguously listed. Part of a single sentence in a standard encyclopedia immediately suggests both the implications of religions for the pursuit of peace and the variety of ideals: "Confucian moral values" are said to be "filial piety, loyalty, love, righteousness, and good faith"; "Buddhist virtues" are "compassion, kindness to all creatures, and remonstration against all evil deeds"; and "Taoism's own ethics" favor "patience, simplicity, contentment."[12] In spite of this variability (cf. V), the probing of religion should not be abandoned, if only because religious leaders and thinkers have grappled with significant problems. Since the aim here is to suggest the intimate relation generally existing between religion and peace, the arbitrary, ethnocentric, not unanticipated decision has been made to concentrate upon Judeo-Christianity.

The perilous search begins with the Ten Commandments as transmitted in Exodus, chapter 20, quoted here in the conventional King James Version. Few Jews and Christians would question their importance as guides to action. Seven actually pertain directly to action, of which six are injunctions concerning interpersonal relations:

Thou shalt not kill
Thou shalt not commit adultery
Thou shalt not bear false witness against thy neighbor
Thou shalt not covet thy neighbor's house, thou shalt not covet thy neighbor's wife
    . . . nor any thing that is thy neighbor's
Thou shalt not steal
Honor thy father and mother

The seventh precept is directed toward action of a more personal character:

Thou shalt not take the name of the Lord thy God in vain

The remaining three Commandments pertain essentially to beliefs:

Thou shalt have no other gods before me
Thou shalt not make unto thee any graven image
Remember the sabbath day to keep it holy

Eight of the Ten Commandments are thus expressed in negative terms, indicating the actions that should not be taken or the beliefs that should not be held, but implying those that should be taken or held. All ten are deeply embedded in the laws and lore of the times. "Remember the sabbath day to keep it holy," for example, is a positive command which in turn is dependent on the belief that the Lord who commanded this action and who Himself set the example as He created the world must be obeyed. With the exception of the taboo on killing, no one of the commandments is directly concerned with the war-peace problem. If all of them, however, were strictly obeyed by everybody, or almost everybody, the presumption is that there would probably be no internal strife: individuals would not quarrel as a result of adultery, false witness, covetousness, or stealing; they would not be overtly aggressive, for example, by being profane; they would lead a satisfactory family existence by honoring their parents and in later life they themselves would be thus honored; and they would share basic religious beliefs concerning the deity and the mode of worship. Gentle leaders would emerge, interpersonal relations would be loving, war would be less likely.

One man's summary of the Old Testament, according to the multifaceted explication he provides for the Hebrew word for "peace," emphasizes that its meaning fluctuated and that it referred to desirable personality traits and interpersonal relations. In his language, peace would be attained if individuals possessed "integrity, lack of pettiness, and possession of one's own attributes." A peaceful society required "an order free from discussion or disputes" as well as "a relationship of cordiality and friendship between persons feeling mutual attraction." Miscellaneous attributes necessary to achieve peace on the individual level included "loyalty, luck, health, security, wealth, joy, life, and justice" and also the kind of poise or equilibrium associated with a mature personality, with "wisdom," and with "the exercise of patience."[13] The main concern of religion in "classical" Judaism, in short, was to achieve peace on an individual as well as on an interpersonal level, for such peace was supposed to replicate "the peace in the divine realm."[14]

From the Christian standpoint, the Old Testament is incomplete and represents a development of actions and philosophy eventually finding their culmination in Jesus and the New Testament. The most important statement concerning the perfectability of man and his behavior unquestionably is found in the Sermon on the Mount.[15] According to one prominent Protestant clergyman, the sermon "provides the only humane policy under which mankind can live."[16] First of all, it reaffirms some of the Ten Commandments, which are then more profusely illustrated or elaborated. In one verse, for example, it is stated "Ye have heard that it was said by them of old time, Thou shalt not kill. . . ." In the next verse warnings are given concerning other aggressive behavior against one's fellow men: "whosoever is angry with his brother without a cause," "whosoever shall say to his brother, Raca," and "whosoever shall say, Thou fool" shall be punished in various ways, including the "danger of hell fire." To actual adultery is added a predispositional, solipsistic injunction: "whosoever looketh on a woman to lust after her hath committed adultery with her already in his heart."

The emphasis in these beatitudes, however, is upon man's relation to his fellows. In effect, Jesus asks His followers to be selfless, tolerant, modest, altruistic, and above all to be motivated at all times and in all situations by love. For at the beginning of the sermon the following, in the recognizable words of the same translation, are blessed: the poor in spirit; they that mourn; the meek; they which do hunger and thirst after righteousness; the merciful; the pure in heart; the peacemakers; they which are persecuted for righteousness' sake; and ye when men shall revile you and persecute you and shall say all manner of evil against you falsely. For the same reason ambiguous utterances (countered by: "let your communication be, Yea, yea; Nay, nay") and hypocrisy (corrected by: "when thou doest thine alms, do not sound a trumpet before thee as the hypocrites do . . . that they may have glory of men'') are condemned. The most important innovation is the counsel to avoid counteraggression after being frustrated by one's peers and, if anything, to turn the agression upon oneself: whosoever shall smite thee on thy right cheek, turn to him the other also; whosoever shall compel thee to go a mile, go with him twain. In the same vein the most germane entreaty for war-peace is Matthew, chapter 5, verse 44:

Love your enemies, bless them that curse you, do good to them that hate you, and pray for them which despitefully use you, and persecute you.

Although theological interpretations of the sermon and of Jesus' other utterances differ, there is, I think, agreement concerning the essence of the message: "the Christian must seek to exemplify the self-effacement of the Saviour"[17]; "man's deeds on earth would be measured against the yardstick of charity and mercy, and he would be judged and appropriately rewarded in the everlasting kingdom."[18] The variations in Christian doctrine introduced by popes and other Catholic theologians as well as by numerous Protestant denominations are beyond the scope of the present treatise. Later in Chapter 7, however, the tenets and practices of one Christian sect, the Quakers or Friends, will be examined in some detail because both in word and deed they have systematically linked their religion to antiwar beliefs and actions.

In order to express religious values a bit more concretely and to relate many of them more or less systematically to the concepts being consistently employed throughout this book, the perfectability of man can be surveyed in terms of his motives, beliefs, attitudes, and skills.

MOTIVES (#s 1a, b, c; 2)

In the spirit of the Sermon on the Mount, the principal attribute of *homo pacificus* is the rejection of violence as a means of attaining goals. In spite of frustrations, counteraggression against the subjectively or objectively real source of the frustration is enjoined. The aggression following failure to attain a goal is to be turned inward or not expressed; or, according to the theory, a substitute response must be sought. The target of aggression is not out-groups, especially potential and actual enemies. The Golden Rule in its most platitudinous form suggests we return good for evil especially when the evil hurts; the perfect person is almost always nonviolent. The ideal of nonviolence in the modern, violent world cannot be mentioned without some reference to its foremost apostle, Mahatma Gandhi, in order to indicate that his doctrine was not an isolated whim or merely a political tactic but reflected a general philosophy and—perhaps surprisingly— admitted exceptions. (See Chapter Appendix 5.1: Gandhi's Nonviolence.)

Homo pacificus is motivated to avoid being lured down the route to war. In the foreseeable future or at least in the West, he constantly strives to be aware of the dangers of war, of the way leaders allow their country to drift toward conflict, of jingoists and sometimes the professional military who believe that war can be not only the ultimate but also the immediate solution to "real conflict." For him the motives attached to earning a living, being in love, pursuing a hobby, and trying to understand the universe are able to compete successfully with the challenge of a war not only when it appears distant but also even when it occurs. Pacifism is his ideal. Pacifism? Ah, *yes*; if the word provokes amazement and cynicism, let it be noted that the doctrine has been called an ideal, and critical reactions, I would plead, should be postponed until later (see Chapters 7 and 8).

The frustrations of *homo pacificus* resulting from the nonattainment of the goals toward which his motives are directed, especially those concerned with basic needs, are at a minimum, but some pain remains. For wisdom and creativity come from suffering; pleasure without pain is difficult to appreciate. *Homo pacificus* eventually dies in the most vivid of imaginary utopias; death or the contemplation of death is the supreme frustration even when attention is paid to declarations or whispers of a hereafter. In the meantime the individual forever strives to prolong life and joy. It is this deeper, more profound motivation that is directed against war; let us live longer, let us be happier, let us concern ourselves with all that is eternal whether here and now or—for believers—later. Perhaps *homo pacificus* believes.

BELIEFS (#s 1a, d, e; 2)

This paragraph contains only the desirable beliefs of *homo pacificus*. War is not inevitable, rather peace is feasible (cf. P). Feasibility includes the conviction that the perfectability of man can be more than approximated: human nature is inclined to select the good, not the evil. We can indeed obey most if not all the Ten Commandments. The pleas and injunctions in the Sermon on the Mount are valid and reasonable guides to human judgments and actions. In the words of a United States president, "our problems are man-made; therefore they can be solved by man."[19] The mistaken belief, as previously indicated, that the victor in war profits from victory is cast out; "the net gains and mutual benefits" from peace are greater.[20] By and large the peoples of the world have become so interdependent that one country or bloc of countries cannot eternally prosper while others suffer.

Beliefs such as the above must be expressed in specific terms comprehensible within each society and for a given zeitgeist. *Homo pacificus* freely and enthusiastically subscribes to a credo embodying them. The credo he considers valid, and indeed it is valid, at least according to the best views of competent authorities. Possible contents of a credo are discussed in Chapter 7 because there—and not here—its role in realizing peace is proclaimed. Leaders, furthermore, require a special catechism as a result of their overall importance and their role in negotiating and in making crucial decisions concerning war-peace. A psychologist has listed assumptions about national security which, in his opinion, are seldom questioned; which should be challenged; and from which, in his and my opinion, leaders must seek to liberate themselves:

1. That national decision-making is predictable from models that assume rationality.
2. That the primary motive of the opponent is aggression, not fear.
3 That we must maintain military superiority.
4. That an invulnerable nuclear retaliatory capability is nothing more than a deterrent.
5. That maintaining the credibility of our deterrent requires a hostile image of ourselves in the eyes of the opponent.
6. That prior commitment from both sides is necessary before either can undertake any tension-reducing action.
7. That inspection is a prerequisite to any disarmament.[21]

Both leaders and followers, as they approach perfection, are skeptical concerning various beliefs prevalent in their society (whether or not they share them), for they recognize that many beliefs are ethnocentric in nature and some are intimately linked to war. The shortcomings and limitations of stereotypes about other countries and ethnic groups are also appreciated since such beliefs are likely to be based upon prejudice and to reflect misconceptions of reality. They have been exposed by peace-loving advocates, including popes[22] and anthropologists.[23]

Finally, self-knowledge is a necessary attribute of *homo pacificus*. His possession of insight lessens the possibility that he will project onto other persons his own shortcomings and misgivings. The path to such wisdom is strewn with the hazards that result from conscious and unconscious self-delusions which, perhaps, can be avoided only by a mentally healthy individual.

ATTITUDES (#s 1c, e, f; 2)

Embodying a principal theme of Christianity, as already suggested, and of most other great religions is a central attitude toward one's fellow beings, that of love in its most extended sense. Interest, sympathy, empathy, concern—these are some of the English words that try, however inadequately, to characterize that attitude. Even the most supreme egotist presumably worries about his immediate family or his associates, but such a worry itself may be selfishly motivated: if something happens to them, where shall I be? Or, if I do not keep their standards high, what will others think of me? There is no complete escape from the demands of the groups to which everyone is attached. But more is needed than self- or family-centered altruism. *Homo pacificus* is sensitive to the needs of others and, though solipsistically encased, he tries to comprehend them and their needs. This saintly love may prevent him from hurting others in any way, from being harmfully aggressive toward them.

Love, to be effective, is accompanied by other attitudes which can also be variously expressed. A British mathematician and philosopher has suggested that they are "tentativeness, as opposed to dogmatism, in our beliefs; an expectation of cooperation, rather than competition, in social relations; a lessening of envy and collective hatred."[24] Many of these attitudes are consequences of not being ethnocentric: *homo pacificus* judges each person not in terms of a demographic or sociological attribute—such as the "nation," race, neighborhood to which he happens to belong—but as an individual. He avoids generalizing from one particular trait, whether it meets his approval or not, to the entire person. That other individual may have a good or bad trait, but he himself is not altogether good or bad. As ever, fancy words are used or coined to label such an attribute; one writer, for example, states that among the "war-breeding complexes" is one he terms *heterophobia* which consists of "distrust, hatred, and exclusivism" resulting from "differences and conformity" among organized groups.[25]

The "tentativeness" mentioned above suggests that a *homo pacificus* recognizes that, wherever he looks, differences between peoples and between individuals within any group inevitably appear.[26] These differences include every conceivable aspect of human thinking, feeling, and behavior. Beneath overt appearances lurk latent variations (cf. V). Even somewhat superficial recitals of life histories of so-called pacifists, beginning with William Penn, including Leo Tolstoy, and ending with the Berrigan brothers, vividly indicate how each came to reject war for unique reasons associated with his personality, milieu, events, and experiences (cf. V). [27] *Homo Pacificus* feels more comfortable in the presence of these differences when he believes they have a satisfactory explanation. The explanation can range from an appreciation of a genetic factor in the case of an individual to geographical factors in the case of countries. Many countries , he knows, reflect varying traditions and cultures that in turn may have been partially determined by the capacity of the land to sustain a population of a particular size or to encourage or discourage special types of economic activities.[28]

SKILLS (#s 1b, d, f; 2)

More than any other skill *homo pacificus* possesses not only appropriate beliefs and attitudes but also the ability to tolerate frustration—I repeat myself deliberately, the point is so important—without experiencing hatred toward the "real" frustrators or at least without feeling impelled to express his hostility or aggression overtly or destructively. Letting loose aggressive or destructive impulses is on occasion essential if only to achieve catharsis, but the social effect is likely to be counterproductive (cf. P). Since the other cheek is not turned automatically, this skill is acquired through experience and is accompanied by a reinforcing, broad philosophy concerning other persons and society.

Among the traits promoting the learning necessary to prevent harmful or false stereotypes from validating a false conception of reality is plasticity or the absence of dogmatism and of rigidity (cf. P). For these traits have been shown, at least among limited samples of human beings (usually American college students) and almost always only through paper-and-pencil question-naires, to be associated modestly with tightly organized beliefs, resistance to accepting new information, and a general intolerance of ambiguity.[29] Elasticity and resilience are necessary, especially when the individual adapts to a quickly changing milieu.

Homo pacificus skillfully avoids the kind of discrepancy frequently existing between war-peace attitudes or beliefs on the one hand and action on the other hand. His favorable attitude toward peace rather than war is accompanied by suitable actions, sometimes because—as argued above—he is truly convinced that achieving peace is important and feasible.[30] He has the courage to act on the strength and content of his convictions, as most conscientious objectors come to realize is required when they are punished for refusing to bear arms during a war. Other diverse skills also bring satisfaction and hence strengthen the individual's inclination toward peace. A social scientist, for example, suggests that increasing the enjoyment of the environment and promoting "pro-life rationality, diversity, and ex-perimentation" helps each person to realize his human potentiality.[31]

The qualifications of leaders as they would formulate foreign policy, carry out diplomatic missions, and conclude a compassionate peace after a war are probably too diverse to be specified, a platitude very well-founded when even a glance is cast at the different personalities of Nobel Laureates designated as peacemakers; for example, Theodore Roosevelt as compared with the two Irish women leading the peace movement in Northern Ireland in the mid-1970s. General knowledge like that possessed by the intellectual elite or the well-educated does not appear, by and large, to be useful; for with exceptions (Masaryk, Wilson, Léon Blum, Nehru, Disraeli, and Glad-stone), "forays by intellectuals into the political domain have usually ended rather disastrously."[32] Fine terms (truth, honesty, graciousness, and sincerity), even when spoken by a Nobel Peace Prize winner,[33] sound inspiring but are too general and removed from the problem. A generaliza-tion, such as that "sympathy with others helps us to see things from their point of view,"[34] is true enough but utterly banal. Beyond having the psychological attributes characterizing *homines pacifici* in general, as delineated in the Sermon on the Mount, fortitude clearly is demonstrated by a leader who leads rather than follows. Unlike most leaders who have been competently investigated,[35] he is not imprisoned in the situations into which he has been pitched by circumstance or, for that matter, by his own past policies.

CHAPTER APPENDIX

5.1 GANDHI'S NONVIOLENCE (#s 1a, d, e; 3a)

In the words of one of his followers, Gandhi's doctrine of nonviolence was an overt declaration of a series of beliefs fostering "(1) faith in God; (2) faith in the goodness of human nature; (3) infinite patience and capacity to suffer; (4) the capacity for infinite sacrifice; (5) fearlessness; (6) complete abstinence from the use of coercion; (7) unfailing adherence to truth; (8) purity of heart to inspire confidence; (9) gentleness and politeness, and (10) perpetual readiness for compromise."[36] Obviously these ten attributes constitute a philosophy of religion, human relations, and personality. In Gandhi's view, therefore, nonviolence as a principle can be salient and effective only when it is the expression of an individual whose rich personality is so well integrated that the principle governs virtually all of his actions.

Secondly, Gandhi himself on four occasions—the Boer War in South Africa, the Zulu Rebellion of 1906 in South Africa, and both World Wars—participated in war and advised others to do so. "The alternatives before us," another sympathetic follower has stated as a summary of his views, "are not violence versus nonviolence, but only direct violence versus indirect violence, or violence versus cowardice and fear."[37] Gandhi believed violence admissible when its nonuse would sacrifice a more important value: when a sufficient number of people was not prepared and could not be persuaded to believe in and practice what he considered to be the true doctrine of nonviolence; when the target of nonviolence was not likely to be influenced. Thus he advocated nonviolence against the British because he believed that they and his followers shared similar values and that they, unlike the Japanese, would or could be affected by nonviolent tactics.[38] And so, *homo pacificus* is nonviolent with exceptions.

NOTES

1. Adam Curle, *Making Peace*. London: Tavistock Publications, 1971. P. 25.

2. Irving Louis Horowitz, *The Idea of War and Peace in Contemporary Philosophy*. New York: Paine-Whitman, 1957. P. 38.

3. B. F. Skinner, Freedom and the control of men. In George Kateb (ed.), *Utopia*. New York: Atherton Press, 1971. Pp. 57-75.

4. George Kateb, *Utopia and Its Enemies*. Glencoe: Free Press, 1963. P. 8, italics deleted.

5. J. C. Flugel, *The Moral Paradox of Peace and War*. London: Watts, 1941. P. 5.

6. Gerado Zampaglione, *The Idea of Peace in Antiquity*. Notre Dame: University of Notre Dame Press, 1973. Chaps. 3, 4.

7. Santiago Genovés, *Is Peace Inevitable?* New York: Walker, 1970. P. 145.

8. Richard A. Falk, *A Study of Future Worlds*. New York: Free Press, 1975. P. 97.

9. Pope John Paul II, Address to the United Nations General Assembly. *New York Times*, 2 October 1979, pp. B4-5.

10. S. D. Goitein, The concept of mankind in Islam. In W. Warren Wagar (ed.), *History and the Idea of Mankind*. Albuquerque: University of New Mexico Press, 1971. Pp. 72-91.

11. Florian Znaniecki, *Modern Nationalities*. Urbana: University of Illinois Press, 1952. P. 175.

12. Wing-tsit Chan, Taoism. *Encyclopedia Britannica*, 1962, 21, 797.

13. Zampaglione, op. cit., pp. 185-87.

14. Nahum Glatzer, The concept of peace in classical Judaism. In Erich Fromm and Hans Herzfeld (eds.), *Der Friede*. Heidelberg: Verlag Lamber Schneider, 1961. Pp. 27-38.

15. Matthew 5:1-7:27.

16. Martin Niemöller, Comments. In Edward Reed (ed.), *Beyond Coexistence*. New York: Grossman, 1968. Pp. 115-17.

17. Roland H. Bainton, *Christian Attitudes toward War and Peace*. New York: Abingdon Press, 1960. P. 263.

18. Zampaglione, op. cit., p. 207.

19. John F. Kennedy cited by Walter C. Clemens, Jr., *Toward a Strategy of Peace*. Chicago: Rand McNally, 1965. P. 23.

20. Cf. Mark A. May, *A Social Psychology of War and Peace*. New Haven: Yale University Press, 1943. P. 28.

21. Charles E. Osgood, Questioning some unquestioned assumptions about national security. In Milton Schwebel (ed.), *Behavioral Science and Human Survival*. Palo Alto: Science and Behavior Books, 1965. Pp. 13-21.

22. Pope John XXIII cited by Clemens, op. cit., p. 253. Also Pope John Paul II, op. cit.

23. Robert Redfield, The ethnological problem. In George B. Huszar (ed.), *New Perspectives on Peace*. Chicago: University of Chicago Press, 1944. Pp. 60-84.

24. Bertrand Russell, Science and human life. In James R. Newman (ed.), *What is Science?* New York: Simon and Schuster, 1955. Pp. 6-17.

25. Zygmunt A. Piotrowski, Is permanent peace possible? In Rolland S. Parker (ed.), *The Emotional Stress of War, Violence, and Peace*. Pittsburgh: Stanwix House, 1972, Pp.1-11.

26. Horowitz, op. cit., p. 40.

27. Nicholas Gillett, *Men Against War*. London: Victor Gollancz, 1966. Mark Lieberman, *The Pacifists*. New York: Praeger, 1972.

28. Cf. Charles C. Colby, The geographical problem. In George B. de Huszar, *New Perspectives on Peace*. Chicago: University of Chicago Press, 1944. Pp. 28-38.

29. Milton Rokeach, *The Open and Closed Mind*. New York: Basic Books, 1960. Jeffrey L. Sanders, The relationship of dogmatism to the nonrecognition of perceptual ambiguity. *Journal of Psychology*, 1977, 95, 179-83.

30. Hans Kreitler and Shulamith Kreitler, Crucial dimensions of the attitude towards national supranational ideals. *Journal of Peace Research*, 1967, 4, 105-24.

31. Herbert L. Leff, *Experience, Environment, and Human Potentials*. New York: Oxford University Press, 1978. P. 410.

32. Lewis A. Coser, *Men of Ideas*. New York: Free Press, 1965. P. 135.

33. Dominique Pire, *Vivre ou Mourir Ensemble*. Brussels: Presses Académiques Européennes, 1969. P. 166.

34. J. C. Flugel, Some neglected aspects of world integration. In T. H. Pear (ed.), *Psychological Factors of Peace and War*. New York: Philosophical Library, 1950. Pp. 111-38.

35. Betty Crump and Bruce M. Russett, Introduction. In Bruce M. Russett (ed.), *Peace, War, and Numbers*. Beverly Hills: Sage, 1972. Pp. 9-17.

36. T. K. N. Unnithan, On non-violence. In International Peace Research Association (ed.), *Proceedings of the International Peace Research Association, Inaugural Conference*. Assen: Van Gorcum, 1966. Pp. 279-87.

37. Giuliano Pontara, The rejection of violence in Gandhian ethics of conflict resolution. *Journal of Peace Research*, 1965, 2, 197-215.

38. Raj Krishna, *Non-violence, War, and Peace*. Ahmedabad: Harold Lask Institute of Political Science, 1964. P. 8.

6.
National and International Perfection

Before surveying the perfectability of the individual in the last chapter, it was necessary to point to the close relation between such an aspiration and the society in which it is to be realized. Now we return to the society itself, to the "nation," and to international relations. The "nation," I would repeat, is conceived of as a collection of individuals whose interactions affect all of its members including hermits and schizophrenics. Leaders produce policies that influence not only their constituents but also, in almost every instance, the relations of those constituents to the leaders and followers of other countries. Governments have both domestic and foreign policies, and the two usually interact. For this reason, then, national and international orientations cannot be separated and are dealt with together in this chapter.

The leaders of any country who formulate a plan for the future are in effect elusively seeking perfect human beings or a more perfect or at least a less imperfect society in which they are to live. President Nyerere of Tanzania has stipulated that self-reliance must be the goal of his people. Specifically this has meant regulating various institutions ranging from the economy to the education system so that his followers would become less dependent upon the outside world and would be able themselves to produce and consume what they themselves need. Under these circumstances Tanzania, it has been hoped, would be less prone to be attacked or to go to war. But in 1979 Tanzanian soldiers and Uganda exiles toppled General Amin in Uganda and afterwards helped to restore law and order there. The link between the domestic goal and the foreign policy might have been a humanistic value such as dignity or self-respect applicable inside and outside Tanzania's boundaries.

UTOPIAS (#s 3b, 4)

When men's imaginations soar and when, whether "out of hope and despair"[1] or some other reason, they create utopias, they necessarily concentrate upon what they consider to be the perfect national or international community (cf. P).* The community achieves perfection because of its perfect leaders, perfect influentials, and perfect followers. Generally, utopianists (that is, those who write about utopias, the inhabitants of which are utopians) favor a nirvana of peace or at least no devastating conflicts within their own ideal setting. Seriously or not, they believe they have clues to the perfect society.

These utopian creations, consequently, merit attention since they reflect the serious views of intelligent writers. The dreams concerning a Golden Age in the past or the future should provide clues to national and international settings through which the possibility of war might be diminished. Utopias reflect a yearning to escape from an imperfect society or to achieve perfection by reconstructing that society.[2] They are, moreover, not confined to the past or to the West, as messianic cults in our society and so-called "cargo cults" in the South Pacific, respectively, suggest.[3]

Utopias can be so broadly defined that they include any aspiration of mankind or any plan for the ideal society, ranging from Plato's *Republic* to a psychologist's slightly fascinating description of *Walden Two* in our time.[4] They "may well be a sensitive indication of where the sharpest anguish of an age lies"[5]—war obviously produces anguish—and they suggest possible solutions to some of the problems;[6] hence in general they ought to delineate ways to pursue peace via perfection. Or so one would hope. With few exceptions, however, such hopes are dashed.

The utopianists are vulnerable to attack, as is any project which criticizes existing conditions. They largely—though not completely, as will be indicated—avoid the problem of how peace is to be attained. Many utopias, we are told by their progenitors, exist in isolation or isolate themselves so that no out-group looms with which wars might be fought; they are islands, they are separated from the rest of wicked mankind by insuperable barriers, generally they "have but a nebulous past and no future," they are just "suddenly there, and there to stay."[7] Or the assumption is made that violence must be employed to achieve the state of perfection. That ideal state, moreover, probably cannot be maintained, even if achieved, except through a political system that is oppressive. Also, from the standpoint of critics, the utopianists would achieve goals that are unacceptable or, if accepted, would jeopardize other values.[8]

---

*See pages 11-12 for an explanation of the cross-referencing system.

Let us, nevertheless, attempt to lift ourselves into the clouds and at least glimpse a vision of what might be,[9] even perhaps as Jews throughout centuries dreamed of a homeland that in reality seemed both remote and impossible.[10] Techniques for initially achieving utopia can sometimes be discerned in some utopian writings. Individuals are forced, or they are persuaded or convinced without the use of force to become citizens of utopia, or they may be allowed voluntarily to join an already established utopian community.[11] Sir Thomas More believed it was necessary to renounce private property to realize his utopia,[12] but he did not suggest what would motivate property owners to make the sacrifice or the leaders of the state to persuade them to do so. Morris's utopian England was to be achieved by bloody fighting and revolution,[13] which is yet another form of the just war, the war that allegedly achieves peace. Marxists, including Marx himself as well as Lenin, certainly indicated the need for a revolution in order to transfer power from the bourgeoisie to the working classes, but in their writings they did not provide detailed strategic or tactical plans. We now know that Marxist states in this century have been achieved only through violence and, alas, have not put an end to violence and oppression in the postrevolutionary years. At any rate, the utopianists of the nineteenth century deliberately summoned their followers to some kind of action in order to produce the utopia they sought.[14]

Peace for utopianists by and large implies the prevention of conflict within the utopian society. Attention, therefore, tends to be concentrated exclusively upon perfecting human beings, not so that they can avoid war but so that they can achieve worthwhile values in their individual roles. Saint-Simon, for example, believed that, if desires were satisfied, there should be "no lust for dominion over others"; and Fourier argued that there would be "no eruption in destructive hostility" if there were outlets for frustrated impulses through "emulation among rival work and love groups" and, to divert murderous impulses, through the slaughtering of animals.[15] These hints concerning internal peace may be desirable on a national basis, but they provide no mechanism to achieve peace between countries.

Some utopianists, such as Plato, stray far from pursuing international peace because their interest in a utopia stems in part from having everyone in a state of "constant readiness for war"; and others, like More, simply accept war as inevitable.[16] No help comes from many writers, such as Huxley and Orwell, who for various and understandable reasons have become so disillusioned with human beings and with society that their projections into the future have been labelled "antiutopias"; they would alert their readers to "the future of horrors of mechanization and collectivism" without providing practical solutions.[17]

The description of each utopia is almost always lengthy; the creator becomes infatuated with his fantasy and provides whatever information tickles his fancy. To convey the flavor of this genre, an arbitrary selection has been made from among the many utopianists. In Chapter Appendix 6.1 attention is focused upon the most influential of the English and American utopianists, More and Bellamy, respectively; for the sake of amusement, the uninfluential, redoubtable H. G. Wells is added.

More, it can be seen in that appendix, is primarily concerned with the perfectability of an elitist group of individuals. On that level he assumes they enjoy a variety of gratifications, none of which stems from prior frustrations or involves subsequent aggressions. His utopians avoid many frustrations because they are served by slaves and because they have been gently, though firmly socialized during childhood. As nationals they are so dependent on slaves that it is difficult, centuries later, to draw any useful lessons applicable to modern countries. We are not likely to produce peace-prone individuals by reestablishing slavery, but it is useful to be reminded that perhaps nonaggression at least can be nurtured. War itself is to be avoided through military preparedness, not a novel procedure and not, as has been pointed out previously, a very promising one; it is declared only in behalf of a just cause and then it is waged both ruthlessly and compassionately.

In his romantic treatise which was once a best-seller, Bellamy presents a fait accompli, a collection of socialist states that have been slowly achieved without bloodshed. He stresses the close relation between the form of the state and its citizens' propensity toward war-peace. Individuals are made peace-prone by being given the opportunity to express their normal impulses in peaceful ways.

In a sense Wells himself has declared his utopia an impossible goal because to achieve its ideals he has had to place it on another planet. He has forcefully made a case for an environment which encourages beliefs different from existing ones and which eliminates nationalism in favor of a world state. Good Fabian that he is, he also advocates gradualism, aided by just wars.

In spite of the criticisms that can be levelled against utopianists, it is well to appreciate their interest in child rearing and the kinds of personalities they believe must inhabit their ideal state. They thus stress the connection between individuals and the state or international relations they would create and foster. The crucial criticism I think is contained in a trenchant, somewhat glib analysis not only of utopias but also of philosophies concerned with the nature of the ideal state: only a "minimal state" is justified. For in such a state citizens are treated "as inviolate individuals" whose rights and dignity are respected. It "allows us, individually or with whom we choose, to choose our life and to realize our ends and our conception of ourselves, insofar as we can, aided by the voluntary cooperation of other individuals possessing the same dignity."[18] In contrast, utopianists would impose a more or less similar pattern upon everyone, for this is the consequence, the author thinks, when the state is more than minimal. The argument, it should be evident, states that individual differences are significant (cf. V). Somewhat melodramatically, the reader is provided with a long list of persons beginning with "Wittgenstein, Elizabeth Taylor, Bertrand Russell, Thomas Merton, Yogi Berra" and ending with "Thomas Jefferson, Ralph Ellison, Bobby Fischer, Emma Goldman, Peter Kropotkin, you, and your parents," followed by a challenge and a long list of rhetorical questions:

Is there really *one* kind of life which is best for each of these people? Imagine all of them living in any utopia you've ever seen described in detail. Try to describe the society which would be best for all of these persons to live in. Would it be agricultural or urban? Of great material luxury or of austerity with basic needs satisfied? What would relations between the sexes be like? . . . The idea that there is one best society for *everyone* to live in, seems to me to be an incredible one.[19]

This critic of utopias and similar projects himself merits criticism. Obviously individual differences always persist and obviously, therefore, no single arrangement will ever satisfy everyone: the universal consensus and social harmony assumed by the utopianists[20] are unrealistic. Whether satisfaction and elasticity are achievable by a minimal state remains an unanswerable question, however telling the author's strictures against regulation appear to be. He himself avoids the war-peace problem except in one brief section which discusses the justification for a preemptive attack or a preventive war only in terms of probability, the potential enemy's past behavior, and the various decisions that might be involved.[21]

A valuable conclusion emerges from the utopianists' desire to achieve perfection: leaders and followers can consider themselves not nationalists but citizens of the world without losing their patriotism (cf. P). They believe "all elements of the human race have fundamental interests in common, and that boundaries between nations should have no more significance in the modern world than the dividing lines between the states of the American Union."[22] As one pacifist sentimentally has expressed her credo:

I am a good American, but far more deeply and happily I feel myself a citizen of the world. I am at home wherever there are people. Wherever I go, I know I shall find cruel, sly, dishonest, unpleasant people; and everywhere I shall find magnanimous, generous people with keen minds, honest, open, serviceable people, who want to help, who want to make friends. . . . I am a patriot and my fatherland is this dear, dear earth, sole home of life in infinite space.[23]

ETHNOPEACE (# 4)

An apology, but not an abject one for the subheading: just as the scientific or the psychological views of laymen are called, respectively, ethnoscience or ethnopsychology, so this neologism directs attention to the conditions relating to war-peace that are considered desirable by non-utopianists and especially by followers when their international orientation is salient.

Let us begin with science. Actually the distance between utopias on the level of fantasy and those presumed to have some relation to scientific knowledge is not great, since both stem from their progenitor's view of reality as perceived either personally in the case of fantasy or collectively by researchers in the case of science. One has, or should have, greater confidence in scientists than in the creators of fantasy because presumably a scientist's perception and conceptualization of objective reality is likely to be more valid than what emerges from unbounded imagination. An American organization, the World Order Institute in New York, once assembled social scientists from various countries, including the Soviet Union, and asked them to name the "five basic values" to achieve a world order. In addition to peace (or the absence of war) and the resolution of conflicts without violence, they pointed to four goals: ecological stability, economic well-being, social justice, and the opportunity for nationals somehow to participate in decisions affecting them.[24] All four seem highly relevant to reducing frustrations and enabling individuals to realize their aspirations or potentialities and hence to be less war-prone. The specific means to attain these objectives varied from writer to writer, but one overall utopia, in my opinion, received almost unanimous consent. A political scientist shall be the spokesman:

A world system composed of sovereign states cannot deal effectively or equitably with the problems facing humankind. Some form of global integration is needed to facilitate the shaping of policy and the sharing of resources. Without such integration, the difficulties of today seem destined to become the nightmares of tomorrow. But as matters now stand the state system remains ascendant, and continues to control the instruments of violence as well as the existing procedures for peaceful change. Whether the issue is preventing nuclear war, maintaining world food or oil supplies, eliminating poverty and repression, or avoiding dangerous levels of air or water pollution, we most urgently require that which is most lacking, namely, the capacity and willingness of national governments to be enlightened, to think and act globally rather than nationally.[25]

For lay ethnopeace, there are survey data drawn from samples of Americans before, during, and after World War II. The salience of the war-peace problem, the predictions and attitudes concerning the possibility of being involved in war, indeed the analysis of war's causes seem to have been a function of ongoing events during the investigation and also of the wording of the questions themselves. A gigantic analysis of samples from ten countries during the 1960s revealed a strong interest in peace and a fear of nuclear war. To attain peace, economic reforms and the improvement of the United Nations tended to be favored, although there was great variability from country to country (cf. V). The most sweeping generalization that could be extracted from the voluminous report was the following: "The sample as a whole showed a considerable level of consensus concerning a set of peace philosophies that can be characterized as liberal and structural, as opposed to conservative and power-oriented ones."[26] Vox populi, vox dei? I think not, but at the very, very least this rough-and-ready approach indicates that, when properly or doggedly questioned, views about war-peace and ways to attain peace can be extracted from men and women perhaps everywhere. No blueprint is provided, only hopes and prayers; usually a world without war can be imagined, however vaguely and uncertainly (cf. P). (See Chapter Appendix 6.2: Surveys on War-Peace.)

HUMAN RIGHTS (#s 3, 4)

The perfect society would protect human rights. Why should the platitutde be acceptable and so often repeated? Two reasons are impressive. First, those rights, whatever they are, express the experience of mankind or at least a large part of mankind regarding the conditions necessary to promote human welfare or happiness (cf. E). They are postulated because, in the words set forth in the American Convention on Human Rights, they are "based upon attributes of the human personality."[27] Other less psychological justifications are also convincing. If "the central core of justice is . . . the exclusion of arbitrariness and, more particularly, of power," then this same "axiom of justice holds for states as for individuals," from which it follows that "what is just for our own state or nation must be equally just for other nations in similar circumstances."[28] Justice, therefore, must be made concrete by specifying the goals everyone is entitled to attain and the frustrations they should not have to endure.

Secondly, since rights are related to the promotion of human welfare and welfare in turn is related to peace, attention is thus focused on the societal conditions that need to be perfected. The American Declaration of Independence asserts, in its most famous phrase, that among the "unalienable rights" of men are "life, liberty, and the pursuit of happiness" because a regime that condemns individuals to death for trivial transgressions, that permits some or many of them to be slaves, and that keeps most of them in such misery that they can neither pursue nor attain happiness is to be condemned for committing, in the language of the Nuremberg tribunal, "crimes against humanity"—and, again, such deprived persons are likely to be war-prone. According to a contemporary German statesman, freedom consists of more than "the absence of war and force," for there must also be "freedom from oppression, from hunger, and from ignorance."[29] Years before a president of the United States publicly and doggedly championed human rights, the Secretary-General of the United Nations, Dag Hammarskjöld, stated:

> We know that the question of peace and the question of human rights are closely related. Without recognition of human rights we shall never have peace, and it is only within the framework of peace that human rights can be fully developed.[30]

This view has been echoed again and again, most recently by Pope John Paul II: " . . . the spirit of war in its basic primordial meaning springs up and grows up, grows to maturity when the inalienable rights of men are violated."[31] For present purposes the chicken-and-egg problem can be avoided by seeking to uncover the nature of the rights that both produce and result from peace.

As it was perplexing to face the vast and relevant subject of religion in the quest for perfection, so a similarly baffling question now arises: how can those human rights be uncovered (cf. I)? The guide of the American Convention on Human Rights mentioned above can be followed and some rights can be deduced, with a dash of recklessness, from the nature of homo sapiens. Undoubtedly, for example, an arbitrary frustration is less endurable than one which can be explained or seems unavoidable. Therefore, individuals, probably everywhere, have the right to know why they are being arrested, why they are detained in prison, and so on. Another approach, not a very fruitful one, is to query individuals directly. While it is true that most persons have their own private conception of an ideal society, surveys tend, by and large, to produce banalities or variations too numerous to function as guides. When samples of university students in eleven diverse countries, for example, were asked in 1969-1970 to "try to imagine a society of which you really approve," the best summary of "the three most frequent responses" seemed to be that they subscribed to the slogan of the French revolution: freedom, equality, and fraternity among men. The usual fluctuations from country to country appeared; thus 37 percent of the Japanese sample and 79 percent of the French sample agreed that "in an ideal society work and play should be indistinguishable."[32] Evidently ordinary mortals find other matters more salient or pressing than contemplating the good society; when molested by investigators, they emit clichés.

To progress, it is more fruitful to draw on a vast heritage that gives a clue to the embodiment of human needs in societal rights throughout the ages, whether the original proponent is thought to be Plato or the Magna Charta or a revision embodied in one of the many declarations issued since the end of World War II. From some standpoints any statement about human rights is in part a restatement of previous statements; for example, for Christians and Jews those implied in the Ten Commandments, and also, for Christians, those in the Sermon on the Mount (cf. P). Understandably the literature on human rights is vast, and almost all of it is concerned with the history or legal interpretation of the documents expressing those rights. From an authoritative account called *Human Rights in the World*,[33] the impression is gained, nevertheless, that certain rights are mentioned again and again, mentioned in fact so often that they must spring from truly deep yearnings of men and women everywhere.

No, not everywhere, for perforce all the standard documents come from our own civilization and hence may or may not reflect values prevalent in traditional societies elsewhere. In fact, one of the documents cited in this section and frequently in Chapter Appendix 6.3, the Universal Declaration of Human Rights, may not be as "universal" as its title proclaims, even though its drafters had at their disposal replies to a UNESCO questionnaire on the subject received from "various thinkers and writers" thoughout the world.[34] The declaration was initially influenced by Western diplomats who sought to affirm human rights in the abstract and, to a lesser degree, by Soviet diplomats who wished to protect individuals from insecurities resulting from social conditions. According to students of Islam, however, it scarcely embodies the view of that great religion which stresses that "God has bestowed upon man certain essential and unalienable natural rights, which he must however harmonize with the interests of the community, based on the imperative of justice prescribed by the Koran."[35] The "concept of man differs fundamentally from society to society, with resulting implications for political institutions and social control"[36] and hence, I add, for the human rights supposedly promoted or safeguarded by such institutions and such control. Even if these criticisms are true, the values of the West keep diffusing everywhere (whether or not the peoples elsewhere seek them), and hence the experience of the West to some degree is universally applicable. Perhaps, too, many of the values are in fact relevant within non-Western contexts or at least, as in contemporary China, raise challenging problems.

In actual fact, virtually every contemporary, formal declaration concerning human rights is built upon and hence borrows ideas from one or more of its predecessors. At the American Convention on Human Rights in 1969, for example, twenty-six rights and freedoms from the European Convention on Human Rights and its protocols in 1959 were included in its declaration, a single one was not included, and only eight were added.[37] The latter eight, moreover, can be found in other international statements.

But where to begin to extract propositions about human rights from the common deluge at our disposal? Perhaps only because I was concerned with organizations seeking to propagate them during World War II, I succumb to a personal, arbitrary prejudice and as a very, very loose framework select the Four Freedoms, first enunciated by Franklin D. Roosevelt and then embodied by him and Winston Churchill in the Atlantic Charter: freedom from want, freedom of speech and expression, freedom of every person to worship God in his own way, and freedom from fear. Slightly interesting is the fact that decades later, when President Jimmy Carter undertook his well-publicized, if ineffective, campaign in behalf of human rights, he singled out three rights whose meaning but not phrasing closely resembles all four of these freedoms: "right to be free from governmental violation of the integrity of the person" (cf. freedom from fear); "right to fulfillment of such vital needs as food, shelter, health care, and education" (cf. freedom from want); "right to enjoy civil and political liberties" (cf. the remaining two).[38] These freedoms, however, seem insufficient. A fifth is needed which, as proposed by sources as diverse as the American Declaration of Independence and a modern Chinese philosopher,[39] can be called the freedom to enjoy life. The fivefold division of the rights is admittedly far from perfect, yet these rights are specifically related to human needs. Conceivably, moreover, there is even a connection between them and the values considered desirable in traditional societies, provided the values have been sensitively grasped from the standpoint of those in-groupers who actively pursue them.[40]

In elaborating the five rights and especially in Chapter Appendix 6.3 (Documents on Human Rights), evidence is derived from five sources:

I: Universal Declaration of Human Rights adopted and proclaimed by the General Assembly of the United Nations on 10 December 1948. That declaration, besides influencing subsequent declarations, embodies most of the statements contained in other declarations in the West and hence in a real sense is a summary of Western thought or aspirations. It was explicitly praised and cited by Pope John Paul II when he addressed the United Nations General Assembly in 1979.[41]

II: International Covenant on Economic, Social, and Cultural Rights adopted by the General Assembly of the United Nations on 16 December 1966.

III: International Covenant on Civil and Political Rights adopted by the same body and on the same date as the covenant above.

IV: American Convention on Human Rights adopted by a majority of the members of the Organization of American States on 22 November 1969.

V: UNESCO Committee on the Philosophic Principles of the Rights of Man. The committee, on the basis of the replies to the questionnaire mentioned above and of its own deliberations, in 1947 formulated fifteen rights which it believed "to be implicit in man's nature as an individual and as a member of society and to follow from the fundamental right to live."[42]

Although their intention has not been implemented and probably never can or will be, the five documents have the value of having been assembled by different committees from different countries. They are, I think, the best guides we have, at least for our generation, to this aspect of political perfection.

Freedom from want refers to the opportunity to satisfy basic needs such as food, clothing, and shelter and to find the means to achieve these satisfactions. *Homo pacificus* requires this freedom in order to survive and indeed to survive above a subsistence level. Without freedom from poverty, the other freedoms are either useless or meaningless, and individuals may not even be interested in obtaining additional human rights. "Wants" motivate actions, but basic wants that are inhibited lead to frustration and perhaps also to rebellion and war. The concrete requirements of this human right are suggested in Chapter Appendix 6.3.

Freedom of speech and expression is usually heralded with a brave, loud, and long blast when that phrasing or some verbal equivalent is included among human rights. In different words: "all the differing ideologies of the world" must have the opportunity to be expressed and communicated.[43] These rights are desirable not only because they are part of the best Anglo-Saxon tradition—not necessarily a strong argument in their behalf when one thinks of colonialism—but also because they pay homage to the unique impulses of each person. Instrumentally he satisfies basic and derived needs in more or less distinctive ways, and to do so he must be able freely to communicate with, and to receive communications from, the persons and groups of his own choice. Without this freedom, political power cannot be utilized to attain significant goals.[44] From the outset the infant cries or screams at will, and no one ordinarily would curb this symptom of bodily need or exaltation. In every society individuals are dependent upon one another and hence must request assistance to satisfy needs. Each person expresses himself somewhat differently. Unless he knows that he always or at least frequently has the opportunity to give vent to what he requires as a result of what he believes to be his own needs and those of his primary group, he will somehow feel frustrated or repressed. He must be both willing and able, without fear of punishment, to have an opportunity to criticize followers and leaders, and to indicate dissent from the prevailing mores and from policies leading to war rather than peace (or, to be fair, vice versa). There must also be "adequate guarantees for the freedom and opinions of the minorities."[45] The perfect government is one with leaders permitting such freedom and exercising no negative sanctions (punishments) against its expression.

No negative sanctions? Even in utopia there is ethical relativism (cf. P). As has been frequently said, freedom of speech does not include the privilege of falsely shouting "fire" in a crowded theater. Whether pornographic exhibitionism, so characteristic of our times at least in the civilized lands of the West, is to be included under freedom of expression is a topic I leave to other generations to decide. A distinguished United States Supreme Court justice and advocate of both civil liberties and peace has declared that "man is selfish, predatory, and aggressive; and he will always need regimes of law and order to police him."[46] Whether "man" should be so glibly and externally characterized is not of immediate interest; but the second clause of the assertion cannot be ignored. "Law and order" means the curbing of some aspect of speech and expression. Obviously a man in jail has his freedom curtailed, he does not have access to his family and peers or to the mass media of his choice. The limitation of his freedom serves another, a more pressing value, that of the life or rights and privileges of the other persons against whom he has transgressed or could transgress. No values are absolute; on occasion one value must be sacrificed in behalf of another. Perhaps, however, this freedom of speech and expression comes as close as any to qualifying for an exemption from relativism, as John Stuart Mill in his noble essay "On Liberty" has argued. (Details are given in Chapter Appendix 6.3.)

The freedom to criticize governmental policies that may lead to war is a privilege relatively easy to exercise, at least in democratic countries during periods of peace. But has *homo pacificus* the right to argue against the war effort when once his country is at war, officially or unofficially? To be consistent, a believer in freedom of expression must agree that he certainly should speak out; yet by doing so he may well bring injury upon himself and his immediate peers. Again the dissenter must select the better, the higher value—and that is no easy task. A far profounder problem confronts the individual after the declaration of war; being a conscientious objector, for example, raises difficult questions dealt with elsewhere in this book.

Similarly difficult is a human right of "expression" involving not words but deeds, "the right to rebellion or revolution," according to the UNESCO committee.[47] Here is a variant of the just war or the use of violence under specified conditions as proclaimed by Thomas Jefferson in the Declaration of Independence: when a "form of government" destroys people's "unalienable rights" and when there has been "a long train of abuses and usurpations" seeming to lead to "absolute despotism," then "it is their right, it is their duty, to throw off such government, and to provide new guards for their future security." Whether this dictum prevents or facilitates even greater violence in interstate war is a question which must be raised and to which no definitive answer exists.

Freedom of expression as well as of speech implies other rights. Citizens must be able to participate in their governments, particularly through freely electing the officials who will govern them. They must be able to enjoy the cultural fruits of their society and to be properly or appropriately educated. They must be granted the privilege of pursuing whatever legitimate career they believe suits their needs and personality. They must be able to determine their own political, economic, social, and cultural existence; but the rights of those who disagree, the minority, must be respected. They must be identifiable as distinct persons and have the right to marry and establish a family. Obviously, in short, free expression includes a multitude of activities.

Freedom of every person to worship God in his own way transcends the freedom of expression because of the importance and special status of religion. This freedom is required for institutional and personal reasons. It is clear that various religious institutions exist throughout the world, but the validity of a religion cannot be established in the manner of a scientific proposition. Throughout the ages, therefore, different approaches to man's eternal problems have evolved, each of which claims to be the true church and the embodiment of the deity. Since no clear-cut way exists for men to make the best decision, each individual must be free to worship as he pleases. Pope John Paul II has cogently expressed the rationale for this freedom:

The practice of religion, by its very nature, consists primarily of those voluntary and free internal acts by which a human being directly sets his course toward God. No merely human power can either command or prohibit acts of this kind. But man's social nature itself requires that he give external expression to his internal acts of religion, that he communicate with others in religious matters, and that he profess his religion in community.[48]

In addition, the relationship each person believes to exist between his god and himself is highly valued and hence dare not be obstructed.

Freedom from fear refers to the emotions resulting from the failure to reach various goals or from anticipating a failure to do so. It is essential to understand the psychological importance of these seemingly negative emotions. Fear of a realistic danger and neurotic anxiety concerning the unknown—a distinction Freud has emphasized[49]—are unpleasant states of affairs ordinarily to be avoided. Little wonder, therefore, that Roosevelt and Churchill tried to motivate their own nationals to cooperate with the war effort against the Axis powers and hopefully to attract Axis nationals to the side of the United Nations by including this freedom in their clarion call. The right to feel generally secure requires a system of laws that are never arbitrary, that guarantee fair and impartial trials in recognized courts, and that protect the family and minorities. It would be misleading not to point out also that both fear and anxiety can serve as sources of motivation to achieve the goal of their removal.

There is one frustrating fear, as we have reminded ourselves in the last chapter while discussing motives, which can never be, perhaps, completely eliminated and that is the fear of death. It can, however, be mitigated. Presumed in all freedoms and in most statements on human rights is a concern for health: as expressed in one of the International Covenants, "the right of everyone to the enjoyment of the highest attainable standard of physical and mental health."[50] When such a right exists, the incidence of diseases decreases and hence death is likely to be delayed. Otherwise only religion or resignation provides a way to cope with the fear of death when that fear is disturbing.

Freedom from fear is a right recognized outside the West. An Indian scholar, for example, believes that "great thinkers like Manu and Buddha" emphasized "five freedoms or social assurances" which could counteract fear. They are freedoms from violence, want, exploitation, violation or dishonor, and early death and disease. In addition there are five individual "virtues" that seem closely related to diminishing fear: absence of intolerance; compassion or fellow feeling; knowledge; freedom of thought and conscience; and freedom from fear and frustration or despair.[51]

Another probably universal fear is that of losing one's freedom completely and becoming a slave; hence the various modern declarations prohibit slavery as an institution. Excluded from a requirement banning "forced or compulsory labor," nevertheless, are the following conditions: when such labor is a punishment for a crime and the sentence is imposed "by a competent court"; when it is required by a person detained by a court or conditionally released from such detention; when it is part of military service or service imposed upon conscientious objectors; when there is an emergency or a calamity threatening the community; or when it "forms part of normal civil obligations."[52]

The ban on slavery, which at first appears so self-evident, raises a perplexing problem. Can slaves be happy (cf. I)? They cannot be happy, according to one viewpoint:

> . . . happy slaves are something of a myth. They may be politically unaware, but that is not to say that they are happy, and they normally live in circumstances conducive to misery. They are, in general, angry, resentful, and embittered; if they show a grinning face, it is for self-protection. . . . it is right to change the condition of the happy slave. If he does not want to change, it may well be that he does not know, in his present state of ignorance, that change is possible or what it might portend.[53]

But, the devil's advocate must ask, suppose the so-called happy slave believes himself to be happy; then who is to gainsay that subjective appraisal of his own hedonic state? One ought to be able to accept his or anyone's appraisal of himself and conclude therefore that he has achieved perfection: he claims to have no "wants," he is free from them, and consequently he is not likely to become belligerent to win his freedom. According to the quotation above, nevertheless, the happiness of such a person is likely to be a delusion: he does not know enough to experience divine discontent and to demand that his untapped potentialities be realized which then would make him—make him what? Would it make him happier, really happier? If he were to become a master rather than a slave, would the added responsibilities make him more or less happy? From a psychological standpoint an infinite number of desires can be created within human beings. When once created, they become needs, the satisfaction of which presumably must be attained. And so it is by no means clear that the rising expectations created in so-called developing countries by contact with the West and in so-called developed countries by commerce and its seductive handmaiden, advertising, lead to greater human satisfaction. We have here, in short, an ancient problem: a simple versus a complicated existence. The issue, I think, remains unsettled and will be ever so. Having introduced the problem with an anti-slavery edict, I end this paragraph with the opposite viewpoint. St. Paul has written: "Servants, be obedient to them that are your masters . . . knowing that whatsoever good thing any man doeth, the same shall he receive of the Lord, whether he be bond or free."[54] Correct on ethical rather than theological grounds?

On an international level, freedom from fear is also important because "a nation with a high level of hostility and anxiety will tend to depend 'irrationally' on more arms for protection, instead of releasing any of its sovereign power to a world government."[55] Translated, the sentence must mean that anxious and hostile national leaders are motivated to reduce their own anxiety and hostility through the security allegedly obtained by armaments rather than by international cooperation.

So far attention has been paid to fears that might be removed or mitigated. There is one fear, however, that should be augmented: the fear of war itself. The basis for this fear *homo pacificus* judges to be realistic: whatever gains a war may bring in the short run (political, ideological, power-oriented, security-attaining, even economic)[56] usually are self-defeating in the long run. Hatreds and impoverishment persist beyond the generation that has been victorious or defeated. The only danger resulting from the fear of war could be an assertion by leaders that the reality of war can be no worse than its anticipation or the alleged consequences of not engaging in war, and that therefore they must plunge recklessly ahead.

Freedom to enjoy life must be expressed in various ways because of its subjective character. Rephrasing it as "the right to enjoyment"[57] leaves the problem unchanged and on an abstract level. In the various Declarations are found words and phrases such as: utilizing fully and freely wealth and resources; having rest, leisure, and holidays; self-expression; access to the best aspects of civilization; at least a minimum education; developing one's potentialities. (See again Chapter Appendix 6.3.) Perhaps the flavor of this freedom is thus conveyed.

CAVEATS CONCERNING RIGHTS (#s 4, 5)

I do not suffer from the delusion that all possible rights and freedoms have been mentioned in the previous section and that those which have been mentioned have been properly squeezed under the five freedoms arbitrarily selected. They have been formulated abstractly—deliberately so—and hence it must be acknowledged that concrete details vary from society to society and from individual to individual (cf. V). Developing societies, for example, must have the rights "to be civilized according to the pattern" they themselves develop and, when vestiges of colonialism remain, to retain their land "with its many-sided associations and meanings."[58] These two rights could be called variants, respectively, of the freedom of expression and the freedom from want, but they call attention more dramatically to the unique problems to be resolved.

Variability is especially conspicuous in the case of freedom from want: one man's delicacy is another's taboo. The secondary or derived wants change over time. Modern Chinese leaders in particular recognize the "malleability" of human nature and hence do not feel they are violating human rights when they find "no a priori reasons . . . to deny either the possibility or the desirability of almost unlimited creation (molding) of people's social natures to induce personality traits or skills"[59] in the direction of their own social philosophy.

The five freedoms are closely interrelated and interdependent (cf. P). Freedom from want, for example, removes one source of fear concerning personal security and may then affect the political content of what people wish to be free to express. Freedom of speech and expression is necessary if there is to be freedom for every person to worship in his own way. One freedom may preclude another, just as the need for law and order means that some freedom of expression must be curbed. Leaders in nondemocratic countries often contend that to achieve freedom from want it may be necessary, temporarily at least, to sacrifice freedom of speech and expression so that a developing economy can function more efficiently. Another balancing of the values inherent in human rights occurs "in time of public emergency which threatens the life of the nation and the existence of which is officially proclaimed"; then, according to the International Covenant, it is permissible for states to "take measures derogating from their obligations," provided that certain rights (such as not being "subjected to torture or to cruel, inhuman or degrading treatment or punishment") are retained.[60]

Of course there is danger here: leaders may create or exacerbate a crisis in order to curtail major aspects of freedom.

The decision to rank one freedom above another is difficult and baffling, for eventually or immediately it is necessary to raise the question concerning the distribution of rights among mankind. Actually, anyone who questions, even in a whisper, the proposition that rights should be distributed equally is usually considered a scoundrel, especially by those who secretly agree with him. But the problem is too closely related to war-peace to be ignored.

No prolonged argument seems possible when the issue is raised concerning religious freedom and freedom from fear. Everyone, adherents to democratic principles are ready to assert, should enjoy them. The same is true of freedom of speech and expression, except for the unusual circumstances that have been specified. With freedom from want the situation is more complicated. First, it is to be noted that the daily toll of persons, largely children, dying from malnutrition on this planet is about fifteen thousand and that perhaps one-fourth of the world's population must undergo "the cycle of hunger, sickness, and death."[61] There is evidence suggesting that the quantity of food now being produced is not enough to provide an adequate diet for all mankind. The situation would worsen if food were more equally distributed since then the population in the developing countries where the incidence of hunger and starvation is high would explode—their birthdate is about double that of affluent countries. Even more persons would require food. The popular way to refer to this neo-Malthusian dilemma is to use the analogy of a lifeboat on the sea that already is filled to capacity: if other individuals floundering in the water are picked up, the boat will be swamped, will probably or certainly sink and those aboard will perish; if those in the water are not picked up, they will drown.[62] When philosophers view the challenge of world food distribution, they assert that various human rights must be taken into account, such as the right to be saved from starvation, the right to be the beneficiary of some moral principle like equity, the right to retain personal wealth, the right not to be killed unjustly, and the right of future generations to have access to food resources that could be exhausted by the present generation. For these rights, except that of retaining personal wealth, to be realized, the affluent countries must modify some of their policies and hence some of their rights, a topic to be considered later when freedom from want is discussed again in Chapter 7.

The question persists: is everyone entitled to equal rights? The basic assumption behind the Universal Declaration of Human Rights of the United Nations, which Pope John Paul II virtually paraphrased in his address before the United Nations in October 1979, provides a fruitful clue to a positive reply: "all human beings are born free and equal in dignity and rights,"[63] and therefore "everyone is entitled to all the rights and freedoms set forth in this Declaration, without distinction of any kind, such as race, color, sex, language, religion, political or other opinion, national or social origin, property, birth or other status."[64] This statement does not assert, as does the American Declaration of Independence, that "all men are born . . . equal"; clearly they are not so born from a genetic standpoint. What is being asserted is that, regardless of initial ability and of status however defined, all persons supposedly must have the opportunity to enjoy the human rights previously enumerated: there must no discrimination. To prevent discrimination resulting from the inequalities of genetic constitution and traditional status, therefore, there must be laws and regulations ensuring more or less equal opportunity. It is not assumed that inequality will be erased; rather, the opportunity to enjoy human rights is to be assured. The aim is to prevent either the innately gifted or the environmentally impoverished from being unable to achieve their potentiality. It is clear that this ideal cannot be completely achieved, but the efforts of the present age (for example, by means of affirmative action), though introducing complications in their own right, move officialdom and many persons in that direction. In the "liberal democratic West," therefore, it is acknowledged that "the exercise of individual rights must be curtailed somewhat to permit equality of opportunity also to flourish,"[65] which means once more that one right must be abrogated in behalf of another. The rich cannot be permitted the right to grow richer and richer at the expense of the poor, for then the latter will become even more discontent and hence presumably war-prone.

Even less respectable is another query: does equality of opportunity sacrifice the gains which might accrue to a privileged elite who through science and art are able, as a result of their privileged position, eventually to contribute to the welfare of all mankind? We do not know (cf. I); and we also do not know whether those suffering from discrimination or exploitation are thus deprived of an opportunity to make similar, maybe even superior contributions. Inequalities in any society have to be justified on some basis,[66] whether it be age (infants have fewer rights than adults to determine their daily routine) or actions (convicted criminals lose many of their rights when committed to a prison). Societies leaning toward the egalitarian seek to safeguard rights they value. In contemporary China, according to the analysis already cited, equality is sought in the realm of rights in general and particularly with reference to the opportunity to enter an occupation and be educated; the distribution of property and other material goods; status—but exceptions are explicitly noted when required by the general welfare.[67] In general, therefore, some inequality is bound to persist (cf. P)—but this does not mean that there must be a sharp, painful, and unjust contrast between extreme luxury and abject poverty or that the basic and many of the derived needs of everyone shall remain unsatisfied.

The fact seems to be that any social-policy decision involves a choice among values. It is generally believed that "some values are better than other values," and that somehow there are "criteria, albeit difficult to express, for evaluating values themselves," even though "at any given time the scale of values can only be vaguely perceived" (cf. I). The political scientist being quoted illustrates his point in a challenging manner: "A taste for string quartets is better than a taste for champagnes; it is better to enjoy poetry than pornography; it is better to want to commune with un-spoiled nature than to like Sunday driving on parkways."[68] The value of peace, however, does not have to be intuited, for under almost all circum-stances its consequences are probably "better" than those of war. Writing as a columnist, another political scientist has contended that Americans "need not be ashamed to put détente above the immediate promotion of human rights in the Soviet Union or China," for "as Kant knew, and President Kennedy once put it, there is a human right to peace, which détente enhances."[69] And yet, as indicated in the last chapter, even Gandhi specified conditions under which his principle of nonviolence could be violated.

We thus discover or remind ourselves of a general principle applicable elsewhere whenever the ethical or even the practical implications of a policy are an issue: every principle guiding action is likely to have exceptions or, in slightly different words, it is not a universal (cf. P). What can be said about the right to live? The exception to this right may be, according to some persons, the exercise of euthanasia, abortion, or contraception under certain circumstances. A principle can function flawlessly up to a point, and then an exception is approved; and the exception itself invokes another principle. Thus it is vitally important, leaders in a democracy sometimes insist, to speak out in behalf of human rights everywhere (which rights may or may not be vaguely listed); but then the other leaders who are accused of violating the rights resent this attempt to interfere with their domestic affairs. They maintain in effect that they themselves are better acquainted with the needs and beliefs of their own citizens than an outside critic who would impose his own standards upon them. Hostility thus arises which may be one step in the direction of war. The value of no war collides with that of human rights. No war in turn is an all-powerful value until someone raises the cry of the just war, and a just war in turn means that killing is justified under some circumstances which embody yet another set of values. The Carter administration attempted to promote human rights outside the United States without provoking hostility. According to an official state-ment at the time, "when it becomes necessary to address human rights conditions in another country . . . the first step is to raise the matter in private with the government involved" and hence that government can "respond in private."[70] But the policy was not or could not be executed successfully; the president's pleas were publicized by himself, his administration, and others; and foreign leaders often responded with hostility and without appreciably improving their treatment of dissenters and minorities.

Another complication in evaluating human rights is perhaps less controversial than the issue of inequality. "Everyone," according to the Universal Declaration cited, "is entitled to a social and international order in which the rights and freedoms set forth in this Declaration can be fully realized."[71] Conceivably, however, reasonably perfect states that ensure their citizens most of the important human rights may not be able to offer them protection from other states. The invasions of Denmark and Norway by Germany during World War II or perhaps the colonization of some traditional societies in Africa and Asia are cases in point. The perfect state, in short, may demand internal imperfections if it is to survive; or else it can exist only in a perfect international world.

Finally, the existence of rights, unless unrealistic anarchism is assumed, also involves duties and obligations. In fact the fine documents frequently cited in this section and in Chapter Appendix 6.3 make at least passing reference to such possibilities. "Everyone has duties to the community in which alone the free and full development of his personality is possible"— but the "duties" are not specified, except as "limitations . . . determined by law solely for the purpose of securing due recognition and respect for the rights and freedoms of others and of meeting the just requirements of morality, public order, and the general welfare in a democratic society."[72] Elsewhere, "responsibilities" are defined in terms of the "community," the "family," "mankind," and "the security of all."[73] Behind the vague, sweet words seems to be the central thought that individuals and hence their rights are interdependent; consequently, complete freedom in any sense is neither attainable nor desirable. A sad sentence with which to end a discussion of perfection, but so be it.

CHAPTER APPENDIXES

6.1 MORE, BELLAMY, AND WELLS (#s 1, 2, 3, 4, 5, 6)

The choice of utopias at which to glance is arbitrary, but should cause no grief: many utopias appear to differ from one another not in broad outline but only with respect to details so that their flavors can be relatively easily conveyed. A modern psychologist, for example, has skillfully assembled what he considers to be the "structural requirements for utopia":

1. An economic and political system based mainly on an Equity 2 norm [each member of a society should have access to vital goods and services, regardless of the member's individual contribution or status] of the distribution of resources and power.

2. A high level of resources and ecologically sound practices relative to population level.
3. A system of socialization, education, cultural norms, and everyday contingencies of reinforcement that promote full ecological consciousness and prepare and encourage all people for full participation in making central decisions that affect them.
4. Societal commitment to pro-life rationality, diversity, and experimentation.[74]

At a minimum an allusion is made to all four of these requirements by most utopianists. The first one refers in effect to a human right, freedom from want, to be considered again below; the second, to the removal of frustrations, already frequently mentioned in these pages; the third, in part to socialization (cf. Chapter 7) and to democracy; and the fourth, essentially to a freedom to enjoy life, also trumpeted in this chapter. Missing is a reference to war and the means of averting it; but presumably these requirements can be implemented only in a peaceful world.

Sir Thomas More (1487-1535) places his utopia upon an island where "a small number of men can hinder the descent of a great army."[75] The inhabitants achieve "tranquility," for they do not suffer from "fear of want" and no man possesses "pride that makes him fancy it a particular glory to excel others in pomp and excess." How can such persons be produced? First, each "country family" (a unit containing no fewer than forty persons) possesses two slaves who are prisoners of war, criminals, and the poor from neighboring countries. The utopians do not slaughter the animals they eat, but require the slaves to do so, since they "think that pity and good nature, which are among the best of those affects that are born with us, are much impaired by the butchering of animals." The slaves also perform "all the uneasy and sordid services" required to prepare meals and to tidy the kitchen thereafter; they drive the oxen and generally look after their masters on a trip. Thus the utopians spare themselves many of the chores of existence and diminish their frustrations.

Children are carefully reared. They are nursed by their own mother or, if the mother dies or is ill, by a nurse who "offers herself cheerfully." Before the age of six they eat with their nurses, thereafter and until they are married, they serve the meals; "if they are not strong enough for that, [they] stand by . . . in great silence, and eat what is given them."

Music is one of the important sources of joy. It also facilitates tranquility during meals. The utopians eschew hunting, fowling, and gaming since these activities involve violence. Some of the pleasures they enjoy "belong to the body and others to the mind":

The pleasures of the mind lie in knowledge, and in that delight which the contemplation of truth carries with it; to which they add the joyous reflections on a well-spent life, and the assured hopes of a future happiness. They divide the pleasures of the body into two sorts; the one is that which gives our senses some real delight, and is performed, either by recruiting nature, and supplying those parts which feed the internal heat of life by eating and drinking; or when nature is eased of any surcharge that oppresses it; when we are relieved from sudden pain, or that which arises from satisfying the appetite which Nature has wisely given to lead us to the propagation of the species. . . . Health is the greatest of all bodily pleasures. . . . They also entertain themselves with other delights let in at their eyes, their ears, and their nostrils, as the pleasant relishes and seasonings of life, which Nature seems to have marked out peculiarly for man.[76]

These tranquil creatures "think pleasures are useless things, and believe that if the common ties of humanity do not knit men together, the faith of promises will have no great effect." As a result "they accustom themselves daily to military exercises and the discipline of war, in which not only their men but their women likewise are trained." Although "they detest war as a very brutal thing," they go to war to help their friends but only when they are convinced that the conflict is "unavoidable" and the cause is "just." An example of such a cause: "when the merchants of one country are oppressed in another, either under pretense of some unjust laws or by the perverse wresting of good ones." What the utopians seek in war is what would have been granted if the war could have been prevented, or otherwise they "take so severe a revenge on those that injured them that they may be terrified from doing the like for some time to come." During the conflict they ruthlessly kill designated persons among the enemy but give "double" the reward if such persons are captured alive. They are also humane: "they never lay their enemies' country waste," "they hurt no man whom they find disarmed, unless he is a spy," they never plunder although they obtain reparations from a conquered enemy in the form of money or land.

Edward Bellamy (1850-1898), writing as if he were looking backward from the year 2000 to 1887 and mixing his description of utopia with what now appears to be a dripplingly sweet romance between the transplanted, dreaming narrator and a beauteous utopian, makes his native Boston into a utopia which in effect is a kind of gentle state socialism.[77] This relation between leaders and followers has been achieved with "absolutely no violence" because "the change had been long foreseen," with the result that "public opinion had become fully ripe for it, and the whole mass of the people was behind it." The rest of the world is similarly organized so that there are "no wars." An "international council" regulates "the mutual intercourse and commerce of the members of the union and their joint policy toward the more backward races, which are gradually being educated up to civilized institutions." Every nation, moreover, enjoys "complete autonomy within its own limits." This socialist state saves money that would have been spent on "military or naval expenditures" and hence develops social and educational institutions; in the absence of "self-service," not soldiers but workers are motivated by "service to the nation, patriotism, passion for humanity." Thus universal state socialism gradually changes and automatically produces peace in a miniature Boston and throughout the world.

The writing of H. G. Wells (1866-1946) is so clever that is is difficult particularly with the perspective of time to take him seriously.[78] At any rate, "no less than a planet will serve the purpose of a modern Utopia," he declares as he introduces his type of fabian socialism. This planet, a duplicate of Switzerland's topography, serves two purposes. First, being a planet, it is free from the possibility of outside attack which, he says, competing utopias are not. The country has "a different literature, a different philosophy, and a different history," because "character and mental gifts" encounter "happier chances there," with the beneficial consequence that great persons are not handicapped by the milieu into which they are born and hence can realize their greatness. "There were wars" in this utopia, "but they were conclusive wars that established new and more permanent relations, that swept aside obstructions, and abolished centres of decay"— in different words, the wars were just. And so in reality the changes are gradual, each generation steps "closer and closer to the problem of the Thing in Being." Eventually, then, a "modern Utopia will have done with yapping about nationality," so that there can be a "World State" which will "absorb all existing governments and fuse them with itself." No details are provided concerning methods of child rearing; instead Wells, in a section on "Women in Modern Utopia," advocates essentially a program not of eugenics but euthenics: before "the State" permits parents to have children, they must demonstrate that they are economically and morally qualified to have them. Otherwise he expects every woman to bear children and to rear them in homes that are intact, with the state paying the mother to safeguard their "being and welfare." The goal should be to have "eight or nine well-built, intelligent, and successful sons and daughters" whose "study and training" will last until the age of twenty.

6.2 SURVEYS ON WAR-PEACE (#s 3, 4)

Slightly more than a half year before Pearl Harbor, 42 percent of an American sample claimed they had "given some thought to what should be done to maintain world peace," but their concrete proposals were vague, with the most frequently mentioned one being "a union of the democracies or a world union; international federation" (33 percent). After being in the war half a year, 24 percent could give no answer to a question concerning what "we and our Allies" should do "to prevent future wars"; only two positive suggestions were advanced by an appreciable number: "federation of all nations" (15 percent) and a "stronger standing army" (14 percent). Two surveys, one in November of 1942 and the other two months later, demonstrate how question wording can affect responses. In the first, 25 percent seemed pessimistic concerning the future because they agreed with the view that "in spite of all our efforts for peace, nations just can't live together, so we might as well expect a war every few years"; 71 percent might be called optimistic because they disagreed with that statement. In the second survey, 57 percent (not 25 percent) were pessimistic because they agreed that "there will always be big wars" and 34 percent (not 71 percent) were optimistic because they agreed that "after the war . . . we will be able to end all wars between nations."[79] Less than a year after the war, a sample was asked to indicate what they believed to be "usually the main cause of war." When the responses were coded, the following were mentioned: greed (81 percent); human nature (15 percent); differences and misunderstanding (7 percent); certain people or groups (20 percent); certain countries, politics, armaments (10 percent).[80]

On a broader basis is a volume embodying the views of 9,000 adults and students from, respectively, 11 and 5 different countries. In the late 1960s they were queried concerning the state of the world they anticipated in the year 2000. They answered no fewer than 200—yes, 200—questions, 25 of which related directly to the peace. The findings are presented in over 700 pages, only the relevant of which are sketched here.

When asked to state the "best thing that could happen . . . between the year 2000 and today," a majority or close to a majority of the adult samples, with the exception of those in Spain and India, chose "world peace, disarmament, united world." Even greater majorities, except for India again and this time also Japan, selected "nuclear or nonnuclear war" as the "worst thing that could happen" in the same intervening years.[81] Although, as the principal writers in this treatise emphasize, both the validity and reliability of such a broad survey are open to question, at least on a phenomenological level it seems clear that, with the exceptions noted, a conscious yearning for peace was clearly discernible.

The adult samples in the same study were drawn from Czechoslovakia, the Federal Republic of Germany, Spain, Great Britain, India, Japan, Norway, the Netherlands, Poland, Finland, and Yugoslavia. Although there were minor fluctuations from nation to nation, the three leading proposals to obtain peace in the future were: "hunger and poverty should be abolished all over the world," "we should have increased trade, exchange and cooperation between countries that are not on friendly terms," and "we should improve the United Nations so as to make it more efficient than it is today." It is significant that the first two hopes refer to economic or basic needs and the third to the one worldwide organization dedicated to preserving the peace. On the other hand, the least popular proposal was one advocating that "an economy based mainly on private ownership should be introduced all over the world," preceded by "countries should have less to do with each other and become more self-sufficient" and "people should become more religious all over the world."[82] It appears as if these samples had little confidence either in traditional capitalism or religion as a way of attaining peace. With one exception, virtually everyone in the eight samples for which data are available (no information is at hand for the German, Indian, and Polish groups), believed that "in the year 2000 scientific knowledge will make it possible to organize the world so that there can be no wars"; the exception was the Japanese sample, but even there 71 percent subscribed to that belief.[83] Out of a factor analysis of the responses to eighteen of the twenty-five proposals that was based upon seven of the countries, two factors were extracted and then flamboyantly and arbitrarily named Leninist and Dullesian (after the United States secretary of state under President Eisenhower). The former stressed that peace could be attained through "the complete equality of nations, the sovereignty of nations, the joining of all workers," in short, "socialist internationalism." The latter sought a peace via "military unification and integrated defense, military assistance, defense of national interest, individualism, and religiousness." The "Leninist peace ideology" tended to be supported, not unexpectedly, by the samples in socialist and nonaligned countries and generally appeared slightly more frequently among workers than among the rest of the population.[84] In this instance, therefore, ethnopeace differences depended upon the nationality and economic class of the samples.

Other differences in the survey may be noted. Although nationality was a more critical determinant of attitudes and beliefs, there was a tendency for the five student samples (drawn from the Federal Republic of Germany, Great Britain, New Zealand, Sweden, and the United States) to be more pessimistic in general about the future than the older samples.[85] Persons with relatively little power in their societies—as determined by their activities, knowledge of events, and satisfaction—were prone to be more pessimistic regarding disarmament in the future.[86] The notion of a world state secured greater support in the larger countries and among the lower strata than, respectively, in the smaller countries and among the upper strata.[87]

Another investigator employed a different technique but reached fairly similar conclusions.[88] He began with the assumption that "everywhere" people possess the same values if in "different degrees." Then he distinguished between instrumental and terminal values: the former refer to modes of action, the latter to "end-states" desired in their own right. He believes that each "grown person" has "about" eighteen terminal values and many more instrumental ones. He first collected long lists of terminal values from reviews of literature on the subject, introspection by himself, and one hundred adults, all American sources. Instrumental values he designated by reference to a standardized list of traits, again with an American bias. Eventually he emerged with eighteen of each type, admittedly on an "intuitive" basis. Data were obtained in 1968 from a cross section of American men and women over twenty-one and also from comparable groups of college men in the United States, Australia, Canada, and Israel. Each person ranked the two lists of eighteen values.

All samples gave a high ranking (among the first four) to only one terminal value, and that was "freedom"; the first for the adult American and the student Israeli sample was "a world at peace," whereas the American, Canadian, and Australian college men ranked that value toward the bottom. All groups ranked "a world of beauty" near the very bottom of the eighteen terminal values. Over and over again differences between and within the samples appeared; thus even American males and females disagreed with respect to some of the values (for example, "a comfortable life" was ranked fourth by males, thirteenth by females). Not surprisingly, American blacks ranked "equality" near the top, whites near the bottom.

The data concerning instrumental values are similar. "Honest" was ranked first by all available samples, "imaginative" at or close to the bottom. The ranking of "loving" went from one extreme to another: among American adults, males fourteenth, females ninth; and among the college men, American eleventh, Australians fourth, Canadians third, and Israelis eighth.

6.3 DOCUMENTS ON HUMAN RIGHTS (#s 2, 3, 4)

In the citations that follow, reference to the five documents mentioned in this chapter will be made by means of their roman numerals rather than through the usual footnotes. For handy reference, the simple code is repeated here:

    I. Universal Declaration of Human Rights
   II. International Covenant on Economic, Social and Cultural Rights
  III. International Covenant on Civil and Political Rights
  IV. American Convention on Human Rights
   V. UNESCO Committee on the Philosophic Principles of the Rights of Man

The arabic numbers after roman numerals I, II, III, and IV in parentheses refer to the article in the document from which the citation comes; an additional arabic number or numbers or a letter in lower case indicates the section of the article. For V, the arabic number is that assigned to the human right being discussed or the explanation by the committee itself. Document I is the basic document to be cited; II and III are included because they are closely related to I; IV because a few statements are not expressed as well or at all in the other three documents; and V because it represents a condensation of so many diverse viewpoints. The aim is to cull from each document the most eloquent and germane statement related to the problem at hand or to that of war-peace.

Freedom from want: On a fundamental level, "everyone has the right to work, to free choice of employment, to just and favorable conditions of work and to protection against unemployment." More specifically, "everyone, without discrimination, has the right to equal pay for equal work" and "to just and favorable remuneration ensuring for himself and his family an existence worthy of human dignity, and supplemented, if necessary, by other means of social protection" (I, 23). All individuals must have "safe and healthy working conditions"(II, 7b) and they should have "the right . . . to participate in the collective determination of the conditions of their work, as well as the right. . . . to understand the general significance of the work done" (V, 3). Also on a fairly basic level: "everyone has the right to a standard of living adequate for the health and well-being of himself and of his family, including food, clothing, housing and medical care and necessary social services, and the right to security in the event of unemployment, sickness, disability, widowhood, old age, or other lack of livelihood in circumstances beyond his control"; in addition, "motherhood and childhood are entitled to special care and assistance" (I, 25). More secondary or derived are the rights of individuals "to own property alone as well as in association with others" (I, 17) and to have "equal access to public service" (I, 21: 2).

Freedom of Speech and Expression: "Everyone has the right to freedom of opinion and expression," which "includes freedom to hold opinions without interference and to seek, receive, and impart information and ideas through any media and regardless of frontiers" (I, 19). Similarly every individual should be accorded "freedom of thought, conscience, and religion" (I, 18); "freedom of peaceful assembly and association" (I, 20); and "freedom of movement and residence within the borders of each state" as well as "the right to leave any country, including his own, and to return to his country" (I, 13). At the outset of the essay, "On Liberty," John Stuart Mill noted that "the struggle between Liberty and Authority is the most conspicuous feature in the earliest portion of history with which we are familiar" and then shortly thereafter he indicated the danger of censorship:

. . . the opinion which it is attempted to suppress by authority may possibly be true. Those who desire to suppress it of course deny its truth; but they are not infallible. They have no authority to decide the question for all mankind, and exclude every other person from the means of judging. To refuse a hearing to an opinion, because they are sure that is false, is to assume that *their* certainty is the same thing as *absolute* certainty. All silencing of discussion is an assumption of infallibility.[89]

Details are provided in the Declarations concerning the implementation of this freedom. Politically, "everyone has the right to take part in the government of his country, directly or through freely chosen representatives,'' with the understanding that ''the will of the people shall be the basis of the authority of government''; that will ''shall be expressed in periodic and genuine elections which shall be by universal and equal suffrage and shall be held by secret vote or by equivalent free voting procedures'' (I, 21: 1,3). Other instrumental rights include those of being able ''freely to participate in the cultural life of the community, to enjoy the arts, and to share in scientific advancement and its benefits'' (I, 27: 1). ''Everyone has the right to education'' which shall be ''directed to the full development of the human personality and to the strengthening of respect for human rights and fundamental freedom'' and to the promotion of ''understanding, tolerance and friendship among all nations, racial, or religious groups'' (I, 26: 1, 2). Within each country, moreover, an ideal right is proposed: ''all peoples have the right to self-determination'' and therefore they may ''freely determine their political status and freely pursue their economic, social and cultural development'' (III, 1:1). Whether such self-determination should be exercised when it deprives a minority of some of its rights is a question illustrating again the problem arising when rights or actions are not immediately compatible.

In addition, the individual's individuality is to be recognized: ''every person has the right to a given name and to the surnames of his parents or that of one of them'' (IV, 18) and also ''to a nationality'' (I, 15). He or she has ''the right to marry and to found a family,'' inasmuch as ''the family is the natural and fundamental group unit of society and the State'' (I, 16: 1, 3). The Conference on Security and Cooperation in Europe (the so-called Helsinki Final Act) which was signed by the principal countries of that continent in 1975 calls for the ''freer'' movement of people and information, a human right that includes access to the mass media, travel, family re-unification, and cultural and educational exchanges.[90]

Freedom from fear: many general and specific fears are to be mitigated. The most general statements of all—''everyone has the right to life, liberty, and security of person'' (I, 3) and ''to social security'' (I, 22)—suggest that all fear should be abolished, which of course is an impossibility. More realistically it seems that fear is really to be diminished, not abolished, except that ''every human being has the inherent right to life'' and hence ''no one shall be arbitrarily deprived of his life'' (III, 6: 1). For this reason many rights pertain to legal matters: ''everyone has the right to recognition everywhere as a person before the law'' (I, 6), ''all are equal before the law and are entitled without any discrimination to equal protection of the law'' (I, 7), ''no one shall be subjected to arbitrary arrest, detention, or exile'' (I, 9), ''everyone is entitled in full equality to a fair and public hearing by an independent and impartial tribunal, in the determination of his rights and obligations and of any criminal charge against him'' (I, 10), ''everyone charged with a penal offense has the right to be presumed innocent until proved guilty" (I, 11: 1), there should be "freedom from ex post facto crimes" (III, 6: 2). Presumably persons with these rights will be neither fearful nor anxious concerning their other rights. In short, "every man has an equal right to justice" (V, 10). The Universal Declaration of Human Rights itself explicitly states in a final article that "nothing in this Declaration may be interpreted as implying for any State, group, or person any right to engage in any activity or to perform any act aimed at the destruction of any of the rights and freedoms set forth herein" (I, 30). One way of achieving such an objective is to permit dissenters to have the right to abandon their "existing citizenship and to assume the citizenship of any country which is prepared to accept him as a citizen" (V, 13). Finally, "no one shall be held in slavery or servitude; servitude and the slave trade shall be prohibited in all their forms" (I, 4).

Another set of rights would alleviate the fears of individuals in specified groups: "marriage must be entered into with the free consent of the intending spouses"; "special protection should be accorded to mothers during a reasonable period before and after childbirth"; "children and young persons should be protected from economic and social exploitation" (II, 10: 1-3); and "in those States in which ethnic, religious, or linguistic minorities exist, persons belonging to such minorities shall not be denied the right, in community with other members of their group, to enjoy their own culture, to profess and practise their own religion, or to use their own language" (III, 27). Other aspects of living must be protected so that individuals will not experience the stress of fear: the right "to the enjoyment of highest attainable standard of physical and mental health" (II, 12: 1); "to seek and to enjoy in other countries asylum from persecution" (I, 14: 1); not to be "subjected to torture or to cruel, inhuman or degrading treatment or punishment" (III, 7); not to be subjected to arbitrary interference with . . . privacy, family, home or correspondence, nor to attacks upon . . . honor and reputation" (I, 12).

Freedom to enjoy life: the Declarations refer to the right "to enjoy and utilize fully and freely . . . natural wealth and resources" (II, 25); "to rest and leisure, including reasonable limitations of working hours and periodic holidays with pay" (I, 24); of "self-expression" and "full access to the enjoyment of the technical and cultural achievements of civilization," that is, "to share in progress" (V, 9, 15). The "right to a certain minimum of elementary education" (V, 6) or, better, the right to an education "necessary for developing the latent faculties and enabling the individual to function as an effective member of society"[91] are means to achieve this goal of enjoyment.

NOTES

1. Melvin J. Lasky, *Utopia and Revolution*. Chicago: University of Chicago Press, 1976. P. 9.

2. Lewis Mumford, *The Story of Utopias*. New York: Boni and Liveright, 1922. P. 3.

3. Mircea Eliade, Paradise and utopia. In Frank E. Manuel (ed.), *Utopias and Utopian Thought*. Boston: Houghton Mifflin, 1965. Pp. 260-80.

4. B. F. Skinner, *Walden Two*. New York: Macmillan, 1948.

5. Frank E. Manuel, Toward a psychological history of utopias. In Manuel (ed.), op. cit. pp. 69-98.

6. Francis Golffing and Barbara Golffing, An essay on utopian possibility. In George Kateb (ed.), *Utopia*. New York: Atherton Press, 1971. Pp. 29-39.

7. Ralf Dahrendorf, Out of utopia. In Kateb (ed.), op. cit., pp. 103-26.

8. George Kateb, *Utopia and its Enemies*. Glencoe: Free Press, 1963. P. 18.

9. Cf. Margaret Mead, Towards more vivid utopias. In Kateb (ed.), op. cit., pp. 41-56.

10. J. L. Talmon, Utopianism and politics. In Kateb (ed.), op. cit., pp. 91-101.

11. Robert Nozick, *Anarchy, State, and Utopia*. New York: Basic Books, 1974. Pp. 319-20.

12. Northrop Frye, Varieties of literary utopias. In Manuel (ed.), op. cit., pp. 25-49.

13. William Morris, *News from Nowhere*. London: Routledge and Kegan Paul, 1970. Pp. 87-111.

14. Judith Shklar, The political theory of utopia. In Manuel (ed.), op. cit., pp. 101-15.

15. Manuel, op. cit.

16. Lewis Mumford, Utopia, the city, and the machine. In Manuel (ed.), op. cit., pp. 3-24.

17. Adam Ulam, Socialism and utopia. in Manuel (ed.), op. cit., pp. 116-134.

18. Nozick, op. cit., pp. 33-34.

19. Ibid., pp. 310-11, Nozick's italics.

20. Dahrendorf, op. cit.

21. Nozick, op. cit., pp. 126-27.

22. McN. Edward Burns, The movement for a world republic. In Erich Fromm and Hans Herzfeld (eds.), *Der Friede*. Heidelberg: Verlag Lamber Schneider, 1961. Pp. 157-75.

23. Emily Greene Balch cited in Mercedes M. Randall (ed.), *Beyond Nationalism*. New York: Twayne Publishers, 1972. P. 241.

24. Jeurgen Dedring, *Recent Advances in Peace and Conflict Research*. Beverly Hils: Sage, 1976. Pp. 55-56.

25. Richard A. Falk, *A Study of Future Worlds*. New York: Free Press, 1975. P. 2.

26. John Galtung, The future. In H. Ornauer, H. Wiberg, A Siciński, and J. Galtung (eds.), *Images of the World in the Year 2000*. Mouton (The Hague): Humanities Press, 1974. Pp. 45-120.

27. Preamble. The four documents cited in this section as well as in the next section and especially in Chapter Appendix 6.3 (Universal Declaration of Human Rights; International Covenant on Economic, Social and Cultural Rights; International Covenant on Civil and Political Rights; and the American Convention on Human Rights) have been conveniently reprinted in A. H. Robertson, *Human Rights in the World*. Manchester: Manchester University Press, 1972. Pp. 185-223, 249-273.

28. Morris Ginsburg, *On Justice in Society*. Ithaca: Cornell University Press, 1965. P. 196.

29. Willy Brandt, *Der Wille zum Frieden*. Hamburg: Hoffmann und Campe, 1971. P. 261.

30. Quoted by Jacob Blaustein, Human rights. In Andrew W. Cordier and Wilder Foote (eds.), *The Quest for Peace*. New York: Columbia University Press, 1965. P. 315.

31. Pope John Paul II, Address to the United Nations General Assembly, 2 October 1979. As transcribed by the *New York Times*, 3 October 1979, pp. B4-5.

32. Otto Klineberg et al., *Students, Values, and Politics*. New York: Free Press, 1979. Pp. 86-88.

33. Robertson, op. cit.

34. UNESCO, *Human Rights*. New York: Columbia University Press, 1969. P. 7.

35. Graduate Institute of International Studies (Lausanne, Switzerland), "Human rights" in Islamic thought. In Marcel Boisard, *Islam and the West*. Private document, 1978. Pp. 33-37.

36. Donald J. Munro, *The Concept of Man in Contemporary China*. Ann Arbor: University of Michigan Press, 1977. Pp. 1-2.

37. Robertson, op. cit., pp. 123-24.

38. U.S. Department of State, *Human Rights and U.S. Foreign Policy*. Washington: Department of State publication 8959, 1978. Pp. 7-8.

39. Chung-Shu Lo, Human rights in the Chinese tradition. In UNESCO, op. cit., pp. 186-90.

40. For example: Hoyt Alverson, *Mind in the Heart of Darkness*. New Haven: Yale University Press, 1978.

41. Pope John Paul II, op. cit.

42. UNESCO, op. cit., p. 268.

43. F. S. C. Northrop, Towards a bill of rights for the United Nations. In UNESCO, op. cit., pp. 182-85.

44. John Lewis, On human rights. In UNESCO, op. cit., pp. 54-77.

45. Don Salvador de Madariaga, Rights of man or human relations? In UNESCO, op. cit., pp. 47-53.

46. William O. Douglas, *International Dissent*. New York: Random House, 1971. Pp. 12-13.

47. UNESCO, op. cit., p. 271.

48. Pope John Paul II, op. cit.

49. Sigmund Freud, *The Problem of Anxiety*. New York: Psychoanalytic Quarterly Press; W. W. Norton, 1936.

50. International Covenant on Economic, Social, and Cultural Rights, Article 12, section 1.

51. S. V. Puntambekar, The Hindu concept of human rights. In UNESCO, op. cit., pp. 195-98.

52. International Covenant on Civil and Political Rights, Article 8, section 3.

53. Adam Curle, *Making Peace*. London: Tavistock Publications, 1971. Pp. 4-5.

54. Ephesians 6: 5,8.

55. Elbert Russell, Factors of human aggression. *Behavior Science Notes*, 1972, 7, 275-312.

56. Dean G. Pruitt and Richard C. Synder, Motives and perceptions underlying entry into war. In Pruitt and Synder (eds.), *Theory and Research on the Causes of War*. Englewood Cliffs: Prentice-Hall, 1969. Pp. 15-34.

57. Lo, op. cit.

58. A. P. Elkin, The rights of man in a primitive society. In UNESCO, op. cit., pp. 226-41.

59. Munro, op. cit., pp. 57-83.

60. International Covenant on Civil and Political Rights, Articles 4, 7.

61. William Aiken and Hugh LaFollette (eds.), *World Hunger and Moral Obligation*. Englewood Cliffs: Prentice-Hall, 1977. P. 1. Also James Rachels, Vegetarianism and "the other weight problem." In ibid., pp. 180-83.

62. Garrett Hardin, Lifeboat ethics. In Aiken and LaFollette (eds.), op. cit., pp. 11-21.

63. Pope John Paul II, op. cit.

64. Universal Declaration of Human Rights, Article 2.

65. Munro, op. cit., p. 163.

66. Leonard W. Doob, *Panorama of Evil*. Westport: Greenwood, 1978. Pp. 149-50.

67. Munro, op. cit., pp. 161-75.

68. Robert Dorfman, An afterword. In Laurence H. Tribe et al. (eds.), *When Values Conflict*. Cambridge, Mass.: Ballinger, 1976. Pp. 153-73.

69. Stanley Hoffmann, Rights and diplomacy. *New York Times*, 31 December 1978, p. E15.

70. U.S. Department of State, op. cit., p. 11.

71. Universal Declaration of Human Rights, Article 28.

72. Ibid., Article 29, sections 1, 2.

73. American Convention on Human Rights, Article 32.

74. Herbert L. Leff, *Experience, Environment, and Human Potentials*. New York: Oxford University Press, 1978. Pp. 63, 408-10.

75. Thomas More, Utopia. In Charles M. Andrews (ed.), *Famous Utopias*. New York: Tudor, 1937. Pp. 127-232.

76. Ibid., pp. 191-94.

77. Edward Bellamy, *Looking Backward*. Boston: Houghton Mifflin, 1887.

78. H. G. Wells, *A Modern Utopia*. New York: Scribner's, 1905.

79. Hadley Cantril, *Public Opinion 1935-1946*. Princeton: Princeton University Press, 1951. P. 783.

80. Ibid., p. 1025.

81. Galtung, op. cit.

82. Ibid.

83. Karel Kára and Jan Rehak, War and peace as conceived in various social groups. In Ornauer et al. (eds.), op. cit., pp. 316-352.

84. Uolevi Arosalo, Social structure and ideologies of peace. In Ornauer et al. (eds.), op. cit., pp. 503-25.

85. H. Wiberg, Age groups and the future. In Ornauer et al. (eds.), op. cit., pp. 279-315.

86. Knud S. Larsen, The powerful, the powerless, and the future. In Ornauer et al. (eds.), op. cit., pp. 421-440.

87. Kjell Skjelsbaek, Young believers in a world state. In Ornauer et al. (eds.), op. cit., pp. 475-501.

88. M. Rokeach, *The Nature of Human Values*. New York: Free Press, 1973. Pp. 1, 7, 11, 27, 30, 55, 57-58, 70, 89-90.

89. John Stuart Mill, *On Liberty*. New York: Norton, 1975. Pp. 3, 18; Mill's italics.

90. U.S. Department of State, op. cit., p. 15.

91. Humayun Kabir, *Human rights*. In UNESCO, op. cit., pp. 191-94.

Part 3:
REALIZATION

7.
Individual
Realization

From time to time the analysis of reality and perfection in the two previous parts of this book has been unable to avoid the topic of realization. For it is virtually impossible to mention what is and what should be without suggesting the means to be or not to be employed to achieve change and, in this instance, to pursue peace. Now the focus is directly upon means, but without neglecting the real and the ideal.

The analysis of realization begins with the individual. To achieve perfect human beings or at least to nullify some or many of the attributes of *homo maleficus* and thus to facilitate those of *homo pacificus*, changes within individuals must take place. Psychologically, therefore, realization means learning, unlearning, relearning. Almost all human experience and systematic evidence indicate that such significant changes are usually slow (cf. P).* Traditions are as difficult to alter as the languages persons speak. Most motives, beliefs, attitudes, and skills, when well established, are likely to resist change. Some change, nevertheless, is possible. In the West each generation tends to deplore some of the manners and actions of its predecessors. Pronunciations shift, and new words are introduced into a language, generally serving the function of enabling speakers to refer economically to new conditions or new objects in their environment.

On occasion, ways of living are altered. An additional touch of optimism arises from the fact that not all mankind is *maleficus* (cf. V). As previously noted, some men hesitate to kill even when the norm to do so exists. Historically, the "picture" of the human being is "mixed": he has exhibited not only bestiality, cruelty, and sadism but also nobility, self-sacrifice, heroism, and martydom.[1] Individuals, therefore, have the potentiality of being less imperfect than they are (cf. P).

---

*See pages 11-12 for an explanation of the cross-referencing system.

The realization of *homo pacificus* can spring from varying sources. A Thomist may maintain that peace is attainable only when men recognize their dependence upon Divine Providence for guidance and conduct themselves "in such a way as to cast the principles of human brotherhood in a Heavenly Image," whereas a pacifist may insist that the same goal can be achieved by retaining "the selfless life and the ascetic life" as "practical ideals."[2] Or some vegetarians are convinced that respect for the lives of animals can generalize to human beings and that therefore peace depends upon a philosophy arising out of the food one eats or rejects. No one of these or other dicta, I contend, is either completely right or wrong. Each may facilitate one or more of the attributes of *homo pacificus* in different individuals. When groups of persons are involved, the interactions are so complex that the outcome often seems virtually unpredictable, and multivariance characterizes the thicket of possibilities (cf. M). Finally, individual, national, and international orientations are interrelated. To achieve peace, for example, heads of state may be compelled to forego certain national aspirations such as the acquisition of territory or the preservation of what they consider to be national sovereignty; the sacrifices are frustrating for them and hence the unresolved conflict may eventually be intensified,[3] so that in effect the pursuit of peace can lead to war.

SOCIALIZATION (#s 1, 2, 3)

Whether the tree must grow as the twig is bent is not a debatable subject. Controversy arises when the attempt is made to decide exactly how to bend that twig to achieve the tree being sought or to suggest what the shape of the tree should be; or, if the botanical metaphor may be continued apologetically for another clause in order to recall evidence from Chapter 2, to locate the roots that eventually give rise to nonagressive fruits (cf. I). On the basis of their inborn and acquired potentialities some persons become more bellicose than others and hence the challenge, when peace is to be sought, is to affect as many of them as possible so that one tendency and not the other is facilitated. A highly motivated peace advocate maintains that in our society a distinctive "military-industrial personality" exists whose attributes, according to him, research has demonstrated to be the following:

He has generally been subjected to a variety of faulty disciplines in childhood, including anxious, hypocritical, inconsistent, punitive, and restrictive treatment. Coming from a strict family, he has usually lived in a strict environment and attended strict churches and schools, so that his original faulty discipline has been reinforced all the way down the line. Finally, he is attracted to the kind of job which further reinforces his compulsion to obey.[4]

Suppose the above characterization were really valid and it were more than a statistical manipulation of current paper-and-pencil studies inflicted largely upon American college students. If so, then so-called human nature could be, as it were, improved by developing persons with the traits exactly the reverse of those above. Or at least we would know what psychological objectives to avoid if *homines pacifici* are to emerge and if *homines malefici* like Genghis Khan, Hitler, and other psychopaths and sociopaths are to be avoided. But not all experts accept the prescription and not all parents are able or willing to carry it out.

On the positive side, moreover, we are not certain what traits we would have *homines pacifici* possess (cf. I). A so-called "intropunitve" person, for example, "feels genuine sympathy for the underdog; he himself has deep feelings of inferiority and unworthiness; he is given to self-blame, he empathizes quickly and keenly with the suffering of others, and finds happiness in helping improve the lot of his fellow men."[5] The outcome of any one of these attitudes is similar: a bond with other persons, probably the kind of love advocated in the New Testament. It is to be doubted, however, whether all persons could or should have these traits. First, because genetic differences and varied early experiences, inevitable as they are, can never permit one procrustean bed for all; and secondly because variety in a society is desirable if there is to be creativity and stimulation.

In addition, we are faced with the complex problem of the relation between early childhood practices and adult personality, a problem—indicated in the last chapter—tentatively explored by More for his utopia and ignored by Bellamy and Wells. Even when we can point to a goal and even when we wish children to be so socialized and educated that as mature men and women they will obey the Ten Commandments, follow the injunctions of the Sermon on the Mount, and possess the personality traits, motives, beliefs, attitudes and skill outlined in Chapter 5 as possible attributes of perfect persons, we have no guaranteed recipe to follow to achieve the goal. Consider one of those attributes, tolerance. Possibly in the West that desirable trait may emerge when the individual comes from a home in which parents have a permissive attitude toward him and his harmless misdemeanors, when he has felt welcomed and loved and hence has no unconscious hostility toward them, when he accepts their authority without fear or criticism, when in brief he has been reared in an atmosphere of flexibility.[6] We have here at least a glimmering of how to achieve a trait assumed to be desirable but—always a *but*—more than tolerance is needed in a *homo pacificus*, and other desirable traits may require socialization methods at odds with those employed in tolerance's behalf. We know or think we know that an attribute acquired at an early age may flip the adult in either direction. A harshly disciplined child may become a rigid adult and then, in the way of all flesh, treat his own children similarly. Or he may rebel against the discipline he endured as a child, relax as an adult, and then discipline his children as benignly as possible. In spite of these reservations, we must cling to the view that early childhood traits persist and that therefore an efficient way to create *homines pacifici* is to try to cultivate the desired traits at the outset (cf. P).

The desired traits, however, cannot be taught like the multiplication table or even patriotic attitudes. For the relevant knowledge or feelings and also the ways of behaving are unobtrusively learned. As is so often said, parents and older siblings function, deliberately or not, as models for the younger child. Formal education is also affected by the family; generally the child returns home each day from primary school so that he is simultaneously affected by parents and teachers. He is likely to learn to love his neighbors as himself not by hearing the familiar precept but by watching his parents behave cordially toward them—and of course provided those neighbors treat him kindly. He becomes self-sufficient or responsible when he is assigned tasks in the household which bring him gratification and for which he alone is made responsible; failure to discharge the obligation may be punished, but not in a manner to produce trauma.

Three difficulties are immediately apparent. In the first place, the parents and others in the milieu who act as models must themselves be willing and able to discharge these roles effectively (cf. P). Ordinarily, intolerant models cannot be expected to produce tolerant followers. Again the way of all flesh continues: were education for world citizenship to be the goal, how could the current generation expect children to learn attitudes and beliefs different from those of teachers and parents who have authority over them?[7] For this reason, the approach to war-peace through psychological devices is justifiably open to criticism by political scientists and others especially addicted to the behavior of groups. The criticism is pungent but not completely convincing if somehow even minute changes can be produced in the models. Parents, after all, do not always precisely reproduce their kind, just as mass media both reflect and affect their audiences. The only bumper sticker ever receiving my complete admiration read: "Insanity is inherited, you get it from your children."

In the second place, in spite of the myth of happy childhood oft-maintained by sentimental tradition, a degree of frustration inevitably accompanies socialization (cf. P). The child's every want cannot be satisfied, either immediately or ultimately. Especially in a modern society, moreover, he is subject to a large variety of influences besides those of his parents and his immediate peers, as a result of which he may come to acquire dispositions at variance with those of his models. It is pointless to refer to the fact that every individual has the potentiality to be aggressive; obviously, there is a cerebral basis for aggression since its activation depends upon other ongoing processes within the brain.[8] On a social rather than a neurological level his aggressiveness resulting from the petty or major frustrations of socialization (in addition to those both during adolescence and adulthood) must somehow be channeled away from hostility toward persons in his milieu as well as from himself and instead be utilized to promote constructive behavior, however "constructive" is conceptualized. The frustrations of early childhood may be inevitable, yet they need not be severe; hence *homines pacifici* are at least conceivable. The same contradiction, however, lingers: the very frustrations inherent in socialization, even when or because they have been severe, may stimulate the adult in later life to pursue peace more avidly: he knows from personal experience what hell can be.

Thirdly, the insight gained from surveying anthropological data derived from traditional and simpler societies that have been reported in earlier chapters cannot be easily or automatically transferred to modern, industrialized societies which require adults to live quite differently. The kind of training needed to develop a nomadic hunter, for example, must be dramatically different from that to which a person must submit who eventually works in a factory five days a week from nine to five and spends a large part of his spare time passively watching the inanities of television. Even on their own level, as reported in Chapter 3, it is apparent that the nonaggression appearing in seven "nonliterate" societies is the culmination of a series of events quite different in each society. They too provide no panacea, no simple path to this single component of perfection.

My conclusion concerning socialization and the pursuit of peace, however, is neither dismal nor despairing. We know, I repeat, that there is a vital connection between those desirable traits and child-rearing practices—*and that is no small intellectual achievement*. I place the last clause in italics to emphasize the significance of the achievement. Instead of assuming fatalistically that we are destined, ordained, doomed to be the personalities we eventually become, we now appreciate that events more or less under our control are decisive, even if we cannot specify the details (cf. I) or overcome the complexities inherent in mulitvariance (cf. M). In the future, furthermore, we shall perhaps be more competent in these respects as additional research leads to slightly better generalizations than we now possess. Conceivably, for example, parents can be taught, if they are willing, to teach their children forms of behavior that will make the entire family more peace-prone (for an illustration, see Chapter Appendix 7.1: "Family Adventures toward Shalom"). At the moment we can only say that psychological deprivation during early childhood is likely, with exceptions, to produce a deformed adult. With some confidence we can suggest that certain conditions must prevail within a society if parents are to function as *homines pacifici* in their role as leaders, followers, and parents and if their children are themselves to be socialized to become less imperfect.

It is discouraging, nevertheless, to chronicle our inability, as it were, to cultivate leaders who will and can effectively pursue peace (cf. I). Although

Marxians and many others, politely or impolitely, justifiably or not, sneer at the notion of great men, we must agree again that under some circumstances the powerful, the charismatic, yes, the skillful leader exerts a tremendous influence on his followers. We must also remind ourselves that dedicated persons, such as Gandhi in behalf of nonviolence and freedom or Nader in behalf of American consumers, "can mobilize enormous resources to mount campaigns for change,"[9] even when they are private persons without any connection to government. We have, nevertheless, no schools for leadership in the Platonic sense, except in the vague way that most leaders in developed countries attend colleges or universities which obviously are not directly dedicated to training for leadership. Even if such schools existed, furthermore, their administrators would not have suitable or compelling curricula available. Military, naval, and aviation academies are able to educate officers for their armed services because the skills required to perform the duties can be specified; but what corresponding skills should or must political leaders possess? So-called foreign service centers provide training in administration, history, and the social sciences; such knowledge is valuable, yet not a substitute for leadership skill. The surveys of the skill components in Chapter 2 and of leaders and officials in Chapter 4 have emitted no magical formulas.

Still it accomplishes little to exaggerate our ignorance. If it is true, for example, that every person commits "the common error of assuming that the way he sees the world is the only possible one,"[10] then surely an awareness of this tendency would be essential for leaders. Other very tentative hints can be squeezed out of available research. At one extreme we have the following commonsense suggestions concerning effective leaders: they should be capable of making sound judgments concerning war-peace; they should not be in poor health, insane or otherwise mentally ill, or too old; nor should they be suffering from sleep deprivation while making decisions.[11] At the other extreme is a summary of experimental studies in the laboratory: "when preparatory information induces a decision maker to become vigilant concerning potential risks before they materialize, he will develop more effective reassurances and contingency plans, which will enable him to display higher tolerance for stress when a postdecisional crisis actually occurs."[12] Jargon aside, the "vigilance" here suggested is desirable since a decision maker can then search "painstakingly for relevant information," assimilate it "in an unbiased manner," and appraise "alternatives carefully before making a choice." He *may* thus arrive at a better and more realistic decision than if he were to follow any one of these alternatives:

   i. "unconflicted adherence" to his previous stand
  ii. "unconflicted change": uncritically adopting a changed policy
 iii. "defensive avoidance" by procrastinating, shifting responsibility, rationalizing, or being selectively inattentive

iv. "hypervigilance": frantically trying to find a decision without considering all the relevant facts and alternatives.[13]

Otherwise there is the usual cornucopia of studies and recollections, each of which is of limited value but contributes information of possible utility in the future (cf. E). In somewhat oversimplified language: leaders can be offered a manual containing the tricks of the trade, but they cannot be told which ones to employ in a given situation. Let there be no groan: excellent lawyers have emerged from law schools that emphasize not principles but the case method.

Psychoanalysts often have melodramatic theories concerning the desirable and undesirable traits of leaders. Three chapters ago I noted that one member of the craft traced the ills of leaders to their dominating fathers. Here it can be reported that another analyst proposes without evidence that war-peace leaders have another disability: they allegedly suffer from "psycho-sexual impotence" or a secret fear of impotence because impotence in some instances "contributes to pacific tendencies," but the unconscious fear of it is "a common cause of war-mindedness and grandiosity."[14] Maybe yes, maybe no; but however could one, as the same writer admits, ever institute an assessment program that could secure the "cooperation" of potential leaders even if we had more reliable or objective ways of detecting such impotence?

Leaders begin life as followers. Whatever can be accomplished to improve the number and quality of *homines pacifici* among followers, consequently, will facilitate also the selection of peace-prone leaders. In addition, however, leaders require special attributes not to be pigeonholed once and for all: those attributes vary both with the society in which the leaders function and with society's problems at the moment when they assume power (cf. V). We seem to be on the trail of a will-o'-the-wisp which cannot be grasped but which must be forever sought. For otherwise, if we keep insisting that our knowledge is inadequate, we shall continue to emerge with leaders having attributes closer to Hitler and Nixon than to Gandhi and Lincoln.

MORAL EQUIVALENTS (#s 1, 2, 3a)

If conflicts within and between individuals are inevitable, and if frustrating scarcities, real or symbolic, must always persist, some tendency toward aggression—one, but only one of the components of war—is likely. That tendency can be minimized when the frustrations are diminished. Aggression can be expressed nonviolently, presumably provided certain socialization patterns exist within the society. But can adequate outlets be provided for whatever aggression remains so that individuals will be less war-prone? That question raises the problem of what has been called "the moral equivalent of war," the famed phrase originated by William James and now part of the vocabulary of many social scientists, reformers, and political leaders.

In respectful deference to James, I return to his original essay[15] and thus avoid some of the loose interpretations that have been given his phrase. He begins by saying that "the war against war is going to be no holiday excursion or camping party." Yes, war is becoming "absurd and impossible from its own monstrosity." Though written in 1910, these initial strictures of his remain true today. He goes on to a more controversial thesis: in "a permanently successful peace-economy," however, certain "martial virtues" are desirable and must persist, which he believes to be "intrepidity, contempt of softness, surrender of private interest, obedience to command." "Antimilitarists" will not achieve their end so long as they "propose no substitute for war's disciplinary function, *no moral equivalent* of war." In addition, he notes sharp inequalities among men "by mere accidents of birth and opportunity." And so both to retain the martial virtues and to rectify somewhat the inequality, he suggests:

If now—and this is my idea—there were, instead of military conscription, a conscription of the whole youthful population to form for a certain number of years a part of the army enlisted against *Nature*, the injustice would tend to be evened out. . . . The military ideals of hardihood and discipline would be wrought into the growing fibre of the people; no one would remain blind, as the luxurious classes now are blind, to man's relations to the globe he lives on, and to the permanently sour and hard foundations of his higher life. . . . Such a conscription, with the state of public opinion that would have required it, and the many moral fruits it would bear, would preserve in the midst of a pacific civilization the manly virtues which the military party is so afraid of seeing disappear in peace. We should get toughness without callousness, authority with as little criminal cruelty as possible, and painful work done cheerily because the duty is temporary, and threatens not, as now, to degrade the whole remainder of one's life. I spoke of the "moral equivalent of war." So far, war has been the only force that can discipline a whole community, and until an equivalent discipline is organized, I believe that war must have its way.

Clearly James's proposal, as he himself so unequivocally writes and as has been pointed out long ago[16] before the meaning of his phrase was distorted, seeks a substitute for war without sacrificing the "military" and "manly virtues" associated with it. He considers the virtues both inevitable and desirable, an assumption that can or must be challenged as the inventory of *homo pacificus* is assembled. Are intrepidity, obedience to command, and all the rest consonant with peace-proneness? Another assumption, the one commonly associated with James's phrase, is that activities can be designed that will in fact drain off excessive aggression and substitute laudable activities.

Would that we possessed adequate data concerning the validity of the second or drainage assumption. The evidence, as shown in Chapter 3 and particularly in Chapter Appendix 7.2, gives us some but really very little confidence in the proposition that individuals will direct less external aggression against out-groups if given an opportunity to express it internally against nature. First, the opportunity to combat nature, as it were, is limited. Modern political leaders like President Carter have twisted the doctrine slightly and have proposed that followers battle to conserve energy or to halt inflation, but so far suitable outlets have not been provided. Sports have been suggested as a substitute for aggression against one's peers in everyday life or against out-groups, but this evidence also is not unequivocal (see Chapter Appendix 7.2: Drainage via Sports). In the United States and other countries, young and sometimes older people have been attracted to peace corps and similar organizations. Their efforts to assist peoples in developing countries have usually been fruitful and appreciated. Is there any reason, however, to believe that these idealistically motivated persons would have been eager to go to war to dispose of their energetic enthusiasm? If perhaps a good experience overseas has made them less war-prone, there is no evidence to suggest that they themselves have influenced their own leaders at home or that the war proclivity of their own foreign offices has been appreciably diminished. The attractions of war for some persons, it must be guessed, are likely to remain greater than those afforded by sports or other peacetime activities. Even a seasoned antimilitarist believes that "a probable effect" of removing the threat of war might be an increase in other types of "organized aggression" and possibly also "an increase in individual acts of violence,"[17] equivalents of war perhaps, but not moral ones.

We shall never—too strong a word?—have the kind of methodologically elegant evidence really required to test James's hypothesis (namely, one nation with and another without activities that allegedly function as moral equivalents) because no two countries are ever sufficiently similar (cf. V, I). The very idea that the people of a nation have a reservoir of energy that can be drained off in peaceful rather than belligerent ways may be only a provocative metaphor; human predispositions, though interconnected, frequently involve goals that are not easily interchangeable (cf. M). There is no surefire way to dispose of aggressive impulses. Although the expression of aggression may reduce the impulse momentarily,[18] one devotee of the experimental literature contends that "the catharsis hypothesis" has not "fared well" in the laboratory.[19] Not completely convincing evidence from available research likewise indicates that by and large, with a notable exception, expression or release leaves the aggressive impulses unchanged or even may increase their strength. The exception is aggression directed against the perceived source of the frustration;[20] presumably the athlete knows that his opponent on the playing field is not the frustrator, whereas the patriot believes or is made to believe that the potential or actual enemy abroad is hurting or threatening him and his country. Within recent years the most international of sporting events, the Olympic Games, increasingly has become a warlike struggle for national prestige rather than a peaceful way to bestow honors upon talented athletes who, it was hoped, would diffuse the resulting goodwill to their own leaders and peoples back home.

James's provocative hypothesis, therefore, has implications for war-peace, but drainage alone will not solve the problem of war. More of mankind's personalities and more of mankind must be positively harnessed or changed. There is no panacea at hand, but a central thought emerges: peace requires the sacrifice of some of the "ideals" allegedly associated with war and unrealizable by peaceful equivalents (cf. P). Again, as ever, values must be weighed, and the losses from peace are so much less than those from war that we can easily spare ourselves any fleeting grief.

CREDOS AND ACTION (#s 1a, d, e; 2)

Individuals are more likely not to discharge aggressive impulses against their fellow men or to wage war when they have strong beliefs and attitudes opposing violence and war (cf. P). Beliefs are helpful because they can function as self-fulfilling prophecies; as already indicated, persons convinced that war can be controlled by men or their governments are prone to be motivated to act in behalf of peace. Attitudes in turn can be significant milestones on the route to action. In Chapter 5 some of the general beliefs and attitudes of *homo pacificus* have been outlined. Now the moment has come, as promised there, to indicate their content in greater detail. Here the need for a credo is stressed, for a credo by definition contains the ideals of its adherents, can easily be committed to memory, and hence may affect action. Admittedly the war-peace problem cannot be solved by words alone, yet words—as will be vigorously argued in the last chapter—can be of some assistance. In addition, it appears as if interim credos favoring war have been stronger than those in behalf of peace:

Men fight with creeds as well as with guns. And before the fighting begins it is their creeds that raise the banners of war. Men fight for territory, dominion, spoils, it is true, but they must be sustained by their creeds.[21]

Certainly we possess perfectly good credos that advocate peace, especially those provided by religions. The Ten Commandments and the Sermon on the Mount are again relevant because they offer Christians and potentially all human beings guides to the perfection of men on earth and for eternity. Let the word be given to Erasmus who could well have been addressing the princes of all denominations:

I will only urge princes of Christian faith to put aside all feigned excuses and all false pretexts and with wholehearted seriousness to work for the ending of that madness for war which has persisted so long and disgracefully among Christians, that among whom so many ties unite there may arise a peace and concord.[22]

It is obvious that Christian and other religious credos have not brought peace to this war-torn world. Christianity, as Erasmus also indicates, has "rarely achieved the results expected"[23] and indeed, like almost all other religions, has cooperated "mightily with the state in practising the morality of power"[24] and not that of love. Again and again and again, as thousands of cynics and noncynics have observed throughout the ages, "God is always invoked by both sides" during a war,[25] so that the value of any religious credo is thereby diminished. All churches, including even those that would be universal like Roman Catholicism and Islam, are linked intimately to the countries in which they function. The nationals on each side of a conflict require and hence are reassured that they are receiving divine assistance. According to a Trappist monk:

It is curious that in the twentieth century the one great political figure who has made a conscious and systematic use of the Gospel principles for nonviolent political action was not a Christian but a Hindu. Even more curious is the fact that so many Christians thought Gandhi was some kind of eccentric and that his nonviolence was an impractical and sensational fad.[26]

This discrepancy between religious doctrines and actions is recognized throughout Western society. An angry critic, writing before World War II ended, exploded: "The wholesale murder, torture, persecution and oppression we are witnessing in the middle of the twentieth century proves the complete bankruptcy of Christianity as a civilizing force, its failure as an instrument to take instinctive human passions and to transform them from an animal into a rational social being."[27] A clergyman could respond by claiming that religion is not responsible for such evils: human beings have free will and many of them, the evildoers, have chosen the wrong alternatives. But then the argument could continue: why have not the tenets of religion been sufficiently strong to induce men to select the right paths? And so on.

It requires no great imagination to document the failures of organized religion. Many Christians as well as adherents of other religions and indeed atheists may subscribe, ostensibly or sincerely, to peace when they are directly questioned about their beliefs and attitudes, but their actions in time of war belie or are inconsistent with these predispositions. Similarly the trite but useful expression, "Sunday religion," refers to the failure of the faithful to practice the noble sentiments to which they presumably subscribe when they attend church and respond to clergymen there. Most of them are able to repeat the creed in prayer or in other forms quite accurately, and they may also conscientiously obey the edicts of the church on the appointed day of worship and on other holy days, but in everyday existence—which for leaders include the momentous decisions concerning war-peace—those principles are weaker than other guides, they do not become salient, or they do not influence behavior either appreciably or at all. Each of us, I imagine, has had the experience of listening attentively to a sermon, of agreeing with every word of it, and then an hour or a day later of being unable to recall its contents in any significant detail.

The failures of religion, nevertheless, must not be exaggerated; the credo in the Sermon on the Mount or any other religious doctrine that cries out for peace cannot be completely disparaged because all men do not follow the message. Some persons have been good Christians in deed as well as in thought, and wars might have been even worse or more frequent if the vision of peace had not been held up as a standard, or if guilt had not sometimes resulted from transgressing what is judged to be God's will. The noble credos of mankind (the Eightfold Path of Buddhism, the four goals of Hinduism, the Magna Charta, the Declaration of Independence, the Bill of Rights, the Communist Manifesto) have had a profound effect upon men's thinking and, yes, their actions. All credos should not be abandoned because some have been imperfectly implemented. Rather, ones powerful enough to become determinants of behavior must be found or designed (cf. P).

But first it is necessary to inquire why peace-promoting credos have not been more effective. Their competitors have been louder and more insistent: peers, leaders, and the mass media. Actually principles other than those in the credos have promoted opposition to war. First, a simple illustration. According to their own explanations—subject to polite doubt—Americans who participated in a peace demonstration in Washington during 1962 claimed they had been motivated by one of the following: to reduce a feeling of isolation or helplessness, as well as uncertainty about the future; to engage in political action for its own sake; to ease a sense of guilt concerning previous inactivity in behalf of peace; or to strike a blow for what they called in effect "purity of humanitarian principles, a combination of idealism and protest."[28] A psychologist believes that "a live memory of having suffered great human losses acts as a deterrent to war"[29] and therefore presumably provides a reason for acting in behalf of peace. During the first 150 years of the Christian era, the apostles opposed war not for pacifist reasons, but because they wished to withdraw from the world, to disavow any action interfering with the purity of true believers, or to show concern not with the affairs of the present world but with the hereafter.[30]

The form of expression and not the content of credos may be responsible in part for their relative failures. In general, credos, though they linger on within the society or within the peoples for whom they were originally intended, are likely to be most influential immediately after they have been formulated and proclaimed, or for a brief period thereafter. Their formulators have caught the spirit of the times, the zeitgeist, and hence are able to evoke the relevant responses. To be effective, therefore, the thought and recommended actions of a credo must be not only fairly closely related to the reality people perceive but must also be phrased or rephrased in the idiom of the times for which they are intended. A credo's words and phrases must enable disciples to retain its content, which then can be frequently salient in appropriate situations and lead to relevant actions. A *modern* credo is needed to inspire both followers not to fight and leaders not to make decisions requiring violence and mass killing.

The distinction just repeated between followers and leaders points to another question: for whom is a credo likely to be efficacious? Just as it is possible that the credo holding the Roman Empire together may have influenced only the elite and not "the masses,"[31] so it might be contended that modern credos should alert and influence leaders exclusively. The obvious fact, however, has been previously emphasized that, except in rigid dynasties, leaders emerge from the ranks of followers and that they themselves even in authoritarian lands are always affected by their followers who at a very minimum set limits within which they are compelled to function. For these reasons, then, a credo must seek to have more or less universal appeal. The word "universal" cannot be too strongly emphasized, for the war-peace problem obviously transcends national boundaries: wars are fought between peoples.

What should a modern credo assert? The precise contents are difficult to specify (cf. I). "The most apparent needs," according to a philosopher who attempts to analyze what he calls "nonmilitary defense," are for all citizens of a country to examine carefully the aspects of existence they cherish and wish to preserve or extend;[32] these might be the basis for a formulation. In addition, a credo must express the genuine yearnings of mankind and suggest ways to achieve them. Some yearnings can be located in current public-opinion surveys, but the opinions thus measured tend to be superficial and ephemeral. Enduring values provide another foundation for a credo and they can be ascertained, perhaps, by consulting two sources: the opinions of modern-day thinkers and scholars on the subject; and the recommendations of the truly great throughout history. (See also Chapter Appendix 7.3: Miscellaneous Credos.)

For the first source a convenient and illustrative clue can be obtained from the deliberations in the summer of 1973 of twenty-two men of goodwill from eleven different countries: some had had practical experience in diplomacy or international relations and others were social scientists concentrating upon international affairs. Again and again one or more of them asserted that "mankind needs a credo to inspire agreement and enthusiasm and to be transmitted through the educational systems and the media.'' The following propositions emerged as candidates for inclusion in such a credo:

1. The only status quo worth preserving is the status quo of nonviolence.
2. A nation's most sacred obligation to other nations is to negotiate differences.
3. Do not expect all countries to be like yours.
4. Peaceful coexistence is possible.
5. Humanitarian principles transcend national boundaries.
6. In the affairs of men irreducible values are those involving human rights, equal rights, and self-determination.[33]

For the second source, reliance has been placed upon the usual Judeo-Christian ethics; the principles enunciated by Buddha,[34] Confucius,[35] and the modern statesman Nehru;[36] and also some of the canons of perfection outlined in Part 2 of this book. A very arbitrary, somewhat ethnocentric synthesis, minus the poetry, might suggest the following headings for such a credo:

I. *The nature of the individual*

The individual controls his own destiny within limits. He inevitably differs from other persons. For human beings to live in harmony they shall not kill, they shall tell the truth, they shall not look for scapegoats. Indeed they must recognize and avow their own shortcomings and mistakes and contemplate the distance between their own ideals and their present achievements.[37] Some conflict or disagreement between individuals is unavoidable, but violence is never necessary.[38]

II. *The nature of nations*

Men may love their country dearly without believing that it is always right or that it possesses absolute sovereignty. All governments are charged with the responsibility of safeguarding human rights and of insuring, in diverse ways, that their citizens be given the opportunity to satisfy their basic and acquired needs by possessing the five freedoms: from want, of speech and expression, to worship God in their own way, from fear, and to enjoy life.

III. *The nature of international relations*

Differences between nations can and must be settled by arbitration or negotiation, never through violence. The welfare of all nations is intertwined. Every country has its own traditions and customs that must ever be respected. Peace is not only desirable, it is also possible. War is not inevitable, it should and can be outlawed.[39] Some values should be sacrificed to attain peace, for peace is almost always the supreme value.

This outline of a credo is both incomplete and platitudinous. It is in the nature of platitudes, however, to express well-worn truths likely to elicit or facilitate assent. An effective credo, as already indicated, requires the expression of such platitudes in ringing, catchy tones that appeal to individuals if it is to be easily remembered. In a sense, let us admit, the credo should contain slogans—"life, liberty, and the pursuit of happiness"; "government of the people, by the people, and for the people"— which are temporarily meaningful. But how can they be made more meaningful? I could imagine that repeating "war is a social trap" (wars look necessary at the moment but prove disastrous in the long run)[40] might make an impression but would not be convincing when the enemy, as it were, is at the gates. Probably the task of composition should be turned over to a first-rate, inspired poet whose allegedly sensitive antennae can respond to mankind's needs and aspirations.

NONVIOLENCE AND QUAKERS (#s 1, 2, 3, 4)

Credos provide only statements of beliefs and attitudes which encourage but do not necessarily produce actions conducive to peace rather than war. What can the individual—yes, the individual in all his uniqueness and individuality—do to render a peace-prone credo effective? In a democracy, in theory at least, the answer is simple and obvious: elect or support leaders who adopt policies and make decisions that avoid war. What those policies and decisions should be will be considered in the next chapter. I would remind myself, however, that the will of the people in a democratic society may appear to favor peace in the polling booth, yet they may elect leaders who eventually lead them into war. In 1916 President Wilson was returned to office with an inspired, inspiring slogan, "He Kept Us Out of War," and less than a half year later he embroiled the United States in World War I. Of course conditions may change rapidly, and elected leaders can say, as Wilson did, that events in the interim make war unavoidable. Followers may tend to agree as a result of what they are told. They themselves are also affected by events. Thus there was a dramatic shift in American public opinion from a predominately isolationist stand before the Japanese attack on Pearl Harbor to one of belligerency immediately afterwards.[41] The very few who believe that wars may be made to appear necessary or alluring after they occur but that the aftermath is almost certain to be disastrous may seek to avoid participation in conflicts, either directly or indirectly, at all costs.

A person with a strong belief in an antiwar credo may act in accordance with a doctrine of nonviolence, one form of which is to declare himself a conscientious objector. The case for nonviolence in general has been eloquently stated by an activist social scientist whose arguments are based upon four assumptions. First, he concedes, conflict may be inevitable, whether between individuals, groups, or countries; and indeed it may occasionally serve a useful function[42] (cf. P). Secondly, the proposed ways to solve political conflicts—such as negotiation, revolution, or world government—have so far not proven to be "sufficient."[43] Thirdly, no permanent solution to international conflicts has been universally successful.[44] Fourthly and finally, any pacifist or nonviolent action involves risks and "serious inadequacies"[45] (cf. P). Unquestionably both the first and fourth assumptions are by and large correct: the inevitability of conflict and the risk of any pacifist policy and the courage it demands. The second and the third, on the other hand, may have been valid in the past, but perhaps— yes, *perhaps*—the future could be different from the past (cf. E).

Another type of argument against violence is advanced by a theologian who challenges what he believes to be its two basic assumptions: (a) the high value given to material wants whenever consumption increases and the downgrading of spiritual values; and (b) the belief that "man has come of age" and hence no longer needs religion and a personal God.[46] Such assumptions, he thinks, require and enable modern men to seek their goals violently. Evidence beyond journalistic intuition for this contention is impossible to collect.

The most telling indictment against violence, aside from the suffering it produces, purports to be a fact and functions as a warning: "violence begets violence."[47] Is this so? On the level of the individual, violence in the form of aggression will be repeated, presumably, if the aggressor is rewarded rather than punished. On the level of the group, individuals or collections of individuals will imitate or repeat violent behavior, again presumably, if they observe, respectively, that those who have been violent or they themselves have been rewarded rather than punished for so behaving. The principle, therefore, has been too broadly stated; the conditions under which the begetting operates have not been specified.

What does nonviolence mean in practice? The theologian cited above who truly tolerates no exception to the doctrine of nonviolence employs the language of battle to describe "the spiritual welfare" in which he would have Christians engage against "injustice, oppression, authoritarianism, the domination of the state by money, the exaltation of sex or science, etc.":

We are to wage the warfare of faith, our only weapons those Paul speaks of: prayer, the word of God, the justice of God, the zeal with which the gospel of peace endows us, the sword of the spirit. . . . The fight of faith demands sacrificing one's life, success, money, time, desires. In the United States, for instance, the fight of faith demands that the blacks be accepted totally, that they be granted full equality, and also—because they have been oppressed and insulted—that their arrogance, their insults, and their hatred be borne. The fight of faith is perfectly peaceable, for it is fought by applying the Lord's commandments.[48]

We have here an affirmation of Christian principles that would distinguish between sexual love (eros) and unselfish love (agape),[49] and hence nonviolent actions must strive to realize goals embodying the latter rather than the former. Perhaps introspection or the judgment of one's peers can determine into which category an act falls, but more objective guides seem desirable. At one extreme of specificity, the activist social scientist cited at the outset of this section has made available a convenient, breathtakingly complete manual of 902 pages listing no less than 198 nonviolent methods that have in fact been utilized by individuals and small groups not only in behalf of peace but also in connection with labor disputes, minority grievances, peasant struggles, colonial liberation movements, objections to national policies, revolutions against tyrants, and so forth. Each action merits consideration in its own right, and therefore all 198 are listed in the author's own words in Chapter Appendix 7.4 (Manual of Nonviolence). In almost all instances the heading is self-explanatory. This impressively long list demonstrates without any doubt that under almost all conceivable circumstances the individual favoring nonviolence has techniques at his disposal through which the goal of the moment or that of his peers or government conceivably can be attained. The list merits careful scrutiny; then the manual itself can be examined for concrete illustrations of how each method has been employed and hence perhaps can be used once again.

No surefire guide is available, however, to determine in a given situation which method or methods should be selected from this bundle of 198 possibilities (cf. I). The decision must depend on the goal being sought, the skill of the protagonists and their capabilities, the strength of opposing forces, and other factors (cf. M). Peace advocates suggest that it is generally expedient for the individual or individuals to join a group already active nonviolently in behalf of peace,[50] if of course such a group exists.

In passing it may be noted that those refusing to fight in a war or to cooperate with a war effort except in ways they themselves specify (such as ambulance duty) probably demonstrate a high degree of consistency with respect to their beliefs, attitudes, motives, and actions. This consistency may be idiosyncratic: each pacifist expresses his convictions for different reasons. American males imprisoned for not participating in the Vietnam War revealed that, although they "were proud of having accomplished what they set out to do in going to prison, none denied the psychic cost of their months in custody."[51] Many pacifists are satisfying their own consciences even when they realize their sacrifice is futile. In the words of an historian of Christian thought, "conscientious objectors have never been numerous enough to stop a war."[52] It takes courage, obviously, to oppose the regulations of one's country and to be faced with the possibility of unpopularity and imprisonment after refusing to be drafted into any army. In the words of an American president, "Wars will exist until that distant day when the conscientious objector enjoys the same reputation and prestige that the warrior does today."[53]

The general question as to whether nonviolence succeeds in achieving its objectives when employed by individuals or groups—its utilization by governments is considered in the next chapter—is too broad to be answered affirmatively or negatively. The tendency for simulated pacifism to be "relatively ineffective" in a laboratory game involving electric shocks and the transmission of information among American freshmen and sophomores, even though the nonpacifists knew they would not be shocked by the pacifists and hence had nothing to fear,[54] is only slightly interesting but certainly, as the experimenters themselves admit, hardly conclusive for "real-life" situations. A proponent of nonviolence admits that passive resistance in defense of political freedom involves "suffering, tragedies, and setbacks as well as dignity, heroism, and successes." Quite rightly, however, he also maintains that "even failure after an heroic struggle by civilian defense is preferable to any outcome of a major nuclear war."[55] It is possible, moreover, to point to instances in which passive resistance played a role in preventing military coups that had been planned or were in progress against authorities in the Soviet Union in 1917, Germany in 1920, Japan in 1936, Cuba in 1959, and the French in Algeria in 1961.[56] And in 1974 such resistance helped topple the colonels who had been ruling Greece. Gandhi himself found no reason, from an historical perspective, to believe that "the sight of suffering on the part of multitudes of people will melt the heart of the aggressor and induce him to desist from his course of violence."[57] On the other hand, force may achieve short-run objectives—after the robbery the hypothetical starving man eats, the strikers prevent strikebreakers from working and eventually win their demands, the slaves revolt and gain their freedom—but, the advocate of nonviolence asserts, the consequences of such actions may be less desirable in the long run.

In the absence of general social approval, two conditions may sustain those resorting to nonviolence, including conscientious objectors. First, their conviction concerning the tactic of pacifism must stem from their own central values embodying a philosophical or religious view, such as that of some American clergymen whose public stand during the Vietnam War (issuing public statements, writing letters of protest to officials, signing petitions) was at variance with that of their own congregations.[58] Gandhi is reported to have added: "Just as one must learn the art of killing in the training for violence, so one must learn the art of dying in the training of nonviolence."[59] The second requirement may be some kind of support or encouragement from one's own peers, no matter how small the number.

The Quakers (Friends) provide themselves with a set of beliefs as well as social support. They have been outstanding among Christian groups who have been pacifists or "at least antimilitarist" for many centuries;[60] consequently, it is profitable to examine them carefully. At the outset, however, it should be clear that they are not perfect models. Not all Friends have refused to participate in or to assist war, and they have also "generally" approved of police when the power of the law "impartially" safeguards the rights of criminals and society.[61] Large numbers, moreover, have accepted military service in the two World Wars.[62] Such deviations, significant as they are, however, do not detract from the overall strategy and tactics of this denomination.

The opposition of the Friends to militarism and war springs originally from religious tenets which are core values in their attempt to become *homines pacifici* and which are so strong that their beliefs and attitudes are frequently converted into action:

We declare our faith in these abiding truths taught and exemplified by Jesus Christ: Every individual of every race and nation is of supreme worth. Love is the highest law of life. Violence is to be overcome by positive good will expressed in individual behavior and in the institutions of law and justice and freedom.[63]

The Quaker credo or declaration, therefore, comes from the Holy Scriptures. If any single phrase could summarize the Quaker ideal, it would be that of leading the true Christian life.[64] One section of the New Testament in particular is often quoted as evidence for Christian teaching: "These shall make war with the Lamb, and the Lamb shall overcome them; for he is Lord of lords and King of kings; and they that are with him *are* called, and chosen, and faithful."[65] In their own words, Friends seek to possess certain positive attributes to avoid certain negative ones. Among the positive are beliefs in the oneness of man, in the sacredness of human personality, in the creative nature of love, in the necessity for self-examination, and in the supreme worth of every individual of every race and country. They are determined to be friends rather than to win friends, and they seek an inner peace which means a serenity of soul and a tranquility of mind and conscience. Negative qualities to be avoided are a lust for power, denial of human dignity, atheism, and the cult of violence.[66]

The idea of peace thus plays a central role in Quaker philosophy. An individual is accepted into membership only when he is "willing to follow the Quaker method regardless of where it may lead."[67] The "Peace Testimony" consists of subscribing to the belief that it is both desirable and "always" possible to settle international disputes peacefully.[68] Although admittedly few young men become conscientious objectors, this Testimony has been considered "in many ways the glory of Quakerism." It has prevented its members from succumbing to "the idolatry of nationalism."[69] Psychologically, the Testimony must be important because every Quaker knows there are others who share and support his beliefs.

Concretely, what is the Testimony? It is, as a fifth- and sixth-grade primer for Quakers suggests, the conviction that "peace for the world begins with peace in our own lives."[70] Furthermore, nonviolence means that men treat one another with affection[71] and hence that pacifists who themselves do not have an "inner sense of peace" cannot effectively work for peace.[72] Aside from such inner peace, Friends seek a "public order and security commanded by the laws of a sovereign government."[73]

The way of life propounded in the New Testament, according to the American Peace Society's Constitution of 1928, requires more than a set of steadfast beliefs. The beliefs must be reinforced by "a healthy public opinion" regarding war, amicable discussions on public issues, and adequate machinery for peacemaking and peacekeeping. Negative and positive sanctions must be utilized. Negatively, the Friends are called upon to correct injustices nonviolently; to decide whether they contribute to warmaking in any way though their occupations, their standards of living, and the taxes they pay; to refuse military training and induction into the armed forces; and in general to subscribe to "civil disobedience." Positively they are asked to seek out facts required to comprehend public issues and to be effective "in action"; to function as volunteers in movements promoting peace education and action; to look for opportunities to engage in such action, especially by lending their support to the various Meetings of the Friends and their organizations; to appeal to others, particularly to churches, to renounce war and war-related activities; and, in short, "to speak and act courageously for peace regardless of personal cost." A specific Quaker technique to resolve conflicts is considered in the next chapter. At their Meetings, as the divine services of Quakers are called, efforts are made to determine whether members have actually carried out Quaker principles and programs of action. Written answers are requested yearly to such questions as, "Do you faithfully maintain our testimony against military training and other preparation for war and against participation in war as inconsistent with the spirit and teaching of Christ?"

The Friends thus have a set of principles embodying their convictions, an organization providing support and encouragement, and also methods for achieving their objectives. Their beliefs are linked to deep religious values as well as to paths through which the beliefs and values can be converted into action. A skeptic must quickly add, however, that wars persist; relatively few persons have flocked to the Quakers so that public policies have not been appreciably affected. "A realistic testimony," one of their own number has said, "cannot ignore the fact that men want, in addition to peace, a reasonable degree of freedom, security, and justice."[74] No Friend, I presume, would deny the importance of these other values, and they are indeed explicitly and implicitly affirmed in other Quaker statements. Their realization, however, requires changes in national and international relations, topics to which attention will now be paid.

CHAPTER APPENDIXES

7.1 "FAMILY ADVENTURES TOWARD SHALOM" (#s 1, 2, 3)

The title of this Chapter Appendix is the subtitle of a booklet published by the Ecumenical Task Force on Christian Education for World Peace and sponsored by a group of Protestant organizations in the United States.[75] It "offers activities for children and adults to enjoy together in and around the home," so that "people of all ages" can "grow in the values and skills of living toward the Shalom vision." *Shalom* as a concept "encompasses God's intention for the world and for all creation: a vision of peace, justice, right relationships, and well-being for all people."

In order to help meet the challenge "to act and live in our daily lives in ways that affirm peace, right relationships, and well-being" and to enable people to "grow in attitudes, values, and skills in living toward the Shalom vision," the authors and editors have devised or assembled a series of very ingenious exercises suitable for families. "Try This" is the title of the manual, and before trying each exercise the head of the family is told for which ages it is suitable, how long it will take, its "biblical roots" (the exact location in the Old or New Testament), and in some instances the materials that are required (for example, "You will need: construction paper, pencils, scissors, paste"); then detailed justification and instructions are provided.

The exercises are described under six headings. To indicate concretely the flavor of this enterprise, those headings are reproduced below together with the snappy title (in parentheses) of one of the exercises under each heading as well as *part* of its description. The selection of the exercises has had to be arbitrary; hence the interested reader is advised to consult the book.

Understanding the Biblical Vision of Shalom

(Agreements Within the Family Covenant) Work out family agreements about what the family will do together or about things each member agrees to do to make life more pleasant for the others. Be sure everyone has a part in the decision about what the agreements will say. Small children may not be able to agree to help support the family, but they can help in many ways at home. . . . A realistic set of agreements, made and kept, gives all members of the family a good feeling and increases self-confidence and mutual trust as well as feelings of closeness.

Valuing All People

(Where Is It From?) Place a globe or world map on the living room floor. [Let] each member, in turn, attach one end of a long string to an object that has come from another country—such as a banana sitting on the kitchen counter. Talk with other members of your household about where this object might come from.

Creative Conflict

(Everyone a Winner) Pick a problem that has caused a conflict in your family recently or that has come up frequently. Instead of seeing it as a conflict between two adversaries, you are going to look at it as a problem to be solved by the two sides working together.

Participating in Creative Change

(S.W.A.K.) Many families have enriched their own lives and really helped another human being by becoming "pen pals" with someone WHO NEEDS A FRIEND.

You may want to write to a prisoner who feels alone and forgotten, or to someone in another part of the world.

Caring for and Sharing the World's Resources

(Hold a Fast) The purpose of this fast is to experience a little of what it is like not to have enough to eat. In talking about it, note that the extended fast, for the purpose of cleansing the body and gaining religious insight, is also a part of our Judeo-Christian heritage.

Choosing to Live by the Shalom Vision

(Awareness Stretching) Watch a TV documentary about life in another part of the world together. Discuss what would be the good things and the difficult things about living in that area. What gifts does that culture have to share with the rest of the world?

Some of these suggestions may sound simplistic or sentimental, but in context they are, in my opinion, eminently defensible. They are clearly written. Virtually all of them seem appealing as well as practical: a family, when properly motivated, can actually carry them out. Many of them are fun, so that children and their parents will not become bored. Even more important are their basic assumptions: the home can be the place where the basic orientation toward peace (the *shalom* in the subtitle) can be taught, the psychological bases for peace can be cultivated, particularly among those who presumably are both loved and trusted. Equally noteworthy is the fact that many of these exercises involve not simply words but actions. In fact all of them require everyone in the family to participate, certainly a propitious condition for learning.

7.2 DRAINAGE VIA SPORTS (#s 1, 2, 3)

American anthropologists reported after World War II that the Japanese authorities in Truk previously had successfully substituted baseball for war as a way of giving expression to tribal rivalries and hostilities.[76] Magical incantations formerly employed in battle by some Zulus in South Africa have been transferred to attempts to be victorious in football matches.[77]

On the other hand, observing the overtly aggressive sport of American football has been shown in one study to increase and not decrease aggressive tendencies. A sample of spectators was interviewed before a game and a comparable one afterwards as they, respectively, approached and were leaving the stadium. Responses to questions concerning customary hostility, irritability, and resentment on the whole increased regardless of whether the preferred team had won or lost or whether the interviewees claimed to be indifferent to the game's outcome. A similar technique revealed no shift among spectators watching a relatively nonaggressive sport, a gymnastic meet.[78] An investigation of twenty societies—all traditional except for the

Hutterites—suggests an absence of any relation between war activities and their emphasis or nonemphasis on combative sports defined as follows: those requiring two persons who have either (a) potential or actual body contact and inflict real or symbolic bodily harm, or (b) no contact, harm, or territorial gain but engaging in "patently warlike activity" through the use of simulated or actual weapons.[79] Similarly, for the period 1920-1970 there was no relation between attendance at American sporting events on the one hand and United States participation or nonparticipation in an ongoing war. If the popular interpretation of James's phrase were correct, during a war period attendance at football games (definitely combative) should have decreased and at baseball games (relatively noncombative) should have increased. In the same period there should have been more persons participating in betting on races (noncombative on the whole) and fewer in hunting (combative).[80]

The kind of evidence just reported is unimpressive. The first study of Americans attending a football game and a gymnastic meet may have found "no support for a catharsis effect," but participation obviously was vicarious and not direct. The other investigations stem, statistically, from correlations that do not establish causal relations; they necessarily are based upon arbitrary if reasonable definitions of combative sports; and they do not indicate whether aggressive impulses finding direct or indirect expression in sport are the ones that could have been channeled into the pursuit of war. As one writer who has surveyed existing knowledge states, "there is no conclusive evidence one way or another as to the consequences of aggressive [sporting] contests."[81] Merely playing a game may draw off physical energy, but only when the game taps significant motives and beliefs in an appropriate social context, as in the case of baseball on Truk, can it conceivably function as a substitute for war. Sports, moreover, tap other motives besides aggression.

7.3 MISCELLANEOUS CREDOS (#s 1, 2, 3a)

Credos are likely to be found in religious groups. One, for example, suggests that "the voice of peace" expresses itself within "our conscience" beginning with "I am the Peace; like wisdom I have been born of God, I am the daughter of God."[82] "Articles of Faith," according to another writer, are statements concerning the goal ("faith in human harmony"), the means ("faith in facts"), the tool ("faith in human intelligence"), the method ("faith in science"), and the motive ("faith in democratic or humanistic motivation").[83]

Credo-like statements that seem relevant for the construction of a curriculum have been made by a peace-loving Italian judge (1885-1927) who chose Umano as his nom de plume to signify a concern for humanity. He proposed certain " 'strategic imperatives' for those intent on preventing further killing among nations." Two of his admirers have provided the following summary of those imperatives:

Depict the horrors of war at every opportunity.

Demonstrate the illogicality . . . of governments that settle domestic disputes by law while urging their peoples to settle disputes among nations by force.

Ridicule governments that buy arms while indulging in philanthropy.

Insist that the spectacle of modern war is . . . monstrous in comparison with the past: ancient rulers led their fighters personally, while today's leaders send their best young people to death while they themselves stay comfortably at home.

Call whoever insists that the reason for the hatred among peoples which makes wars is due to the struggle for existence a bully.

Curse those venal publicists who by building up trivial incidents prepare the minds of the people for war.

Preach peace whenever possible but do not make the mistake of thinking that this will work without the realization of the only ideas which will succeed, namely, that of peoples working together in agreement.[84]

7.4 MANUAL OF NONVIOLENCE (#s 2, 3)

The self-evident phrasing and numbers in all instances are those of the manual's author as are all the headings and the subheadings.[85]

I. The methods of Nonviolent Protest and Persuasion
    A. Formal Statements
        1. Public speeches
        2. Letters of opposition or support
        3. Declarations by organizations and institutions
        4. Signed public statements
        5. Declarations of indictment and intention
        6. Group or mass petitions
    B. Communications with a Wider Audience
        7. Slogans, caricatures, and symbols
        8. Banners, posters, and displayed communication
        9. Leaflets, pamphlets, and books
       10. Newspapers and journals
       11. Records, radio, and television
       12. Skywriting and earthwriting
    C. Group Representations
       13. Deputations
       14. Mock awards
       15. Group lobbying
       16. Picketing
       17. Mock elections
    D. Symbolic Public Acts
       18. Displays of flags and symbolic colors
       19. Wearing of symbols

20. Prayer and worship
21. Delivering symbolic objects
22. Protest disrobings
23. Destruction of own property
24. Symbolic lights
25. Display of portraits
26. Pain as protest
27. New signs and names
28. Symbolic sounds
29. Symbolic reclamations
30. Rude gestures
E. Pressures on Individuals
31. "Haunting" officials
32. Taunting officials
33. Fraternization
34. Vigils
F. Drama and Music
35. Humorous skits and pranks
36. Performances of plays and music
37. Singing
G. Processions
38. Marches
39. Parades
40. Religious processions
41. Pilgrimages
42. Motorcades
H. Honoring the Dead
43. Political mourning
44. Mock funerals
45. Demonstrative funerals
46. Homage at burial places
I. Public Assemblies
47. Assemblies of protest or support
48. Protest meetings
49. Camouflaged meetings of protest
50. Teach-ins
J. Withdrawal and Renunciations
51. Walk-outs
52. Silence
53. Renouncing honors
54. Turning one's back
II. The Methods of Social Noncooperation
A. Ostracism of persons
55. Social boycott
56. Selective social boycott
57. Lysistratic nonaction [refusal of wives to have sexual intercourse with their bellicose husbands]

    58. Excommunication
    59. Interdict [suspend religious services]
  B. Noncooperation with Social Events, Customs, and Institutions
    60. Suspension of social and sports activities
    61. Boycott of social affairs
    62. Student strike
    63. Social disobedience
    64. Withdrawal from social institutions
  C. Withdrawal from the Social System
    65. Stay-at-home
    66. Total personal noncooperation
    67. "Flight" of workers
    68. Sanctuary
    69. Collective disappearance
    70. Protest emigration
III. The Methods of Economic Noncooperation: (1) Economic Boycotts
  A. Action by Consumers
    71. Consumers' boycott
    72. Nonconsumption of boycotted goods
    73. Policy of austerity
    74. Rent withholding
    75. Refusal to rent
    76. National consumers' boycott
    77. International consumers' boycott
  B. Action by Workers and Producers
    78. Workmen's boycott
    79. Producers' boycott
  C. Action by Middlemen
    80. Suppliers' and handlers' boycott
  D. Action by Owners and Management
    81. Traders' boycott
    82. Refusal to let or sell property
    83. Lockout
    84. Refusal of industrial assistance
    85. Merchants' "general strike"
  E. Action by Holders of Financial Resources
    86. Withdrawal of bank deposits
    87. Refusal to pay fees, dues, and assessments
    88. Refusal to pay debts or interest
    89. Severance of funds and credit
    90. Revenue refusal
    91. Refusal of a government's money
  F. Action by Governments
    92. Domestic embargo
    93. Blacklisting of traders
    94. International sellers' embargo
    95. International buyers' embargo
    96. International trade embargo

IV. The Methods of Economic Noncooperation: (2) The Strike
    A. Symbolic Strikes
        97. Protest strike
        98. Quickie walkout (lightning strike)
    B. Agricultural Strikes
        99. Peasant strike
      100. Farm workers' strike
    C. Strikes by Special Groups
      101. Refusal of impressed labor
      102. Prisoner's strike
      103. Craft strike
      104. Professional strike
    D. Ordinary Industrial Strikes
      105. Establishment strike
      106. Industry strike
      107. Sympathetic strike
    E. Restricted Strikes
      108. Detailed strike
      109. Bumper strike
      110. Slowdown strike
      111. Working-to-rule strike
      112. Reporting "sick" (sick-in)
      113. Strike by resignation
      114. Limited strike
      115. Selective strike
    F. Multi-Industry Strikes
      116. Generalized strike
      117. General strike
    G. Combination of Strikes and Economic Closures
      118. The hartal [temporary suspension of all economic activity]
      119. Economic shutdown
V. The Methods of Political Noncooperation
    A. Rejection of Authority
      120. Withholding or withdrawal of allegiance
      121. Refusal of public support
      122. Literature and speeches advocating resistance
    B. Citizens' Noncooperation with Government
      123. Boycott of legislative bodies
      124. Boycott of elections
      125. Boycott of government employment and positions
      126. Boycott of government departments, agencies, and other bodies
      127. Withdrawal from government educational institutions
      128. Boycott of government-supported organizations
      129. Refusal of assistance to enforcement agents
      130. Removal of own signs and placemarks
      131. Refusal to accept appointed officials
      132. Refusal to dissolve existing institutions

C. Citizens' Alternatives to Obedience
    133. Reluctant and slow compliance
    134. Nonobedience in absence of direct supervision
    135. Popular nonobedience
    136. Disguised disobedience
    137. Refusal of an assemblage or meeting to disperse
    138. Sitdown
    139. Noncooperation with conscription and deportation
    140. Hiding, escape, and false identities
    141. Civil disobedience of "illegitimate" laws
D. Action by Government Personnel
    142. Selective refusal of assistance by government aides
    143. Blocking of lines of command and information
    144. Stalling and obstruction
    145. General administrative noncooperation
    146. Judicial noncooperation
    147. Deliberate inefficiency and selective noncooperation
        by enforcement agents
    148. Mutiny
E. Domestic Government Action
    149. Quasi-legal evasions and delays
    150. Noncooperation by constituent governmental units
F. International Governmental Action
    151. Changes in diplomatic and other representation
    152. Delay and cancellation of diplomatic events
    153. Withholding of diplomatic recognition
    154. Severance of diplomatic relations
    155. Withdrawal from international organizations
    156. Refusal of membership in international bodies
    157. Expulsion from international organizations
VI. The Methods of Nonviolent Intervention
    A. Psychological Intervention
        158. Self-exposure to the elements
        159. The fast
        160. Reverse trial
        161. Nonviolent harrassment
    B. Physical Intervention
        162. Sit-in
        163. Stand-in
        164. Ride-in
        165. Wade-in
        166. Mill-in
        167. Pray-in
        168. Nonviolent raids
        169. Nonviolent air raids
        170. Nonviolent invasion
        171. Nonviolent interjection

172. Nonviolent obstruction
173. Nonviolent occupation
C. Social Intervention
   174. Establishing new social patterns
   175. Overloading of facilities
   176. Stall-in
   177. Speak-in
   178. Guerrilla theater
   179. Alternative social institutions
   180. Alternative communication system
D. Economic Intervention
   181. Reverse strike
   182. Stay-in strike
   183. Nonviolent land seizure
   184. Defiance of blockades
   185. Politically motivated counterfeiting
   186. Preclusive purchasing
   187. Seizure of assets
   188. Dumping
   189. Selective patronage
   190. Alternative markets
   191. Alternative transportation system
   192. Alternative economic institutions
E. Political Intervention
   193. Overloading of administrative systems
   194. Disclosing identities of secret agents
   195. Seeking imprisonment
   196. Civil disobedience of "neutral" laws
   197. Work-on without collaboration
   198. Dual sovereignty and parallel government

NOTES

1. Roland H. Bainton, *Christian Attitudes toward War and Peace*. New York: Abingdon Press, 1960. P. 235.

2. Irving Louis Horowitz, *The Idea of War and Peace in Contemporary Philosophy*. New York: Paine-Whitman, 1957. P. 43.

3. John W. Burton, *Peace Theory*. New York: Knopf, 1962. Pp. 72-73.

4. Norman Z. Alcock, *The Emperor's New Clothes*. Oakville: CPRI Press, 1971. P. 16.

5. Gordon W. Allport, *The Nature of Prejudice*. Cambridge, Mass.: Addison-Wesley, 1954. P. 438.

6. Ibid., pp. 426-28.

7. Mark A. May, The psychological foundations of peace. *Annals of the American Academy of Political and Social Science*, 1944, 235, Sept., 128-34.

8. Carl Sagan, *The Dragons of Eden*. New York: Random House, 1977. P. 62.

9. Richard A. Falk, *A Study of Future Worlds*. New York: Free Press, 1975. P. 253.

10. Robert Jervis, *Perception and Misperception in International Problems*. Princeton: Princeton University Press, 1976. Pp. 409-10.

11. Jerome D. Frank, *Sanity and Survival*. New York: Random House, 1968. Pp. 53-62.

12. Irving L. Janis and Leon Mann, Coping with decisional conflict. *American Scientist*, 1976, 64, 657-67.

13. Ibid.

14. Edward Glover, *War, Sadism, and Pacifism*. London: Allen and Unwin, 1933. P. 108.

15. William James, The moral equivalent of war. In Leon Bramson (ed.), *Memories and Studies*. New York: Longmans, Green, 1924. Pp. 267-96.

16. Walter Lippmann, The political equivalent of war. *Atlantic Monthly*, 1928, 142, 181-87.

17. Margaret Mead, The psychology of warless man. In Arthur Larson (ed.), *A Warless World*. New York: McGraw-Hill, 1963. Pp. 131-42.

18. Leonard Berkowitz, *Aggression*. New York: McGraw-Hill, 1962. P. 197.

19. Albert Bandura, *Aggression*. Englewood Cliffs: Prentice-Hall, 1973. P. 149.

20. Berkowitz, op. cit., pp. 227-28.

21. R. M. MacIver, *Towards an Abiding Peace*. New York: Macmillan, 1943. P. 102.

22. Desiderius Erasmus, *The Education of a Christian Prince*. New York: Columbia University Press, 1936. P. 256.

23. Gerado Zampaglione, *The Idea of Peace in Antiquity*. Notre Dame: University of Notre Dame Press, 1973. P. 3.

24. John Somerville, *The Peace Revolution*. Westport: Greenwood, 1975. P. 73.

25. L. W. Bernard, *War and Its Causes*. New York: Holt, 1944. P. 442.

26. Thomas Merton, *On Peace*. New York: McCall Publishing Co., 1971. P. xxvii.

27. Emery Reves, *The Anatomy of Peace*. New York: Harpers, 1945. P. 76.

28. Frederic Solomon and Jacob R. Fishman, Youth and peace. *Journal of Social Issues*, 1964, 20, no. 4, 54-70.

29. Zygmunt A. Piotrowski, Is permanent peace possible? In Rolland S. Parker (ed.), *The Emotional Stress of War, Violence, and Peace*. Pittsburgh: Stanwix House, 1972. Pp. 1-11.

30. Ralph Luther Moellering, *Modern War and the Christian*. Minneapolis: Augsburg Publishing House, 1969. Pp. 34-35.

31. Crane Brinton, *From Many One*. Cambridge: Harvard University Press, 1948. Pp. 40-41.

32. Arne Naess, Nonmilitary defense. In Quincy Wright, William E. Evan, and Morton Deutsch (eds), *Preventing World War III*. New York: Simon and Schuster, 1962. Pp. 123-35.

33. Leonard W. Doob, The analysis and resolution of international disputes. *Journal of Psychology*, 1974, 86, 313-26.

34. K. Satchidananda Murty and A. C. Bouquet, *Studies in the Problems of Peace*. Bombay: Asia Publishing House, 1960. P. 111.

35. Helmut G. Callis, Mankind and world order in Chinese history. In W. Warren Wagar (ed.), *History and the Idea of Mankind*. Albuquerque: University of New Mexico Press, 1971. Pp. 27-32.

36. Daniel Frei, *Kriegsverhütung und Friedenssicherung*. Frauenfeld: Verlag Huber, 1970. P. 27.

37. Cf. Robert Gordis, A report from the theological participants in the convocation. In Edward Reed (ed.), *Beyond Coexistence*. New York: Grossman, 1968. Pp. 242-43.

38. Cf. Mortimer J. Adler, *How to Think about War and Peace*. New York: Simon and Schuster, 1944. P. 60.

39. Cf. Cord Meyer, Jr., *Peace or Anarchy*. Boston: Little, Brown, 1947. P. 232.

40. John Platt, Social traps. *American Psychologist*, 1973, 28, 641-51.

41. Hadley Cantril, *Public Opinion 1935-1946*. Princeton: Princeton University Press, 1951. Pp. 977-78, 1172-73.

42. Gene Sharp, "The political equivalent of war"—civil defense. *International Conciliation*, 1965, Nov., no. 55, 7.

43. Gene Sharp, *Exploring Nonviolent Alternatives*. Boston: Porter Sargent, 1970. Pp. 2-4.

44. Sharp, "The political equivalent of war"—civil defense, op. cit., p. 13.

45. Ibid., p. 8.

46. Jacques Ellul, *Violence*. New York: Seabury Press, 1969. Pp. 35-43.

47. Ibid., pp. 95-96.

48. Ibid., p. 165.

49. Ibid., p. 167.

50. Alcock, op. cit., pp. 157-62.

51. Lewis Merklin, Jr., *They Chose Honor*. New York: Harper and Row, 1974. P. 306.

52. Bainton, op. cit., p. 248.

53. John F. Kennedy quoted by George S. Tamarin, Dialectics of prestige and human existence. *Proceedings of the International Peace Research Association*, 1970, 3, 138-69.

54. Gerald H. Shure, Robert J. Meeker, and Earle A. Hansford, The effectiveness of pacifist strategy in bargaining games. *Journal of Conflict Resolution*, 1965, 9, 106-17.

55. Sharp, "The political equivalent of war"—civilian defense, op. cit., pp. 56-57.

56. Adam Roberts, Civil resistance to military coups. *Journal of Peace Research*, 1975, 12, 19-36.

57. Cited by Leo Kuper, *Passive Resistance in South Africa*. New Haven: Yale University Press, 1957. P. 84.

58. Harold E. Quinley, The Protestant clergy and the war in Vietnam. *Public Opinion Quarterly*, 1970, 34, 43-52.

59. Narayan Desai, The Gandhian concept of peace education. In M. Rafiq Khan (ed.), *Proceedings of the International Peace Research Association Fifth General Conference*. Oslo: International Peace Reseach Association, 1975. Pp. 1-7.

60. Elbert W. Russell, Christianity and militarism. *Peace Research Reviews*, 1971, 4, no. 3, 1-77.

61. Howard H. Brinton, *Friends for 300 Years*. Wallingford, Pa.: Pendle Hill, 1952. P. 163.

62. Anonymous, *Faith and Practice of New England Yearly Meeting of Friends*. Cambridge: New England Yearly Meeting of Friends, 1966. P. 39.

63. Anonymous, *The Friends Peace Testimony*. Philadelphia: Friends Coordinating Committee on Peace, n.d.

64. C. H. Mike Yarrow, *Quaker Experiences in International Conciliation*. New Haven: Yale University Press, 1978. Pp. 1-8.

65. Revelation 17:14.

66. Anonymous, *Speak Truth to Power*. N.p.: American Friends Service Committee, 1955. Pp. 28-32, 40-42. Brinton, op. cit., p. 49. Anonymous, *The Friends Peace Testimony*, op. cit. Anonymous, *Faith and Practice of New England Yearly Meeting of Friends*, op. cit. Benjamin Seaver, *Three Definitions of Peace*. Philadelphia: Friends Peace Committee, 1967.

67. Howard H. Brinton, *Guide to Quaker Practice*. Wallingford, Pa.: Pendle Hill, 1950. P. 8.

68. Wolf Mendl, *Prophets and Reconcilers*. London: Friends Home Service, 1974. Foreward, no p.

69. Cynthia Arvio et al., *Quakerism*. Pomona, N. Y.: The Back Benchers, 1966. P. 17.

70. Christine Taylor, *Introduction to Quakerism*. Philadelphia: Religious Education Committee, Friends General Conference, 1965. P. 14.

71. Albert Bigelow, *The Voyage of the "Golden Rule."* Garden City: Doubleday, 1959. P. 33.

72. Brinton, *Friends for 300 Years*, op. cit., p. 166.

73. Seaver, op. cit.

74. Miriam Levering, Reaction. In Lyle Tatum (ed.), *The Peace Testimony of Friends in the 20th Century*. Philadelphia: Friends Coordinating Committee on Peace, [1966?]. Pp. 19-21.

75. Ecumenical Task Force on Christian Education for World Peace, *Try This: Family Ad-*

ventures toward Shalom. Copyright 1979 by Discipleship Resources, P. O. Box 840, Nashville, Tennessee 37202. Used by permission.

76. George Peter Murdock, Baseball. *Newsweek,* 1948, 32, no. 9, 69-70.

77. Norman A. Scotch, Magic sorcery, and football among urban Zulus. *Journal of Conflict Resolution,* 1961, 5, 70-74.

78. Jeffrey Goldstein and Robert L. Arms, Effects of observing athletic contests on hostility. *Sociometry,* 1971, 34, 83-90.

79. Richard G. Spies, War, sports, and aggression. *American Anthropologist,* 1973, 75, 64-86.

80. Ibid.

81. Berkowitz, op. cit., p. 204.

82. R. Coste, *Dynamique de la Paix.* Paris: Desclée, 1965. P. 156.

83. Theo. F. Lentz, *Towards a Science of Peace.* New York: Bookman Associates, 1955. Pp. 85-86.

84. Edgar Ansel and Lillian T. Mowrer, *Umano and the Price of Lasting Peace.* New York: Philosophical Library, 1973. Pp. 34-35, italics deleted.

85. This list is reprinted by permission of the author from Part Two, The Methods of Nonviolent Action from Gene Sharp, *The Politics of Nonviolent Action* (Boston: Porter Sargent Publisher, 1973, three volume paperback 1974), Porter Sargent Publishers, Inc., 11 Beacon Street, Boston, MA 02108. Pp. 119-435.

8.
National
Realization

One goal to be achieved both nationally and internationally, if *homines pacifici* are to emerge and if war is thus to be avoided, is perfectly clear: the realization and protection of human rights, the five freedoms as they have been previously outlined on a lofty, abstract level. Consider as an example the freedom from want. This freedom is postulated as desirable whether the form of government be democracy in pure or modified form; whether it be communism in the Soviet Union, the People's Republic of China, or any so-called Iron Curtain country; or even whether it be fascism as envisioned by Hitler, Mussolini, or a Latin American dictator. People's lives are to be improved so that they are hopefully freed from want. In fact, the degree to which wants are satisfied and the distribution of such satisfactions throughout the society vary with the type of system, which in turn may affect both domestic and international tranquility. In this sense the cliché that "bad states lead to war"[1] rings partially true.

A metaphor in connection with the world food supply and the freedom from this pressing want has been mentioned in Chapter 6: should the harsh ethics of a crowded lifeboat prevail, should the starving be allowed to die in view of the alleged fact that the supply is insufficient?[2] The answer must be *no* on moral, political, and social grounds. Ethically, even aesthetically, it is repugnant to allow people to starve and die if they can be saved. Most persons in affluent countries cannot tolerate the thought of tragedy even when it is communicated to them in abstract, statistical form or when they cannot perceive identifiable victims. For this reason they would push the awareness of the misery of others out of consciousness or else rationalize a repugnant state of affairs by trying to believe that, as a general principle, people deserve their present status, whether that status is enviable or deplorable. Avoidance, however, is difficult and often impossible. Politically, it is clear that hunger and starvation result in large measure not only from wars but also from past and present exploitation of developing countries by the developed ones; hence the arguments against all forms of imperialism, colonialism, and neocolonialism are convincing.[3] Socially, starvation is a threat to everyone: the victims are basically frustrated; if they have the strength, they are prone to engage in various forms of violence, not excluding war.

Certain practices, consequently, must be changed if freedom from want is to be realized. According to one estimate, Americans waste about 10 percent of the food they buy. With a change in habits, the food or money thus saved could be used to alleviate starvation, at the sacrifice of the right to do what one wishes, including being wasteful.[4] Around 90 percent of the food value in grain is lost when it is not consumed in that form but as fodder for animals which are eventually eaten. Americans use about 78 percent of their grain to feed cattle (the corresponding figure for the Soviet Union is less than 30 percent) and they are consuming greater quantities of meat each year.[5] Were they to become vegetarians (except for fish which are not fed by human beings) or to eat just enough meat to compensate for protein and other deficiencies that would not be supplied by legumes, the world's food problems could be even more dramatically mitigated; but again at the sacrifice of the right to do what they wish, including eating or overeating meat. Countries receiving food to alleviate hunger and starvation might be forced to agree to limit their population through contraception but at a sacrifice of doing what they wish with respect to family size, sexual activity, or the edicts of religion or philosophy. Sending food from one area to another is costly and consequently an additional burden for taxpayers who are asked to make this sacrifice at the expense of other ways in which their money could be spent (cf. P).* Obviously a choice of values and policies must be made.

Any national and international goal, however, is easier to formulate in the abstract than to realize in reality. A political scientist notes an "absence of any marked concern with machinery to enforce" the rights which have been bravely set forth in Chapter 6. Thus the International Convenant on Civil and Political Rights, even if it were ratified by major and minor nations, would have to be administered by a committee whose jurisdiction and decisions could not be compulsory and which would not even be permitted to issue an adverse report as a mild sanction against a country violating the rights it proclaims.[6] With virtually no exception, all modern governments have been unable at some point to refrain from engaging in war or from being war's victims, a generalization quickly substantiated by a backward glance at the development of modern Europe. After the Bolshevik

---

*See pages 11-12 for an explanation of the cross-referencing system.

Revolution at the end of World War I, there were those who believed, in Lenin's terms, that the state would wither away and hence that at least the leaders of the Soviet Union would be less inclined to have their country engage in war. We know now, however, that the power of the Soviet state has increased and, whether it or hostile powers in the outside world have been responsible, that government has had to follow the example of those other governments which both prepare for and wage major and minor wars. The People's Republic of China has been struggling to create a better life for its people; whether it will be able to steer away from big wars, not border clashes, we do not momentarily know. Perhaps a strong case can be made for some form of regionalism in any pluralistic country containing diverse cultural groups. For with some degree of autonomy, as among the Jura in northwestern Switzerland,[7] local folkways and mores can be retained without appreciably sacrificing the efficiency and satisfaction associated with the larger national group. Hostility toward a centralized government and the possible desire of regional leaders and followers to achieve greater autonomy through violence or with the help of outsiders may thereby be avoided. At any rate, as we begin a discussion of realization, it is perhaps refreshing to know that we do not know and hence to examine the state of our ignorance.

STATE OF KNOWLEDGE (4c, e)

Science continually progresses, so that the facts and theories of yesterday are often outdated today or tomorrow. Evidence for this assertion is easy to come by, whether one turns to theoretical physics, biochemistry, or any aspect of modern technology. Similarly the environment changes: resources are exhausted, pollution occurs, new ways to utilize resources are discovered. Utopia cannot be static,[8] there must be provision for change and improvisation, which means that wars probably can be avoided only by utilizing different means required by the new conditions.

Have social and psychological sciences or, specifically, the disciplines concerned with government, international relations, and hence the war-peace problem advanced in the manner of the other sciences? By and large a negative reply must be given, and it is well to face bluntly this discouraging state of affairs. Innovation is needed.

It seems strange, however, to cry out for innovation. Mankind has been trying and experimenting for centuries to find the pathways to peace (cf. P). Why is not the heritage more effectively passed on, so that we can transcend the mistakes of the past? For one thing, we do not know what history teaches: events in the past are too complex and unique and also too multi-variant to enable even the sagacious to eke satisfactory generalizations from them (cf. V, M). The lessons of the past have been learned by the generations experiencing them but not necessarily by later generations who grasp those lessons only verbally or after they have passed through innumerable hands or heads and who therefore have not suffered, tolerated, or enjoyed the actual experiences.

After this dose of skepticism and defeatism, is it possible to inject a few feeble notes of cheer by suggesting what the social and behavioral sciences have to offer policy makers who would realize peace? Oversimplified or glib recipes are to be avoided (see Chapter Appendix 8.1: Assertions Concerning Realization). First of all, there are very general propositions which can be of assistance. One solidly based generalization receives, I think, universal assent: every modern nation is dependent on the rest of the world. The existence of international trade, the fluctuation of currencies on national exchanges, the flood of tourists[9] are facts indicating the nature of the one world that is developing. The phenomenal growth of international organizations, both governmental and nongovernmental, especially since World War II, provides additional evidence of this interdependence. This trend may not produce the millennium, we unhappily realize, but at a minimum it suggests that most national leaders and some followers recognize their own limitations and that again no man is an island, nor can a country be one except in a geographical sense.

Social changes do take place, in spite of the fact that they are as difficult to achieve as far-reaching alterations in personality. "The force of tradition" plays a double role for war-peace: individuals are reluctant to commit "foolish and dangerous acts" which depart from tradition and may lead to war, but they also resist innovations that might help abolish war.[10] Available data, obviously not completely adequate, suggest the reckless generalization that "almost nothing in the world" [sic!] is capable of changing the "images of 40 percent of the population in most countries" even within a decade or two. But over longer periods of time—two decades or more, especially from one generation to the next—cumulative events can have greater impact.[11] This delay and then the eventual change must result in part from the interaction between the majority and minority within a society: first the majority opposes change, but then slowly the opposition loses some of its following and becomes a minority.

The writings of a small number of utopianists have been hastily surveyed in Chapter 6. In addition, many utopian communities and contemporary communes have challenged the religious, political, economic, and social assumptions of current institutions by seeking to create real utopias rather than literary fantasies. They have been motivated by the belief that "it is possible for people to live together in harmony, brotherhood, and peace."[12] All that seems salvagable from their experience, aside from the fact that some Americans can have such an optimistic belief, is that some of the communities have been able to survive "at least 25 years." There are grounds for hope. Like most of the literary utopianists, the leaders and followers of these enterprises have not grappled directly with the problem of war-peace on an intersocietal basis; they have simply withdrawn from society.

At first glance other knowledge derived from the social sciences appears similarly far removed from reality although with patience useful tidbits can be extracted. A challenge, for example, has been tossed to anthropologists: "Just how do we use what we have learned about Hungarians and Brazilians, or Samoans, to decrease the incidence of violent conflict?"[13] There are several answers. One has already been given: data from these and other societies indicate that social change is slow, to which may be added the contrary fact that under some conditions it can be rapid (cf. P). A second reply: the fact of cultural diversity throughout the world and within most countries has been so well documented that policy makers are likely to take the relativity of values and practices into account (cf. P). At their peril, will they dare to pass judgments to the effect that one group is inferior or superior to another or to ignore cultural nuances? A third suggestion stems from the anthropological insight that the changes in "human nature" required to help resolve the war-peace problem[14] are wrought through an interaction between initiatives of leaders and the needs of followers (cf. P). The last point can be illustrated by referring to intermarriages between ethnic groups within a given state. They are perhaps desirable for the country as a whole since cross-cultural contact is thus established and the married pairs become, as it were, a communication channel between the two cultures. Where there is communication—all the *buts* will be considered later—amity may be more likely to reign and hence the need for the expedient of war may decrease. We know that in the West, perhaps everywhere, such marriages produce difficulties over and beyond the ones confronting any marriage, and the difficulties may be compounded for the children. If the modal attitude within the society is tolerant or permissive, however, the strain will be less.

In previous chapters the predisposing and precipitating causes of war have been carefully examined. Does such knowledge facilitate the realization of peace? The predisposing causes, it may perhaps be recalled, have been analyzed largely on the basis of anthropological evidence. One of six emerging propositions has been evaluated in the last chapter, that of the connection between "early and later gratifications." Our knowledge here, as I have repeatedly emphasized, is encouraging but tantalizing: we have no thoroughly tested, practical guides.

Let us turn to the other predisposing causes, except for that of military expenditures which will be considered in the next section. For the sake of exposition, we might charitably assume that the relations suggested in Chapter 3 are sound and do not require the modifications and qualifications with which they have been adorned in that chapter. "Primitivity" tends to be associated with peace rather than war; but surely no one dreams of making modern societies, virtually all of which are complex, "primitive" in order to achieve peace. Measures being proposed in the West and to a lesser degree implemented to meet the energy crisis may compel individuals to be less dependent on sophisticated modes of transportation, heating, and cooling as well as on various gadgets, yet the sum total of these changes has little relevance to "primitivity" in the anthropological sense and hence to the war-peace problem. If anything, the search for fossil fuels appears to make heads of government more bellicose to attain or retain whatever it is they believe to be necessary for their security. The generalization mentioned in Chapter 3—that a nomadic society emphasizes self-reliance and achievement (desirable for individual warriors) and an agricultural or pastoral society obedience and responsibility (desirable for members of an armed force)—is not the least bit compelling in the present context. Modern societies encourage both kinds of traits, or at least one type in some persons and the other in others, and both guerrillas and trained armies are utilized. Similarly, if primitivity is correlated with isolation, it becomes immediately clear that the modern world is shrinking so that isolation in almost any form, for better or worse, is quickly disappearing.

The same criticisms are applicable to "political centralization" which is loosely associated with warfare. The trend by and large everywhere is toward increased centralization, with an expanded capability to wage war emerging as a consequence. Possibly the vigorous demands for some degree of local autonomy—by the regional movements mentioned in this chapter and by groups such as the Basques and Catalans in Spain—may lead to some political decentralization, yet it is by no means evident that subunits with more political power produce less war-proneness in the country as a whole. Possibly—let us stretch our imagination—leaders in centralized governments which grant autonomy may be more inclined to avoid war since they are less assured of cooperation by the autonomous units.

The relation of the fourth factor, "internal conditions," to war proclivities in the modern world is too complicated to affect war-peace policy. The "moral equivalent of war" has not been discovered and perhaps the very concept, as previously noted, is based on a false assumption concerning the drainage of aggression. Violence within almost every country is obviously not on the wane at the present and—if an immoral glance is cast at the proposition—no one would propose encouraging crime and terror to drain off war-prone tendencies.

Finally, among the "combinations" associated with war, the trio of private property, "frustrated personality," and "egoistic morality" sounds promising because—except perhaps for private property in many countries —all three seem changeable; yet the techniques to facilitate the changes are not clear. Again, however, some of the reforms are too remote from modern societies. Although it may possibly be true, for example, that matrilocal residence promotes peace, as suggested in Chapter Appendix 3.2, it is inconceivable that even current protests concerning the rights of women will persuade modern leaders (whether female or male) to favor this form of residence to avert war. The lesson to be learned from the analysis of the predisposing causes of war and indeed from anthropological research hovers once more around the fact of multivariance which cannot be too often repeated: wars ultimately result from so many different causes that one dare not fixate upon one or even several of them and say, in effect, "change this or these," and peace will be realized (cf. P, M). All that can be recklessly concluded, on the basis of what is known anthropologically, is that perhaps radical reforms in social institutions and in socialization practices are necessary to attain peace. We are uncertain of what those changes should be, though we catch a very faint glimpse of them as other peoples are surveyed.

Slightly more encouraging, specific, and potentially fruitful, although also multivariant, are the analyses dealing with the precipitating causes of war. Here the approach must be eclectic but can be decisive: mitigate the conflicts at hand that seem to be leading to war. Two investigators have examined the serious conflicts between and within states between 1944 and 1969 and suggest that they have all begun with a dispute which then may or may not have moved into phases they label prehostilities, hostilities, posthostilities, a continuing dispute, and perhaps a settlement. At each point, in theory at least, peace could have been maintained or restored. During the initial dispute, while neither party contemplated military action, the goal could have been to keep the dispute nonmilitary and to have settled it then and there. Or after hostilities ceased, the goals could have been to prevent the resumption of hostilities, to restrict the scale or scope of potential hostilities, and obviously to settle the dispute once and for all.[15] Similarly, a careful analysis of the bloody massacres in four modern African countries (Algeria, Rwanda, Burundi, and Zanzibar) leaves the impression that the polarization leading to the conflicts might have been mitigated and the massacres avoided[16] if—if, if certain measures had been taken before it was too late. But again the cases and the measures seem unique (cf. V).

From such descriptive, somewhat commonsensical analyses, nevertheless, it seems clear that leaders are not only able but must also be willing to intervene at some crucial points to prevent a conflict from escalating. The apple, we know, will fall from the tree when it is overripe unless someone picks it beforehand; knowledge about gravity forecasts only that it will hit the ground but does not indicate whether the event will be prevented. Then, too, it can be dangerous to extrapolate from the past into the future. In the indicated situations, conflicts have followed a particular course, but they may not do so in the future (cf. E). We know only that various techniques have been tried in the past and are available. They range from violence to diplomacy and include actions against the potential or actual aggressor (sanctions, blockades) or in behalf of the weaker country (economic aid, mutual assistance treaties).[17] What is not clear is the circumstances or set of circumstances under which any one or more of these methods will be effective; and, to be sure, ethical issues also intrude.

In Chapter 4 reference has been made to "the fog of military estimates" in order to suggest that the multivariant nature of international relations practically precludes a high degree of rationality in making war-peace decisions. The futility of depending upon actuarial reasoning can be illustrated by the doctrine of appeasement (cf. E). Should the leaders of one country appease those of another to avoid war? After the nationalization of the Suez Canal by Egypt, Prime Minister Eden feared that Britain would be accepting "a second Munich" or "a second Rhineland" unless he took some drastic action "to reverse the Egyptian moves."[18] The action was taken with disastrous consequences both for Britain and his own career. A broader perspective from the past ought to prove more helpful. When a statistical analysis is made of forty international wars fought between 1815 and 1945, it is not surprising to discover that the winners tended to be stronger as measured by available wealth and to have lost fewer lives in battle in absolute terms or relative to their total populations. What may be surprising are the following facts: "about 1 war in 5 was won by the party with less wealth"; "in only slightly more than half the cases" did the winner suffer less in absolute life loss; and in 25 percent of these wars the loser "lost a smaller percentage of its population." In short: a country "with either more revenue or a lower population loss rate" seemed favored to win "by about 3 or 4 to 1," and the odds increased to "almost 5 to 1" when the country was favored in both respects.[19] During the 150 years beginning in 1816, the fatalities of the Western nations initiating a war were on the average about half of those suffered by their opponents; but they were victorious only 71 percent of the time.[20] Such marked deviations from actuarial trends probably cause officials to distrust the lessons of the past or perhaps recklessly or hopefully to ignore them. According to one historian, moreover—and I suppose that any honest historian or social scientist could make a similar statement—"in public issues men rarely pay much attention to historians, as historians have the best of reasons for knowing."[21] Leaders are tempted to disregard precedents or whatever basic knowledge, according to scholars, is available by convincing themselves that the present problem is unlike others in the past in some or many respects, or that they themselves are better able to find a more optimal solution. If history in actual fact teaches mankind something, these same officials may find the lessons difficult to extract, and they are not eager to profit from them. In addition, when precise information is lacking concerning the enemy's military potential and financial strength or concerning the casualties the other side and their own countrymen are willing to tolerate (cf. I), the leaders may be tempted to exaggerate their own strengths and to minimize the enemy's weaknesses.

The technique of simulation is available ostensibly to rescue policy makers from the perils of multivariance and uniqueness (cf. M. V). In Chapter 4 that technique, although it has certain methodological advantages, has been criticized because in war games or diplomatic games atypical persons may be the participants, and the outcome may not be sufficiently closely related to real-life situations. Anyone who has participated in, or simply observed a simulation, however, is likely to be impressed with the way in which the participants quickly become emotionally involved in the intellectual exercise; they begin to act as if the game were real. Being actively involved, they retain much of what they have learned, and at a minimum they usually report that they enjoyed the experience and some claim to have profited from it. Simulation, moreover, has the advantage of being a rigorous intellectual exercise so that possible relations between variables can be ascertained.[22] In theory, therefore, leaders can employ simulation to help them predict the outcome of the various decisions they are able to make, and then perhaps they can be better able to lead their country away from war. But, it must be cynically added, in the same way the technique may enable them to determine the decision which would frighten a real or hypothetical enemy. Suppose that in the present or the future, according to valid and reliable data fed into a supercomputer, the printout reads, "you are likely to win." Under these circumstances what is to prevent a leader from resorting to war since into the computer's calculation, we assume, have gone all imaginable factors ranging from military strength to the popular support to be elicited from followers? Nothing, the answer must be—unless he and his clique have principles preventing them from inflicting damage on other human beings, whether they be compatriots or enemies. There is no compelling reason to accept the optimistic, unproven, unprovable belief that the diffusion of game theories (based on the mathematical manipulation of data obtained from simulation exercises) to policy makers will help to "undermine the legitimacy of the war-waging state"[23] and will induce them to abandon a win-lose strategy in favor of some intermediate choice benefiting both parties and producing a minimum of losers.

And so a practical, discouraging note must be struck: it is not to be anticipated that research findings, however solidly grounded, will instantly affect policy decisions (cf. P). According to one suggestion, their influence depends upon the skill with which the findings are communicated, the "amount of inference" required to apply those findings to the problem at hand, and the relation of the research to the "conventional wisdom" of the policy makers.[24] Perhaps the most formidable obstacle is the last, since leaders are often prone to consider themselves omniscient. They may well be, as it were, correct: after they have sought advice and facts from their advisers, they are usually left with a multivariant, complicated set of possibilities, the consequences of which may not have been delineated by the research or experience (cf. M). The possible gains, losses, and risks in any situation, even when weighted by research, cannot be easily computerized and, even when they are, the computer's wisdom needs to be interpreted.

What would or what does happen when so-called experts are asked directly to recommend policies? We know this occurs within government since specialists from the various disciplines are employed or called upon as consultants. We do not know, definitively or generally, however, whether their recommendations spring from their disciplines, from common sense, or from a combination of the two. The panel of 150 so-called Western experts mentioned in Chapter Appendix 4.10—natural and social scientists, engineers, writers—was asked to indicate and then to evaluate the "realistic effective measures that might be undertaken in the future in order to reduce the overall probability of the occurrence of another major war."[25] The evaluation consisted of three judgments: the desirability of each measure; its effectiveness if implemented; and the probability of its being implemented. The three most desirable measures were: "buildup of Western-bloc conventional forces"; "increased security of command-and-control and retaliatory capability"; and "development by both sides of invulnerable delayed-response weapons that are incapable of surprise attack."[26] No one, I imagine, would consider the three proposals either innovative or surprising; they are merely undiluted pleas for deterrence through armaments. The three measures considered least desirable were: "creation of buffer zones to avoid direct confrontation of major powers"; "recognition of Communist China and East Germany—creation of a realistic policy"; and "U.S.-initiated unilateral steps toward disarmament." Fine, *but* the "probability" that China would be recognized was rated "medium" and not "low" or "high"—and shortly thereafter the People's Republic was recognized and admitted to the United Nations.[27] Then in 1868-1969 a panel of thirty-four persons , whose fields were largely social science but included one each from religion, medicine, business, and science, was given a series of detailed questionnaires; similar results emerged. The participants revealed close to unanimous agreement or disagreement concerning some trends (for example, disagreement that "There will be a major military attack on the United States during the 1980s"), considerable variability regarding others (agreement that "Nuclear armaments will proliferate"), and little or no consensus regarding others (agreement that "There will be a nuclear war").[28] Do such studies discredit experts as sources of wisdom because they make mistakes or because they do not always agree with one another? It could be, of course, that some experts are more expert than others and that seeking a consensus is not a sensible exercise. Professionals in the sciences and in engineering also do not always achieve unanimity, an observation not likely to bring much consolation either to the expert social scientists or to the policy makers who consult them.

DETERRENCE (# 4e)

The only gain of civilization for mankind is the greater capacity for variety of sensations—and absolutely nothing more. And through the development of this many-sidedness man may come to finding enjoyment in bloodshed. In fact, this has already happened to him. Have you noticed that it is the most civilized gentlemen who have been the subtlest slaughterers, to whom the Attilas and Stenka Razins could not hold a candle, and if they are not so conspicuous as the Attilas and Stenka Razins, it is simply because they are so often met with, are so ordinary, and have become so familiar to us? In any case civilization has made mankind if not more bloodthirsty, certainly more vilely, more loathsomely bloodthirsty. In former days he saw justice in bloodshed and with his conscience at peace exterminated those he thought proper to kill. Now we do think bloodshed abominable and yet we engage in this abomination, and with more energy than ever. Which is worse? Decide that for yourselves.[29]

The indignation comes not from a modern reformer but from Dostoevsky writing in 1864. It is an appropriate introduction to contemporary attempts to combat the evil of which he speaks. The first effort is to reconsider the problem of deterrence in the light of the evidence already presented in Chapter 3 which indicates that military expenditures have not functioned as deterrents. Since extrapolation from the past to the future is always perilous, may it not be, nevertheless, that in this era the strengthening of one country's ability to wage war will inhibit a potential enemy country from starting a war?

In the present century deterrence has been an official policy of most powerful countries. They hesitate to disarm for fear that the opposing country or countries will be in a more favorable position to attack and destroy or conquer them. Instead they engage in lengthy negotiations, such as the SALT treaties between the Soviet Union and the United States whose aim has never been complete disarmament but limited deterrence, to be achieved by attempting to diminish and perhaps to equalize the military strength of the contending parties.

Realistically it is necessary to recall that the superpowers occupy their position of strength as a result of the technological changes since World War II.[30] They have used the threat of punishment against each other and against other countries to maintain their superiority in arms and matériel and thus also ostensibly to prevent attack.[31] In the words of a controversial

Nobel Laureate, written years before he achieved self-propelled prominence as the American secretary of state, "Perhaps the basic problem of strategy in the nuclear age is how to establish a relationship between a policy of deterrence and a strategy for fighting a war in case deterrence fails."[32] According to another prominent person experienced in advertising, government, and diplomacy, however, not nuclear weapons, even though they be "essential," but "ideas, faith, and understanding" can lead to peace— "our salvation" cannot be purchased with dollars.[33] The mild protest against force and the too obvious declaration in favor of ideas are laudatory; but are nuclear weapons "essential," whether or not they can produce a peaceful world? Two writers cleverly if not convincingly reduce the difference between the Soviet Union and the "Western" conception of war-peace to a chicken-and-egg reaction: leaders in the former country believe that "if all agree to abolish the chickens (war), all problems as to the armament eggs— inspection, compliance, control, international police, and so on—become easily manageable," whereas the position of the latter is that "if you agree gradually to abolish the eggs (armaments), the chickens of war that hatch from them will gradually disappear in the process, and the war problem will become manageable."[34]

Three problems challenge a doctrine of deterrence. First, "the mere possession of force in itself cannot maintain peace,"[35] as the anthropological and contemporary evidence in Chapter 3 suggests. Additional actuarial reasoning is at hand. According to an economist, threats or efforts to increase bargaining power—not only through deterrence but also through "retaliation and reprisal, terrorism and wars of nerve, nuclear blackmail, armistice and surrender, as well as in reciprocal efforts to restrain that harm in the treatment of prisoners, in the limitation of war, and in the regulation of armaments"[36]—have not succeeded in the past or, if they have succeeded, they have succeeded only temporarily (cf. E). Deterrence, nevertheless, cannot be thus dismissed so summarily. As indicated many pages ago, the Swiss were able to remain neutral during World War II in part because of their concentrated but potentially effective military strength. Both Switzerland and Sweden continue to use what might be called defensive deterrence to maintain their neutrality; this entails very heavy expenditures on military equipment so that potential enemies appreciate the losses they will suffer if they ever were to attack.[37] On the other hand, the presence of the Norwegian army did not deter the Germans from invading Norway in World War II.

Deterrence, secondly, can be effective only if the "nation's threat to retaliate (or intervene in behalf of an ally) is believable."[38] German leaders apparently were convinced that the Swiss would actually adhere to their proclaimed intention to resist and to blow up strategic tunnels. In general, the leaders who are to be deterred must be convinced or have evidence indicating that a counterattack by their forces will be futile or too costly.[39] Nowadays credibility requires that both sides appreciate fully the dangers of nuclear war, that they accurately estimate probabilities rather than react emotionally to "mere possibilities,"[40] and that they rationally appreciate the factors for and against military action.[41] Toward this end announcements are made concerning new weapons; the latest devices, especially planes, are displayed to military and naval attachés or on ceremonial occasions. Another form of deterrence is to give or sell weapons to friendly, usually smaller or developing countries. Leaders both in the West and East have justified the policy of arming others by arguing that "military aid and sales programmes indirectly benefit their own security, provide a lucrative source of income, win economic and political influence, stabilize the balance of power in a given area, spread the increasing capital costs of their own military equipment programmes, or work towards the standardization of equipment, communications, and procedures throughout alliance structures."[42] Among these reasons, it is immediately clear, deterrence looms large: if arms are sold to one country, it will hopefully not be threatened or invaded by the donor's enemies. Also the friendship allegedly won by the gift or the sale may strengthen that donor's bargaining power in international negotiations. Credibility, however, cannot be based upon the complete truth: political and military leaders guard their offensive potential most zealously and employ spies or secret agents to try to ascertain classified information concerning a potential enemy. The information thus obtained, if considered valid and impressive, may also function as a deterrent or a temptation.

Thirdly, there is the question of whether the goal of deterrence is realistic. Deterrence in all probability leads to an arms race: leaders in the opposing country react violently without necessarily increasing their military expenditures, and this reaction in turn evokes a more violent response within the country initiating the chain of events.[43] In addition, a complete defense against the superweapons of the modern age is impossible. Casualties are bound to be heavy even if the most sophisticated defenses effectively shield large numbers from being killed or wounded.[44] Without complete disarmament, therefore, lethal potentialities persist. According to a New Zealand political scientist, the existence of the deadly weapons that are supposed to deter rests on the further assumptions that the men actually in charge of government or the armed forces will make "cool" judgments during a crisis and not fire those weapons; and also that, if one individual in an official capacity " 'fails,'' his colleagues will function as a " 'fail-safe' device" and prevent catastrophe. He believes, however, on the basis of fragmentary research, that both assumptions are "almost certainly false."[45] He may be exaggerating, but he is correct in pointing to the great risks.

In the present circumstances, however, it seems impossible to avoid increases in military strength as a form of deterrence whenever a crisis is at hand or appears—or is made to appear—imminent. In the winter of 1979-1980, for example, the president of the United States increased military expenditures after Soviet forces moved into Afghanistan since he and his advisers believed American interests in the Middle East, and particularly in Middle Eastern oil, were threatened. Not to have attempted to take measures which might deter the Russians from extending their expansion would have incurred the wrath of many Americans and their allies. In a psychological sense, there seemed to be no alternative other than to follow a policy of deterrence and simultaneously to implement the policy peacefully by cutting off certain strategic supplies to the Soviet Union and to boycott the Olympic Games in Moscow. In general, when leaders think or imagine their country may be attacked, they feel they must seek to ward off the attack by being prepared to go on the offensive or to suggest that the attack will fail. Past experience with deterrence almost inevitably produces responses weaker than those evoked by anxiety at the moment.

The same situation exists in connection with poison gas and other chemical weapons. Several nations, including the Soviet Union and the United States, have subscribed to the Geneva Protocol of 1925 which bans them, but they have reserved the formal right to employ them in order to retaliate if the protocol is violated by an enemy. In the meantime, therefore, deadly chemicals as well as defenses against them (gas masks, suitable clothing, and so on) are being stockpiled. Whether the threat of chemical "retaliation" is an effective deterrent depends in part on where the fighting conceivably might occur, since civilian populations do not have protective equipment and hence would suffer the consequences of an attack or a counterattack.[46]

Most impressive or depressing are the figures for military expenditures, as demonstrated too easily by a few examples from the decade starting in 1967. Almost everywhere expenditures increased, with countries of the world spending in real terms nearly 20 percent more in 1976 than ten years earlier. Those expenditures toward the end of the decade were about two-and-a-half times the money allocated to public health although, it must be added, over 6 percent more was assigned to education than to military preparations. Developing countries, however, allocated only about half as much for health and education as they did for the military. Even after adjusting for inflation, conventional arms trade increased during the decade.[47] Surely these vast sums have not made war any less likely; or has a balance of power thus been achieved (cf. I)?

The doctrine of the balance of power is another form of deterrence and rests upon the assumption that alliances between various countries against other countries prevent the leaders of both sides from resorting to war because as a consequence they come to believe that neither side has enough to win. But World Wars I and II have shown the futility of such a belief. An alliance between a weaker power and stronger ones may not prevent the former from being attacked, as the leaders of Czechoslovakia learned to their sorrow in 1939 when their allies, France and England, did not combat the invasion by the German armies. According to two qualified scholars, even though "more than 8,000 peace treaties and hundreds of peace plans" have been ratified and proposed, no "dependable and effective" method of peace enforcement has ever been devised, so that again and again peace-keeping organizations have been impotent; the leaders of nations have either refused "to underwrite international companies" or have violated "solemnly contracted pacts."[48] Apparently, therefore, power can be balanced only relatively.

In passing it is impossible to repress the thought that military officers, no matter whether their devotion to peace is sincere or not, must have some urge to use the weapons being stockpiled as deterrents. Simulated battles during field exercises are not quite as satisfactory as real engagements. Even in a laboratory environment it has been shown that the presence of aggression-producing objects (such as guns) may elicit aggressive behavior more frequently than harmless ones.[49] Possibly Costa Rica has been able to avoid becoming embroiled in Central American and other wars because it has no army but supports two symphony orchestras.

Many persons, as their muffled cries suggest, are convinced that un-limited or limited deterrence has not been notably successful as a technique to avoid war. Although what would have happened in the absence of deterrence is unknown (cf. I), they point to the apparent failure of various post-World War II approaches by the United States to halt the arms races and to diminish international disputes: containment under President Truman; massive retaliation under President Eisenhower; multi-deterrence under President Kennedy; and old-fashioned deterrence accompanied by negotiations leading, hopefully, to disarmament under Presidents Ford, Nixon, and Carter. When superpowers agree to disarm or not to strengthen their military potential in certain specified respects, their leaders assume that such parity functions as a deterrent; the other side will not attack because its leaders know that their strength is no greater than their opponent's. The rub comes in defining parity; and so the negotiators haggle for years to try to arrive at precise figures concerning the number and types of planes, warships, missiles, and so forth, each side will agree to have or not to have. The negotiations perforce are permeated with suspicion: can we trust them to carry out the treaty, have we adequate ways to detect violations, will they not violate the spirit of the agreement by manufacturing new weapons not included in its provisions? In addition, the technical details essential to maintain parity and surveillance cannot be computerized to yield a single interpretation concerning relative strengths, with the result that within a country like the United States, where differing opinions are freely expressed, experts on disarmament disagree as to whether their country is gaining or losing its military power and hence its defense and deterrence capabilities.

As one keen political observer noted at the start of the United States Senate debate over SALT II in the late spring and summer of 1979, most legislators, being "rank amateurs" concerning the technical details contained in a treaty, must rely on experts for guidance; but the experts come to different conclusions on these issues, even though they have the same data at their disposal. In the final analysis, consequently, their judgment concerning a treaty is likely to depend upon the "ideological predilections."[50] There is no infallible, scientific guide to disarmament and deterrence (cf. P, I).

The clear-cut alternative to deterrence could be unilateral disarmament. This tactic, however, is considered dangerous and, in democratic countries, not politically feasible[51] because it weakens the disarming country and allegedly lays it open to attack. A stimulating, academic proposal once received commendable attention when its author offered detailed and, he thought, practical unilateral measures to achieve a final objective, namely, total disarmament. The plan was called Graduated Reciprocation in Tension-Reduction, the acronymn for which was GRIT, considered by its progenitor to be "both easily remembered and full of persistence."[52] A superpower like the United States unilaterally and publicly should announce a relatively minor but significant retrenchment in its armament without jeopardizing its security in any far-reaching fashion; it would do nothing more until its opponent (in this instance the Soviet Union) would make a similar reduction; then it would reduce its military potential a bit more and await a corresponding change by the other side; and so on. By announcing the reduction in advance, by not requiring that its opponents make a corresponding reduction, and by carrying out the reduction as announced, the leaders of the country initiating the policy would gradually build up trust among the decision makers of the other country. Nuclear deterrents under such a plan would be abandoned last of all; until that point was reached, however, the proposed unilateral initiatives would not prevent the United States from counteracting aggression with conventional weapons and "with appropriate graded conventional" counterattacks.[53] Without demanding a quid pro quo, announcements concerning unilateral actions should explicitly include invitations to reciprocate. International agencies might also be strengthened by the same procedure: nations could unilaterally submit their problems to the United Nations.[54] The arguments in favor of gradualism thus expressed are most appealing and convincing; yet, as a skeptical, anonymous reader wrote in the margin of the copy of the book I borrowed from the Yale library, "won't work." He might well have written "hasn't worked significantly."

Must "won't work" be the final judgment not only for GRIT but also for all attempts to halt the arms race in any form? Perhaps not. Perhaps the Cuban missile crisis in 1962 validates GRIT and other hopes, for then at least a series of reciprocating withdrawals prevented the incident from developing into a war between the Soviet Union and the United States. The United States in 1969 unilaterally renounced biological warfare and the development of appropriate biological weapons; this led to a convention in 1972 in which the same measure was considered by other nations.[55] On the whole, however, leaders in their international orientation continue to use the conventional methods of deterrence, propaganda, diplomacy, negotiation—and the arms race continues, international tensions rise and fall but never bring security or peace on a more lasting basis. Should we agree with Dostoevsky, whose sour notes introduced this section?

LIMITED NONVIOLENCE AND THE JUST WAR (#s 4e, 5)

Nonviolence as a technique available to individuals who would protest or act against war and other miseries has been appraised in the last chapter. Here attention is directed to what is arbitrarily called another aspect of nonviolence which cannot be sharply separated from the first form, that is, the national policy of nonviolent resistance as "a possible substitute for war."[56] Like the manual of nonviolent techniques for individuals previously outlined in Chapter Appendix 7.4, another treatise, this time in German, suggests how goals ordinarily requiring military measures conceivably can be achieved nonviolently. The "alternative to civil war," as the subtitle and title, respectively, bravely proclaim, gives way to "nonviolent resurrection."[57] If their country is invaded, another writer asserts in the same vein, the civilian population simply refuses to cooperate with the aggressors: "The deployment of troops can be delayed by obstructionist activities at the docks if major troop shipments come by sea, by refusal to operate the railroads, or by blocking highways with thousands of abandoned automobiles," and such resistance together with informal contacts may make the invading soldiers less brutal and even evoke strains of sympathy within them. Also "the invader's parades of troops throughout the cities may be met with empty streets and shattered windows, and his public receptions boycotted." If the leaders of the belligerent country know in advance that the weapon to be employed against them will be passive resistance, they may decide not to invade because they conclude the operation will be too difficult or because they believe it will be ineffective.[58]

Does limited nonviolence succeed in achieving its objective? An enthusiastic advocate of the technique has cited eighty-five cases (including nine "against war and war preparations") which, as he indicates, suggests that the technique has been employed in the West and East, both to defend and oppose governments, and by majorities as well as minorites. The list begins with "Gandhi's fast in Calcutta, 1947" and ends with "Popular resistance and demonstrations, and political noncooperation by Czechs and Slovaks following the Warsaw Pact invasion in August, 1968."[59] Obviously there have been some successes, partial successes, and failures in the short and the long run (cf. E). One observer and supporter of nonviolence is reported to be convinced that the successes of nonviolent action in conflicts between states have not been "unambiguously positive,"[60] clearly an understatement. The belligerents with weapons may have been somewhat less violent when confronted with civilians without weapons perhaps because it may be more difficult to hurt or kill a defenseless opponent.[61]

Of very doubtful efficacy has been the use of sanctions to deter the leaders of a country from waging war or from achieving some other undesirable objective. Sanctions did not prevent Mussolini in 1935 from invading and conquering Ethiopia. In the 1930s they did not inhibit the Japanese from following an expansionist policy, and instead stimulated them to expand southward and increased their determination to declare war on the United States.[62] By themselves incompletely applied sanctions did not significantly affect the economy or majority rule in Rhodesia during the 1960s and 1970s.[63] Perhaps, it has been suggested, sanctions are not effective because the decision to apply them probably indicates that the leaders of the sanctioning countries are not sufficiently motivated to take greater risks. What often happens is that the leaders of the country being punished are able to find alternative if more difficult or inconvenient ways to meet their country's economic needs; and leaders of the sanctions-proclaiming countries may be reluctant, for political or economic reasons, to enforce the punishing regulations.

If it is true that nonviolence alone is seldom completely effective, whether employed by small or large groups, then it must follow that some violence may be required on occasion to achieve desirable ends (cf. P). For this reason alone consideration must be given to what is being called here limited nonviolence. At issue is a variant of the ancient and tricky problem of the relation of means to ends. It is perhaps too glib to assert that "means are always justified—if they are justified at all—by their ends."[64] For the ethical argument is compelling:

Force in itself is neither right nor wrong. It depends on how it is used. It can be used morally and it can be used immorally. . . . although organised evil has often increased its power by war and established tyranny, organised evil has also often been restrained by war.[65]

Once more the value of the just war arises, and the peaceful doctrines of philosophers and, as indicated in Chapter 4, theologians often crumble—deliberately or otherwise—on this cross. In classical times, Aristotle believed war to be justified only in order to defend the city-state, to establish harmony over people for their own good, and to control political units deserving to be enslaved; somewhat similarly, Cicero considered wars just when they had been declared and proclaimed and when their objective was revenge or self-defense.[66] The motto of a council at Poitiers in the year 1000 was *guerre à la guerre*, which means that the officials of the Church considered themselves obliged "to oppose war by warlike means, that is, by the intervention of troops under religious leadership."[67] This recommendation of war as being *sometimes* the lesser of two evils can be found in the Old Testament—the "holy war" that is "declared, led, and won by Yahveh himself[68]—and it has also appeared in Christianity from the very beginning.[69] The Gospel according to St. John is quoted in which it is said that Jesus "found in the temple those that sold oxen and sheep and doves, and the changers of money sitting and when he had made a scourge of small cords, he drove them all out of the temple . . . and poured out the changers' money, and overthrew the tables."[70] Chronologically Christian ethics first stressed pacifism in the early years of the Church in order to emphasize the dissociation between earthly and heavenly existence. Then the just war was sanctioned as a result of the close association between the Church and the state; also Europe was being invaded by peoples considered "barbarians" and hence it was necessary to restrain evil. The Crusades of the Middle Ages thus sought to impose Christianity upon heathens.[71] During these centuries the Papacy effectively regulated and controlled warfare between local European rulers;[72] hence the conflicts could be to some degree interpreted as having divine sanction through the Pope. In Chapter 6 it has been suggested that Sir Thomas More would have his utopians wage war under specified, just circumstances. John Calvin listed five conditions for a just war that have been summarized as follows: "to inflict public vengeance by a king, to preserve the tranquility of a territory, to suppress disturbers of the peace, to rescue victims of oppression, and to punish crimes."[73] Muhammad, as mentioned earlier, initially stressed the unity of mankind but later attempted to establish a church that would be "exclusive and militant."[74]

A legal war, according to the Dutch jurist Hugo Grotius in the seventeenth century, was one that had been formally declared; but a war not formally declared could also be legal if it was in a just cause. For him a war was just when it was fought to right an injury received; hence he recognized self-defense, the recovery of property, and the inflicting of punishment as just causes.[75] In an eighteenth-century classic on "The Laws of Nations," Emer de Vattel, a Swiss jurist and once a diplomat employed by the King of Saxony, discussed what he called the "justificatory reasons" for carrying on war. In the first instance and in the last analysis, he strongly insisted that "a right of so momentous a nature," namely, declaring war, "can belong to the body of the nation, or to the sovereign, her representative"; but it "belongs to nations no farther than is necessary for their own defense and for the maintenance of their rights"; and it includes "the right to security," "defensive war . . . against an unjust aggressor," and the obligation "to succor and assist, by all possible means, a nation engaged in a just war."[76] Finally reference can be made to an American Civil War general and lawyer who conscientiously reflected the viewpoint current in large sections of British and American jurisprudence during the nineteenth century: wars he considered justified as a result of "injuries received or threatened." They should have three objectives: "to secure what belongs or is due to us," "to provide for our future safety, by obtaining reparation of injuries done to us," and "to protect ourselves and property from a threatened injury."[77]

With such an overpowering tradition it is not to be wondered that justifications for the just war linger within society. Like the Social Democratic Party in Germany during World War I which renounced its antiwar policy because it did not wish to commit political suicide by not sharing in a possible German victory or by being accused of contributing to a defeat,[78] most religious leaders dare not consistently advocate and adhere to the peaceful principles of their own faith. In addition they themselves also have a national orientation and share the aspiration and prejudices of their followers and political leaders. The implicit assumption by some pacifists that "the ethics of nonviolence" will shortly win worldwide support[79] does not seem to be valid.

Using force, even if limited and in a good cause, however, is dangerous. Dictators suppress violence through the use of violent methods—there is an old Chinese proverb to the effect that "kill one, frighten ten thousand"—but the violence thus momentarily suppressed may eventually be expressed against the regime or, when the regime tumbles (as in modern Italy, Spain, and Iran), against struggling factions within the society. After terror is employed to combat terrorism, as often happens or seems necessary in law-abiding countries, the society—as the cliché would have it—is damaged as much by the cure as by the disease.[80] Similarly, any change wrought by violence, particularly revolution, may be viewed skeptically: force utilized internally may provide the skill and attitudes conducive to its external use.

And yet, say the oppressed before a bloody or bloodless coup as well as the victims of modern terrorists, force may be the only means available to achieve what might be called justice or even peace. Consider the lives that probably would have been saved, even so late in World War II, if the attempted assassination of Hitler in July of 1944 had been successful. Dramatically the question must be asked: "If a Gandhian is attacked, may others defend him by means he morally rejects?"[81] As previously indicated, Gandhi himself countenanced force under some circumstances; and so too, it has been pointed out, have various Christian theologians; President Nyerere of Tanzania; the utopianists, More and Wells (but not Bellamy); Thomas Jefferson; and also a UNESCO committee.[82] Even St. Augustine who abjured violence in self-defense admitted exceptions: one may sacrifice oneself and fight "in defense of the innocent victims of unjust attack";[83]

a city or people should be punished when its citizens have not previously been punished for doing wrong; and stolen properties should be restored.[84] And of course it is undoubtedly senseless to stand by when a mad dog, figuratively or literally, is threatening to attack.

Force, constrained force, limited violence, therefore, cannot or should not be cast aside merely because violence ordinarily is to be condemned. A perfect society, as the Quakers agree, requires police to prevent psycho- and sociopaths from infringing upon the liberties and lives of others. The existence of such a force, however, does not mean that police may shoot at sight, whimsically arrest individuals, or raid private homes without a warrant; rather they have the right to intervene when the violence occurs or threatens. The United Nations peacekeeping forces in various parts of the world, as will be argued in the next chapter, are perhaps essential to avoid further bloodshed; they must return fire in self-defense under carefully prescribed circumstances.

The Chapter Appendixes consider in some detail two instances in which a limited use of violence achieved what probably would be considered by most persons to be praiseworthy ends: Denmark during World War II and the South Tyrol thereafter. The Danes used only limited force against the German army, the Nazi authorities, and some of their own compatriots in order to prevent Danish Jews from being seized by the authorities. (See Chapter Appendix 8.2: Rescue of Jews by Danes.) They were successful for a variety of traditional, humane, economic, and contemporary reasons; hence the lesson to be drawn from their heroism is that limited nonviolence is not a technique to be unfurled unless a combination of probably unique factors is propitious (cf. V, M). The German-speaking South Tyroleans in northern Italy have probably gained most of the autonomy and other privileges they sought from the Italian government because their demands appeared just to some leaders in the international community; because the Italian leaders were both generous and more preoccupied with other political and economic problems; because they pressed their claims vociferously through established political channels and public protests; *and* because real violence on one occasion—the dynamiting of power plants and public buildings (though without loss of life)—frightened the Italian authorities. (See Chapter Appendix 8.3: the South Tyrol and the Italians.) Another unique historical occurrence, in short, but the violence was limited and was combined with other factors.

The more general question to raise is whether—or when—limited violence should be used to prevent or settle international conflicts. Immediately there is a challenge: "to admit that pacificism cannot stop Hitler from his deeds does not commit us to the position that war is a solution to the problems which created a Hitler."[85] Some of those problems presumably are eliminated in the perfect society in which the five freedoms previously discussed are realized in whole or in part. Less basically, moreover, concrete measures are needed to prevent, deter, and mitigate conflict; thus arises, it is said, the need for an international military and police force.[86] Reluctantly I have evidently pushed myself into the company of those who believe that, under some unspecified conditions, violence or a just war seems necessary or desirable. The concomitant risks both in the present and the future of such a policy, however, are staggering. The short-run gains from the use of force, other than in a policing action, are admittedly tempting, against which the longer-run considerations as well as the horror of violence-begetting-violence are to be reckoned. I must repeat a last-minute warning: even the worst conceivable tyrant believes or at least asserts that his war is just.

NATIONALITY AND HUMAN RIGHTS (#s 5, 6)

The beliefs prevalent within the society in which he lives as well as the actions he is permitted or required to carry out help determine whether the individual becomes a *homo pacificus* or *maleficus*. A fruitful assumption is to agree again with utopianists, many clergymen, and other persons of goodwill who say in effect that states are likely to be "bad" and to lead to war when they encourage the belief in unlimited sovereignty (accompanied, as suggested in Chapter 3, by the metaphor of "national honor") as well as when they inadequately safeguard human rights.

The danger of sovereignty has been previously but mildly stated, as the reality of nationalism was described. Now the case against both the belief in sovereignty and the actions to which it gives rise must be vigorously stated:

Self-determination is an anachronism. It asserts the sacred right of every nation to do as it pleases within its own frontiers, no matter how monstrous or how harmful to the rest of the world. . . . Families are entirely free to do many things they want to do. They can cook what they like. They can furnish their homes as they please. They can educate their children as they see fit. But in a Christian country no man can marry three women at the same time, no man living in an apartment house can set fire to his dwelling, keep a giant crocodile as a pet, or hide a murderer in his flat. If a person does these or similar things, he is arrested and punished. . . . Clearly, he is absolutely free to do everything he wants in all matters which concern himself and his family. But he is not free to interfere with the freedom of others. His freedom of action is not absolute. It is limited by law.[87]

The leaders of virtually every nation, in short, tend to believe that they must determine their own destiny; hence they resent any interference by outsiders with what they consider their own privileges, especially—as noted in Chapter 6—when they are accused of violating the human rights of their own citizens. For a similar reason, many leaders and followers are prone to resort to almost any kind of action, including war, in order to protect the sovereignty of their "nation." All members of the United Nations subscribe to its Charter: in principle they have agreed to "settle their international disputes by peaceful means in such a manner that international peace and security, and justice, are not endangered" and also therefore to "refrain in their international relations from the threat or use of force against the territorial integrity or political independence of any state or in any other manner inconsistent with the Purposes of the United Nations."[88] Wars, nevertheless, continue. The formal explanation for this contradiction resides in the fact that every government, considering itself sovereign, remains "for the most part legally free" either to accept or reject any solution which relates to itself and which would change an existing situation.[89]

How, then, can the belief in unlimited sovereignty be weakened? For realistic reasons suggested in Chapter 3, it is not to be anticipated that patriotism, sovereignty's nonidentical twin, will ever disappear: love of country is an extension both of the self and of the love of family, and it provides the individual with stability and continuity (cf. E). Can it be that "a pure and intense patriotism" is "entirely compatible" with a friendly feeling toward other nations and need not hinder cooperation with them?[90] Perhaps achieving internationalism through individual stages is "dangerous and uncertain"; on the other hand, such internationalism may have to rest "only on satisfied nationalism."[91] When God chose Israel as the Chosen People, it is said, "His universality or His concern for the rest of mankind" was not abdicated.[92] *Homo pacificus*, as was mentioned when attitudes were first discussed in Chapter 2, can have a national or patriotic as well as an international orientation.[93] Pride and love of an in-group can be on a smaller scale and can remain intense when not directed toward the "nation" as a whole but toward one of its subdivisions such as a region, a community, or even a neighborhood.[94]

On the level of the individual, less ego- and ethnocentrism are likely to produce less jingoistic patriotism and less rigid adherence to the doctrine of unlimited sovereignty (cf. P). The less egocentric the person, the better able he is to comprehend others inside and outside his own group. The less ethnocentric, the less inclined he will be to judge others from his standpoint and to be intolerant of their differences. With such a world view he can learn to curb his own self-centered impulses and hence not require or demand unlimited sovereignty for his country. Both on an individual and national level, psychological sacrifices are required in behalf of a presumably more compelling value, that of peace. Ultimately such a system of beliefs and attitudes is to be acquired in the schools and, as stressed in Chapter 10, via the mass media and other vehicles of communication.

Nonegocentric and nonethnocentric attitudes and beliefs, however, do not emerge from parents, teachers, journalists, and so on, as a result solely of hopes and prayers. Basic human needs must be satisfied, meaningful goals must be attained both by leaders and followers within each country. To dampen sovereignty, it is necessary to ask whether such a dream, the mere expression of which seems sentimental and moralistic especially to Marxists and others priding themselves on their realism, can be realized? Three of the previously mentioned documents proclaiming human rights—the United Nations' International Covenant on Economic, Social, and Cultural Rights; the United Nations' International Covenant on Civil and Political Rights; and the American Convention on Human Rights—also suggest means for achieving those rights. The suggestions are not embodied in a blueprint. Rather they cover a wide range of possible actions, short of encouraging revolution or war. Although they do not fit into neat categories, it seems useful to summarize an alphabet-length list of the most important ones in order to indicate what might be accomplished within countries as, for better or worse, these rights now exist. (See Chapter Appendix 8.4: Implementing Human Rights.)

These declarations do not quite reach the point of rejecting the present "ideology of 'sovereign equality' " that does not permit other states of the United Nations itself to intervene upon occasion. They seem to perpetuate the present system—illustrated particularly by the relations between the Soviet Union and the United States—of simply regulating and institutionalizing contacts between any two countries. And yet, if actually executed, they would sweep away most of the evils of nationality, patriotism, and nationalism—and leave only the good behind. It is frustrating, aggravating, yes, sinful, to possess the knowledge of these means to pursue peace and to see many, most of them, deliberately overlooked and sabotaged. Little wonder that the gods and we feel discouraged.

Words, words, words. Another happy phrase has been coined to describe an international goal that transcends the implementation of the twenty-six proposals in Chapter Appendix 8.4: "autonomous interdependence." What is needed is a general sort of relation among groups (whether they be states, communities, or smaller groups): a relation by which one group accords another recognition and respect; a relation which encourages each to follow its own cultural and political preferences; but a relation which does not deny interdependence in such specific areas as trade, communication, the sharing of scarce resources, the exchange of skilled persons, security, weather forecasting, and so forth.[95] Such a "peaceful new order" would have "a natural harmony" and be able to tolerate "competitive features" in nonviolent forms (for instance, in trade and in striving for individual excellence).[96] Even under such semiutopian circumstances, however, unlimited sovereignty as a principle would be invoked; hence that nasty topic remains the central preoccupation of the next chapter.

CHAPTER APPENDIXES

8.1 ASSERTIONS CONCERNING REALIZATION (#s 3, 4)

A psychologist has pronounced the following dictum:

Both the anthropological and the attitudinal studies would suggest that peace requires at least the abolition of private property (especially, and perhaps only, in land and other natural resources), more permissive and rational treatment of children in particular and of one another in general, and better living conditions and effective methods for developing moral maturity, which considers others as well as oneself.

. . . . we need more compassion in human relations, which means valuing personality more than property at least, and less compulsion in subordinating human rights to property rights, if we want peace.[97]

The validity of such a prescription for peace is open to question and hence cannot be dogmatically submitted to policy makers with or without reservations. The analysis of war's predisposing causes in Chapter 3 indicates some relation between socialization and war-peace, but—as emphasized again in the text of that chapter—the precise "treatment" to be recommended is not completely clear. Also "better living conditions" would indeed remove some sources of frustration but not all. Finally, there is no reason to single out "private property" as the archvillain unless it can be shown that its existence produces poverty among the propertyless or unless its pursuit is another reason for declaring war or expanding an imperialistic empire. It is true, however, that the relief from poverty, which the prescription implicitly recommends, points to the freedom from want, one of the ways in which progress toward perfection might be achieved. The ending of the dictum, moreover, is vague and really nothing more than a pious prayer.

Similarly, part of the elephant is observed by many writers without comprehending the nature of the beast. One writer singles out limiting the population in order to reduce "social restlessness" and violent tendencies.[98] Another believes "an abiding peace" can be achieved only through economic reforms, among which he lists removing major barriers to international trade and maintaining "relatively stable parities between the monetary units" of different nations.

Some psychiatrists, as indicated from time to time in this book, use the technical terms of their profession to describe the war-peace problem. One of them, for example, finds a similarity between "psychotic delusions" and the idea of national sovereignty expressed "so glibly" by political leaders. Specifically, he suggests, chauvinistic nationalism on the political level is similar to neurotic fixation on the individual level; isolationism to schizophrenic asocial withdrawal; and sovereignty to manic delusions of grandeur or narcissism.[99] If national ideas are psychotic and if the original definition of "psychotic" is to be retained, then surely the psychotic ideas must belong to psychotic leaders and their followers; nevertheless it is to be doubted whether ideas that are classified in a metaphorical sense as psychotic really spring from psychotic persons or even should be called psychotic. No evidence is submitted to demonstrate that nationalism, sovereignty, or war could be alleviated by resorting to the kinds of treatment found useful in the treatment of psychotic patients.

8.2 RESCUE OF JEWS BY DANES (#s 1, 2, 3, 4)

In the fall of 1943 large numbers of Danes prevented the Nazi authorities, then in control of their country, from seizing more than 6 percent of the 8,000 Jews who had heretofore not been harmed and who were to have been deported to concentration camps in Germany and probable death.[100] They very rarely employed violent means to accomplish this feat; the German army and police could easily and painfully have crushed them. Instead they warned Jews concerning the danger confronting them. Then they hid some of them and transported almost all the rest to neighboring Sweden which, after the intervention of Niels Bohr, willingly accepted them. There is "no simple answer" to the question of why the Danes, and nationals in no other European country other than Belgium and Bulgaria, resisted the Nazis. At first the Danes had no organization to conduct the operation and no special training; yet they expressed both "unanimously and effectively" in word and deed their "deeply held moral convictions."[101]

First of all, the Danes were following their own "century-old" tradition of democracy which accorded all citizens, including Jews, human rights in every sphere of existence. Interviewed twenty years later, one Dane said:

I never think of a man as a Jew or not. It makes no difference to me. At that time I was helping people in trouble. I did the same for the Jews as I did for Allied fliers, saboteurs, and others who had to get to Sweden.[102]

And another:

It was the natural thing to do. I would have helped any group of Danes being persecuted. The Germans' picking on the Jews made as much sense to me as picking on redheads.[103]

In fact, many Jews and Danes had intermarried, and generally Jews had been absorbed into Danish society.

In this atmosphere the Danes who actively or passively engaged in the rescue operation knew they were being supported by virtually all their peers. The plight of the Jews was well publicized throughout Denmark and "there was scarcely an organized body which did not express its profound indignation to the German authorities."[104] The Danish king protested. The bishop of the Lutheran Church of Denmark proclaimed that the historical kinship between Jews and Christians required his followers to "raise a protest" against the Nazi actions. A theologian at a university stated that his countrymen not only faced "a question of right and justice for the Jews" but also that "justice and freedom in Danish life" were "at stake."[105] Preexisting organizations among teachers, students, priests, journalists, physicians, businessmen, and members of the resistance movement provided practical assistance. Threats were hurled upon any Danes who cooperated with the Nazis or who sought to betray the rescue operations. In fact the Danish Nazi party in March 1943 had received only 3 percent of the popular vote and had always been a minority party.

Contemporary events played a role. Initially in 1940 the Danes did not resist the Nazi invasion and were treated well as they cooperated with the German authorities. Gradually they became disenchanted as economic conditions in Denmark worsened and as they came to appreciate "the bestial character of Nazism."[106] Helping the Jews, therefore, was a way of protesting. Before the Nazis decided to round up the Jews in 1943, a resistance movement had come into existence. Danes resented the fact that the Germans were planning to break the promise they had made, as they invaded Denmark, not to discriminate against Jews.

The rescue operation, moreover, occurred soon after the Germans had suffered significant military defeats in North Africa and the Soviet Union, so that it began to look as if they would lose the war. Some Danes ferried Jews to Sweden because they were paid to do so or out of "love of adventure"; but these motives were not conspicuous. Even so-called "luck" was involved. A few but important German officials gave advance warning concerning the plan to seize the Jews; having been stationed in Denmark they wished silently to sabotage the plans either because they had been influenced by the Danes or because they anticipated resistance from significant sectors of the Danish population. In fact, special Nazi officers had to be sent to Denmark from Germany to try to carry out Hitler's decision to liquidate the Jews.

8.3 THE SOUTH TYROL AND THE ITALIANS (#s 2, 3, 4)

The South Tyrol (Alto Adige in Italian) is a small alpine, basically agricultural region south of the Brenner Pass in northern Italy with an area of

2,857 square miles and a population of about 375,000. It was ceded to Italy after World War I, in accordance with the secret Treaty of London (1915), as one of the territorial rewards for joining the Allies in fighting Germany and Austria-Hungary.[107] At that time about 87 percent of the inhabitants had German as their mother tongue and possessed a distinctively Germanic culture; of the rest, about 9 percent were Italians and 4 percent Ladins. During the reign of Mussolini, the Tyroleans were oppressed in innumerable ways: Italian became the compulsory language of instruction in the schools; almost all German names of towns and cities as well as those on street signs and tombstones had to be Italianized; traditional dress could not be worn; opposition to the regime was severely and sometimes cruelly punished.[108] The land, as the Tyroleans expressed it, was "colonized," so that the percentage of Italians rose to about one-third.[109] Force, however, was not effective: the Tyroleans were not deterred; they continued underground to cultivate the German language, and they remained fiercely loyal to their Germanic traditions. Italy was on the losing side in World War II, but the victorious powers permitted her to retain the South Tyrol. Austria, however, was designated the protective power for the region. In spite of an agreement between the Italian and Austrian governments in 1946, Tyroleans believed they were not able to achieve the legal rights therein specified. Although German again became the language of instruction in the schools, the area was flooded with Italians from other parts of Italy who monopolized the civil service posts and who became the leading merchants and shopkeepers in the larger towns. These immigrants knew only Italian, so that to communicate with them the Tyroleans were compelled to learn and speak Italian. New housing schemes favored the Italians. The Tyroleans, consequently, remained discontented in spite of the fact that they enjoyed a relatively high degree of prosperity, not only because their principal products—fruit, wine, lumber—found profitable markets in Italy and abroad, but also especially because the number of tourists, largely from Germany, increased year by year. In North Tyrol irredentist claims for the lost South Tyrol continued to be proclaimed for political and patriotic reasons. The atmosphere became so tense that in 1960 Austrian officials, accompanied by South Tyrolean leaders, filed a protest before the General Assembly of the United Nations. A special commission reviewed the case for eight days and instructed the Austrians and Italians to negotiate their differences.

Then in the spring of 1961 there was overt violence. In a series of coordinated dynamite blasts late one night, power stations and lines were disrupted and other property was destroyed, though with virtually no casualties of any kind. The Italian government responded with a show of force. Soldiers were sent into the area to guard power stations, bridges, railroads, and other important installations. A minor precaution was added, since in the Tyrol and elsewhere in northern Italy bombs had exploded in baggage rooms and lockers: baggage had to be thoroughly inspected before it could be deposited. Again the issue of this region was brought before the United Nations General Assembly, and again both sides were instructed to negotiate their differences. Within Italy a mixed commission, with Italians in the majority, was appointed to study the whole South Tyrolean question. Finally in 1972, ten years later, the commission issued its report, a so-called package which eventually was accepted on an all-or-none basis by the Italian parliament and by a slight majority of the Tyroleans' own party. The package contained 115 articles and 97 proposed changes, many of which satisfied major Tyrolean demands. Austria was no longer the protecting power; disputes were to be referred to the international court at the Hague.

By the middle of the 1970s, consequently, peace by and large had been restored. Tyroleans followed most of their old traditions, the mother tongue continued to be German, relations with Italians were on the whole distant but friendly, children at school were no longer resisting the learning of the Italian language, some intermarriages (especially between Tyrolean girls and Italian boys) were taking place. Tyroleans were represented in the Italian parliament by elected members of the South Tyrolean Folk Party which never missed an opportunity to defend the rights of their compatriots whenever they thought those rights were not being fully protected. Throughout the land various groups sought to preserve and foster traditional customs. Tourists, informally, and various groups in Germany and Austria visited the South Tyrol and thus strengthened German culture there. Affixed to the "I" for Italy that must be displayed near to the rear license plate by cars crossing the border into Austria or elsewhere abroad there is often a sentence printed not in High German but in the local dialect, "am a South Tyrolean" or a member of a particular Tyrolean community or region.

How and why, then, has this particular war-peace problem been almost completely resolved? First and perhaps foremost, the Italian government agreed to most of the demands in the "package," so that Tyroleans and their Austrian friends no longer felt their culture was being threatened. Politically they had achieved in fact a high degree of autonomy. Complaints were still heard here and there with reference to the civil service positions which the Italians continued predominately to occupy and concerning preference given Italians for jobs allocated through official labor exchanges. It was also said that local Italian officials did not speak German adequately, but by and large—in the experience of this writer—German was understood and spoken by Italians in crucial places (such as in post offices and on trains and busses), and Tyroleans even had positions on the state and local police forces. Then, in spite of taxes and inflation in Italy, the South Tyrol enjoyed prosperity as a result of the increased influx of tourists and the higher prices obtained abroad for Tyrolean wine and fruit. Those who personally suffered during the fascist regime between the two wars were either very old or dead; and so the hatred, though it still existed on a verbal level, seemed no longer emotionally strong. The two cultural groups, moreover, remained on the whole separated: peasants and cultivators were exclusively Tyrolean, and almost no Italians lived on the land and in the smaller towns or villages. Only in the four large towns or cities did the two groups reside side by side. Most of the day, from six-thirty in the morning until ten at night, radio programs in German and with a Tyrolean orientation were broadcast from the government stations and also, later, from private stations; and Italian television transmissions confined only to evening hours were paralleled by German-language programs. It appears, moreover, as if the issue of South Tyrol was no longer a burning issue in Austria itself, although some irredentist sentiment remained, although cultural propaganda was being sent over the border to South Tyrol, and although Austrian radio programs always carried news about and to the region. As a result, terrorist activities ceased. The Italian government no longer patrolled strategic installations, but wisps of evidence suggested that the Italian inhabitants of the area began to feel that *they* had become an oppressed minority.

It must be added, of course, that many of the ostensible changes in attitude regarding the Italians were only on the surface of Tyrolean behavior; a bit of probing could produce some hostility tinged, though, with less anxiety than formerly. Italian authorities made so many concessions because they must have been concerned with more pressing problems in their country. For Italy had not been able to achieve a stable government; economic conditions had worsened; and Italian terrorists were striking down Italian officials, and industrialists. One of the strongest Italian political parties, the Communist, evinced no interest in the South Tyrolean question. Within the Italian republic, moreover, there were general trends toward decentralization of power for all regions of the country as well as toward a recognition of the right of regional self-determination.

Most important, too, was the display of force in 1961 as well as the protests before the United Nations. The force convinced the Italian leaders that they could obtain peace only by making concessions; enforcing the older regulations through counterforce was too expensive. The violence and the actions before the United Nations brought South Tyrol to the headlines of the media and called attention to the problem on Italy's frontier. Italy as a democratic country could not afford to follow the tradition of Mussolini and perpetrate injustice among the Tyroleans. The South Tyroleans themselves struggled nonviolently to preserve their heritage; but the impetus to significant reform was violence and outside pressure.

8.4 IMPLEMENTING HUMAN RIGHTS (#s 3, 4)

The abbreviations for the three sources and the meaning of the succeeding numbers are the same as those given in Chapter Appendix 6.3. Excluded from the summary below are important, specific proposals regarding legal procedures and types of permissible punishment for individuals, such as the following: "In the determination of any criminal charge against him, everyone shall be entitled to the following minimum guarantees, in full equality." This particular proposal is followed by a list of seven guarantees, the last of which is: "Not to be compelled to testify against himself or to confess guilt" (III, 14: 3).

Some of the ways the rights should be realized are expressed in general, positive, but vague terms, and represent little more than an entreaty to do something:

a. "promote the realization of the right of self-determination and . . . respect that right" (II, 1: 3)
b. "undertake to guarantee" the rights mentioned in the Covenant "without discrimination of any kind" (II, 2:2)
c. "take appropriate steps" to realize "the right of everyone to an adequate standard of living" (II, 11:1)
d. "ensure equality of rights and responsibilities of spouses as to marriage, during marriage, and at its dissolution" (III, 23:4)
e. "undertake to respect" freedom of "scientific research and creative activity" (II, 15:3)
f. give parents or guardians the freedom to educate their children "in conformity with their own convictions" (III, 18:4)
g. for those countries now without compulsory and free primary education, to "work out and adopt" a suitable and sufficiently speedy "plan of action" (II, 14)

Specific, positive recommendations are made on a national level to improve or change existing institutions, including:

h. take "economic and technical" steps to achieve human rights, "particularly the adoption of legislative measures" (II, 2: 1) or "other measures" (III, 2:2)
i. improve "methods of production, conservation, and distribution of food" by utilizing "technical and scientific knowledge," by disseminating that knowledge, and by "developing or reforming agrarian systems . . . to achieve the most efficient development and utilization of natural resources" (II, 11: 2a)
j. prevent, treat, and control "epidemic, endemic, occupational, and other diseases" (II, 12: 2c)
k. promote "the conservation, the development, and the diffusion of science and culture" (II, 15: 2)

l. facilitate "full and productive employment" as well as overall development by means of "technical and vocational guidance and training programs, policies, and techniques" (II, 6:2)

m. safeguard "the right of everyone to form trade unions and join the trade union of his choice" (II, 8: 1)

n. develop "an awareness of human rights among the peoples" belonging to the Convention (IV, 41a)

o. use "the same communications outlet" to reply to an injury caused by "inaccurate or offensive statements or ideas disseminated to the public in general by a legally regulated medium of communication" (IV, 14: 1)

Negative injunctions of a general and specific type are also proposed:

p. "the State may subject" the rights conforming to the Covenant "only to such limitations as are determined by law only insofar as this may be compatible with the nature of these rights and solely for the purpose of promoting the general welfare in a democratic society" (II, 4)

q. the "fundamental human rights" already existing in a nation may not be restricted or derogated by using the "pretext" that such rights are not at all or fully recognized in the Covenant (II, 5: 2)

r. "prior censorship" of information and ideas related to "the right to freedom of thought and expression" shall not be exercised, except that public entertainment affecting "the moral protection of childhood and adolescence" may be restricted and also "any propaganda for war and any advocacy of national, racial, or religious hatred" under specified conditions may be "considered as offences punishable by law" (IV, 13)

s. the injunction against suppressing "the enjoyment or exercise of the rights and freedom" in the Convention applies to groups and to individuals (IV, 29).

t. states, groups, and persons do not have "any right to engage in any activity or to perform any action aimed at the destruction" of the human rights or the freedoms mentioned in the Covenant (II, 5)

u. a procedure involving the establishing of fact, the writing of a report, and its publication shall be followed in dealing with "a petition or communication alleging violation of any of the rights" protected by the Convention (IV, 48-51).

v. submit to an international official such as the Secretary-General "reports on the measures" adopted to achieve human rights (II, 16)

w. inform other parties to the Covenant if they derogate rights embodied in that Covenant "in time of public emergency" and under specified conditions (III, 4)

x. participate in a Human Rights Committee that shall "receive and consider communications to the effect that a State Party claims that another State Party is not fulfilling its obligations under the present Covenant" (III, 41: 1).

y. establish (for the American States) a "Court of Human Rights which, among other duties, shall grant parties injured through the "violation of a right or freedom . . . fair compensation" (IV, 63: 1, 2).

z. use "such methods as the conclusion of conventions, the adoption of recommendations, the furnishing of technical assistance, and the holding of regional meetings and technical meetings for the purpose of consultation and study organized in conjunction with the Governments concerned" (II, 23)

NOTES

1. Kenneth N. Waltz, *Man, the State, and War*. New York: Columbia University Press, 1954. P. 122.

2. Garrett Hardin, Lifeboat ethics. In William Aiken and Hugh LaFollette (eds.), *World Hunger and Moral Obligation*. Englewood Cliffs: Prentice-Hall, 1977. Pp. 11-21.

3. Michael A. Slote, The morality of wealth. In Aiken and LaFollette (eds.), op. cit., pp. 124-47.

4. James Rachels, Vegetarianism and "the other weight problem." In Aiken and LaFollette (eds.), op. cit., pp. 180-93.

5. John Arthur, Rights and the duty to bring aid. In Aiken and LaFollette (eds.), op. cit., pp. 37-48. Also Rachels, op. cit.

6. Ernst Haas, *Human Rights and International Action*. Stanford: Stanford University Press, 1970. Pp. 2, 6.

7. Michel Bassand, The Jura problem. *Journal of Peace Research*, 1975, 12, 139-50.

8. George Kateb, *Utopia and its Enemies*. Glencoe: Free Press, 1963. Pp. 77-78.

9. Valene L. Smith (ed.), *Hosts and Guests*. Philadelphia: University of Pennsylvania Press, 1977.

10. William Field Ogburn, The sociological problem. In George B. de Huszar (ed.), *New Perspectives on Peace*. Chicago: University of Chicago Press, 1944. Pp. 115-42.

11. Karl. W. Deutsch and Richard L. Merritt, Effects of events on national and international images. In Herbert C. Kelman (ed.), *International Behavior*. New York: Holt, Rinehart and Winston, 1965. Pp. 132-87.

12. Rosebett Moss Kanter, *Commitment and Community*. Cambridge: Harvard University Press, 1972. Pp. 3, 32, 236, 245.

13. Waltz, op. cit., p. 52.

14. Ibid., p. 40.

15. Lincoln Bloomfield and Robert Beattie, Computers and policy making. *Journal of Conflict Resolution*, 1971, 15, 33-46.

16. Leo Kuper, *The Pity of it All*. Minneapolis: University of Minnesota Press, 1977.

17. E. Leslie, Some thoughts on international peacekeeping. *Canadian Defense Quarterly*, 1978, 7, no. 3, 18-22.

18. Fred Charles Iklé, *Every War Must End*. New York: Columbia University Press, 1971. Pp. 112-14.

19. Steven Rosen, War power and the willingness to suffer. In Bruce M. Russett (ed.), *Peace, War, and Numbers*. Beverly Hills: Sage, 1972. Pp. 167-83.

20. J. David Singer and Melvin Small, *The Wages of War, 1816-1965*. New York: Wiley, 1972. Pp. 370-71.

21. F. H. Hinsley, *Power and the Pursuit of Peace*. London: Cambridge University Press, 1963.

22. Robin Jenkins, Perception in crises. *Proceedings of the International Peace Research Association*, 1968, 1, 155-75.

23. Anatol Rapoport, The application of game theory to peace research. *Impact of Science on Society*, 1968, 18, no. 2, 111-23.

24. John R. Raser, Deterrence research. *Journal of Peace Research*, 1966, 3, 297-327. Cf. Leonard W. Doob, The utilization of social scientists in the Overseas Branch of the Office of War Information. *American Political Science Review*, 1947, 41, 649-67.

25. Olaf Helmer, *Social Technology*. New York: Basic Books, 1966. P. 68.

26. Ibid., pp. 68-71.

27. Ibid., pp. 28, 64, 68-72.

28. Raul de Brigard and Olaf Helmer, *Some Political Societal Developments*. Middletown: Institute for the Future, 1970. Pp. 11-12, 50-54.

29. Fyador Dostoevsky, *Notes from the Underground*. Garden City: Doubleday, 1960. P. 199.

30. Oran R. Young, *The Politics of Force*. Princeton: Princeton University Press, 1968. P. 47.

31. Raser, op. cit.

32. Henry A. Kissinger, The problems of limited war. In Charles R. Beitz and Theodore Herman (eds.), *Peace and War*. San Francisco: W. H. Freeman, 1973. Pp. 98-108.

33. Chester Bowles, *The New Dimensions of Peace*. New York: Harpers, 1955. P. 380.

34. Walter Millis and James Real, *The Abolition of War*. New York: Macmillan, 1963. Pp. 107-08.

35. R. G. Bell, *Alternative to War*. London: James Clarke, 1959. P. 29.

36. Thomas Schelling, *Arms and Influence*. New Haven: Yale University Press, 1966. Pp. v-vi.

37. Richard A. Falk, *A Study of Future Worlds*. New York: Free Press, 1975. P. 97.

38. Dean G. Pruitt and Richard C. Snyder, Restraints against the use of violence. In Pruitt and Snyder (eds.), *Theory and Research on the Causes of War*. Englewood Cliffs: Prentice-Hall, 1969. Pp. 101-13.

39. John R. Raser and Wayman J. Crow, A simulation study of deterrence theories. In International Peace Research Association (ed.), *Proceedings of the International Peace Research Association Inaugural Conference*. Assen: Van Gorcum, 1966. Pp. 146-65. Also Herman Kahn, *On Thermonuclear War*. Princeton: Princeton University Press, 1961.

40. Charles E. Osgood, *An Alternative to War or Surrender*. Urbana: University of Illinois Press, 1962. Pp. 54-55.

41. Bert V. A. Röling, La paix par la dissuasion. In Centre de Sociologie de la Guerre (ed.), *La Paix par la Recherche Scientifique*. Brussels: Editions de l'Institut de Sociologie, 1970. Pp. 225-57.

42. George Kemp, Arms transfers to developing countries. *Proceedings of the International Peace Research Association, Second Conference*, 1968, 2, 254-68.

43. Nazli Choucri and Robert C. North, *Nations in Conflict*. San Francisco: W. H. Freeman, 1975. Pp. 249, 278.

44. Norman Z. Alcock, *The Emperor's New Clothes*. Oakville: CPRI Press, 1971. Pp. 33-44.

45. John R. Raser, The failure of fail-safe. In Milton J. Rosenberg (ed.), *Beyond Conflict and Containment*. New Brunswick: Transaction Books, 1972. Pp. 127-46.

46. Matthew Meselson, Chemical weapons and chemical arms control. *Bulletin, American Academy of Arts and Sciences*, 1978, 32, no. 1, 14-21.

47. U. S. Arms Control and Disarmament Agency, *World Military Expenditures and Arms Transfers 1967-1976*. Washington: U.S. Arms Control and Disarmament Agency, 1978. Pp. 1-8.

48. S. Strauz-Hupé and S. T. Possony, *International Relations*. New York: McGraw-Hill, 1950. P. 848.

49. Leonard Berkowitz and Anthony LePage, Weapons as aggression-eliciting stimuli. *Journal of Personality and Social Psychology*, 1967, 7, 202-07.

50. Richard Rovere, Affairs of state. *New Yorker*, 28 May 1979, 124-26.

51. Amitai Etzioni, *The Hard Way to Peace*. New York: Crowell-Collier, 1962. Pp. 15-60.

52. Osgood, op. cit.

53. Ibid., p. 92.

54. Ibid., p. 128.

55. Meselson, op. cit.

56. Gene Sharp, *Exploring Nonviolent Alternatives*. Boston: Porter Sargent, 1970. P. 42.

57. Theodor Ebert, *Gewaltfreier Aufstand*. Freiburg: Verlag Rombach, 1968. P. 11.

58. Gene Sharp, "The political equivalent of war"—civilian defense. *International Conciliation*, 1965, no. 555.

59. Sharp, *Exploring nonviolent alternatives*, op. cit., pp. 115-23.

60. Theodor Ebert cited by Rainer Kabel, *Mobilmachung zum Frieden*. Tübingen: Katzmann Verlag, 1971. P. 106.

61. Cf. Michael Walzer, *Just and Unjust Wars*. New York: Basic Books, 1977. Pp. 332-34. See also Chapter Appendix 2.2.

62. Chihiro Hosoya, Miscalculations in deterrent policy. *Journal of Peace Research*, 1968, 5, 97-115.

63. Richard C. Porter, Economic sanctions. *Journal of Peace Science*, 1978, 3, 93-110.

64. Max Lerner, *Ideas for the Ice Age*. New York: Viking, 1941. P. 37.

65. Bell, op. cit., p. 17.

66. William Ballis, *The Legal Position of War*. Hague: Martinus Nijhoff, 1937. Pp. 16-28.

67. Strauz-Hupé and Possony, op. cit., p. 208.

68. Ralph Luther Moellering, *Modern War and the Christian*. Minneapolis: Augsburg Publishing House, 1969. Pp. 20-21.

69. Jacques Ellul, *Violence*. New York: Seabury Press, 1969. Pp. 1-12.

70. John 2: 14-15.

71. Roland H. Bainton, *Christian Attitudes toward War and Peace*. New York: Abingdon Press, 1960. Pp. 14-15.

72. Myres S. McDougal and Florentino P. Feliciano, *Law and Minimum World Public Order*. New Haven: Yale University Press, 1961. P. 133.

73. Donald A. Wells, *The War Myth*. Indianapolis: Bobbs-Merrill, 1967. P. 35.

74. S. D. Goitein, The concept of mankind in Islam. In W. Warren Wagar (ed.), *History and Idea of Mankind*. Albuquerque: University of New Mexico Press, 1971. Pp. 72-91.

75. Ballis, op. cit., pp. 112-13.

76. E. de Vattel, *The Law of Nations*. Philadelphia: Johnson and Co., 1865. Pp. 292, 301-05, 324.

77. H. W. Halleck, *International Law*. San Francisco: H. H. Bancroft, 1861. Pp. 313-15, 328-34.

78. Waltz, op. cit., p. 135.

79. Mulford Sibley, *The Political Theories of Modern Pacifism*. Philadelphia: Pacifist Research Bureau, 1944. P. 56.

80. Richard Clutterbuck, *Living with Terrorism*. London: Faber and Faber, 1975. P. 17.

81. Robert Nozick, *Anarchy, State, and Utopia*. New York: Basic Books, 1974. P. 139.

82. UNESCO, *Human Rights*. New York: Columbia University Press, 1949. P. 271.

83. Cited by Ralph B. Potter, Jr., The moral logic of war. In Beitz and Herman (eds.), op. cit., p. 9.

84. Ballis, op. cit., pp. 42-43.

85. Wells, op. cit., p. 103.

86. Robert Bosc, *Sociologie de la Paix*. Paris: Les Editions Spes, 1965. Pp. 176-77.

87. Emery Reves, *The Anatomy of Peace*. New York: Harpers, 1945. Pp. 192, 196.

88. Article 2, sections 3, 4.

89. Study Group on the Peaceful Settlement of International Disputes, *Report*. London: David Davies Memorial Institute, 1966. P. 2.

90. William McDougall, *Janus*. New York: Dutton, 1927. P. 48.

91. Lindsay Rogers, The League of Nations and the national state. In Stephen Pierce Duggan (ed.), *The League of Nations*. Boston: Altantic Monthly Press, 1919. Pp. 82-95.

92. Eliezer Berkovits, Jewish universalism. In Wagar (ed.), op. cit., pp. 47-71.

93. Cf. Adam Curle, *Making Peace*. London: Tavistock Publications, 1971. P. 15.

94. Leonard W. Doob, *The Plans of Men*. New Haven: Yale University Press, 1940. Pp. 328-29.

95. Curle, op. cit., p. 261.

96. Sondra Herman, *Eleven Against War*. Stanford: Hoover Institution Press, 1969. P. 8.

97. William Eckhardt, Primitive militarism. *Peace Research Reviews*, 1974, 6, no. 2, 63-78.

98. Zygmunt A. Piotrowski, Is permanent peace possible? In Rolland S. Parker (ed.), *The Emotional Stress of War, Violence, and Peace*. Pittsburgh: Stanwix House, 1972. Pp. 1-11.

99. Kenneth Appel, Nationalism and sovereignty. *Journal of Abnormal and Social Psychology*, 1945, 40, 355-62.

100. Helen Fein, *Accounting for Genocide*. New York: Free Press, 1979. Pp. 69, 70, 114, 144-52. Harold Flender, *Rescue in Denmark*. New York: Simon and Schuster, 1963. Leni Yahil, *The Rescue of Danish Jewry*. Philadelphia: Jewish Publication of America, 1969.

101. Thomas Merton, *On Peace*. New York: McCall, 1971. P. 165.

102. Flender, op. cit., p. 115.

103. Ibid., p. 124.

104. Fein, op. cit., p. 148.

105. Ibid., p. 146.

106. Flender, op. cit., p. 256.

107. Dennison T. Rusinow, *Italy's Austrian Heritage 1919-1946*. Oxford: Clarendon, 1969. Pp. 9-11.

108. Leonard W. Doob, *Patriotism and Nationalism*. New Haven: Yale University Press, 1964. Pp. 21-22.

109. Adolf Leidlmair, Bevölkerung und Wirtschaft seit 1945. In Franz Huter (ed.), *Sudtirol*. Vienna: Verlag für Geschichte und Politik, 1965. Pp. 560-80.

9.

International Realization

Conceivably almost all persons within a country could achieve perfection, their "nation" could be close to perfection, and yet they could be compelled to endure a war resulting not from the decision of their own leaders but from havoc wrought by an invading army representing a less perfect country with less perfect inhabitants. Belgium, as its good people freely admit, is perfect in neither respect, but surely its leaders and followers are not in any other than a metaphysical sense responsible for the misery most of them endured as German forces swept through and occupied their land in both World Wars. It is necessary, consequently, to consider how relations between countries can be improved in order to increase the probability of realizing peace.

Once again let there be no optimistic hope that panaceas are forthcoming, only the pursuit and encouragement of innovation are contemplated. Glances backward toward people in their milieu, as previously surveyed, must continue. Thus the predisposing causes of Belgium's plight in the two wars must be sought throughout Europe and perhaps also in North America, the precipitating causes in German leaders and the Germans themselves. But the emphasis here will be upon the relations between leaders of countries, international organizations, and peacekeeping operations.

NEGOTIATION, MEDIATION, AND INTERVENTION (#s 4e, 5)

When conflicts or disagreements occur between leaders, either because they themselves or their followers seek incompatible goals, peace can be pursued by direct negotiation or with the help of outside mediators or intervenors. The official negotiators may be the heads of states or their deputies, such as foreign ministers or ambassadors. For the world as a whole, the Security Council and particularly the Secretary-General of the United Nations function as the agents attempting to extinguish the "brush fires," in the phrasing of one United Nations official, that have plagued so many countries since World War II. According to Article 99 of the United Nations Charter, the secretary-general "may bring to the attention of the Security Council any matter which in his opinion may threaten the maintenance of international peace and security." The council has passed resolutions urging parties to a dispute to reach accord, sometimes in accordance with principles its members have indicated; the secretary-general has visited parties in conflict and has often brought their representatives together in meetings over which he or his representative has presided. Also, regional organizations have tried to settle conflicts among their members and in some instances have succeeded. The Organization of African Unity, for example, has functioned in various ways in connection with boundary disputes: the intervention of the Ethiopian emperor and the president of Mali enabled Morocco and Algeria to reach an agreement concerning their dispute in 1956; Sudan performed the same function in achieving a ceasefire between Somalia and Ethiopia in 1964, but a "Good Offices Committee" under the chairmanship of Nigeria did not prevent the outbreak of hostilities in 1977; the president of Guinea induced Upper Volta and Mali to sign "a permanent peace agreement" in 1975.[1]

Negotiators, whether the country's leaders or their representatives, are constrained by a host of factors: the traditional or momentary foreign policies of their governments, the effect of any settlement upon their followers at home, their own personal motives, and above all the boundaries within which they are permitted to bargain with their antagonists (cf. P).*[2] In theory, they have at their disposal a repertoire of threats they can employ in behalf of their demands: slackening of cultural relations, economic measures, breaking of diplomatic relations, and ultimately a declaration of limited or all-out war. Or, from the opposite standpoint, corresponding rewards may be proffered. When a recent American secretary of agriculture called food "a tool in the kit of American diplomacy," he was suggesting quite crudely and honestly that American diplomats could offer food as a lure for cooperation or could threaten to withdraw food if confronted with noncooperation. In the present analysis it is assumed that one, both, or all the negotiators seek to avoid war. How can that objective be realized other than through bribes or threats?

Every successful negotiation—successful in the sense of avoiding armed conflict—is likely to contain unique components (cf. V). Unquestionably, for example, personality factors play a role in any negotiation. From 1960 to 1974 the scholarly journals emitted "more than 500" studies on bargaining

---

*See pages 11-12 for an explanation of the cross-referencing system.

as investigated in the antiseptic conditions of the laboratory where conditions are less hectic and less varied than in real life;[3] almost all of them sought to link personality or personality traits to interactions among the participants and to the outcome. The results have been inconsistent and not compressible into easy generalizations. This state of affairs is not surprising when, as has been suggested, the role of personality factors depends upon the negotiator's attitudes toward one another, their formal relations, their expectations, and the tactics employed during the negotiations,[4] all of which appear in an almost infinite number of combinations (cf. M, V).

Even the momentary situation, sometimes referred to as "the-shape-of-the-table" problem (named after the prolonged arguments in 1969 by the Vietnamese and American negotiators concerning, literally, the table which for them had symbolic significance as they met in Paris to try to bring their war to a close) may play a crucial role. Other more or less mechanical factors include the seating arrangements, the number of negotiators on each side, the hours spent each day in negotiating, the parliamentary or other procedures during the meetings, and so forth.

And now a sigh. Just as a first-rate cook knows which ingredients, their proportions, the order in which they should be brought together, the mode of mixing them, the kind of receptacle into which they are to be poured or placed, and the length of time the emerging dough should be baked in order to make a tempting, delicious cake or pie, so there ought to be similarly specific and valid knowledge concerning the optimal conditions required for each of the negotiation factors just mentioned in order to ensure the success of a negotiation (cf. I). Sometimes the shape of the table is important, sometimes it is not; sometimes brief sessions, sometimes long sessions are fruitful; sometimes the meeting of one diplomat or leader from each side leads to a peaceful settlement, sometimes it is better to have their staffs also participate actively; sometimes it is wise to seek agreement on specific issues and thus to segmentalize the conflict, at other times it may be essential to reach for agreement on the totality. We know, tentatively, only the parameters of the problem. The variables demand unqiue weighing in each negotiation.

In the West, for example, "secret diplomacy" has an evil connotation and is frequently avoided. In 1954, however, the representatives of the Italian and Yugoslav governments settled a long-standing conflict over Trieste after prolonged deliberations and in a manner apparently satisfactory to both countries. During the negotiations, the participants later recalled, all of the diplomats considered it essential to maintain absolute secrecy. They were discussing territorial questions; and government leaders, they knew, believe it "almost impossible" to retreat from positions once their views have become public. Secrecy thus permitted the participants to be flexible and "to negotiate seriously."[5] Obviously the representatives of these two countries wished to resolve the dispute without going to war. In other situations, success may depend upon either a public confrontation or upon leaking news of a negotiation to journalists in order to exert pressure upon one's opponents. When diplomacy is conducted in conferences or through multilateral negotiations, the proceedings are usually public and thus, it is said, time is saved and followers know what is being done in their name. But public debates, as in the United Nations General Assembly and Security Council, become little more than a formal ritual, with the critical decisions being made informally or secretly before the terms are legally approved. One United Nations official has stated, off the record, his belief that only about one-tenth of the decisions of the Security Council are made at its public meetings. The public debates of the United Nations agencies, including the Security Council and the General Assembly, however, are not charades, for at the very least, when reported by the mass media, they keep leaders and followers informed about the issues and problems provoking a dispute.

The techniques of negotiating are as varied as those in any human inter-action, even when constrained by tradition or protocol (cf. V). Their complexity is compounded by the fact that usually the negotiators represent different cultures and hence evaluate actions differently. Perhaps in some situations, for example, it is wise to begin a negotiation with a set of demands from which one is willing to retreat somewhat and thus give one's opponent the impression, the illusory impression, that he has gained something by bargaining. In some societies, however, such a concession could be interpreted as a sign of weakness.

Faint lights, nevertheless, shine through the gloomy fog of uniqueness. Some insight into the process of negotiating, some generalizations are available. It may be shrewdly guessed that background factors are generally more important than the personality or technical variables mentioned above. According to reasonably solid evidence, the leaders of countries are more likely to settle disputes peacefully if the values and way of life of their peoples are compatible than under the reverse conditions (cf. P). They may develop "a pluralistic security community" if they both have "rising capabilities," if they anticipate "joint economic growth," and if they have "an unbroken social communications network with a wide range of trans-actions."[6] Other conditions have been associated with successful negotia-tions in various situations, both in the laboratory and in industry, many of which have implications for the pursuit of peace. Styles of negoti-ating, for example, may reflect not only the idiosyncracies of the negotiators but also their cultural backgrounds which induce them to propose, at least at the outset of a negotiation, either abstract and lofty or detailed and concrete ways to settle a dispute. The parliamentary procedures of the West permeate most international negotiations especially when many individuals participate, as in the United Nations General Assembly. Whether or not such formality—"my esteemed colleague" (a reference to an opponent or an enemy)—assists understanding is a moot question.

One or more of the factors alleged or likely to be helpful in a negotiation may be lacking or some disturbing event intrudes in medias res, with the result that negotiations end or war breaks out. The absence of common cultural traditions or of a history of trust and friendship has made negotiation between the Arab states and Israel sometimes impossible, always difficult and prolonged; whereas the presence of such traditions and an amicable history enable Canada and the United States to negotiate, usually quickly and always successfully, whatever differences arise between them. In both instances variations in the same factors, respectively, cause the differences to arise or not to arise.

How can the conditions of negotiations be improved so that peaceful settlements will be facilitated? The factors hindering success can be isolated, at least on a very abstract level: the "unintentional" ones arising from ignorance, lack of understanding, or the inability to diagnose the situation at hand; gaps between reality and perception resulting in "emotional distortions" and "ideational divergences"; and difficulties emerging from bargaining tactics and other actions during the negotiation.[7] This scholarly generalization, though doubtless valid in retrospect, is likely to receive at the most a polite and skeptical smile from a seasoned diplomat; it will not help him, he believes he knows, when he sits down to participate in a bargaining exchange. In the future, however, negotiators could be more thoroughly trained to appreciate and anticipate such factors. In addition, they may conceivably be inspired by some of the newer approaches to negotiation and mediation described later in this section.

The problems of third parties, mediators and nonbinding arbitrators who intervene in a conflict either on their own initiative or upon invitation of the opposing parties, are similar to those confronting negotiators. Mediators and arbitrators, however, always seek to resolve the conflict peacefully, whereas each negotiator would have his own side victorious and may use war as the ultimate threat. The United Nations Secretary-General also attempts to function as a peacemaker and peacebuilder. In addition, diplomats and leaders from various countries may discharge third-party functions. American policy between the World Wars was to avoid mediation and participation in most world affairs and to hope that somehow peace could be retained by the system of alliances then in effect. The policy has been drastically changed since World War II. American officials have attempted to deter aggression and what they consider to be injustice in many lands, and to intervene militarily as in Korea and Vietnam. Friendly countries have been strengthened through military, economic, and financial aid; through participation in NATO; and more dramatically, if not always successfully, through mediation. The role of two American secretaries of state in the Middle East conflicts has been motivated in part by humanitarian considerations but certainly also has been affected by the so-called Jewish lobby and other political pressures in the United States and by American interest in oil from the Arab countries.

In face-to-face meetings mediators from the diplomatic profession usually but not always employ fairly formal procedures since the protagonists are contrained by their goverments' instructions. In general, both they and intervenors must have prestige and be trusted by the participants. Their own motivation must be high. They must have concrete and accurate knowledge about the conflict at hand as well as about principles concerning human behavior and society. They must have confidence in themselves and their techniques. Obviously they must be impartial. They must be able to withstand frustration and possess the attributes of patience, flexibility, sympathy or empathy, intelligence, and tact. These godlike qualities are described more fully in Chapter Appendix 9.3: Qualifications of Mediators and Intervenors.

In any case, in the present century both formal negotiation and mediation are not always—should one say seldom?—successful and therefore techniques are being sought that are more likely to stimulate creativity. For this reason within recent years private persons, without attempting to supplant official diplomacy, have attempted to intervene in conflict situations. They have brought together individuals, either officials or ordinary citizens, and have tried to induce or help them, somehow, to arrive at either a better understanding or a solution or resolution of the problem at issue. Two summaries and critical evaluations of current techniques have appeared[8] and hence only a relatively swift résumé need be given here. Generally these "unofficial diplomats," as they have been called, have certain advantages not possessed by accredited diplomatic mediators. They may provide a specially designed setting in which representatives of the parties in conflict can interact privately and with more or less complete confidentiality. New ideas can be advanced and dissected without official sanction and without commitment. Channels of communication between specialized groups can be created: for Soviet and American intellectuals and particularly for scientists by the Pugwash Conferences;[9] for disarmament experts, churchmen, writers, businessmen, scholars, and "unofficial" officials of various sorts from the same two countries by the Dartmouth Conferences[10] and by numerous professional, international societies; for journalists by the International Press Institute;[11] for persons interested in religion by the Commission of the Churches on International Affairs;[12] for humanitarians by the International Committee of the Red Cross;[13] and for diplomats functioning off the record and other specialists by the Center for Mediterranean Studies in Rome.[14] During the Vietnam War, diplomats from neutral countries and two American journalists sought vainly to end the war by ascertaining unofficially the terms one of the parties was willing to accept and to offer the other.[15]

Notable successes through mediation, at least on the surface, have not been scored. One of the American organizers, for example, has modestly and candidly evaluated the Dartmouth and Pugwash Conferences:

It's probably incremental rather than fundamental. Certain things that pop up might not come to view otherwise. The conferences are valuable, I think, atmospherically. It's quite possible that the Soviets attach considerable importance to it.

Such being the case, they come to it perhaps better briefed by their government than we are by ours. As a consequence, we get a rather good reading of what's going on in the minds of the Soviet government: what their expectations are; what the issues are that they'd like to try out on us.

In this way a number of issues with respect to the test ban were aired very early. There's no doubt in my mind that the Dartmouth Conference had some part to play in the eventual treaty that came about. The same could also be said of the Pugwash Conference and of a number of other probes that were going on. All these efforts, I think, were useful. That is not to say that if there were no Dartmouth, if there were no Pugwash, you would not have had a test ban. Of course you would have. But something else would have had to take their place.[16]

And an official of the International Press Institute which assembles persons from the mass media to discuss the significance of current events has stated:

It is difficult to measure the direct or indirect impact of these meetings. Sometimes the real effect appears only years afterward, when the literature devoted to a specific period or event is published, and the findings of these meetings are analyzed by theoreticians. Sometimes, meetings are only poorly covered by the news media, but later extensive treatment appears in specialized periodicals. Other times, on the contrary, media coverage is satisfactory, but academic appreciation is poor. It is impossible to predict accurately a meeting's consequences, since so many factors influence reactions.[17]

Another technique, "controlled communication," brings together minor government leaders representing unofficially the parties in dispute who freely discuss their disagreements and agreements in a permissive atmosphere and who at appropriate moments are offered suggestions by participating social scientists concerning social-science principles or other ways to analyze the difficulties at hand. The participants themselves have been affected, but no international dispute has thereby been settled.[18] In 1966 the approach was used in an effort to resolve the Cyprus conflict, without obviously averting the tragedy begun there in the summer of 1974. I, too, sought to bring Cypriotes together in a workshop, a plan which was not carried out because it was to have been implemented a few days after the coup against the Makarios government and on the very day the Turkish army arrived there.[19] There was no guarantee that this plan would have been any more successful than the previous attempt. Colleagues and I, moreover, conducted a workshop for Ethiopians, Kenyans, and Somalis with reference to their border disputes. Our lack of success was shown by the fact that in one of the contested areas, the Ogaden, armed conflict broke out eight years later between the Ethiopians and Somali guerrillas.[20] We also recruited fifty-six Protestant and Catholic volunteers from Belfast to attend a workshop in Scotland in 1972. We did not focus upon the basic political and economic problems of Northern Ireland, but merely sought to have the two groups interact in the hope that, after experiencing under our guidance the ways groups function, they would establish associations and organizations back home which would contribute to a better understanding between members of both communities. The effects of this experience upon the associations between the two communities seem to have been minimal.[21]

Intervention by means of a workshop, however, remains promising, I think, for three reasons. In the first place, as suggested above, it is too early to say that all past efforts have been complete failures; seeds may have been planted in the minds of some participants, as it were, and they may have yielded fruits which we have been unable to observe and which may become apparent later on (cf. I). Then possibly the method may prove more useful in the future, at least that is my modest faith. Also the theory behind the procedures and the procedures themselves throw light, perhaps, on why conventional approaches often do not succeed.

The last point merits detailed examination. For illustrative and, I trust, not egotistical reasons I use my own not completely original method as an illustration, if only because I am well acquainted with it. The underlying theory suggests that, although individuals are slow to change or to be creative, under some circumstances rapid changes and creativity can be induced. They are likely to be influenced when they have been transplanted out of their usual milieu, when somehow they have been induced to view a situation quite differently from the way they have in the past or the present, or when a central change within them—as in a conversion—has repercussions for their other values and attitudes (cf. P).[22] To facilitate changes and creativity through a workshop, persons of goodwill from both sides of a conflict are carefully recruited and then transported out of their normal environment. For a period of roughly two weeks they live together and hence interact intimately. During the first half of the exercise they are helped to understand one another and to appreciate some of the normal processes characteristic of human interaction, such as projection, identification, and rationalization. During the second half, when a degree of mutual trust has been established, they attempt first to discover the fundamental factors in the conflict and then they seek somehow to achieve a creative solution. Fine-sounding words? No, I insist, as I would indicate by means of an analogy to which I have resorted many times in an effort to explain the rationale to potential participants in workshops, to officials whose permission was needed to allow other participants to attend, to students and colleagues, and to readers. For years I believed it was my own creation, but in essence it is not.[23] If two persons are in a room and one wants a window open and the other shut, there can be either what is fashionably called a zero-sum game (one wins, the other loses) or there can be a compromise (the window is open or shut only halfway or partially). But if both can be truly honest and resort to a psychological analysis, they may discover that the individual seeking to have the window opened really desires fresh air and the one seeking to have it closed wishes for reasons best known to himself to avoid a draft. Then a creative solution may emerge: a window in another room or a door is opened so that the first person receives fresh air and the second escapes a draft. If groups in conflict keep insisting that each must possess a given territory, a zero-sum situation exists; possibly, possibly they may discover that it is not the territory they "really" wish but some other goals each can achieve without intruding upon the other. In every case, the participants to a dispute may cling stubbornly to their surface demands until a third party points out, or helps them to appreciate, their own more basic goals.

The first question to answer before undertaking such a workshop is whether anything can be gained by an intervention and, if so, whether the time is ripe to attempt one. During an actual war it is highly unlikely that the antagonists will be willing or able to confront one another; the decision to declare an armistice must come from leaders; perhaps after the end of hostilities new ideas for peacebuilding can emerge. My own conviction concerning the selection of participants can be briefly stated. When the goal is to affect decision makers—as in a jurisdictional dispute—persons should be invited who have access to them but who themselves are not discharging that role. Those in power are usually not available because they cannot afford to be away from their posts for any length of time, because they fear the political consequences of having contact with the "enemy," and so forth. Even if they were to attend a workshop, moreover, they necessarily would represent the official views of their government and hence they would be unable psychologically to relax and be creative. This recruiting criterion, however, has a potentially crippling disadvantage: the participants may be affected by the experience of the workshop but have insufficient influence back home to affect policy decisions. For this reason, some organizers of workshops prefer to have decision-making officials actually participate *if* that is possible. When a different goal is sought—such as a change in what is taught in schools in order to promote understanding between parties in conflict (one of the objectives that seemed feasible in Cyprus before the crises in 1974)—persons who either have relevant power or qualifications to achieve that goal should be asked to participate.

The role of the intervenors during a workshop also depends upon the goal or goals to be achieved, and these can be either "problem-solving" or "process-promoting."[24] The former is directed toward discovering a possible solution to the conflict, the latter to enabling the participants to acquire knowledge and skills that will be useful in their back-home interactions and may conceivably be relevant to mitigating or even resolving the conflict. We used a so-called Bethel problem-solving approach with our eastern African participants: the aim was to have them interact in such a way that trust and understanding would emerge during the first week. In the Belfast workshop we reluctantly resorted to a modified Tavistock or process-promoting technique: to enable the participants to organize associations of both Protestants and Catholics in strife-torn Belfast, we sought to have them understand how groups function. This objective we felt might be attained not by lecturing but by having the participants experience what it means to move from one group to another and to organize new groups composed of persons with different values or statuses. In the workshop, for example, we did not simply tell our fifty-six men and women that behavior varies with the group in which one is participating. Instead, within the course of a morning and part of an afternoon, we first broke them into small groups based on age (seven subgroups, each of which contained persons of roughly the same age), then on religion (Protestant, Catholic), and finally on sex (male, female). In each instance we did not announce the basis on which the subgroups had been formed. The participants themselves soon discovered their varying common interests as they spontaneously developed their own agenda, and thus they came to realize that they had been behaving differently as they moved from group to group.

Again, as our friendly critics suggest, it is possible, by isolating participants either by removing them from their normal milieu as we have done or by having them interact intensely in their usual environment, to change attitudes, feelings, or knowledge relatively quickly. They may, however, be only ostensibly polite to one another; they may develop friendships and understandings limited to the unusual, detached context in which they have been placed. The practical question in the pursuit of peace is whether the change will have an effect upon leaders in power and hence ultimately upon the conflict itself, or whether associations or committees are actually organized back home that will improve relations between the parties in conflict (cf. P). So much depends upon what the participants have learned and their consequent motivation to utilize the new information as well as upon the problems confronting them in their normal milieu. We might have had an important effect upon our friends from the Horn of Africa were it not for the fact that immediately after the workshop a coup was staged in Somalia and a new government came into power; eventually in Ethiopia the Emperor was deposed. Those changed conditions possibly affected whatever influence our participants could have exercised. The Belfast workshop seems to have affected some of the fifty-six volunteers who attended both in their private and public lives,[25] yet the effects were contaminated by publicity we received afterwards from a few persons adversely affected by the Tavistock method which had served its pedagogical purpose quite well but at the expense of a regrettable aftermath.

A different, very promising technique has been evolved by the Quakers; in fact their method of mediation or intervention dwarfs all contemporary efforts by private organizations or individuals.[26] Aside from their religious convictions, their attitudes toward nonviolence, and a strong motivation to act upon their beliefs, as previously indicated, they also assume that communication through their impartial offices will clear away misunderstandings and bring about a resolution of some conflicts. They have a long history of attempting to use their techniques of conciliation to settle or mitigate disputes and otherwise to reduce human suffering. They sought to stop the war between the Indians and the colonists in Rhode Island in 1675; to bring about peaceful settlement between the American colonies and England shortly before the Revolution; to prevent the conflict between Germany and Denmark over Schleswig-Holstein in the middle of the last century; to avert the Crimean war; to help rescue Jews and others from the Nazis; vainly after World War II to aid in abating bitter hostilities in the Middle East and also the deep differences between eastern and western blocs of countries, especially in connection with Berlin.[27] Recently their main effort has been to function as third-party conciliators between parties in conflict, such as in the disputes between India and Pakistan over Kashmir since independence or the civil war in Nigeria starting in 1966.

The first step is taken when one or more Friends feel "concerned" and have a religious impulse to "put God's love into action in some concrete situation of need." That concern is then appraised at a Quaker Meeting. There they examine the conflict in practical terms by considering their own available resources to deal with the problem, the experience of other Friends in the area, the avenues of communication to policy makers, and the members' general knowledge of the controversy. The original motive is thus transformed into action, or else a decision is reached that intervention is not likely to be fruitful. If the decision to attempt reconciliation is favorable, the procedure to follow is adopted. A conference may be called, for example, or a more indirect method may be employed. Here attention is focused upon that indirect method. Representatives establish contact with the parties in conflict and seek to clarify the issues. One Quaker leader reported informally his own activities in the Middle East in 1967:

Well, I went around asking people in Cairo, Jerusalem, Amman, and Beirut certain questions. The conventional things that Quakers have done—working with refugees, children, etc.—seemed not to be urgent needs. . . . The thing that everyone agreed upon was that the real nub of the problem was the political conflict situation . . . So we began to play with the idea of perhaps developing a kind of Quaker statement, reflecting the points of view of the different parties. . . . What we did then was to undertake a series of visits around the area and for the moment I couldn't tell you exactly how many times I've been around that circuit in the last three years.[28]

In short and in general: after securing the facts, including the emotional attitudes of both sides, an effort is made to formulate a solution that will be acceptable to both and to convey that message to the responsible leaders. By 1970 a committee of American Friends carrying out their mission in the Middle East had written fifteen drafts of a document[29] that was later published as a long report. The background of the conflict between Israel and her Arab neighbors was given in detail. This was followed by a presentation of various viewpoints ranging from those of the United Nations and the "Great Powers" to those of the Palestinian Arabs and the Israelis, including "World Jewry" and the oil companies. Then four suggestions for attaining "a practical peace settlement" were offered (psychological and emotional disengagement, military disengagement, structuring of a political settlement, and peacebuilding). At the end there appeared the assertion that some kind of peace was possible as well as "a Quaker expression of concern and an affirmation of peace" accompanied by appeals to the United Nations, the Arab states, and Israel.[30] There are, however, situations in which one side is more powerful than the other and no misunderstanding exists. Under these circumstances, some Quakers concede, confrontation rather than reconciliation ("awareness of latent or patent injustices") is sought, which in effect almost means taking sides.

The Quakers are able to function as mediators because of their worldwide reputation not only for impartiality but also for the impressive deeds associated with them. As humanitarians they bring relief in the concrete form of food and medical supplies to areas in need (for instance, to the Irish during the potato famine of 1848, to German children after World War I, and to the Biafrans at the end of the civil war in Nigeria in 1970). They have centers in various countries, particularly one at the United Nations in New York City, that try to function in connection with incipient or actual conflicts and that also administer relief. Their numerous efforts to promote contacts between peoples of different countries and thus to increase understanding will be mentioned in the next chapter. The distinguishing characteristic of all their efforts has been the unselfish, courageous religious motive, namely, somehow to help mankind. As a result, they have been almost always respected and admired by parties in conflict and have received the gratitude of those they have assisted.

Unquestionably assistance has been given, but have conflicts been mitigated by the Friends? Like all other efforts at mediation, no clear-cut evaluation is possible (cf. I). Available reports are blunt; thus in connection with the problem of East and West Berlin, the international affairs representative in Germany for the American Friends Service Committee reports that "needless to say, it was hardly the aspiration of the writer's two year's work to make a dramatic impact on the complex, many-layered situation surrounding a divided Germany."[31] Again, we do not know whether Quaker efforts might not have had some small, nonascertainable effect upon the conflicts that continued after or in spite of their best efforts.

No matter what third-party technique of mediation is employed, whether face-to-face contact or communication at a distance, the mediator may be in a position to facilitate understanding or agreement of some kind through the use of specific rhetorical devices. In a volume "intended to stimulate a mediator who is looking for some ways to loosen up a conflict situation or move it forward" and considered by its authors to be "not an answer book, but a toolbox," no fewer than sixty-three such devices have been collected on the basis of common sense and experience in mediations.[32] The suggestions are very concrete and are offered in the snappy tradition of *How to Win Friends and Influence People* or any other best-selling, self-improvement paperback. (See Chapter Appendix 9.1: "The Rational Approach".) In a similar vein, but on the level of individuals rather than groups, "a balance sheet schema" has been outlined which might enable leaders to make wiser decisions by offering them greater insight into themselves and the consequences of their decisions. It is recommended that they estimate the gains and losses for the self and one's significant contemporaries as well as an appraisal of whether a decision will be approved by the self and by those other persons.[33] In effect this means probing all available consequences (that is, trying to be "rational" in the sense mentioned in Chapter 4), which may or may not be feasible when war-peace is the problem. In their clinical practice, the authors of the schema report, they have contributed to the resolution of conflict between individuals by helping and counseling them as they filled out such a balance sheet. In other instances they have instructed their clients to role-play, first, the feelings they would have if they were to make one decision rather than another; and then, secondly, those feelings they imagine they would have as a result of coming to the second decision. The gap between these techniques and the decisions of political leaders, however, is great. And yet, mediators might be able to help leaders think through in advance the consequences of decisions and the feelings they attach thereto. In short, do they *really* want the window open or shut?

I permit an optimistic bias to be expressed. A large leap forward is made when some technique, whether touched upon in the foregoing discussion or not, facilitates the discovery of areas of agreement between antagonists.[34] An advocate of workshops has written:

. . . the conflict behaviour of communities and states comprises alterable components such as perception of external conditions, selection of goals from many possible values, choice of different means of attaining goals, and assessment of values and means in relation to assessments of costs of conflict.[35]

The emphasis should be on the "alterable components," for the parties in conflict must come to perceive their relations no longer in "unpeaceful categories" but in "a peaceful one"[36] (cf. P). Just as leaders are provided with memoranda concerning the economic, social, and political matters relevant to a pending negotiation, so conceivably, I say in dreams, workshops could be staged in advance to uncover the emotional issues likely to hinder negotiations and to uncover possible solutions. The findings could then be communicated to the participating decision makers who might or might not find them helpful. In any case, the search for innovative techniques must continue if the "defective social institution" of warfare is to be exposed and if peace is to be truly pursued.[37]

WORLD ORGANIZATIONS (#s 5, 6)

"It may be true that war will exist so long as the will to war exists, and that there can be no peace without the will to peace, but the absence or presence of international organizatons, such as councils and tribunals, is *part* cause of the existence of the will to war or the will to peace"[38] (cf. E). This view by a prolific, celebrated literary critic serves to introduce a banal but significant fact: almost wherever the search leads—whether to the past or present proposals of scholars, reformers, and sometimes even political leaders—some type of world organization is believed to be indispensable to the pursuit of peace. (cf. P) (See Chapter Appendix 9.2: Dreams Concerning a World Organization.) Underlying all, or almost all the proposals and indeed the world organizations themselves during this century are similar central ideas. First and most emphatic of all, in the words of an American general and president, "there can be no peace without law."[39] The same theme recurs again and again: "indisputably" history is supposed to demonstrate that "only one method" can compel men to accept "moral principles and standards of social conduct," that is, "Law"[40] (cf. P). The perennial villain of sovereignty appears in this context, for "we" must choose between it and "international law."[41] Lawyers and others who speak and write of the need for the rule of law describe in great detail the kind of "enforceable world law" that is needed to achieve such a goal. One stimulating treatise by two wise lawyers suggests several "principles" as guides. Essential, they think, are regulations against international violence that are "explicitly stated in constitutional and statutory form"; judicial tribunals to interpret and apply the antiviolence laws; "a permanent world police force" to "forestall or suppress" violators of the law; complete disarmament of all nations; "effective world machinery . . . to mitigate the vast disparities in the economic condition of various regions." These principles require that every nation or almost every one participate in the world peace authority. Conceivably they could be embodied in revisions of the United Nations Charter; or else there could be a new authority in "parallel" to the United Nations or a brand new world organization.[42] To avoid violence and war, in short, an authority is needed to which parties in conflict refer their disputes for compulsory arbitration; its decisions must be enforceable.

Two principal criticisms can be levelled against plans that would extend international law. They assume that existing laws, originally formulated to deal with a world that did not have to contend with current problems (energy shortages, newly independent countries, nuclear warfare), can be amended and brought up to date. Then, in the words of the ancient fable, who will bell the cat? It is all very well to advocate the rule of law, but how can the leaders of countries be convinced, first, that their government should join an organization or subscribe to a principle and, secondly, that it will obey the edicts?[43] Formally joining or agreeing in principle offers virtually no problem, but the rub comes sooner or later in practice. Few conflicts of any significance, as mentioned in Chapter 4, have been referred to the International Court of Justice; by and large, consequently, the court has not been accepted by all nations "as a normal method of settling their legal disputes."[44] The members of any society voluntarily surrender certain individual rights (such as the impulse to insult a deadly bore or to drive over the speed limit) because from earliest childhood on they are taught the advantages of such sacrifices. Similarly, the leaders and followers of modern nations must agree to relinquish whatever it is they mean by absolute sovereignty in return for a world order. The challenge is to make that reward seem more compelling than the appeals of nationalism. In the case of the latter, as cannot be too often repeated, the individual experiences so many immediate and meaningful rewards (those associated with a more or less common culture, a common language, a set of traditions) that, as a result, he appreciates the connection between his own welfare and his "nation." But an international body? When there is peace, such a body seems far removed from one's everyday existence and therefore unworthy of sacrifice. In the words of the moving song, when will they ever learn?

Or what will persuade them to learn? One scholar is convinced, largely on the basis of his analysis of the United Nations' International Labor Organization, that certain prerequisites have to be met if the "universal sharing" of values is to be achieved (cf. P). In my words, rather than his, a proposal fostering any human right must be considered desirable, if it is to be accepted, by the leaders in power and by many followers in the relevant countries; it must be broad in scope, it must be expressed so specifically and accompanied by procedures so concrete that the investigation and evaluation of violations are feasible; and it must be protected by some sort of international machinery.[45] These are of course ideal criteria and in effect they restate in less legal language the principles of "enforceable world law" reported two paragraphs ago. The outline sounds glorious until enforcement is mentioned; then comes the hitch: aspects of sovereignty must be relinquished.

A system of international law is facilitated by the undeniable fact that countries in the modern world are interdependent. Like it or not, the developing countries are slowly beginning in many but not all respects to resemble those in the West and in the Soviet bloc, with the result that they import materials considered strategic or relevant to their own rising expectations. Almost any international action, therefore, has repercussions far beyond national boundaries. Changes in the domestic policy of one country may also affect those of others, notably in connection with trade and monetary policies. When catastrophes occur, the International Red Cross and various governments seek to assist the victims. Few would question the contention that any international body like the United Nations, if peace is to be retained or attained, must face and try to solve the problem of raising "the living standards of the world's people."[46]

Various international organizations now exist whose functions are supposed to be, either directly or indirectly, that of peacekeeping, peacemaking, and peacebuilding. It is through them presumably that peace should be pursued more vigorously and effectively than it is at the present time; without any doubt whatsoever they must be strengthened. During two decades starting in 1951 the number of United Nations organizations remained constant, but the number of international nongovernment organizations increased by 73 percent and the number of international governmental organizations by 103 percent.[47] One of the knotty problems, therefore, for any world organization and for the United Nations in particular is the relation between the regional entities, such as NATO, the Warsaw Pact countries, the Arab League, the Council of Europe, the Organization of American States, the Organization of African Unity, on the one hand, and the central or worldwide organization on the other. From afar the arguments in favor of regional organizations seem compelling. Their members are located close to one another, they share common problems, they may follow similar traditions. Article 52 of the United Nations Charter, as already mentioned, states that "nothing in the present Charter precludes the existence of regional arrangements or agencies for dealing with such matters relating to the maintenance of international peace and security as are appropriate for regional action, provided that such arrangements or agencies and their activities are consistent with the Purposes and Principles of the United Nations." The proliferation of these regional organizations, however, has been motivated in part not by a desire to secure peace on a worldwide basis but as a reaction to the cold war and the consequent faith in deterrence through strength, by a loss of faith in the United Nations, and generally by the belief that coexistence is both necessary and desirable.[48] Instead of being stepping stones to the United Nations, they have come to assume some of its power and to render it less effective. The Soviet Union and the United States in particular have challenged the competence of the Security Council to judge situations they consider to be in their own spheres of influence,[49] which means they prefer their own regional organizations or bilateral negotiations. According to one view, therefore, the effectiveness of the United Nations in the future may depend upon reducing the competition offered by the various regional defense systems.[50] It may also be argued that these regional groups have been contributing to peace: some of their specific accomplishments have been mentioned earlier in this chapter; and their very existence means that member countries have relinquished somewhat their claim to absolute sovereignty, a positive step in the pursuit of peace.

The closest approximation to world government at present is of course the United Nations itself. As an organization it is imperfect and hence must be continually reevaluated. It includes all countries other than the two Koreas and Namibia. In addition, Switzerland has refused to participate for fear that in some way its role as a peaceful neutral might be jeopardized. The moment a country has shaken off its colonial power, it has applied immediately for membership and has been accepted. The formal description of United Nations machinery—submitting the dispute to the Security Council or the General Assembly by a party to the dispute or any member of the United Nations; debating the merits and demerits of the claims set forth by the contending parties; establishing special machinery to deal with the problem; achieving a cease-fire through various means; setting up procedures to settle the dispute (direct negotiation, referral to the International Court, establishment of a subsidiary organ); appointing a mediator or a small commission[51]—gives the vivid impression that the organization is equipped to deal with conflicts and even to settle them. For example: Article 38 of the Charter states that "the Security Council may, if all the parties to any dispute so request, make recommendations to the parties with a view to a pacific settlement of the dispute." Article 39: "The Security Council shall determine the existence of any threat to the peace, breach of the peace, or act of aggression and shall make recommendations to maintain or restore international peace and security." In addition, the Council "may decide what measures not involving the use of armed force are to be employed to give effect to its decisions'' (Article 41); but when it has determined that peaceful measures "would be inadequate or have proved to be inadequate,'' it "may take such action by air, sea, or land forces as may be necessary to maintain or restore international peace and security'' (Article 42). What more could a utopianist demand if he were asked to design a utopian world government? We seem to have here almost a perfect document, as perfect in its international implication as is the Sermon on the Mount for the individual in his interpersonal relations.

What, then, has gone wrong; why has not the United Nations Security Council exercised its authority rather than wait, as it usually does, until a party to the conflict brings the problem formally before that body? It is clear that actions by the United Nations have not prevented many of the major post-World War II disputes from resorting to violence and war. A glance backwards at the United Nations' predecessor, the League of Nations, is somewhat helpful. In 1935 Mussolini commanded his representatives to walk out of the league when Italy's invasion of Ethiopia was condemned; the Italian armies conquered the country; the league took no effective action other than to declare a boycott of Italy to which only lip service was paid. How could Mussolini's armies have been halted? Actually —a fact now overlooked—the league was able to settle thirty-five of the sixty-six disputes occurring between the two world wars, but only "if and when both litigants wanted to accept the arbitration awards and if and when . . . they did not exploit their disputes as a pretext for aggression."[52] Similarly the United Nations' principal difficulty has arisen largely from East-West controversies and from the decisions of the superpowers frequently to ignore available United Nations machinery. When the parties in conflict have called upon the United Nations (the dispute between the Netherlands and Indonesia in 1962, for example), that machinery has generally functioned effectively.

Being unable or unwilling to deal with the basic difficulty of the United Nations, friendly and unfriendly critics have sought ways to improve its functioning through superficial or sweeping changes in the way it now functions. The superficial include additional publicity and attention-getting through the mass media, displaying the United Nations flag more frequently, and composing an international anthem; lip service is paid to the possibility of developing "a second tongue for all."[53] Among the sweeping proposals is one to strengthen and enlarge the role of the "good offices" provided by the secretary-general,[54] in spite of the fact that in theory he has in the Charter all the authority he needs, that he almost always is considered to be impartial and neutral, and that he has or can acquire all the expertise needed to be effective. The United States State Department has favored "timely Council involvement in all situations endangering international peace" on an "earlier and more regular basis."[55] In actual fact, the definition of the secretary-general's functions has fluctuated with the views of the occupant of the position. At the outset, the great powers were supposed to cooperate to enforce the peace among the small powers.[56] Then in the days of Dag Hammarskjöld the United Nations tried to steer clear of East-West controversies and to concentrate upon minor conflicts between small nations not aligned with the big powers, upon problems arising from the liquidation of colonialism, and upon relatively minor and tangential disputes during the cold war.[57]

In sorrow, on the other hand, a perspicacious Canadian has become convinced that the United Nations is "unreformable." It was established before the nuclear age had begun and was then based on the assumption that the five permament members of the Security Council (China, France, the Soviet Union, the United Kingdom, and the United States) would use their military forces to police the world and thus prevent aggression. The Security Council has only limited military power to enforce its decisions. Every nation, no matter how large or small, has a single and hence an equal vote in the General Assembly. The thirty agencies of the United Nations have not been coordinated and receive very little central direction. In short, the "decision-making structure" of the United Nations has become "entirely unworkable."[58]

A functionalist approach to an unspecified world organization which may perhaps be more effective in the long run would first concentrate upon building organizations with specific functions which transcend national boundaries, such as communications, cultural exchanges, or economic cooperation. Only after "a world community of sentiment" is thereby established should consideration be given to a world government as such.[59] One does not, one should not anticipate planetary uniformity, yet for decades to come differences in cultures, economic development, beliefs, attitudes, and motives among the people of the countries of the world will remain so great that fruitful cooperation on every issue confronting a world organization cannot be anticipated (cf. V). This state of affairs would not suggest that the United Nations should be abandoned. It would merely point to the possibility that its effectiveness will increase as leaders of various countries achieve a more equal footing and understanding. The belief in absolute sovereignty may thus be gradually weakened.

A brief but relevant tangent: are the civil servants within any international organization, including the United Nations, likely to have a national rather than an international orientation? Their immediate impulse presumably is to reflect the interests of their own countrymen, for they have been so reared and in many instances so commanded by the foreign offices and other officials back home. Here is the same problem that arises in any legislative group within a democratic country: do the elected officials represent their constituents or the welfare of the entire country? Some congressmen in the United States place greater emphasis on their national or even international activities than they do on their actions in behalf of their own districts; in so doing, they may run the risk of not being reelected. Within the United Nations one hears again and again the conviction among the working staff that they are international servants and no longer representatives of their home country. In the limited experience of this writer, their conviction seems to be sincere; yet fairly frequently they may be recalled by their governments, and their national loyalty is not easily jettisoned. There is little evidence that members of the Security Council or the General Assembly submerge their national interests in behalf of the world government or world peace especially when matters pertaining to their own country are being discussed or debated, nor indeed are they really expected to do so.[60]

UNITED NATIONS PEACEKEEPING (#s 5, 6)

If the record of the United Nations in peacemaking and peacebuilding is not outstanding, its achievements in the area of peacekeeping are noteworthy. According to one scholar, "the three basic elements of the [United Nations] Charter system for maintaining international peace and security—peaceful settlement, enforcement action, and arms regulations—are closely interrelated. The evolution of peacekeeping has been in many respects a response to the failure to develop the second of these elements as originally planned."[61] Peacekeeping—the word does not appear in the Charter—thus can be considered a substitute for collective security as one step toward peacemaking and peacebuilding (cf. P): it enforces cease-fires and thus provides an opportunity for the parties in conflict to resolve or try to resolve their differences. In short, it exists as an ally to diplomacy, since it permits normal diplomacy to begin, continue, or resume.[62]

The United Nations Security Council has sought to implement its decisions concerning some of the ongoing disputes that have been placed on its agenda by dispatching observers, personal representatives of the secretary-general, mediators, police, and above all military forces to the area in question. The parties to the dispute—often referred to as the host country or countries by members of the staff of the secretary-general—must almost always first agree, however, to accept a peacekeeping force composed of troops and other personnel from the governments offering their services. This procedure was followed even during the chaos in the Congo in 1960 after Prime Minister Lumumba called upon the United Nations to help his regime restore law and order.[63] When Greece in 1946 complained to the Security Council concerning the assistance being given communist guerrillas inside its borders by Albania, Bulgaria, and Yugoslavia, the council first investigated the situation, then could not agree on a resolution as a result of Soviet objections, and hence eventually referred the problem to the General Assembly; that body established a United Nations Special Committee on the Balkans to help settle the dispute; the committee was impotent because it was unacceptable to the Soviet Union and its three allies.[64] In other conflicts, as will be indicated, the council's mandate has been implemented more directly and more successfully. With few exceptions (Britain in Cyprus, France in Lebanon), the superpowers have contributed to peacekeeping, not personnel, but supplies and transportation: for political reasons their personnel have been found unacceptable as peacekeepers either to the disputants or to the Security Council from which the authority of a force comes.[65]

The peacekeeping personnel or forces carry out the council's mandate for an area in various ways. They patrol the borders or regions separating the parties in conflict. They cooperate with the local police or they temporarily function as police in order to safeguard civil liberties and otherwise to enforce the legal system and prevent crime. They report violations of cease-fires or of other agreements such as those concerning troop withdrawals. They interpose troops in a buffer or neutral zone between the armed forces of the factions or the opposing parties.[66]

The significant contribution of United Nations forces in the Middle East, the Congo, and Cyprus cannot be gainsaid, but their role has necessarily been restricted to the Security Council's mandate. From a military standpoint their dependence upon the 38th Floor of the United Nations building in New York City—jargon for the office of the secretariat and the corps of dedicated international civil servants who assist him—creates difficulties for the commander when split-second decisions have to be made regarding the needs of United Nations troops to protect themselves or when changing interpretations concerning the rights and privileges of the disputants are required by new situations. It seems obvious, nevertheless, that ultimate authority must rest not with the military but with civilians who represent the United Nations itself and its participating governments.

Although in July of 1974 United Nations forces, both military and police, were stationed in Cyprus when Turkish troops arrived after the Makarios government had been overthrown by right-wing elements within the Greek community, they used not military means but verbal appeals to try to stop the fighting and the atrocities; the United Nations commanders simply had no mandate to intervene directly. Fighting in fact ceased after United Nations resolutions in New York had been passed and, perhaps more important, after the Turkish army decided to make no further advances following a second offensive. But during the fighting, United Nations personnel succeeded in effecting a cease-fire at the international airport in Nicosia and elsewhere. When fighting stopped, they performed innumerable humanitarian missions, including the exchange of refugees from both sides, and patrolled a buffer zone between the two communities. In the Congo (now Zaire) they did in fact reestablish law and order. Other peaceful goals have been achieved in those two areas and elsewhere: arbitrating water rights; locating missing persons as well as the dead and wounded; the clearing of bombs and mines; restoring electric power; providing medical services; helping to repair damaged houses; protecting and restoring archaeological sites. In Namibia military and civilian forces planned to supervise an election.[67]

Three articles in the United Nations Charter seem to provide ideal machinery for peacekeeping. In addition to Article 42, cited above, which permits military action of all kinds "necessary to maintain or restore international peace and security," Article 48 suggests that "the action required to carry out the decisions of the Security Council for the maintenance of international peace and security shall be taken by all the Members of the United Nations or by some of them, as the Security Council may determine," and Article 49 states that "the members of the United Nations shall join in affording mutual assistance in carrying out the measures decided upon by the Security Council." To date these articles, like the more sweeping ones concerning peacemaking and peacebuilding, have been only partially implemented as a result of suspicions and disagreements among the superpowers. With few exceptions, moreover—for example, the Syrian forces in Lebanon in 1978—the regional organizations have not assumed peacekeeping responsibilities: they have simply agreed "to perform the function of self-defense against armed attack" upon their own members.[68] The handicaps facing the United Nations peacekeeping efforts, consequently, must be considered in some detail.

From a military standpoint, the United Nations lacks a proper organization. A military staff committee was originally established to assist the Security Council with respect to all military matters but, as a result of political differences among members of the council, it has become virtually impotent.[69] The secretary-general has only a single military liason staff officer[70] who by himself lacks the staff to anticipate, plan, and carry out peacekeeping operations. He has no regular army to activate, even though it would appear that the Charter's Article 29 ("The Security Council may establish such subsidiary organs as it deems necessary for the performance of its functions") would permit the creation of such a force. He has no central planning staff and no central staff school. He may not even stockpile weapons since he cannot expend funds that have not been authorized by the Security Council; the weapons and supplies at the United Nations dump in Pisa have previously been used in peacekeeping operations and are frequently out-of-date. Instead he is dependent upon officers and men from the lesser powers only when they are acceptable both to the council and to the disputing powers or host countries.

Peacekeeping is not made any easier by the fact that the secretary-general must usually engage in complicated negotiations of a formal and informal sort with the countries volunteering a military or police force and with the disputing countries or factions. Article 43 of the Charter obligates all United Nations members "to make available to the Security Council . . . armed forces, assistance, and facilities . . . necessary for the purpose of maintaining international peace and security," but it also has not been implemented because, again, of "disagreements among the major powers."[71] A limited number of governments—notably the four Nordic countries (Sweden, Norway, Denmark, and Finland), Canada, Ireland, Italy, Iran, the Netherlands, India, Austria, Brazil, Yugoslavia, and New Zealand—has at one time or another trained forces for peacekeeping operations.[72] The Nordic countries have established a joint training system to standardize peacekeeping procedures and have divided the contents of that curriculum among themselves so that one country assumes responsibility for one or more of the five components: Military Police Duties, Movement Control Duties, Observer Duties, Logistic Duties, and Headquarters Staff Duties.[73] Simulation is (or should be) used during the training. Aside from arousing interest and thus facilitating learning, the exercise emphasizes the numerous variables and hence the different solutions (some no better or worse than the others) associated with situations confronting peacekeeping forces.

The secretary-general's office is able more readily to persuade countries to supply observers rather than troops or police because fewer numbers and fewer risks are involved. The countries mentioned above as well as others volunteer from time to time to send troops for a variety of reasons: the prestige from participating; the opportunity for their armed forces to gain experience and to test equipment abroad; an idealistic desire to advance the cause of peace and to strengthen the international system; a minor reduction in domestic unemployment; the expectation of long-term reciprocity by other nations; and on occasion a financial advantage (reimbursement from the United Nations may be greater than the costs). But there are also disadvantages aside from possible financial losses: the probability of casualties; reduction in defense readiness at home; political complications; and the separation of the force's personnel from their families. Some governments, consequently, prefer a limited involvement. Except for small numbers before 1956 and an occasional officer in an advisory capacity since that time, United States forces have not participated in peacekeeping operations because the American government has not been considered impartial.[74] United States planes, however, have been provided to transfer troops of other countries to the conflict areas where they were being stationed; and sophisticated electronic equipment was effectively operated by the one hundred fifty Americans, comprising the enclave of the Sinai field mission, to detect violations of the Egyptian-Israeli agreement concerning that area. Also directly through financial contributions to particular peace-keeping operations, often without reimbursement, and indirectly to the overall United Nations budget, the United States has given significant financial support to all peacekeeping operations.[75]

Another handicap confronting the United Nations stems from the fact that the office of the secretary-general has no intelligence-gathering organization of its own. It even eschews the military word "intelligence" and substitutes "information," in part to indicate that it does not engage in covert operations to obtain the data it needs. It is dependent, consequently, upon miscellaneous sources, such as governments and the mass media, for the information necessary to guide decisions concerning the mandates to be transmitted to peacekeeping forces. Private individuals may be used to negotiate or carry on conversations with nongovernment guerrilla forces. A field representative of the commander may reconnoiter the area to which United Nations troops are to be sent and thus at least secure basic information about the terrain and its resources.

As a result of the nature of the task and of the constraints placed upon him and the secretary-general, the force commander in the field is faced with very difficult, delicate problems. He must improvise his operating procedure because each situation is unique (cf. V), because he commands an international force from a handful of countries, and because the United Nations has not been able to evolve or require, in military terms, a standard operating procedure. He is, however, assisted by the secretary-general's office which has had years of experience in coping with new peacekeeping challenges. With or without help from a United Nations political adviser attached to his staff, the commander must engage in negotiations with the disputing parties, in order to carry out the United Nations mandate, whether those parties be established governments or guerrilla forces; hence he requires prior training and briefing. His peacekeeping task is further complicated by the fact that any government is privileged to withdraw from his command its own forces for whatever reason it finds compelling, provided permission from the Security Council has been obtained. When a new emergency occurs elsewhere and the United Nations is short of troops or police, some of the commander's force may be dispatched to the other troubled area. A peacekeeping army or police composed of men and women from various nations, moreover, faces a set of intricate problems ranging from not having a common language (which makes communication between units difficult) to arriving with armaments and vehicles requiring different spare parts not easily or quickly available—or not perhaps utilizable when instructions are given, for example, in nonmetric units to mechanics accustomed to the metric system.

The precarious nature of peacekeeping is indicated by the fact that parties to the dispute may require the withdrawal of the force. The Egyptian government made such a request in May 1967; after some diplomatic activity, the request was reluctantly granted; and the six-day war with Israel followed.[76] Previously the Israeli government had not allowed a force to be stationed on its soil.

A particularly difficult problem for the commander and his forces has been that of knowing under what conditions weapons may be employed. The principle seems clear: "With the exception of Korea, all U. N. operations have been based on the premise that peaceful and not enforcement methods will be used to achieve solutions in conflict and violence situations."[77] The definition of self-defense and its implementation while executing a United Nations mandate are, nevertheless, not equally self-evident. When fired upon and if feasible, United Nations forces first issue verbal commands to the offenders, then shoot into the air, and as a last resort may fire upon the recalcitrant or aggressive party. Tear gas has also been countenanced. In some situations, moreover, "force" may be applied: in self-defense; for the sake of safety; to prevent a forced withdrawal; to resist being disarmed or being prevented from carrying out United Nations responsibilities.[78] The killing or even wounding of United Nations soldiers is a sad event not only for the usual self-evident reasons but also because of its unfavorable effects upon nationals back home. Usually, however, the opposing parties hesitate to fire upon a peacekeeping force because they would avoid condemnation by the international community.

The countries supplying troops and police do not or cannot follow standardized procedures. Generally a government volunteering troops must be prepared to equip and supply them, although another country may transport them to the troubled area; for less-developed and poorer countries, logistical support may come from other donors. The force's mandate is seldom amended by the Security Council even when conditions in the field have changed. In addition, that mandate must be renewed every three to six months and the troops themselves, especially volunteers who may or may not sign on for another tour, are rotated at stated intervals, neither of which arrangements makes for stability of operations or facilitates long-range planning.

There are miscellaneous problems that plague peacekeeping operations. The troops of the force commander must have freedom of movement, but they have often been restricted by one or more of the disputants. Supplies must be renewed; on occasion their arrival has been delayed not only by the paperwork required before they can be authorized by the 38th floor and by the time it takes to transport them to the areas, but also by local customs officers. Some of the troops joining the force have been regular soldiers trained in peacekeeping, some have been recruited from a standby force, but others may have had little or no training for peacekeeping as such.

As a result of these handicaps, it is not to be wondered that, according to many critics, the present United Nations peacekeeping must be considered inadequate. The United Nations itself, it should be clear, needs a planning staff and a reserve force of its own when a chain of command and trained personnel are to be quickly assembled and dispatched during an emergency; when a solution is to be found for the "peculiar" problems facing peacekeeping operations; and when cooperation from naval and air forces is occasionally required.[79] Even though, to maintain peace, a police force is obviously needed that is "truly international, highly mobile, and able to decide quickly that action is necessary,"[80] to date the United Nations lacks both the funds and the authorization to have such a force. This state of affairs is likely to remain unchanged as long as the superpowers mistrust one another and as long as voluntary contributions, by some nations and not by others, are needed to pay the high costs of each peacekeeping operation. To be sure, the secretariat attempts to facilitate the work of peacekeeping forces and to interpret their mandates. Even though small, it has been accused—unjustly I think—of being too interested in perpetuating its own existence.

The United Nations Special Committee on Peacekeeping Operations (the so-called Committee of 33, that is, representing thirty-three nations) has been concerned not with planning actual peacekeeping but with disagreements over policy problems. Its members, moreover, have reached no decision on any significant issue largely as a result of acrimony between the Soviet Union and the United States. It has been unable even to agree concerning the contents of a peacekeeping manual.

In this context it is appropriate to refer to the International Peace Academy which has written and published a *Peacekeeper's Handbook* and which informally and unofficially has performed or supplemented some of the United Nations' functions with reference to peacekeeping. Its skeleton staff and consultants include persons who have had practical peacekeeping experience in various parts of the world (retired military officers, retired and active diplomats from different countries) as well as members of university faculties. It has a close, informal connection with the United Nations. Being private and hence independent of governments, it possesses a greater flexibility than United Nations organizations such as UNITAR and UNESCO which must receive official approval before embarking upon new ventures. It has organized international seminars attended by military officers and foreign service personnel from numerous countries, and it has published educational materials in line with its objectives. The seminars, financed by private donors or by governments which generously provide subsidies or pay the tuition fees for the men from their countries who attend, have largely concentrated upon instruction for peacekeeping.

The *Peacekeeper's Handbook* has been designed to help standardize procedures for countries supplying troops and police. It has been used in fact by some of the countries in the course of training their troops for service with the United Nations and also by officers of those troops as they carry out the United Nations mandate in troubled areas. Its aim is "to familiarize the peacekeeper with the practical and physical skills and procedures commonly practised in the United Nations' operations and missions."[81] The *Handbook* concisely summarizes the objective of the training program sponsored by the academy as well as by the countries contributing troops to peacekeeping:

Most of the soldierly qualities developed through the training systems of national armies are basic to any military operation—for instance, you cannot do without discipline or a corporative morale. But where the weapon used is that of negotiation and mediation and not the self-loading rifle, some of those inbred qualities of a soldier need extra emphasis and development. . . . emphasis needs to be placed on the essential qualities of observation, patience, endurance, vigilance, quick reaction and response, initiative and leadership. . . . The professional soldier with all his excellent attributes and training is not necessarily the best peacekeeper.[82]

In spite of all the political and logistical complications, the secretary-general has sometimes been able to dispatch peacekeeping forces to troubled areas within a few days after the Security Council's decision. This feat is accomplished because his office, through anticipating—correctly or not—the decision, has made informal arrangements with the countries supplying the forces. In a few instances the International Peace Academy even more informally has assisted in sounding out governments in advance. Clearly it takes time to alert personnel and provide the logistical support required to mount a peacekeeping force and to make the United Nations presence known in the area; careful preparations are essential. An official of the United Nations, however, has indicated privately that a hastily assembled force has one advantage: the diplomatic haggling encouraged by protracted preparation is circumvented and some efficiency is thereby gained.

Three practical problems associated with peacekeeping are relegated to chapter appendixes: the qualifications of peacekeepers (Chapter Appendix 9.4), the relations between peacekeepers and the host country (Chapter Appendix 9.5), and the relations among the peacekeepers themselves (Chapter Appendix 9.6). Here attention is directed to some of the consequences of peacekeeping. First, countries supplying troops who have not been previously trained in peacekeeping techniques conceivably derive a secondary if not very probable benefit. Their troops, as a result of special instruction and experience in the field, develop skills useful in controlling crowds and the "illegal movement of personnel and weapons" and in maintaining order. In the future they may be equipped by the United Nations with tranquilizers and gasses that cause "temporary incapacitation" without leading to permanent damage.[83] These skills can be utilized back home to quell insurrections and terrorists and thus to bolster a regime, for better or for worse. In an indirect, very minor way, peacekeeping in this respect may strengthen a government's status quo and block revolution or change.

To date, United Nations peacekeeping forces have not contributed appreciably to peacemaking on a formal basis because—again—this function has not been within their mandate. Inevitably, however, they have been the vehicle through which contacts between the disputants have occurred. They always establish or try to establish "a good working relationship with the contending parties,"[84] so that some negotiation, mediation, or arbitration is required on a level "lower" than that at which diplomats have previously operated or are operating.[85] The United Nations itself has recognized the need to combine peacekeeping and peacemaking, so that the secretary-general continually tries to promote negotiations between the parties in conflict by bringing their representatives together. A special representative of his has been stationed in Cyprus who, until the troubles in 1974, presided over the intercommunal talks between the Greek and Turkish communities. In early 1979 engineers from Greek and Turkish Cypriot governments met under United Nations auspices and agreed to construct a common sewage system for Cyprus' capital, Nicosia; but this laudable contact between the two sides had no immediate effect upon the political settlement of the divided country, and the overall negotiations remained deadlocked.

A United Nations peacekeeping force, as has been repeatedly emphasized, requires the prior consent of the host country or countries. The secretary-general does not dispatch a force to prevent what the Security Council considers to be a threat to the peace unless such consent has been previously obtained. This means, therefore, that the council or the United Nations in general must wait until its attention is officially called to a conflict *after* and not before it is already in progress and has often reached "uncontrollable proportions" (Sinai in 1956 and 1973; Lebanon in 1978) or when one or both parties to the dispute seek a settlement with the assistance of the United Nations (India-Pakistan, 1941; West Irian, 1962).[86] Should this policy be changed? To answer the question by ignoring reality, let the undoubtedly valid assumption be made that, if ever there could be a force about to wage a so-called just or preventative war or to use force on occasion in behalf of a "good" cause, such a force should come from the United Nations. It is, however, chilling to recall Marshal Pilsudski's advice to France in 1933: overthrow Hitler while he is still weak. If this had been done, mankind would have been saved untold misery. Such a move, however, would have violated "the *principle* of noninterference in the internal affairs" of a nation; according to that principle, Germany had the "*right*" to choose its own leader and form of government.[87] A United Nations force, rather than France, might have accomplished the mission. It is impossible, nevertheless, to imagine that officials of the League of Nations or the present United Nations or anyone else in authority would have agreed with Pilsudski; Germany's sovereignty—that nasty villain—could not be violated, they would have righteously asserted. Any host country, however, accepts some limitation upon its sovereignty by permitting forces to enter its territory, but this abdication is voluntary.[88] Even if the absolute value of sovereignty were to be modified so that a peacekeeping or peacemaking force could be dispatched without the consent of the parties in conflict, a momentous problem would remain unsolved: is there any reason to believe that the decision of a third party to interfere with the internal or external affairs of another country is important, just, or correct? The interventions by third-party countries are suspect because they have too often been employed to rationalize declarations of war. Who should judge the justification of an intervention before it occurs? The United Nations may be an international body, but its decisions, whether originating in the Security Council or the General Assembly, are made by individuals with biases engendered by their home governments. Perhaps the International Court of Justice might be expected to give a less prejudiced, more judicious decision, but its judges always move cautiously and they are also human and hence fallible. And yet, and yet, as Marshal Pilsudski recommended, the best of mankind judged or could or should have judged Hitler to be evil before he perpetrated more of his evil deeds. Maybe yes, maybe no; it is much easier to identify a conflict and its evil consequences after than before the fact (I).

Some United Nations officials privately believe that peacekeeping to be effective must often be based on what is called a diluted form of consent. In the spring of 1979 when General Amin was overthrown by an outside force consisting of Ugandan exiles and Tanzanian troops, and also later at a summit meeting of the Organization of African Unity that summer, some African leaders who had had no love for that ruthless dictator and who favored the human rights so brutally violated by his regime nevertheless condemned Tanzania for invading Uganda: the principle of sovereignty and the sacredness of existing borders between states embodied in the OAU charter they considered more compelling than that of human rights. The president of Tanzania, Nyerere, argued that Amin had previously invaded his country, which was true enough but not a complete justification for toppling him. No, Nyerere had obtained the consent of the Ugandans in exile, and he could well have assumed that many, perhaps the majority of Ugandans inside Uganda would have consented to the military intervention if they had had the opportunity to express their view. Once more, however, it must be confessed, if invasion in behalf of just causes is to be sanctioned, encouragement might be given to unjust invasions.

By and large the chief accomplishment of the various United Nations peacekeeping forces has been the restoration and maintenance of peace, at least temporarily, wherever they have been dispatched. They have been stationed in a limited number of places where conflict has broken out: in regions of interest both to the Soviet Union and the Western powers (Korea, Cyprus, the Balkans, Lebanon), and in countries newly liberated from colonial rule (Congo, New Guinea). They have not been called upon to function in countries closely connected with the Soviet Union (Hungary; Czechoslovakia) or in countries undergoing civil strife (Northern Ireland, Nigeria).[89] On the other hand, when peacekeeping forces have moved into an area, they have served as a deterrent because, as mentioned above, ordinarily neither party to a dispute wishes to be responsible for shooting them and then to be accused of aggression.[90] As I have listened to United Nations officials, both civilian and military, report the constraints under which they operate, I have been deeply impressed with what their forces have nevertheless been able to accomplish. During peacekeeping interludes, an opportunity is offered the civilian leaders of the host countries to pursue peace, a real peace.

In theory, perhaps in practice, nevertheless, the apparent advantages of peacekeeping—the saving of human lives which are always precious, the alleviation of misery, the possibility of peacebuilding—must be challenged. Will opposing parties reach a more lasting, a more just peace when they have this opportunity to negotiate, more or less leisurely, and come to terms, *or* when in the absence of a peacekeeping force they are more strongly motivated to negotiate in order to bring the ongoing strife to an end? With the exception of the Congo, peacekeeping has not led very quickly to peacemaking or peacebuilding. For almost two decades the presence of a United Nations observer force kept the peace in Kashmir, but India and Pakistan did not resolve their controversy as to who should possess that territory. Similarly another United Nations force prevented bloodshed in Cyprus after July of 1974 and thus enabled the Greek community to restore a bustling, vigorous economy and the Turkish community to establish its own political autonomy and also to strive to achieve a more independent economy; but the basic political problems between the two parties remained unresolved. Peacekeeping, in short, may serve to strengthen the status quo: it removes for the time being the conviction that an international crisis exists since its essential characteristic is "the perpetuation of a dangerously high probability of war";[91] the dispute becomes "an accepted and semi-permamanent part of the way of life in the area" and thus reduces the "sense of urgency" to find a peaceful solution;[92] in fact, "the political relations among the disputants at the time that peacekeeping occurs may be solidified."[93] Even enthusiastic, experienced peacekeepers admit that "peacekeeping by itself inevitably tends to prolong rather than to resolve conflict," but it "contains and constrains violence" and "aims to induce an atmosphere of calm in which a peaceful settlement can be negotiated"[94] (cf.P).

Perhaps, therefore, the parties in conflict ought to feel obligated to resolve their differences when they accept a peacekeeping force, for they thus are the beneficiaries of the funds expended to maintain the force, funds that come at least in part from the governments providing the force and hence from their taxpayers. Possibly also when the Security Council promulgates or renews a mandate, it should specify that the mandate will not be renewed in the future and that, under almost all conceivable circumstances, the force will be withdrawn. Settle your differences, in short, within a finite period or else you run the risk of having the conflict break out again, and then you cannot expect the United Nations once more to bail you out.

It would be pleasant to be able to conclude this chapter on a cheerful, cheering note, but it now appears that all the instruments for peacekeeping, peacemaking, and peacebuilding are imperfect. Conflicts are not submitted for arbitration to the International Court of Justice. Edicts of the United Nations are usually unenforceable. Perhaps it is fair to maintain that the United Nations has been more successful at peacekeeping than at peacemaking or peacebuilding, but peacekeeping is only the first step. Humanitarian efforts to make war slightly more humane fail, as Vietnam has demonstrated. Virtually all peace plans either advocate or assume the reduction or elimination of armaments, or at the very least some form of "controlled disarmament" or "arms control"[95]—with relatively little success except for doubtful gestures like the several SALTs so long and so agonizingly produced. Nevertheless some successes in the pursuit of peace are scored, some conflicts are mitigated, some lives are saved, some barbarities are avoided. Imperfect as they are, the international efforts to establish a world organization or a world community may accomplish something either in the long or the short run. The psychological effects of communications condemning violations of international agreements should not be overlooked:[96] leaders and followers may well experience pangs of conscience when they contemplate abrogating such agreements or after they have done so. And so communication in a broad sense must be considered in the final chapter.

CHAPTER APPENDIXES

9.1 THE RATIONAL APPROACH (#s 3, 5, 6)

Most but not all the suggestions offered in a volume with the intriguing title of *Handbook of Mediation* seek to change the protagonists' mode of judging a conflict by changing their beliefs. The exceptions are directed toward feelings and attitudes and include ideas like the following: reward "constructive work with personal credit"; stimulate "symbolic gestures of good feeling"; organize "a session for 'letting off steam.' "[97] Otherwise the basic assumption seems to be that, as in a court of law, the participants are rational and will change their beliefs either when they are offered new evidence almost in a legal sense or when somehow they are induced to view the conflict in a different light. In detail, as it were, we must understand the consequences of what we shall gain if we win and forego if we lose during a negotiation; just as important, we must understand what they stand to win or lose; they must make the same kind of analysis of themselves and of us; perhaps then both of us can view the conflict in a different light and agree to a more or less satisfactory resolution. Here are examples of the headings in the *Handbook*:

How about preparing and discussing some balance sheets of each party's present perceived choice?
Are the parties aware of the importance of inventing?
How about changing the scope of a proposed agreement?
How about using a simple analogy?
How about asking for contingent offers?
How about making proposed promises more credible?
How about using check lists to stimulate thinking?

This approach has been expressed by the senior author in an earlier publication that also has an inviting title, *International Conflict for Beginners*. The volume offers a so-called "map" which can serve as an accurate summary of its contents. Four questions are asked which are placed below in capital letters. Each gives rise to three other questions, the first of which represents the "Demand" ("the decision desired by us"), the second the "Offer" ("the consequences of making the decision"), and third the "Threat" ("the consequences of not making the decision"):

1. WHO?   Who is to make the decision? Who benefits if the decision is made? Who gets hurt if the decision is not made?

2. WHAT?   Exactly what decision is desired? If the decision is made, what benefits can be expected; what costs? If the decision is not made, what risks; what potential benefits?

3. WHEN?   By what time does the decision have to be made? When, if ever, will the benefits of making the decision occur? How soon will the consequences of not making the decision be felt?

4. WHY?   What makes this a right, proper, and lawful decision? What makes these consequences fair and legitimate? What makes consequences fair and legitimate?[98]

The primer itself advances various suggestions in popular terms for settling conflicts, such as (to quote a few of the chapter headings): "Give them a yessable proposition"; "Making threats is not enough"; "Ask for a different decision"; "Make the most of legitimacy." Similarly, in discussing the Middle East, the same author has suggested that progress in a negotiation can often be made if a conflict is "fractionated" into its component parts.[99]

Thus an omnibus agreement may be impossible to achieve, but the parties may be able to come to terms regarding trade, cultural relations, or a change in boundaries.

In general, this rational approach is a bit glib and somewhat of an over-simplification, yet its aim is praiseworthy: let people know that solutions are possible when they direct their attention to additional factors and possibilities. It has, however, one glaring defect: the mediator or the intervenor is not told precisely when a particular technique should be employed. For this reason, as illustrated above in connection with the *Handbook*, many of the suggestions are phrased tentatively by being introduced with "How about . . . ?" The defect is both understandable and excusable: too many factors are involved in a negotiation to be able to specify at what point a given technique will prove useful. It is extremely valuable, nevertheless, for a negotiator or intervenor to have at his disposal this rich, provocative collection of possibilities from which to choose during the give-and-take of the negotiating session.

9.2 DREAMS CONCERNING A WORLD ORGANIZATION (# 5)

Kant, in an essay called "Perpetual Peace," which largely defended the status quo with respect to territorial boundaries and, to a certain extent, the concept of sovereignty, nevertheless wrote that "a state of Peace among men . . . is not the *natural* state," "the state of Peace must, therefore, be *established*"; hence "the right of nations shall be founded on a federation of free states."[100] Of the twenty-four notable peace plans presented between 1250 and 1890, seven advocated a world state and twelve a federation of European or Christian countries.[101] Other reviews and analyses make essentially the same point, and also sometimes indicate that organizations falling short of being worldwide—bilateral arrangements, regional groupings —may postpone war, but eventually fail to achieve the objective either of reducing international tension or of eliminating war.[102] Many of these noble ideas eventually become amusingly dated. After trenchantly criticizing the various "preventives of war" then being discussed in the 1920s, a distinguished psychologist considered "force as necessary support of law and order"; therefore he advocated as "the police power" of the International Court of Justice and the League of Nations an international air fleet travelling at the speed of 200 or more miles per hour, with commercial planes limited to a speed of 100.[103] Usually modern proposals combine a plea for a world organization with other ideas which may or may not, in my opinion, run contrary to the notion of world government.[104] Some of the plans are worked out in casual detail, as when a lawyer indicates the kind of constitution necessary to achieve what he calls a World Alliance: "my purpose in writing this book is to give the people of the world my recommendation for the establishment of a worthy and dependable international organization to insure permanent peace by honorable means in the entire world."[105] Another writer suggests various properly complicated alternatives for transforming "the world that is to the world that might be." His blueprint projects "a power authority nexus for the year 2000 that has the following relationship to that which exists as of 1974" (the year of his proposals): "A United Nations Organization or its equivalent, with a doubled size and status"; and "a set of universal functional agencies that have four times their present size and status."[106]

9.3 QUALIFICATIONS OF MEDIATORS AND INTERVENORS[107] (# 1, 2, 3c, 5)

Really adequate data are lacking concerning the qualifications of mediators and intervenors since they vary with the conflict in question and the individuals toward whom the effort is directed (cf. V, I). The parameters of the problem, nevertheless, can be explored by bringing together and unabashedly stealing the ideas proposed by experienced persons,[108] by organizations such as the Society of Friends,[109] and to a lesser degree by investigators toiling in the pure but artificial atmosphere of social science laboratories.[110] For purposes of verbal economy in this appendix, mediators and intervenors will be called *facilitators*; the enterprise which they sponsor will be referred to as a *workshop*.

Demographic Characteristics. The effective facilitator requires status that enables him to be considered competent and trustworthy. That status may result from past achievements or from membership in some organization, such as an international group or a university, which itself has the required prestige. Recently individual Americans have had difficulty establishing their credibility because their nationality evokes suspicions concerning a possible affiliation with the CIA. Other demographic attributes are difficult to specify. If participants are prejudiced concerning the competency of women (for example, believing that they should be subservient), then the facilitator should be a male; the battle for female equality can be fought in some other arena or at some other time. Undoubtedly chronological maturity is an asset: it is widely believed that wisdom is acquired with advancing age, at least before the onset of senility. Membership in the same racial or ethnic group as some or all of the participants may be helpful or harmful, helpful by increasing knowledge or trust, harmful by jeopardizing neutrality.

The facilitator must also be trusted by the actual decision makers of the governments in conflict. He must perhaps secure their permission to invite participants to the workshop. He must be able somehow to convince those governments that he has selected competent participants to whom officials will listen after the workshop is over; otherwise whatever is accomplished will not be communicated to those in power and hence will be ineffective.

Motivation. The motivation to facilitate must be very high, for the facilitator is in a precarious role and hence is likely to experience stress before, during, and after the workshop. Beforehand, he must often raise the necessary funds from the sponsoring organization to which he belongs or, if he is operating alone, from other sources. Frequently fund-raising requires convincing one's intellectual inferiors that the project is worthwhile; in any case, begging is not pleasurable and requires stamina. Logistical arrangements, unless there is a competent staff, demand attention to detail that can be both taxing and boring. Since he is responsible for the enterprise, the facilitator may be blamed for whatever malfunctions; he becomes a highly visible and convenient scapegoat, whether or not his role is active or passive. If he fails or some of the participants are dissatisfied with the outcome—and some are bound to be—he may be held accountable; his ability to lead other workshops in the future may suffer. My own limited personal experience in intervention suggests that, try as hard as one can, it may be impossible to convince potential participants as they are being recruited that a workshop can be a rigorous and unpleasant undertaking. Afterwards, consequently, the facilitator may be accused of failing to obtain informed consent and is vigorously attacked.

Motivation as well as other factors in the personality of the facilitator will depend upon the duration of his facilitating role. He may be a professional or semiprofessional, in which case his energies must be continual and his reputation for future work may always be at stake. Or he may intervene on only a single occasion; then the strain may be less and his reputation, if not his pride, largely irrelevant.

The sources of a strong drive are various. The facilitator's profession may be to negotiate or arbitrate; thus are brought into play all the factors related to occupational status and reputation. He may be motivated by religious or philosophical convictions that emphasize the evil nature of force or war. Academic individuals may wish to test theories in order to contribute to knowledge, to the length of their publication list, or to both. Possibly, too, some facilitators seek to demonstrate that their brand of facilitation is superior to that of others toiling in the same vineyard; and they may have conscious or unconscious urges to exercise power over the participants.

Knowledge. Quite obviously the facilitator must be acquainted with the method he would employ to recruit participants and passively to supervise or actively to lead the workshop once it has begun. Organizations like the Friends transmit such information to their facilitators; the chairman at Quaker workshops is reported "to provide a sense of continuity, in much the same way as a 'clerk' at meetings of the Society of Friends acts to provide continuity and direction."[111] Special training centers exist, such as the National Training Laboratory in Bethel, Maine, and the Tavistock Clinic in London, which offer instruction in their particular, distinctive techniques. In any case, the facilitator must have a plan regarding the kind of interaction among the participants he would stimulate and the ways, therefore, in which understanding among them can be obtained. A passive facilitator who plans exercises for the participants must know, either on the basis of theory or practice, the kinds of settings likely to produce mutual trust, to increase self-knowledge, to make participants aware of their own stereotypes or of their tendency to project their own hatreds or insecurities upon their opponents, and so on. In some workshops, particularly those conducted according to Tavistock principles, the facilitators must be acquainted with the roles they play for pedagogical purposes during the exercise; for example, they must appreciate the value of silence and aloofness as psychological techniques.

It is probably useful for the facilitator to be acquainted with aspects of the social sciences. Relevant is a knowledge of conflict and conflict resolution, whether the referent be tension between groups or tension within a particular individual. Knowledge of learning principles may be helpful since the goal of mediation or negotiation, in psychological terms, is to have participants unlearn some modes of thinking or behavior and learn others. Some contact with anthropology is also very desirable so that the facilitator can thoroughly appreciate the relativity of many societal values and hence prevent himself from committing the errors of judgment associated with ethnocentrism. During the workshop, for example, it may be essential to estimate whether a given expression of attitude or a bit of behavior reflects the individual's culture or is peculiar to him. Some kinds of workshops, moreover, are designed to disseminate knowledge from the facilitator to the participants. Knowledge of conflict principles, the social sciences, psychology, and even psychiatry, which initially may have aided him in conducing the workshop, can then serve this second function of enlightening the participants. The facilitator, in addition, may be a so-called resource person who supplies facts pertaining to the conflict under discussion.

Again the facilitator is faced with a dilemma: should he know a great deal or relatively little about the conflict he would help resolve? Like maternal and paternal love, adequate knowledge always seems desirable: the more the facilitator knows about the conflict and its background, in as many subtle respects as possible, the greater will be his competence. Of course the facilitator, however, is also a human being; hence, if his role is to be a passive one, he may be tempted to display his erudition which in turn may antagonize some participants. If he is an outsider from a different society, on the other hand, his knowledge of them, their culture, or the conflict may seem impressive and thus increase rapport. Less knowledge or "simulated ignorance,"[112] nevertheless, may be advantageous: the ego of participants may be flattered by being given the opportunity to correct the ignorance of the prestigious facilitator. Perhaps it is important for active facilitators to be somewhat ignorant but to be aware of their ignorance, for then they too can eagerly participate in the workshop without being blinded by their own preconceptions.

Attitudes. The facilitator must have faith and confidence in himself and in the methods he would employ while mediating or negotiating. He must have such an attitude toward himself to be able to endure the frustrations already mentioned. He must also believe that his techniques can be efficacious, otherwise his own uncertainty may be conveyed to the participants who then may lose confidence in him. But—and there is always a *but*—in my limited experience I have known facilitators who are so enamored of their own methods that they consider them to be absolute panaceas and themselves to be prophets from the school in which they have been trained; the result is that they utilize or try to utilize their approach in situations for which a different medicine might be more suitable.

Confidence, however, cannot be absolute. For whatever he does, the facilitator cannot be certain that he will succeed. The risk of failure is obvious. During the recruiting stage, consequently, he must indicate this latter possibility, while simultaneously encouraging potential participants to attend. He thus finds himself in conflict: to obtain informed consent, he must acknowledge the possibility of failure; to obtain cooperation, he must seem confident. This dilemma is both ethical and psychological, and cannot be easily resolved.

Above all else, the facilitator must display impartiality. If he actually feels impartial, this stance may be relatively easy to convey to the participants. He is, however, subject to human foibles, and hence he may be inwardly convinced that one side is more correct or justified than the other. Whether he then can prevent himself from revealing his bias, perhaps unwittingly through nonverbal gestures, is a challenge difficult to meet.

Skills. The ability to withstand the frustration before, during, and after the workshop is one that is probably embedded deeply in the personality of the facilitator. Some persons, for example, are better able than others to remain calm or undisturbed when hostility is displaced upon them. Probably an individual who is personally insecure for whatever reason will find such hostility unendurable and hence he should never become a facilitator. But, as ever, the argument can be turned upside down: the insecure person may be so highly motivated to achieve success that he is willing and able to tolerate the punishment.

The facilitator, as the concept has been employed, may in fact perform at least four roles in connection with the workshop: he may be an adminstrator who is concerned with logistical and other details; he may plan and direct the workshop; he may assist in carrying out aspects of the plan; and he may function as a researcher who, by participating and observing, attempts to record what occurs. Except for the first role, it is conceivable that certain psychological attributes are desirable in any kind of workshop. Tentatively they may be described as:

a. *Patience.* Conflicts are never resolved instantly, long-winded statements are likely to appear during the sessions, some participants are bound to be stubborn and unyielding. The facilitator must have the fortitude to endure whatever transpires.

b. *Flexibility.* No workshop probably ever functions according to plan; the facilitator must be prepared to shift or alter his technique and not adhere to his preconceived plan. Since a workshop at best is a complicated affair and since no rules exist that can convert a zero-sum situation into one where both sides gain and neither side loses appreciably, the facilitator must be so flexible that he himself can be innovative or be willing to accept innovations from the participants.

c. *Sympathy, empathy.* It is essential under most circumstances for the facilitator to comprehend the intellectual and emotional arguments being advanced by both sides during the workshop. One has to feel one's way into the other person; accomplishing such momentary identification is seldom automatic. Often one or more participants require emotional support in order to carry on—and that support can be provided by the facilitator either during or between sessions.

d. *Intelligence.* One hesitates to include such a vague, catchall term in the inventory of skills, but its inclusion flamboyantly calls attention to a significant problem: the relation between knowledge and creativity. Acquiring principles or procedures is only a first step; then comes the hard intellectual work of actually utilizing them. Certainly knowledge of the situation is essential; but a touch of ingenuity or brilliance must also be added to that knowledge, which touch is not possessed by everyone—just as relatively few persons, if an old-fashioned concept may be permitted, have an IQ over 140.

e. *Tact.* This attribute is about as vague and as important as intelligence. Perhaps it is a way of summarizing all the other skills the effective facilitator should possess, perhaps it refers to an ability to affect participants unobtrusively, or perhaps it should be subsumed under the sense of timing about to be mentioned. Another name for tact could be sensitivity: the ability to observe nuances in others usually produces appropriate and thoughtful behavior by the observer.

Other skills less closely related to personality and more dependent upon experience include:

i. *Administrative know-how*: either alone or by delegating the responsibilities to a staff, arrangements usually must be made to bring the participants together and this in turn involves transportation, housing, and so forth.

ii. *Diagnostic skill*: it is necessary to comprehend through clues and intuition the presence of difficulties within individuals or groups.

iii. *Sense of timing*: undoubtedly there are optimal times at which intervention in a conflict is desirable or undesirable as well as optimal times during the workshop when the facilitator should play an active or passive role. He must be able to summon the conviction that a given technique or exchange of viewpoints or emotions has run its course and that a new procedure must be instituted or a temporary or final stopping point has been reached. Somehow he must have the right touch, the rich hunch.

9.4 QUALIFICATIONS OF PEACEKEEPERS (#s 1, 2, 3, 4, 5)

Above all else peacekeepers must be technically competent and accustomed to military routines. Those specializing in communications, for example, must be acquainted with the latest equipment and be able to utilize it under field conditions. With few exceptions they should receive the regular training given to officers and enlisted men. Peacekeeping then becomes, as it were, a postgraduate course in which the specialized problems associated with that art are taught and practised.

Who should be admitted to such a course? According to the *Peacekeeper's Handbook* of the International Peace Academy, a member of a peacekeeping force should possess the following: patience ("Listen first and speak afterwards"); restraint (he should not express his own emotions when parties to the dispute show anger or ridicule him); advocacy ("ability without force or threats to persuade both sides to avoid violence"); personality ("combine an approachable, understanding, and tactful manner with fairness and firmness"); persuasion and influence, perspective, attitude and approach ("quality of impartiality"); flexibility and speed; humor; vigilance; and alertness.[113] In similar and different words:

Whether the peacekeeper be of the lowest or the highest rank, his success will depend upon his ability to prevent conflict through every means other than force. . . . A lost temper, a threatening attitude, excessive persuasion, all can in a moment render useless the attempts of the peacekeeper.[114]

With some of these angelic qualifications soldiers and particularly officers should be blessed before they are ever assigned to be trained as peacekeepers; others they can perhaps learn through prior training in their home country. No one can quarrel with such a shopping list which possibly can serve as a sort of model or ideal. Two skeptical notes, however, must be sounded.

First, recruiters have no standardized way to ascertain whether the attributes exist among, or have been acquired by, potential recruits. Psychometrics at best provides only the probability, as based on paper-and-pencil measurements, that the individual possesses or does not possess whatever traits or skills are allegedly measured (cf. I). There is also likely to be a discrepancy between what emerges from a questionnaire or even from observations and actual behavior in field situations (cf. E). Secondly, the combination of attributes believed to be desirable or undesirable depends on factors which cannot be controlled or completely foreseen by recruiters: the status of the individual (officer compared with common soldier or policeman); the nature of the task he undertakes (staff work, clerk, guard duty, patrol); and the situation confronting him in the field (dangerous or peaceful).

According to one view, "possibly more important than anything is the peacekeeper's understanding of the problem at the root of the conflict and of the human relationships involved; for this will determine his attitude and approach to the situations and problems that face him."[115] Some non-academic military men may agree that such understanding is desirable but believe that it is "something which cannot always be acquired in advance of the peacekeeper's arrival in the operational area; instead he will more often than not have to acquire his knowledge in the course of carrying out his duties."[116] No one, I think, can question the value of preliminary instruction before the peacekeepers go into the field, and it is equally self-evident that what is learned beforehand has to be modified and sharpened after they arrive in the area of conflict. Some experienced officers, nevertheless, have a different view. They have told me privately that knowledge of the rationale of a peacekeeping effort, of the United Nations, and of the disputants may be important for commanders but not for the common soldier: his job is to carry out orders from someone more knowledgeable than himself. In my opinion this latter argument is probably without merit: there are good reasons why such knowledge is essential for many if not for all members of a peacekeeping force. Their morale is improved, presumably, if they appreciate the importance of what the United Nations through them is seeking to accomplish. Good morale is important, otherwise day-by-day tasks for ordinary soliders are boring. In Cyprus, for example, United Nations soldiers have accompanied Greek and Turkish farmers into a buffer zone both to protect them and to be certain that they were not engaging in any activity of military significance; they simply have stood by, often in the blazing sun, as the men went about their tasks. Soldiers stationed at isolated outposts and not knowing the local language are not only bored but are also lonely. If there are casualties, it is perhaps somewhat heartening to know that they have occurred in behalf of a cause considered worthwhile or at least comprehended. As difficulties with the local population arise, members of the force can distinguish between normal reactions in a culture different from their own and overreactions to the situation at hand. Finally, unless they are well briefed, they inevitably draw their own conclusions concerning events about them—and they may be wrong.

9.5 RELATIONS BETWEEN HOST COUNTRY AND PEACEKEEPERS (#s 4e, 5)

A United Nations peacekeeping force generally benefits the economy of the country where it is stationed. According to one estimate, for example, the force in Cyprus contributed around nineteen million preinflation dollars per year to that nation's economy.[117] Since the funds come both from the United Nations and from the countries whose forces are stationed in the disputed area, they can be considered—though never so phrased—as another minor device for distributing the world's wealth.

Nationals in the host country may be grateful to the peacekeeping forces for enforcing a cease-fire, for the humanitarian missions they have performed, for enabling diplomats to try to make or build peace, for providing eligible husbands, and so on, but resentment may also be present because of the force's isolation and privileged status. Peacekeeping soldiers, being human, may misbehave: they may not be "courteous" to women of the host country, indeed they may compete, as it were, with local men for those women; they have been known to sell on the black market liquor which, because of their membership in the force, they have been able to purchase at duty-free prices. They come from a different culture and so ethnocentric misunderstandings are bound to arise. Also the exact nature of the United Nations mandate may be misunderstood by the local population. During the fall of the Makarios regime and in the midst of the fighting between the Greek and Turkish armies in Cyprus in 1974, for example, some of the Greek Cypriotes with whom I took refuge asked me why the United Nations forces did not stop the slaughter, and I tried to explain to them, incredible as it seemed, that such a role was not part of the United Nations mandate. Also, although both sides may appreciate that the force is only enforcing a cease-fire, or preventing more bloodshed, some nationals feel that they are thus prevented from attacking their enemies. Finally, sometimes members of a force are not completely impartial: for reasons that are understandable or not, they come to sympathize with one of the parties.

It is sad, but not unexpected to note, on the basis of an informal survey of United Nations forces in Cyprus, that the men there seemed to have kept themselves isolated from the inhabitants and hence on the whole they did not come to know the elementary demographic and ethnic facts concerning the country they were policing. Troops from one of the countries who had received prior instruction about Cyprus knew virtually no more about the island after being there than those from two other countries who had not had the instruction. Participation in the force did not "foster international values" among them.[118]

9.6 RELATIONS AMONG PEACEKEEPERS (#s 3c, 4e)

As in most multinational operations, all is not always milk and honey among the peacekeeping forces:

Temporary armies, assembled with great difficulty, lacking permanent skills and accumulated experience, without central discipline, their components unaccustomed to acting in concert, their leaders in want of a clear hierarchy of command and control, their storehouses filled with miscellaneous assortments of equipment, their systems for provisioning inadequate, their continuity preserved only by reliance on mercenaries—these are trademarks that critic and friend alike often attributed to U.N. peacekeepers.

These phrases have been "directly lifted not from studies of U.N. missions but from a classic treatise on armies and warfare in the Middle Ages."[119] An up-to-date, less cute, empirical investigation of the peacekeeping force on Cyprus in 1969-1970—over four years before the ghastly troubles of 1974— revealed the following types of conflict within that force:

1. Difficulties common to all military organizations and hence also to the force on Cyprus: "staff vs. line," "reserve vs. career personnel," and "officer vs. other ranks."
2. Difficulties common to all multinational forces operating under a multinational command and hence appearing also in Cyprus: "official language other than that of some units"; "pay differences between national units"; "negative stereotypes between national units"; and "division of labor."
3. Difficulties peculiar to the situation in Cyprus: "structured strain resulting from the organizational separation of the power of assignment and promotion from the operational unity in which an officer served." Ordinarily duty, promotion, and assignment are "under the same chain of command," but service in the Cyprus force "offered no permanent assignment nor any sort of advancement through U.N. channels."[120]

In addition, cultural differences within the force create problems if not friction. The eating habits of men and women from the various countries inevitably are different; hence they generally have their meals served in their own enclaves.

The difficulties, however, should not be overemphasized. On an informal level contacts among the various nationalities composing the force can also be exciting and stimulating. Some of the problems can be alleviated through a standard operating procedure or through tactful decisions by the force commander. Efforts have been made to equalize the disparities in pay received from the home country while performing the same or similar duties.

NOTES

1. Berhanykun Andemicael, *Peaceful Settlement among African States*. New York: United Nations Institute for Training and Research, 1972.

2. Cf., for example, Ross Stagner, *Psychological Aspects of International Conflict*. Belmont: Wadsworth, 1967. P. 155.

3. Jeffrey Z. Rubin and Bert R. Brown, *The Social Psychology of Bargaining and Negotiation*. New York: Academic Press, 1975. P. viii.

4. Bertram I. Spector, Negotiation as a psychological process. *Journal of Conflict Resolution*, 1977, 21, 607-18.

5. John C. Campbell, *Successful Negotiation*. Princeton: Princeton University Press, 1976. P. 149.

6. Michael Haas, International socialization. In Michael Haas (ed.), *International Systems*. New York: Chandler, 1974. Pp. 51-75.

7. Oran R. Young, *The Politics of Force*. Princeton: Princeton University Press, 1968. Pp. 38-39.

8. Maureen R. Berman and Joseph E. Johnson (eds.), *Unofficial Diplomats*. New York: Columbia University Press, 1977. Also Herbert C. Kelman, The problem-solving workshop in conflict resolution. In Richard L. Merritt (eds), *Communication in International Politics*. Urbana: University of Illinois Press, 1972. Pp. 168-204.

9. Berman and Johnson, Unofficial meetings. In Berman and Johnson (eds.), op. cit., pp. 35-44.

10. Norman Cousins, The Dartmouth Conferences. In Berman and Johnson (eds.), op. cit., pp. 45-55. Also Philip D. Stewart, Improving Soviet-American understanding. *New Ways*, 1979, Fall, 3-5.

11. Ernest Meyer, The bilateral and multilateral meetings of the International Press Institute. In Berman and Johnson (eds.), op. cit., pp. 56-65.

12. Elfan Rees, Exercises in private diplomacy. In Berman and Johnson (eds.), op. cit., 111-29.

13. Jacques Freymond, The International Committee of the Red Cross as a neutral intermediary. In Berman and Johnson (eds.), op. cit., pp. 142-51.

14. Phillips Talbot, The Cyprus seminar. In Berman and Johnson (eds.), op. cit., 159-67.

15. Harry S. Ashmore, An exercise in demi-diplomacy. In Berman and Johnson, op. cit., pp. 130-41.

16. Cousins, op. cit.

17. Meyer, op. cit.

18. Kelman, op. cit. Also Ronald J. Yalem, Controlled communication and conflict resolution. *Journal of Peace Research*, 1971, 8, 263-72.

19. Leonard W. Doob, A Cyprus workshop. *Journal of Social Psychology*, 1974, 94, 161-78.

20. Leonard W. Doob (ed.), *Resolving Conflict in Africa*. New Haven: Yale University Press, 1970.

21. Leonard W. Doob and William J. Foltz, The Belfast workshop. *Journal of Conflict Resolution*, 1973, 17, 489-512.

22. Leonard W. Doob, Facilitating rapid change in Africa. In Arnold Rivkin (ed.), *Nations by Design*. New York: Doubleday, 1968. Pp. 333-86.

23. Mary Follett, *Creative Experience*. New York: Longmans, Green, 1924. Pp. 156-78, especially 169-70.

24. William Foltz, Two forms of unofficial conflict resolution. In Berman and Johnson (eds.), op. cit., pp. 201-21.

25. Leonard W. Doob and William J. Foltz, The impact of a workshop upon grass-roots leaders in Belfast. *Journal of Conflict Resolution*, 1974, 18, 237-56. Also Doob and Foltz, Voices from a Belfast workshop. *Social Change*, 1975, 5, no. 3, 1-8.

26. C. H. Mike Yarrow, *Quaker Experiences in International Conciliation*. New Haven: Yale University Press, 1978.

27. Roland Warren, The conflict intersystem and the change agent. *Journal of Conflict Resolution*, 1964, 8, 231-41.

28. Landrum R. Bolling. Informal comments in Alvin C. Eurich (ed.), *Observations on International Negotiations*. New York: Academy for Educational Development, 1971. Pp. 53-55.

29. Landrum R. Bolling, Quaker work in the Middle East following the June 1967 war. In Berman and Johnson (eds.), op. cit., pp. 80-88.

30. Landrum R. Bolling (ed.), *Search for Peace in the Middle East*. Greenwich: Fawcett, 1970. Pp. 91-104, 111-23.

31. Warren, op. cit.

32. Roger Fisher and William Ury, *International Mediation*. New York: International Peace Academy, 1978. P. 1.

33. Irving L. Janis and Leon Mann, *Decision Making*. New York: Free Press, 1977. P. 137.

34. Cf. Roger Fisher, *Dear Israelis, Dear Arabs*. New York: Harper and Row, 1972.

35. John W. Burton, *Conflict and Communication*. New York: Free Press, 1969. P. ix.

36. Adam Curle, *Making Peace*. London: Tavistock Publications, 1971. P. 19.

37. Margaret Mead, War is only an invention—not a biological necessity. In David Brook (ed.), *Search for Peace*. New York: Dodd, Mead, 1970. Pp. 12-16.

38. Leonard S. Woolf, *The Framework of a Lasting Peace*. New York: Garland, 1971. P. 10, Woolf's italics.

39. Dwight D. Eisenhower as quoted by Grenville Clark and Louis B. Sohn, *World Peace through World Law*. Cambridge: Harvard University Press, 1966. P. xv.

40. Emery Reves, *The Anatomy of Peace*. New York: Harpers, 1945. P. 78.

41. Percy E. Corbett, *Morals, Law, and Power in International Relations*. Los Angeles: John Randolph Yaynes and Dora Yaynes Foundation, 1956. Pp. 26-27.

42. Clark and Sohn, op. cit., pp. xv-xvii, xlii-xliii.

43. Cf. D. W. Bowett, *The Search for Peace*. London: Routledge and Kegan Paul, 1972. P. 5.

44. P. J. Allott, The International Court of Justice. In Study Group on the Peaceful Settlement of International Disputes (ed.), *Report*. London: David Davies Memorial Institute, 1966. Pp. 122-58.

45. Ernst B. Haas, *Human Rights and International Action*. Stanford: Stanford University Press, 1970. Pp. 20-22.

46. Arnold Simoni, *Beyond Repair*. New York: Macmillan, 1972. P. 97.

47. Rainer Kabel, *Mobilmachung zum Frieden*. Tübingen: Katzmann Verlag, 1971. P. 99.

48. R. A. Akindele, *The Organization and Promotion of World Peace*. Toronto: University of Toronto Press, 1976. Pp. 15, 132. Also Said Uddin Khan, The threats to coexistence. In Edward Reed (ed.), *Beyond Coexistence*. New York: Grossman, 1968. Pp. 15-16.

49. Akindele, op. cit., p. 134.

50. Ibid., p. 150.

51. Elmore Jackson, *Meeting of Minds*. New York: McGraw-Hill, 1952.

52. S. Strauz-Hupé and S. Possony, *International Relations*. New York: McGraw-Hill, 1950. P. 825.

53. J. C. Flugel, Some neglected aspects of world integration. In T. H. Pear (ed.), *Psychological Factors of Peace and War*. New York: Philosophical Library, 1950. Pp. 111-38.

54. Leonard W. Doob, The analysis and resolution of international disputes. *Journal of Psychology*, 1974, 86, 313-26.

55. Bureau of Public Affairs, Department of State, Reform of the U.N. system. *Gist*, November 1978.

56. Oran R. Young, *The Intermediaries*. Princeton: Princeton University Press, 1967. Pp. 116-26.

57. Oran R. Young, *Trends in International Peacekeeping*. Princeton: Center of International Studies, 1966. P. 3.

58. Simoni, op. cit., pp. xiv, 65-82.

59. Ernst B. Haas, *Beyond the Nation-State*. Stanford: Stanford University Press, 1964. Pp. 8-14.

60. Simoni, op. cit., p. 51.

61. David W. Wainhouse, *International Peacekeeping at the Crossroads*. Baltimore: Johns Hopkins University Press, 1973. P. 5.

62. Cf. E. Leslie, Some thoughts on international peacekeeping. *Canadian Defense Quarterly*, 1978, 7, no. 3, 18-22.

63. Indar Jit Rikhye, Michael Harbottle, Bjørn Egge, *The Thin Blue Line*. New Haven: Yale University Press, 1974. P. 73.

64. Ibid., pp. 144-46.

65. Larry L. Fabian, *Soldiers without Enemies*. Washington: Brookings Institution, 1971. Pp. 165-84.

66. International Peace Academy, *Peacekeeper's Handbook*. New York: International Peace Academy, 1978. P. IV/13, no. 53.

67. Ibid., Pp. IV/25, no. 103; V/37, no. 119. Also Fabian, op. cit.

68. Norman Z. Alcock, *The Emperor's New Clothes*. Oakville: CPRI Press, 1971. P. 75.

69. International Peace Academy, op. cit., p. II/7, nos. 25, 27.

70. Ibid., p. II/8, no. 33.

71. Akindele, op. cit., p. 75.

72. Fabian, op. cit., pp. 144-70.

73. International Peace Academy, op. cit., p. IX/8, no. 14.

74. Fabian, op. cit., pp. 170-84.

75. Wainhouse, op. cit., p. 604.

76. Rikhye, Harbottle, and Egge, op. cit., pp. 59-63.

77. International Peace Academy, op. cit., p. III/20, no. 61.

78. Ibid., p. IV/16, no. 60.

79. Indar Jit Rikhye, Preparation and training of U.N. Peacekeeping Forces, In Per Frydenberg (ed.), *Peacekeeping Experience and Evaluation*. Oslo: Norwegian Institute of International Affairs, 1964. Pp. 183-97.

80. Louis B. Sohn, Keeping peace in a world without arms. In Arthur Larson (ed.), *A Warless World*. New York: McGraw-Hill, 1962. Pp. 1-10.

81. International Peace Academy, op. cit., p. I/3, no. 7.

82. Ibid., p. IX/2, nos. 1-2.

83. Arthur M. Cox, *Prospects for Peacekeeping*. Washington: Brookings Institution, 1967. Pp. 99, 101.

84. International Peace Academy, op. cit., p. V/6, no. 14.

85. Ibid., p. V/35, no. 110.

86. John Mroz, *Third Party Roles*. Unpublished paper presented to International Studies Association, Toronto, 21 March 1979.

87. Raymond Aron, *Peace and War*. Garden City: Anchor Press, 1966. Pp. 302-03, Aron's italics.

88. Leslie, op. cit.

89. Cf. Rikhye, Harbottle, and Egge, op. cit., pp. 232-33.

90. Cox, op. cit., p. 6.

91. Glenn H. Snyder and Paul Diesing, *Conflict among Nations*. Princeton: Princeton University Press, 1977. Pp. 6-7.

92. Annual Report by Secretary-General U. Thant, 1965, as cited by Lincoln Bloomfield, Peacekeeping and peacemaking. *Foreign Affairs*, 1966, 44, 671-82.

93. David P. Forsythe, *United Nations Peacekeeping*. Baltimore: Johns Hopkins University Press, 1971. P. 97.

94. Rikhye, Harbottle, and Egge, op. cit., p. 16.

95. Walter Millis and James Real, *The Abolition of War*. New York: Macmillan, 1963. Pp. 86-105.

96. Olaf Hasselager, The relevance of international law to civilian defense. *Proceedings of the International Peace Research Association*, 1970, 2, 158-76.

97. Fisher and Urey, op. cit., pp. 29, 33.

98. Fisher, *International Conflict for Beginners*. New York: Harper and Row, 1969. P. 48.

99. Fisher, *Dear Israelis, Dear Arabs*, op. cit., pp. 66-67.

100. W. Hastie (ed.), *Kant's Principles of Politics*. Edinburgh: T. & T. Clark, 1891. P. 88, Hastie's italics.

101. J. C. Starke, *An Introduction to the Science of Peace (Irenology)*. Leyden: A. W. Sitjhoff, 1968. Pp. 194-203.

102. Cf. Betty Reardon and Saul H. Mendlovitz, World law and models of world order. In Charles R. Beitz and Theodore Herman (eds.), *Peace and War*. San Francisco: W. H. Freeman, 1973. Pp. 152-61.

103. William McDougall, *Janus*. New York: Dutton, 1927. Pp. 116, 144-50.

104. William O. Douglas, *International Dissent*. New York: Random House, 1971. Pp. 31-146. Herbert C. Kelman, Social-psychological approaches to the study of international relations. In Herbert C. Kelman (ed.), *International Behavior*. New York: Holt, Rinehart, and Winston, 1965. P. 573. C. Wright Mills, *The Causes of World War Three*. New York: Simon and Schuster, 1958. Pp. 7-38. C. Maxwell Stanley, *Waging Peace*. New York: Macmillan, 1956. Pp. 205-09.

105. William C. Brewer, *Permanent Peace*. Philadelphia: Dorrance, 1940. P. 5.

106. Richard A. Falk, *A Study of Future Worlds*. New York: Free Press, 1975. Pp. 226-27, italics deleted.

107. Leonard W. Doob, Mediation and negotiation: personal skills. This Appendix is a reproduction, with minor changes, of an unpublished paper presented to the Second Annual Meeting of the North American Council of the International Peace Academy, Quebec, April 1978.

108. Burton, op. cit., pp. 60-88. Also Ronald J. Fisher, Third party consultation. *Journal of Conflict Resolution*, 1972, 16, 67-94.

109. H. G. Darwin, Mediation and good offices. In Study Group on the Peaceful Settlement of International Disputes (ed.), op. cit., pp. 72-82.

110. Daniel Druckman, *Human Factors in International Negotiations*. New York: Academy for Educational Development, 1971.

111. UNITAR, *Some Psychological Techniques and the Peaceful Settlement of International Disputes*. New York: UNITAR, 1970. P. 5.

112. Burton, op. cit., p. 62.

113. International Peace Academy, op. cit., p. IX/14, no. 37.

114. Rikhye, Harbottle, and Egge, op. cit., pp. 267-68.

115. Ibid., p. 268.

116. International Peace Academy, op. cit., p. IX/17, no. 37f.

117. Charles C. Moskos, Jr. *Peace Soldiers*. Chicago: University of Chicago Press, 1976. P. 64.

118. Ibid., p. 135.

119. Fabian, op. cit., pp. 35-36.

120. Moskos, op. cit., pp. 79-81.

10.
Communication

Let there be no misunderstanding: devoting a chapter to communication does not mean that communication is the panacea for war-peace problems. There are intractable conflicts not to be resolved by words alone (cf. P).* Hitler's goal to have his Reich last a thousand years and hence his need to subjugate all of Europe could not have been blocked through communication, at least after almost a majority of Germans had permitted him to become their leader and after English and French leaders had appeased him at Munich. The conviction of the Turkish community in Cyprus that before 1974 they were threatened and maltreated by the Greek community and the ancient hostility existing between Catholics and Protestants in Northern Ireland have resulted from stubborn historical, social, political, and economic realities that cannot be erased by verbal exchanges alone. The incredible developments in communication during the present century—the mass media, the jet planes—have enabled messages in every form to be delivered virtually everywhere with dispatch, so that leaders and followers can establish direct or indirect contact without delay; yet these technical advances definitely have not diminished the threat or the actuality of war. Whether the "hot lines" providing instant communication between the leaders of the superpowers will ever enable them to avoid a war we do not know (cf. I).

For better or worse, however, communication is a component of most war-peace problems (cf. P). In negotiation and mediation facts or alleged facts are transmitted from one side to another. Any rhetorical schema that would describe intervention in disputes by third parties[1] is simply a way of prescribing particular kinds of communication. A policy of deterrence assumes that knowledge of a country's military power will be acquired by

*See pages 11-12 for an explanation of the cross-referencing system.

the leaders of the government that is its potential enemy. One of the principal functions of the International Court of Justice, of regional organizations, and of the United Nations itself is to encourage fact-finding either by individuals within their own organizations or by outsiders such as experts or disinterested parties;[2] the facts are then disseminated and hopefully somehow contribute to peaceful decisions. The Nazis found communications useful to justify their actions to their own people and to foreigners and also to serve as a verbal smokescreen to conceal their invasion plans from the staffs of their enemies.[3] If I permit myself to use a popular, ugly verb of our day, both leaders and followers must be mobilized in behalf of peace, and mobilization is accomplished largely through the mass media. Action, moreover, is a form of communication when the activities are communicated to the relevant audience. To prevent Hitler from invading Czechoslovakia in 1938, the French manned their Maginot Line and thus sought to deter the invasion by communicating their intention to declare war on Germany if that action were taken;[4] obviously the news of the maneuver was leaked to the German authorities who did not respond as the French had hoped.

Peace is more likely when leaders and followers have beliefs and attitudes inclining them toward peace rather than war. These predispositions have their origins in what they have previously perceived. What they have perceived in turn results from the ways in which they have been socialized or educated, which consists in large part of various forms of communication ranging from verbal admonitions to models of behavior serving as standards to be learned. Events are filtered through the subtle and seductive language employed by the media and other persons; followers communicate their views by voting, when voting is permitted, by demonstrations, and by other actions. On the one hand, as pessimistically foreshadowed in Chapter 4, it is possible to be convinced that leaders control their followers through the "power" of the written and spoken word; hence peoples have grown not more but less internationally minded as literacy has increased and communication in general has improved. On the other hand, according to a former Spanish diplomat and writer, "the most effective deterrent against a Soviet invasion" of Western Europe is the attitude of individuals in the countries now under Soviet influence; he thinks they would immediately revolt and free themselves from Soviet domination.[5] If his assertion is true, citizens in those eastern countries have communicated their intentions to Soviet leaders partially through verbal utterances, probably more impressively by minor and major actions.

Words and sentences, therefore, may also have a negative effect on the pursuit of peace. The window-open, window-shut metaphor mentioned in the last chapter in connection with mediation and intervention suggests that verbal fomulations may conceal individuals' underlying motives. Merely claiming that a conflict is only a question of sovereignty, for example, beclouds the desire for economic gain. A major component of a successful leader's repertoire, including his so-called charismatic effect upon his followers, can be traced to the style and content of his communications.

One of the five freedoms, that of speech and expression, refers largely to communication; and from some standpoints both verbal facility and the desire to speak up freely may increase as peoples become more westernized.[6] A society possessing this freedom permits citizens who oppose war or trends toward war to declare their viewpoints and their opposition. Before they do so, however, they must have access to relevant information communicated to them by leaders and the mass media. It may well be, as suggested in Chapter 2, that attitudes are less subject to change—and in this sense less inclined to be changed in the direction of war—when they are accompanied by adequate and relevant knowledge. The privilege of speaking freely but recklessly, without knowing the significant facts, is not likely to be effective. Knowledge of the facts does not automatically make men into *homines pacifici*, but it is a necessary first step in that direction—perhaps.

EDUCATION (# 3)

The beliefs and attitudes related to war-peace are transmitted from one generation to the next during socialization which quite obviously includes not only formal schooling but also the informal instruction given in the home, by peers, and through whatever media exist in the society (cf. P). Formal schooling is largely emphasized in this section because of its potential importance in the West and because of the attention schools necessarily pay to war and peace. One of the ways to achieve "lasting peace" is through education thus narrowly conceived.[7] Realistically, however, it is clear that, although what children learn at school may affect their leaders and the policies of their country (that is, what is called the political system), the existing system sets constraints on what educators may transmit. It is discouraging to note that there has been a "gradual upward trend in worldwide military expenditures . . . since World War II" and that "total world military expenditures in 1976 were about two-and-a-half times those for public health"; yet it is possibly encouraging that in the same year "total public education expenditures were 6.5 percent greater than those for military expenditures."[8]

One place to begin an analysis of education is with textbooks in history, geography, civics, social studies, current events, and other related subjects. They guide teaching and inevitably contain versions of wars and values that directly affect relevant attitudes and beliefs regarding peace. These books cannot avoid the subject of war. Still they have the potentiality of stressing not only the bravery and heroism of men and women during wars but also the misery in war's aftermath as well as the progress of mankind, however defined, during periods of peace. Such progress may seem less exciting to restless children and adolescents than the exploits of soldiers or the rhetoric of patriotic clichés ("My only regret is that I have but one life . . . ''), and herein is exactly the pedagogical challenge. The role of the profit motive and of the so-called merchants of death, the munitions makers, need not be exaggerated in describing wars, rather it can be truthfully and realistically presented. American youth can learn about Richard Nixon as well as George Washington, just as histories about Germany can mention the hideous crimes of the Nazis as well as the cultural and scientific contributions stemming from the truly great of that country. Almost any subject, moreover, has implications for war-peace. Learning a foreign language may create a friendly attitude toward the country or countries of its speakers. It would seem to be a moot question, however, whether the study of pure science as such promotes attitudes toward peace. The leaders of the American and French revolutions were supposed to be "well versed" in the science of their time, and Newton stimulated not only scientific progress but also "deep thought about society" that emphasized "the equality and unity of mankind.''[9] If so, then the teaching of science might be expected to aid peace by encouraging clear thinking or by pointing to scientists like Einstein and Pauling as models to be followed in making decisions about international affairs. On the other hand, scientists are generally concerned only with their own subject matter, and their clear thinking may or may not be transferred to other spheres, even though they appreciate the fact that theoretical and sometimes also applied science is international in scope.

New, credible information as such often has the capability of changing attitudes (cf. P). Children who learn in history or geography that customs vary from place to place may become less ethnocentric and hence less prone to react unfavorably to persons from other countries. A somewhat extreme illustration in this connection has been reported concerning Australians who were captured by the Japanese during World War II; they are said to have been able to tolerate the harsh treatment they received because their "education" made them realize that the system and not the particular tormentor sanctioned brutality.[10] In general, there exists evidence, though of a preliminary sort, that "benign images of the world and a desire for cooperative involvement in it will more frequently be found among the well-informed segments of the population than among the poorly informed.''[11] The need to increase knowledge concerning peace is illustrated by a Norwegian study indicating that in the early grades children gradually learned about war-peace (especially weapons, killing, fighting), but that their knowledge concerning war increased faster than their knowledge about peace, probably because they were not being given an opportunity to acquire "an active peace concept.''[12]

Years ago a political scientist pointed out that compiling world histories would facilitate the creation of "common world perspectives.''[13] This

Nirvana, however, has its problems. The irrationality of wars generally is exposed when past wars are examined, and yet—what patriotic American does not approve of the violent revolution that enabled the thirteen colonies to secure independence from England? Then, on a realistic basis it may be anticipated that some school boards or whatever authorities select textbooks will howl with rage and reject a book that appears "unpatriotic." Of course very biased accounts of past events can be expurgated or corrected, but the fact remains that some past events cannot and should not be suppressed if an account is to be objective, even if reading about those events can keep old hatreds alive. Certainly some of the beliefs prevailing in a society must be exploded in textbooks when peace is to be pursued. A devoted peace advocate, for example, believes it is essential to expose four of the "most serious myths of our age," which he considers to be "the possibility of defense, the sanctity of nationalism, the virtue of economic growth, and the beneficence of foreign aid."[14] Although the reader and perhaps I myself may agree that these shibboleths should be debunked because they promote the kinds of beliefs and attitudes leading to war and although, therefore, the arguments advanced may seem convincing, conservative forces in the society will assert that such views undermine our youth and destroy the foundations of our mighty country. In addition, possibly one or more of the so-called myths may on occasion promote peace and not war; thus there *may* be some virtue in economic growth and foreign aid. In short, it is not easy to find a textbook in history or a related discipline which does not come under attack by some group within modern society.

Pour moraliser les peuples il faut les éclairer ("To instill morality in people it is necessary to illuminate them"), a French army captain declared before the middle of the last century in a book devoted to pacifist tendencies in European society.[15] Such illumination requires not a series of discrete beliefs with their accompanying attitudes but a coherent credo. The need for such a credo has been stressed in Chapter 7 where a suggested outline of its contents has likewise been given; and the great religions, also as previously mentioned, provide supplementary exhortations and guides. It is discouraging to note, however, that democratic countries have not evolved a suitable set of beliefs, in spite of the fact that we know which beliefs should be in the repertoire of *homo pacificus*: the noninevitability of war; the approximate perfectability of man; the economic advantages of peace; the interdependence of the world's nations. Perhaps we are fearful of imposing dogma or of evolving a stereotyped litany, such as a prayer or "I pledge allegiance to the flag."

Up to this point the target of education has been schoolchildren. No one would dispute the fact that it is also important to communicate information about war-peace to adolescents, college and university students, and adults, especially since leaders who make critical policy decisions for their country are recruited from the general population. Much of this war-peace information comes from the mass media, to be discussed in the next section, but some is transmitted through formal education. During the 1970s, college and university students in the United States could major in or concentrate upon peace studies in twenty-nine institutions. Similar opportunities were being offered in Canada, Sweden, and the United Kingdom. In the Swedish course of study, the following were topics in the curriculum: structure of international systems; problems of armament and disarmament; forms of nonmilitary struggle; refusal of military duty; ideas, institutions, and social change; peace research (analysis and criticism of its development); general conflict development.[16] Graduate study in peace science at an American university, according to its announcement in a record-breaking sentence, "has two basic orientations: one is toward the underlying theory of conflict and conflict management as they relate to interaction of behaving units—nations, communities, cultures, governmental and business organizations, ethnic groups, interest groups, religious institutions and individuals—in their psychological, economic, social, and political contexts; the other is toward the development of methodology and techniques for effective examination of conflict problems and for the design of cooperative procedures to provide guidelines for consistent public policies and groups and private decisions in coping with conflict."[17] Syllabuses for college courses on peace are readily available.[18] Some countries have had one or more peace research institutes: Belgium, Canada, Finland, France, Germany, the Netherlands, Sweden, and the United Kingdom.

In a rapidly changing world, education for peace must adapt itself to new conditions, a point made forcefully by an international group of social scientists shortly after World War II.[19] For pupils and students this means that textbooks must be kept up-to-date. For adults who have finished their formal education, "mass" or "continuing" education outside school or university circles is essential, an effort that obviously must be adapted to the groups and organizations constituting the audience.[20]

A most difficult challenge facing those who would educate for peace is, if I may use an old-fashioned word for personality that has attached to it a moral twist, how to develop a character prone toward peace. Believing that war is evil by itself may not produce appropriate action unless, for example, "latent aggression in children" is reduced.[21] The reduction of such aggression, as has been repeatedly maintained in earlier chapters, depends on removing or diminishing frustrations to which the individual is submitted during socialization and by the events within his society. In addition, the character-building aspects of education via schools, churches (including their Sunday schools), and other institutions, can promote, in the spirit of the Sermon on the Mount and other religious doctrines, the personal and social desirability of expressing aggression "constructively"—and the definitions of "constructively" can be broad or specific. Otherwise we have recipes galore for educating *homo pacificus*, most of which hover around the standards of perfection outlined in Chapter 5. One educator, for example, believes that the key trait to be cultivated is that of "maturity" which he thinks can be achieved by teaching individuals to be aware of the causes of conflict; to be less egocentric; to have their values and actions "consistent" and also flexible; to acquire a stable self-concept; and somehow to be "autonomous."[22] Here is an area of education requiring exploration and—yes—additional research. A fashionable concept, for example, that of "locus of control," refers to the tendency of persons to judge the source of their own actions: do they think they act as a result of external or internal pressures? Those believing in the inevitability of war, one bit of evidence suggests, because they think its roots are part of human nature may also value comfort and leadership more than benevolence and independence, and are perhaps also more likely to be conservative in the sense of being nationalistic, militaristic, or resistant to change.[23] Without entering into a metaphysical dispute concerning the validity or applicability of the doctrine of determinism, possibly peace can be pursued more efficiently when individuals are encouraged to believe and act as if they controlled their own fate.[24]

MASS MEDIA (# 3)

In a perfectionistic sense, *homo pacificus* should be rational, or at least as rational as a human being with conflicting emotions and unconscious motives can be; he understands the outside forces affecting his judgments (cf. P). He is able to derive sound conclusions from factual premises. In a modern society he has insight into the techniques employed by leaders and his peers. He appreciates that even the best of statesmen withhold some information for legitimate or illegitimate reasons. He realizes that the portrait of reality conveyed by the mass media, whether through an apparently straightforward news item or the analysis of a complicated event, is likely to be an oversimplification or at least, from the standpoint of some other observer, a more or less biased account. He knows, moreover, that some of the distortions confronting him are not necessarily intentional: they may reflect unconscious motives of the communicator or they may simply be the expressions of the cultural biases within the society. Whether or not he functions rationally is determined by his early socialization, his mature personality and, in developed countries, by his formal education and the mass media.

These media can be effectively utilized, in behalf of good or evil, for many reasons. Even in many developing countries they are all-pervasive. They are the ultimate source of information concerning events not personally or directly observed. Peers and influentials may also communicate, but they derive much of their information from the press, radio, and even books. Those controlling the media possess, within limits, the capability of ascertaining people's current attitudes and beliefs not only intuitively but also through surveys.[25] They thus are in a position to exploit systematic, if tentative knowledge concerning techniques; for example, they may be able to specify the conditions under which both sides of an issue should be presented[26] or to know in advance when a given communication is likely to boomerang.[27] By implication or direct suggestion they promote almost every conceivable form of action and hence must be included as part of the "power structure" of a community or a country.[28]

It is easy to charge the media with certain responsibilities in connection with war-peace. Certainly they should be expected to present the facts, however facts are defined in particular contexts. But there are so many facts, and facts cannot be communicated without some distortion—distortion in their selection and treatment. Also as important, however, are the frailties of the media's audience, especially in modern society where the number of events, even when adequately reported, tends to exceed most persons' ability to absorb and remember them, or even to be keenly interested in them in the first place. In spite of the pervasive coverage by many of the media—but not by all—public opinion surveys during the middle 1960s, for example, revealed that Americans were very poorly acquainted with simple facts about international relations. For example, a "distressingly large" percentage could not identify outstanding political leaders in the world or could not recognize such terms as NATO, Common Market, or OAS.[29] An impertinent question to the reader: do you know what OAS stands for? Americans, perhaps most persons in the West other than some leaders and military men, are more likely to be concerned with immediate, personal problems than with matters of war-peace. When a national sample of Americans in 1971 was asked to indicate "some ways in which life in the United States is getting worse," for example, only 7 percent referred to war or the military establishment, whereas 52 percent mentioned "behavior and attitudes of individuals in social situations" (use of drugs; "individuals' reactions to modern life and to each other"; young people and hippies); and 48 percent pointed to "sociological problems: institutions, economic, general, living conditions."[30] The billions spent on armaments may be reported, but they are likely to be noted only in passing in an era when the budgets of nations have become as unintelligible as astronomical distances.

In addition, most persons tend to avoid reality when it is unpleasant and affects them directly, including what they might learn from the mass media (cf. P). In the pursuit of peace, it may be argued, the media should continually report the destructive power of atomic, nuclear, chemical, biological, and other weapons[31] as well as the efforts of diplomats, including their machinations, to facilitate or inhibit war. Thus the dangers of war can be ever salient, and perhaps the threat of war provides part of the motivating power to avoid war. At the same time, if such communications produce fear or anxiety, they may be deliberately or unconsciously overlooked, repressed, or forgotten.[32] An American psychologist believes that, as the destructive capability of weapons increases, people become less concerned about the danger.[33] Somehow, in connection with war, it is essential to try to strike a balance between salience and anxiety: salience, so that the communications are perceived; sufficient anxiety, so that leaders and followers alike are motivated to take action against war, and not too much anxiety, lest they avoid the problem (cf. I). A fragment of evidence has been collected in modern Japan: those Japanese who read newspapers became more peace-oriented than those who did not. The investigator assumes a cause-and-effect sequence which may or may not be true; he is probably on sounder ground when he argues that in his country "Conservatives may become peace-oriented like Liberals if they can somehow be activated to participate in community life."[34]

It is also clear that individuals do not always use available information or allow themselves to be influenced by it.[35] Many have a tendency to be more impressed with concrete details than with abstract generalizations, even when the latter are either more accurate or encompassing. A realistic description of the horrors wrought by a nuclear explosion, for example, may have less effect than a vivid report or portrayal of the misery experienced by a single victim.

The potentiality of the mass media to disseminate news very quickly unless blocked by censorship at the source is double-edged as far as war-peace is concerned. Probably radio listeners and television viewers become blasé: cruel events are reported on the same set that provides entertainment and fantasy. And so war itself can be judged with greater equanimity, an attitude not conducive to peace-seeking. In general, moreover, in an age of violence and increasing crime, all of which are reported, usually sensationally, by the mass media, it is to be wondered whether any event, including even the horrors of war, can truly shock audiences. The invasion of one nation by another is no longer as simple as it was formerly: news is quickly reported, and pressure may thus be exerted upon aggressing leaders to desist.[36] If so, then the media have an inhibiting effect on them, for they know that their actions, either immediately or eventually, will be judged everywhere; particularly by leaders in other countries.

The prominence given information promoting internationalism by the mass media and by local groups such as libraries, peace societies, and women's organizations, in comparison with the space or time devoted to military expenditures, varies from country to country (cf. V). A systematic content analysis of one leading newspaper in each of five countries (the United States, Great Britain, France, Russia, and Germany) during the first fifty years of this century suggests that editorials in prestige newspapers accurately expressed the opinion of the elite regarding foreign affairs.[37] Perhaps the great advances in communication since the Industrial Revolution have improved only the speed with which news and views are transmitted but not the content of "what man has to say to man."[38] International communication, moreover, is affected by trade and commerce; the sale of American products overseas, for example, is often accompanied by local advertising that fortifies a business ideology. Were it not for the mass media, however, the consciences of many in developed countries would not be stirred by the plight of persons in developing countries: the protests of African, Asian, and Latin American leaders concerning the misery of their countrymen, which they often justifiably attribute to colonialism and neocolonialism, are continually transmitted to those enjoying superior status.

Other criticisms of the media with reference to war-peace are forthcoming. On the level of national policy it has been speculated that they may "harden public opinion to such a degree as eventually to destroy the freedom of choice" of leaders whether to go to war or accept some other alternative.[39] Actually we are confronted here with what has been cleverly called an instance of "circularity in polyarchy"[40]: leaders affect followers, as a result of which followers affect leaders. Just as the heads of corporations and other large business enterprises deliberately or indirectly influence the content of the mass media in the United States through various pressures, press releases, and personal associations, so leaders of government affect the media they control directly in authoritarian states or indirectly in democracies to secure support for their own war-peace policies. Then they or their successors become more or less prisoners of these creations (cf. P). Thus opposition in the United States to the Vietnam War was first reduced by having Americans gradually become habituated to deeper and deeper involvement: each small step in the process of escalation was presented by successive administrations to the media as "a logical unavoidable result or consequence of a previous small step."[41]

The fashionable description of the mass media, especially American television, is that they are superficial, often mendacious, frequently inaccurate, and always elite-oriented. On the basis of largely anecdotal evidence, scattered opinions, and shrewd intuition, a Norwegian political scientist offers the following "suggested hypotheses" that he considers to be the most telling indictments of the news media, which media allegedly, he thinks, tend:

1. to reinforce the status quo and to exaggerate the importance of individual actions by big power leaders.
2. to present the world as being more conflict-laden than it really is, to emphasize the use of force rather than peaceful means in solving such conflicts, and thus also, more indirectly, to give the impression that conflicts can be averted more easily by preparing for the use of force, rather than by reducing tensions by undramatic means.
3. to reinforce or at least to uphold the divisions of the world between high and low status nations.[42]

The indictment can be almost endlessly prolonged. The media, for example, publicize the kidnapping of prominent persons and the hijacking of planes since acts of terror are considered newsworthy, at least in countries with a free press. Sympathy may thus be evoked and strengthened for the potential victims, so that pressure is exerted upon authorities to accede to the terrorists' demands.[43] In addition, practicing or potential terrorists may become convinced that kidnapping and hijacking are efficacious; another success for violence is thereby scored—and violence via war indirectly may benefit.

It is too glib to assert self-righteously that the mass media should be truthful. As ever, truth is tricky and sometimes must be sacrificed to a higher value, if only temporarily. Whether a mass medium should dwell upon atrocities committed by a potential enemy—yes, atrocities truly committed—and thus to inflame, perhaps to facilitate war and perhaps also additional atrocities is an issue difficult to decide once and for all; yet it is one that has to be faced by those controlling the media. With some ingenuity, moreover, it is relatively easy in democratic countries to deluge the media with communications that publicize an event or to contrive one in order to communicate information regarding war-peace. In this instance "truth" is created, and the media simply report the "news" in a manner of their own choosing.[44] Peace marches in large cities attact attention, but so do murders and assassinations. In 1958 media worldwide carried the story of how a group of Quakers tried to sail a ship into a nuclear bomb area in the Marshall Islands of the South Pacific, in order to voice protest against war in general and that event in particular.[45]

The sophisticated techniques employed in modern psychological warfare all involve some form of communication, more often than not through the mass media.[46] Perhaps it is better in wartime to demoralize one's opponents or one's enemies than to kill them; but demoralization may eventually facilitate killing. In peacetime, large and small nations contribute to a stream of international propaganda (usually disguised behind some obvious euphemism such as information or public relations) which utilize radio broadcasts, printed materials, lobbyists, and public relations counsels to communicate their opinions and policies to friendly and unfriendly nations. The government's special viewpoint may be presented blatantly (for instance, if a touch of ethnocentrism be permitted, the news broadcasts of so-called Iron Curtain countries) or quietly (for example, the BBC World News Service and the Voice of America). These programs would enhance the reputations of their countries by demonstrating their contributions to mankind, as do their overseas libraries, exhibitions, and public lectures. The overall goal is to strengthen positive attitudes and beliefs among friendly and neutral countries and also to discredit unfriendly countries or potential enemies as well as to encourage dissent among citizens of the latter countries.

These forms of communication are difficult to evaluate, for adequate knowledge is lacking concerning the effects upon nationals and their leaders (cf. I). Besides, we never know whether relations with the target country would have been better or worse in the absence of the communications since control situations are lacking: even if such efforts suddenly begin or cease, one is not certain whether whatever changes occur can be attributed to the propaganda or to concomitant events.

While it is true that the mass media are the channels through which information concerning war-peace is transmitted, the context of what is communicated depends not only upon those controlling the media (private interests, governments, reporters, editors, producers, directors, and so on) but also upon the events they consider appropriate to transmit and especially upon the activities of groups and persons having a vested or an invested interest in war-peace problems. It follows, therefore, that the pursuit of peace will and should be fostered by pro-peace activities; thus efforts can be made to combat some of the impressions international propagandists strive to create. Two paragraphs ago the episode of the Quaker ship protesting a nuclear explosion in the South Pacific was mentioned: the test nevertheless was carried out, but people everywhere learned about the protest since what these Friends attempted was courageous and hence at least temporarily newsworthy.[47]

Much more than publicity is needed if peace attitudes are to be learned and strengthened. Quakers have brought students of various countries together in seminars to study the bases for war-peace; they have organized other international seminars concentrating on problems of development; they have sponsored meetings of social scientists who then tried to influence foreign policy; they have assembled junior diplomats to discuss international problems; they have organized international work camps for young people who thus have established contact with one another. These measures have the primary goal of increasing knowledge and changing attitudes in face-to-face situations; secondarily some of their fruits immediately or eventually are reported in the mass media if only in the form of printed reports or books.

The peace movement in the United States began during the nineteenth century as a "largely religious phenomenon"[48] and later was joined by secular groups. In 1944 Pax Christi, a virtually worldwide Catholic organization, was created in order to pray for, study, and work toward peace.[49] Advocacy of peace does or could play a significant role in the sermons, training, and instruction of most religious groups.[50] Similarly other associations, such as the National Committee for a Sane Nuclear Policy (with the acronymn SANE, of course), Women Strike for Peace, Amnesty International, serve an educational function for their members and indirectly if not deliberately increase the flow of peace-oriented information to the mass media. Such privately funded organizations continually arise, present a peace program that sounds sensible at the time, attract and enlighten a number of followers, and may fade slowly out of existence leaving behind a trace or more than a trace of favorable attitudes toward peace. Before World War II, for example, a group calling itself Union Now achieved considerable prominence, particularly in the United States, largely because of the zeal of its founder. After the war, the group's leader recognized the split between the East and West and hence revised his program in the direction of gradualism: "federate the freest fraction of mankind in a Great Union of the Free, and thereafter extend this federal relationship to other nations as rapidly as this proves practicable, until the whole world is thus eventually governed by freedom and union."[51]

Generally, since "much indoctrination" is necessary to prepare individuals for "warlike activities,"[52] advocates of peace deliberately puncture war-promoting communications and substitute ones of their own. Attitudes considered desirable in the pursuit of peace, however, may have undesirable consequences or may be judged otherwise in another era. Not long before World War II, I believed it was necessary to educate Americans concerning the events and propaganda shaping their knowledge and attitudes and that only "a skeptical attitude and the knowledge of the existence of these forces" would make them "less prone to succumb to jingoistic appeals."[53] I cooperated, therefore, with a group of isolationists called the Institute for Propaganda Analysis: we issued curricular materials for high schools (which were still being used thirty years later), a newsletter, and a book; we also sponsored conferences and lectures. It soon became clear to many of us that Hitler and the Nazis were evil beings whose ambitions and actions had to be halted and that perhaps we were injuring what was then called the "morale" of Americans with adverse references to the coming war which, by 1940 or so, began to appear "just."

Publicizing information about the United Nations and thus promoting peace presents special problems. First, there is money: the United Nations does not have sufficient funds to mount adequately an extensive public relations program. With sorrow and indignation let me give one illustration to indicate its deplorable plight. Papers on disarmament which had been prepared for a special session of the General Assembly of the United Nations in 1977 could not be distributed to the full United Nations member-ship because the cost—$220,000—was considered too high. That amount of money, it was pointed out, "is what the world spends on arms every 18 seconds."[54] The United Nations, moreover, is faced with a dilemma in some instances: on the one hand, its activities should be better known to increase its prestige, but on the other hand some information—especially of a military character or involving the delicate relations between a peacekeeping force and the opposing parties—can cause damage if transmitted to the mass media. On its very restricted budget the United Nations employs press releases and radio programs to publicize its activities. Perhaps there should be an international broadcasting system which, among other functions, could provide "every nation with the opportunity to defend its position on any issues before an international audience."[55]

Symbols for the United Nations and peace organizations in general, it has been pointed out, "are virtually lacking": there are no world parks or gardens, for example, and only "a few symbolic world-minded documents."[56] The United Nations, however, does have the beginning of a university; perhaps an international university could have a world appeal by being located on a peripatetic ship.[57] The cluster of United Nations buildings in New York, Geneva, and elsewhere provides a substantial reminder of the international efforts to pursue peace. But it remains true that the kind of simplified incantation for one world—a "Marseillaise" striking an inspring chord on the international level—is lacking.

Tantalizing is the fact that within recent years our knowledge concerning the effective ways to affect individuals progressively increases, but that knowledge has not been adequately utilized toward peaceful ends (cf. P). The success or failure of a communication depends upon its mode of presentation (its content, its probability of being perceived or ignored) and upon the audience's own drives, beliefs, attitudes, and skills. The credibility of the communicator or his medium, for example, may have a profound effect upon its acceptance, but people's own personal characteristics in turn may also determine who or what they consider credible.[58] Principles of this kind have been more successfully and extensively utilized by advertisers than by peace advocates, at least in the Western world. Abundant anecdotal and systematic evidence, however, indicates that the media on occasion are effective in changing attitudes and in adding to the information or mis-information of audiences. A somewhat typical, obvious illustration will suffice. In the middle 1960s, half of the eleventh grade pupils in an American school read a pamphlet on civil defense, the other half did not: more of the former than the latter felt thereafter that nuclear war was likely.[59]

Mass media not only communicate news about war-peace but also pro-vide entertainment often relevant to the same problem. Similarly literature and the arts probably affect people's beliefs and attitudes concerning war—the role of science fiction has been previously mentioned. Again and again there are outcries directed against the vast amount of violence in the dramatic productions on American television. It is thus assumed that this medium affects viewers' conception of violence—and obviously violence has some relation to war-peace. The situation is more complicated. Station owners and producers contend, privately and publicly, that they are simply satisfying the need or desire of their audiences to witness such episodes. By and large, however, the experimental and empirical evidence—largely confined to

American children—offers "substantial testimony" that viewing violence tends to foster aggressiveness.[60] For some children, nevertheless, there is very shaky evidence indicating that TV violence may have a cathartic function by reducing rather than increasing such a tendency toward violence.[61] The methodological tangle is illustrated by a study of American college women which reveals that those with high manifest hostility and low guilt concerning their own hostility, as measured by paper-and-pencil questionnaires, tended to prefer violent TV programs;[62] but it is not known whether the hostility induced them to view such programs or whether the programs contributed to the hostility. The safest conclusion to be drawn is a dialectic one (or another instance of "circularity in polyarchy," the fancy phrase cited a few pages ago): the programs and the viewers interact, with each reinforcing the other so that, short of changing the viewers or the programs, the tendency toward violence probably spirals (cf. V).

Articles and books in behalf of peace are more durable than the electronic media but not necessarily more effective. Novels depicting the miseries of warfare may be widely read, but it is impossible to imagine what effect they have upon their readers and policy makers (cf. I). Certainly the portrayal of trench warfare by Remarque in *All Quiet on the Western Front*[63] did not prevent the rise of Hitler and World War II, and the idiocy of army routines lampooned by Heller in *Catch-22*[64] had no noticeable effect on the way the United States conducted its war in Vietnam. Or are such minor consequences simply unascertainable?

The conclusion must be that in the modern world communication about peace is inadequate (cf. P). Terror, conflict, and wars almost always make better news copy than the pursuit of peace. Whatever their immediate or ultimate contribution to the war-peace problem, the media operate only within the present political and international framework.

CONTACT (#s 3, 4, 5)

Intuitively it is believed that contacts between peoples, however achieved, are likely to promote better understanding and hence to lead them in the direction of peace. Even laboratory subjects are inclined to develop a favorable attitude toward nondescript letters, words, symbols, and faces as they perceive them repeatedly.[65] Similarly, it is claimed, one of the potentials for war, ethnocentrism, decreases when an individual visits a foreign country or meets foreigners at home. The more Canadians, especially French-Canadians, travelled to other provinces or outside their own country, the more tolerant concerning ethnic groups and multicultural diversity they tended to be; but the relationship, though statistically significant, was not very strong, and it is impossible to determine whether travel produced tolerance or tolerance led to travel.[66] The better relations between France and Germany since World War II, in comparison with those following World War I, have resulted from many events and circumstances, included among which probably are increased contacts between various groups such as veterans of the wars, students, and scientists. UNESCO, an organ of the United Nations, seeks to contribute to peace by facilitating contacts between scholars and scientists of different countries, the exchange of persons who seek education abroad, and increased appreciation of the artistic and other cultural contributions each country makes to the world's enrichment.[67] Learning a foreign language is a form of culture contact that ought to promote better understanding. All languages contain subtleties in vocabularly and structure which, when comprehended, provide some insight into the people who speak them and which are difficult and sometimes impossible to translate without resorting to long locutions. As an international language—apparently English—becomes more widespread, negotiations between leaders of countries, interventions by third parties, and debates and contructive actions in the United Nations ought to become more fruitful, or at least some misunderstandings can be avoided if the participants are not completely dependent upon simultaneous translations.

For Americans and perhaps to a lesser degree for other peoples in the Western orbit the number and variety of organizations through which contacts with other peoples can be established and even maintained is staggering. In fact, an efficient, typically American catalogue of such groups was once published called *Pathways to Peace*.[68] The pathways are the affiliates of the United Nations, including UNICEF Christmas cards; the exchange of students and scholars (for example, the Institute of International Education); pen pals and foster parents; CARE packages, Boy Scouts and Girl Scouts and Guides; the Peace Corps, Operation Crossroads in Africa, the Experiment in International Living; and so on—on and on. After describing each group and giving its address, the author frequently concludes his unrestrained hymn of praise with a section called "What You Can Do," in which he offers practical, commonsensible suggestions to increase contacts and presumably thus to encourage peace.

The value of culture contacts, however, cannot be uncritically acclaimed (cf. P). On the topic of language just mentioned, it is clear that violent civil wars occur between peoples speaking the same language: the American Civil War; the Catholics and Protestants in Northern Ireland. In fact it has been suggested, without evidence, that the absence of a common language may foster friendly relations: individuals who understand each other with dispatch may also quarrel quite easily; in contrast, they are likely to be "more careful about what they say" when their communications have to be translated.[69] In addition, not only a common language but also a common religion, a common political ideology, and science of all kinds seem to produce unity within a nation but are not associated with peaceful relations between nations.[70] A previously mentioned study of twenty conflicts beginning with the Han dynasty in 125 B.C. and ending with the eighteenth-century struggles between France and England reveals that the exchanges of culturally influential elites (teachers, students, missionaries, royal brides, entertainers, hostages) occurred more frequently during peaceful than during strife-torn decades;[71] but the reliability of these appraisals is open to question, and presumably during a war elites are not likely to travel back and forth. Even when culture contacts occur, it may be very difficult to prove that they have encouraged changes in attitude, for example, in the direction of an increased international perspective (cf.I).[72] The degree to which 114 nations participated in the United Nations (by making voluntary financial contributions in addition to the national assessment, for instance) and in other governmental international organizations was not related to their participation in nongovernmental organizations;[73] thus contacts among elites of these countries apparently did not induce their leaders to function more actively in other groups associated with world government.

Culture contacts, moreover, may boomerang (cf. V). Jet-travelling tourists may not like the country they visit. Individuals in the host country may be appalled by the behavior of the visitors and then may consider them representative of their compatriots back home when in fact such may not be the case.[74] A collection of detailed anthropological studies suggests that the fabric or the basic values of indigenous cultures by and large have been seriously and permanently damaged or at any rate changed by tourists (two Eskimo communities, the Tonga in Polynesia, a town in the Spanish Basque country, a French Alpine community, three North Carolina coastal towns, Jews in Iran before the downfall of the Shah). Elsewhere, however, the effects can be called at least temporarily beneficial in terms of increased economic opportunities, a strengthening of cultural identity, and a revival of artistic traditions (the Balinese, the Toraja of Indonesia, the Indians of the Southwest in the United States); in other societies at the present time the repercussions are uncertain (the Cuna Indians of Panama, a Catalan community in northwestern Spain). The same studies reveal that generally persons in the host country stereotype their visitors and certainly develop attitudes toward them which may be either friendly or unfriendly.[75]

Just as United Nations peacekeeping forces do not necessarily acquire a favorable or even an accurate impression of the lands in which they serve (previously mentioned in the last chapter), so it is possible that the ever-growing number of multinational corporations or the intergovernmental organizations may not develop "a world outlook" among their employees or the nationals of the countries they serve.[76] The individuals who coordinate and regulate railroad and airplane traffic between adjacent countries or who facilitate the movement of supplies during a war[77] confine their contacts to the task at hand without necessarily improving the political relations between the governments of their countries. Indeed the very basis for encouraging contacts of any kind can be challenged on two scores. First, it is possible that increased knowledge leads to arrogance and not to humility, and so perhaps some nations remain at peace "precisely because they do not understand each other very well."[78] As a summary of the attempts to lessen ethnic prejudice in the United States suggests, contact may produce change in either direction, and the direction in turn is determined by the conditions under which the contact is made, whether favorable or unfavorable; for example, the previous attitudes and expectations of the interacting groups affect the outcome.[79] A propitious contact, it has also been suggested in the same context, is more likely to occur when the individuals or groups have similar status and seek common goals.[80] In addition, some individuals fear the unknown, and consequent contact may reduce such fears; but war may be waged more blithely against persons with whom one is well acquainted for the very reason that they are regarded as "adversaries who can be beaten and are worth beating."[81] In short, contact can be double-edged and, even when friendly attitudes are created among followers or between leaders of government, the understanding on one level does not necessarily produce corresponding changes on the other.[82]

NOTES

1. Cf. Oran R. Young, *The Intermediaries*. Princeton: Princeton University Press, 1967. Pp. 51-61.

2. Study Group on the Peaceful Settlement of International Disputes, *Report*. London: David Davies Memorial Institute, 1966. Pp. 19-22.

3. Leonard W. Doob, *Public Opinion and Propaganda*. New York: Holt, 1948. Pp. 307-08.

4. Glen H. Snyder and Paul Diesing, *Conflict among Nations*. Princeton: Princeton University Press, 1977. P. 317.

5. Salvador de Madariaga, Blueprint for a world commonwealth. In Carnegie Endowment for International Peace (ed.), *Perspectives on Peace 1910-1960*. Pp. 47-64.

6. Leonard W. Doob, *Becoming More Civilized*. New Haven: Yale University Press, 1960. Pp. 200-1.

7. Karl Mannheim, *Man and Society in an Age of Reconstruction*. New York: Harcourt, Brace and World, 1940. P. 123. Psychologists' manifesto. In Gardner Murphy (ed.), *Human Nature and Enduring Peace*. Boston: Houghton Mifflin, 1945. Pp. 454-60.

8. Charles L. Taylor and Michael C. Hudson, *World Handbook of Political and Social Indicators*. New Haven: Yale University Press, 1971. Pp. 1, 4.

9. Melvin Kranzberg, Science, technology, and the unity of mankind. In W. Warren Wagar (ed.), *History and the Idea of Mankind*. Albuquerque: University of New Mexico Press, 1971. Pp. 135-58.

10. John Bostock, Australia. In George W. Kisker (ed.), *World Tension*. New York: Prentice-Hall, 1951. Pp. 1-14.

11. William A. Scott, Psychological and social correlates of international images. In Herbert C. Kelman (ed.), *International Behavior*. New York: Holt, Rinehart and Winston, 1965. Pp. 71-103.

12. Trond Ålvik, The development of views on conflict, war, and peace among school children. *Journal of Peace Research*, 1968, 5, 171-95.

13. Harold D. Lasswell, *World Politics and Personal Insecurity*. New York: McGraw-Hill, 1935. P. 251.

14. Norman Z. Alcock, *The Emperor's New Clothes*. Oakville: CPRI Press, 1971. P. 9.

15. Ferdinand Durand, *Des Tendances Pacifiques de la Société Européene et due Rôle des Armées dan L'Avenir*. New York: Garland Publishing, 1972. P. 117, my translation.

16. John Demeter and Kevin Marion, Peace studies courses. *Peace Research Review*, 1974, 6, no. 1, 1-96.

17. Cornell University, *Graduate Study in Peace Science*. Announcements, 1979-1980.

18. Rafiq M. Khan (ed.), *Proceedings of the International Peace Research Association*, 1975. Oslo: International Peace Research Association, 1975. Pp. 43-52.

19. Hadley Cantril (ed.), *Tensions that Cause Wars*. Urbana: University of Illinois Press, 1950. Pp. 18-19.

20. Sue Carroll, George Lakey, William Mayer, and Richard Taylor, Organizing for social transformation. In Charles R. Beitz and Theodore Herman (eds.), *Peace and War*. San Franciso: W. H. Freeman, 1973. Pp. 415-24.

21. Robert J. Havinghurst, The educational problem. In George B. de Huszar (ed.), *New Perspectives on Peace*. Chicago: University of Chicago Press, 1944. Pp. 162-78.

22. Douglas Heath, What education for a more violent world? *American Association of University Women Journal*, 1970, 63, 160-65.

23. William Eckhardt, Crosscultural theories of war and aggression. *International Journal of Group Tensions*, 1972, 2, no. 3, 36-51.

24. Cf. Hans Vaihinger, *The Philosophy of "As If."* New York: Harcourt, Brace, 1925.

25. Cf. James G. Miller, Psychological approaches to the prevention of war. In Wayne Dennis (ed.), *Current Trends in Social Psychology*. Pittsburgh: University of Pittsburgh Press, 1948. Pp. 274-99.

26. Cf. Ralph K. White, Three not-so-obvious contributions of psychology to peace. *Journal of Social Issues*, 1969, 25, no. 4, 3-39.

27. Cf. Irving L. Janis and M. Brewster Smith, Effects of education and persuasion on national and international images. In Kelman (ed.), op. cit., pp. 190-235.

28. Cf. Martin Oppenheimer and George Lake, *A Manual for Direct Action*. Chicago: Quadrangle Books, 1964. P. 15. This Quaker-inspired manual summarizes nonviolent methods in behalf of civil rights, many of which, as outlined in Chapter Appendix 7.3, can also be employed in connection with war-peace.

29. Milton J. Rosenberg, Images in relation to policy. In Kelman (ed.), op. cit., pp. 278-334.

30. Angus Campbell, Philip E. Converse, and Willard L. Rodgers, *The Quality of American Life*. New York: Russell Sage Foundation, 1976. Pp. 269-70.

31. Linus Pauling, A report from the scientific participants in the convocation. In Edward Reed (ed.), *Beyond Coexistence*. New York: Grossman, 1968. Pp. 233-38.

32. Carl I. Hovland, Irving L. Janis, and Harold H. Kelley, *Communication and Persuasion*. New Haven: Yale University Press, 1953. Pp. 56-96.

33. Charles E. Osgood, Graduated unilateral initiatives for peace. In Quincy Wright, William E. Evan, and Morton Deutsch (eds.), *Preventing World War III*. New York: Simon and Schuster, 1962. Pp. 161-77.

34. Yasumasa Kuroda, Peace-war orientation in a Japanese community. *Journal of Peace Research*, 1966, 3, 380-88.

35. Clinton Pettus and Edward Diener, Factors affecting the effectiveness of abstract *versus* concrete information. *Journal of Social Psychology*, 1977, 103, 233-42.

36. Rainer Kabel, *Mobilmachung zum Frieden*. Tübingen: Katzmann Verlag, 1971. P. 101.

37. Ithiel de Sola Pool, *Symbols of Internationalism*. Stanford: Stanford University Press, 1951. P. 60.

38. Kranzberg, op. cit.

39. Karl W. Deutsch, Mass communication and the loss of freedom in national decision-making. *Journal of Conflict Resolution*, 1957, 1, 200-11.

40. Charles E. Lindblom, *Politics and Markets*. New York: Basic Books, 1977. Pp. 201-13.

41. Isidore Ziferstein, Psychological habituation to war. *American Journal of Orthopsychiatry*, 1967. 37, 457-68.

42. Einar Östgaard, Factors influencing the flow of news. *Journal of Peace Research*, 1965, 2, 39-63.

43. Richard Clutterbuck, *Living with Terrorism*. London: Faber and Faber, 1975. P. 24.

44. Cf. Anders Boserup and Claus Iversen, Demonstrations as a source of change. *Journal of Peace Research*, 1966, 3, 328-48.

45. Albert Bigelow, *The Voyage of the "Golden Rule."* Garden City: Doubleday, 1959.

46. Peter Watson, *War on the Mind*. New York: Basic Books, 1978. Pp. 388-416.

47. Bigelow, op. cit., pp. 241-48.

48. Charles Chatfield (ed.), *Peace Movements in America*. New York: Schocken Books, 1973. P. x.

49. Daniel Frei, *Kriegsverhütung und Friedenssicherung*. Frauenfeld: Verlag Huber, 1970. Pp. 31-32.

50. John Somerville, *The Peace Revolution*. Westport: Greenwood, 1975. Pp. 155-56.

51. Clarence K. Streit, *Freedom's Frontier*. New York: Harpers, 1961. P. 42.

52. R. M. MacIver, *Towards an Abiding Peace*. New York: Macmillan, 1943. P. 6.

53. Leonard W. Doob, *Public Opinion and Propaganda*, op. cit., pp. 285-89.

54. Garcia Robles, cited in *UNITAR News*, 1978, 10, p. 11.

55. Arnold Simoni, *Beyond Repair*. New York: Macmillan, 1972. P. 152.

56. Gordon W. Allport, The role of expectancy. In Hadley Cantril (ed.), op. cit., pp. 43-78.

57. H. P. Hendrikx, Some comments on the prospects of the world university. In Khan (ed.), op. cit., p. 330.

58. Timmothy G. Plax and Lawrence B. Rosenfeld, Individual differences in the credibility and attitude change relationship. *Journal of Social Psychology*, 1980, 79-89, 111.

59. Melvin J. Lerner, The effect of preparatory action on beliefs concerning nuclear wars. *Journal of Social Psychology*, 1965, 65, 225-31.

60. Michael H. Banks, A. J. R. Groom, and A. N. Oppenheim, International crisis gaming. *Proceedings of the International Peace Research Association*, 1968, 1, 85-124. Cf. Leonard Berkowitz, *Aggression*. New York: McGraw-Hill, 1962. P. 254.

61. Robert M. Liebert, John M. Neale, and Emily S. Davidson, *The Early Window*. New York: Pergamon Press, 1973. Pp. 44-48.

62. Lawrence A. Fehr, Media violence and catharsis in college females. *Journal of Social Psychology*, 1979, 109, 307-8.

63. Erich Maria Remarque, *All Quiet on the Western Front*. Boston: Little, Brown, 1929.

64. Joseph Heller, *Catch-22*. New York: Simon and Schuster, 1961.

65. R. Zajonc, Attitudinal effects of mere exposure. *Journal of Personality and Social Psychology, Monograph Supplement*, 1968, 9, no. 2, pt. 2, 1-27.

66. Rudolf Kalin and J. W. Berry, Geographic mobility and ethnic tolerance. *Journal of Social Psychology*, 1980, 29-34, 112.

67. Lloyd Cook, *Intergroup Education*. Westport: Greenwood, 1954. Pp. 322-24.

68. Russell D. Brackett, *Pathways to Peace*. Minneapolis: T. S. Denison, 1965.

69. Kenneth E. Boulding, Integrative aspects of the international system. In Proceedings of the International Peace Research Association (ed.), *Inaugural Conference*. Assen: Van Gorcum, 1966. Pp. 27-38.

70. Ibid. Also Anatol Rapoport, Two views on conflict. In Proceedings of the International Peace Research Association (ed.), op. cit., pp. 78-99.

71. Raoul Naroll, Vern L. Bullough, and Frada Naroll, *Military Deterrence in History*. Albany: State University of New York Press, 1974. Pp. 334-35.

72. Stephen Bochner, Anli Lin, and Beverly M. McLeod, Cross-cultural contact and the development of an international perspective. *Journal of Social Psychology*, 1979, 107, 29-41.

73. Michael P. Sullivan, International organizations and world order. *Journal of Conflict Resolution*, 1978, 22, 105-20.

74. Ithiel de Sola Pool, Effects of cross-national contact on national and international images. In Kelman (ed.), op. cit., pp. 106-29.

75. Valene L. Smith (ed.), *Hosts and Guests*. Philadelphia: University of Pennsylvania Press, 1977.

76. Kurt P. Tudyka, Peace research and multinational corporations. In Khan (ed.), op. cit., pp. 203-12.

77. David Mitrany, *A Working Peace System*. Chicago: Quadrangle Books, 1966. P. 70.

78. Kenneth N. Waltz, *Man, the State and War*. New York: Columbia University Press, 1954. P. 48.

79. Yehuda Amir, Contact hypothesis in ethnic relations. *Psychological Bulletin*, 1969, 71, 319-42.

80. Thomas F. Pettigrew, Racially separate or together? *Journal of Social Issues*, 1969, 25, 43-69.

81. Watson, op. cit., p. 442.

82. C. Wright Mills, *The Causes of World War Three*. New York: Simon and Schuster, 1958. P. 76.

11.
Whither? How?

Perversely this chapter must be the shortest of all, although it is perhaps the most important. For after all the gloomy statements, all the critical comments concerning war-peace generalizations, and all the unanswered rhetorical questions, a timid approach will be made to the problem of basic reform which requires (a) changing human beings into *homines pacifici* and (b) creating the societal conditions that facilitate the emergence of such persons (cf. P).* All else is relatively superficial and can be considered only temporary, palliative means toward these ends. Essential as they are, the peacekeeping and peacemaking—but not the peacebuilding—apparatus of United Nations and of other international organizations as well as increased education, communication, and contact can achieve a more enduring peace only when socialization practices and the economic and political order have been altered.

We dare not, however, adopt a Cassandra-like stance and look askance at these makeshift means: they save lives and every human life is or ought to be precious. And they reduce misery during this present period of war and violence and hence during the lifespan of those who will die before peace can be pursued more vigorously and before the millennium moves a bit closer. Yes, let us outlaw nuclear and other devices. Let us. But will we, can we, and what will they—whoever they are—do? While it may be true, consequently, as suggested in the last sentence of a brilliant critique of just and unjust wars, that "the restraint of war is the beginning of peace,"[1] it is essential to focus our wrath and indignation upon the phenomenon of war itself and not to be distracted completely by moral judgments concerning the means men adopt to fight wars, evil as these means also can be. War is the villain, armaments are only deadly assistants.

---

*See pages 11-12 for an explanation of the cross-referencing system.

Again and again in these pages reference has been made to the ways in which individuals are formed during their early years and to the need to avoid the frustrations they endure as a result of the milieu in which they live. The two are interrelated: parents whose milieu enables them to achieve their significant goals are likely to rear children who, when they become adults, will not be war-prone. One can argue either way: change the milieu in order to change the parents, or change parents in order to change the milieu. Both must be accomplished simultaneously (cf. P).

Although uncertainties persist, I have maintained, we gradually seem to be acquiring the skill enabling us to rear nonaggressive adults. Some knowledge exists, although in practice success is never guaranteed. We have guides from the great religions, from elusive utopias, from the Society of Friends, and from some of our greatest intellectual predecessors concerning the goals we seek in human terms. Perhaps we are less certain of the desirable personality and personality traits than we are of the behavior that is sought. It may seem old-fashioned or utopian to look to the nursery for part of our salvation, but out of the nursery all of us emerge and then as leaders, influentials, and followers we have some impact, for better or worse, upon our society and hence upon present and future generations. We realize full well that we shall always have diversity, diversity among human beings and societies. Hence *homo pacificus* is a literary myth, *homines pacifici* of various kinds are conceivably real.

What we do not know is how to improve the economic and political structure for mankind so that there will be greater equity, less suffering, profounder respect for human rights (cf. I). As individuals, as members of organizations we struggle to find solutions for our economic and political ills; and panaceas are offered by reformers, utopianists, and advocates of diverse economic and political systems. We know that starvation, suffering, even injustice usually spring either from real scarcity or from the exploitation of a large group by a small one, yet we are not certain how to rid ourselves of such evils. The evils appear overpowering even when we are able to admire a stirring landscape, an infant's eagerness, an intellectual accomplishment, a classical sonata, and a magnificent painting. How should we proceed?

This book has grappled frequently, and always I think unsuccessfully, with the problem of the just war (cf. I). It takes no great imagination to point to the evils of violence and war, but completely baffling, I think, is the discovery of the circumstances under which deviations from the principles of nonviolence or pacifism become justified. As a shrewd and experienced observer has reminded us, "there will always from time to time be crazy demagogues like Hitler and technological surprises like the invention of gunpowder or of nuclear weapons,"[2] as a result of which some kind of defense in the form of counterviolence becomes essential. The same observer proposes, "roughly," what he calls a "middle ground" that "allows killing in self-defense but forbids the purposeless massacre of innocents":

Bombers are bad. Fighter airplanes and anti-aircraft missiles are good. Tanks are bad. Anti-tank missiles are good. Submarines are bad. Anti-submarine technology is good. Nuclear weapons are bad. Radar and sonar are good. Intercontinental missiles are bad. Anti-ballistic missile systems are good.

The flavor of the proposal is all that need be conveyed, for the details—like those embodied in any ideology or scheme—are obscure; thus "it is often true that the best anti-tank weapon is a tank and the best anti-submarine weapon a submarine."

The challenge of course is how to attain peace without running the risk of losing the benefits of peace as a result of the machinations of others. There may be protected oases such as Switzerland which "maintains a citizen army . . . posing no threat to its neighbors but ready to fight like hell against anybody who comes with dreams of conquest,"[3] but for the super-powers that country looks as far away from realization as the Sermon on the Mount, exquisite to contemplate as a model but impossible to attain. Impossible? Yes, I think so, or at least until basic reforms within all countries are achieved. And so the eternal questions are unavoidable, even if men everywhere are prepared to recognize a distinction between war and limited violence, even if they are immune from rationalizing their wars by calling them limited in scope. Is there a contradiction between a thought expressed in one sentence by the chief executive in a message to Congress ("There is no more important responsibility for me as President than ensuring the safety and security of our nation") and one proclaimed a few sentences later in the same message ("To prevent war—and to redirect the resources of nations from arsenals of war to human needs—will be a formidable challenge to all mankind in this last quarter of the 20th Century")?[4] Must there be a revolution with a consequent loss of life and possible terror and repression in postrevolutionary days? Should the change be gradual with the strong possibility that those who profit from the evils inflicted on others will never relinquish their power significantly? What sacrifices are the few willing, perhaps also able to make in order to change mankind? Will those in power ever come to realize that to attain their goals war is "inferior to other available means"?[5] These questions are not rhetorical, though as ever they have been rhetorically phrased; and there are no answers to them unless we choose to suffer from the delusion that paradise is attainable or can be easily attained. That is why this chapter has not indeed dispelled the gloom and is so brief, why *homines pacifici* and the good society are elusive, but why both must ever by pursued. Yes, indeed, "a man's reach should exceed his grasp, or what's a heaven for?"

NOTES

1. Michael Walzer, *Just and Unjust Wars*. New York: Basic Books, 1977. P. 335.

2. Freeman Dyson, Reflections: disturbing the universe: III. *New Yorker*, 20 August 1979, 36-80.

3. Ibid.

4. Jimmy Carter in U. S. Arms Control and Disarmament Agency, *Arms Control 1978*. Washington: U. S. Arms Control and Disarmament Agency, 1979. P. ii.

5. Cf. W. Fred Cottrell, Research to establish the conditions of peace. *Journal of Social Issues*, 1955, 11, no. 1, 13-20.

Appendixes

1   PROPOSITIONS

Individual Reality

1. Human nature is sufficiently plastic to give rise to the noble or ignoble behavior associated with *homo pacificus* or *maleficus*.

2. Aggressive impulses and behavior result largely from prior frustrations.

3. Frustration-aggression sequences provide a clue only to limited aspects of war-peace.

4. Belligerency or aggressiveness toward another country increases when individuals believe that failing to arm, to capture or regain a territory, or to win a war means that their important values might not survive or prevail.

5. The threat of war or of protracted hostilities arouses previously reinforced beliefs which then become simplified and polarized and which are likely to influence behavior.

6. War-peace beliefs tend to resist change unless they are contradicted by forceful events.

7. Patriotic attitudes have deep psychological roots and therefore a national orientation is likely to be both strong and salient in most persons from time to time.

8. Skill in hurting others must often be learned.

9. No variable affecting personality ordinarily operates in isolation.

National Reality

10. Nationals are likely to believe that they and their peers share a common cultural and historical background as well as many cultural traits, especially when they use the same language.

11. The leaders of every sovereign government believe they have the right to declare war under circumstances they themselves have the privilege to specify.

12. The more "primitive" the society, the less inclined to wage war its inhabitants are likely to be.

13. The greater the political centralization in a society, the higher the degree of military sophistication.

14. The greater a country's military expenditures, the greater the probability it will go to war.

15. Conditions within a society have a greater effect on foreign policy and war-peace than relations between states.

16. The greater the modal gratification or nonfrustration during socialization, the less the tendency for persons in a society to be war-prone.

International Reality

17. Economic explanations of war provide a setting for war-peace, but fail to distinguish between predisposing and precipitating causes.

18. Precipitating causes of war are numerous and are weighted differently in each conflict.

19. The role of leaders varies with their own personalities and capabilities, their interaction with followers and influential peers, and their relevant out-groups.

20. War-peace judgments and decisions are not likely to be made "rationally."

21. Before or immediately after declaring war, leaders must convince their followers, perhaps also their enemies, that they are going to be, or have been attacked and hence a just war must be waged.

22. On the surface war seems to offer more positive attractions than peace.

23. Present peace machinery would perhaps be adequate if modern states were to refer their disputes to the appropriate peacemaking or peacekeeping organization and if they were then to abide by its resolutions or decisions.

Individual Perfection

24. Plans for the future usually assume that some persons or groups will be improved.

25. Perfect persons arise and flourish under all conditions, but *homines pacifici* are more likely to appear in a "favorable" environment.

26. Every society postulates and tries to achieve ideal human beings.

27. The world's great religions foster doctrines praising peace and tranquility and condemning war and violence, but otherwise their value systems diverge.

28. *Homines pacifici* reject the belief that war is inevitable and accept the belief that peace is feasible.

29. Expressing aggressive impulses on occasion may lead to catharsis, but can be counterproductive from a social standpoint.

30. Plasticity or the absence of both dogmatism and rigidity are traits promoting the learning necessary to prevent harmful or false stereotypes from seeming to validate a false conception of reality.

National and International Perfection

31. The imagination needed to create utopias is stimulated by hope and despair.

32. According to utopianists, leaders and followers can consider themselves not nationalists but citizens of the world without losing their patriotism.

33. Views about war-peace can be extracted from men and women perhaps everywhere; usually a world without war can be imagined, however vaguely and uncertainly.

34. Each generation responds to similar golden thoughts repeated in language suited to its own needs and problems.

35. Utopias assume some degree of ethical relativity.

36. The five freedoms (from want, of speech and expression, to worship God in one's own way, from fear, and to enjoy life) are closely inter-related and interdependent.

37. Inequality in any society is inevitable, but all the basic and many of the derived needs of everyone must be satisfied.

38. Every ethical or practical principle guiding action is likely to require exceptions and not to be universal.

Individual Realization

39. Significant changes in the components of personality and behavior result from learning, unlearning, and relearning which usually occur slowly.

40. Human beings possess the potentiality of becoming less imperfect than they are.

41. Traits considered desirable in later life must usually be developed during childhood.

42. The success of parents and others who act as models for children depends upon the degree to which they themselves are willing and able to discharge those roles effectively.

43. A degree of frustration inevitably accompanies socialization.

44. Peace requires the sacrifice of some "ideals" associated with war and unrealizable by peaceful equivalents.

45. Individuals are more likely not to discharge aggressive impulses against their fellowmen or to wage war if they have strong beliefs and attitudes opposing violence and war.

46. Inspiring credos, though imperfectly implemented, can help promote peace.

47. Conflicts between individuals, groups, or countries are inevitable and may occasionally be useful.

48. Any significant action in behalf of peace involves potential difficulties and risks.

National Realization

49. Some persons or groups must make sacrifices if a more universal and lasting peace is to be achieved.
50. Mankind has been trying and experimenting for centuries to find pathways to peace.
51. Under some circumstances social change is rapid.
52. Policy makers are likely to take into account the relativity of values and practices.
53. Changes in individuals required to resolve the war-peace problem are wrought through an interaction between leaders' initiatives and followers' needs.
54. Wars ultimately result from so many different causes that peace is not likely to be realized after one particular reform.
55. At present, research findings in the war-peace sphere seldom affect policy decisions.
56. No scientific, infallible guides to disarmament and deterrence exist.
57. On occasion violence may be required to achieve desirable ends.
58. Diminished ego- and ethnocentrism are likely to produce less jingoistic patriotism and less rigid adherence to the doctrine of unlimited sovereignty.

International Realization

59. Official negotiators are constrained by a host of factors.
60. Leaders are more likely to settle disputes peacefully if the values and way of life of their peoples are compatible than under the reverse conditions.
61. Changes within individuals are likely to occur when they have been transplanted out of their usual milieu, when they have been induced to view a situation quite differently from the way they have viewed it in the past or the present, or when a central change within them has repercussions for their other values and attitudes.
62. The immediate successes apparently achieved by mediators and intervenors in workshops may have no appreciable effect upon the conflicts they would resolve.
63. Conflicts between individuals or groups may be resolved when the issues are placed in peaceful rather than unpeaceful categories.
64. Some type of world organization is widely believed to be indispensable to the pursuit of peace.
65. Moral principles and standards of conduct are more likely to be accepted by governments when they are legally enforced.
66. International organizations come into existence and function effectively only when officials of the participating governments share significant values.

67. Peacekeeping since World War II has been a substitute for collective security.

68. Effective peacekeeping may delay effective peacemaking and peace-building.

Communication

69. Communication cannot resolve conflicts that appear intractable, but it is a component of virtually all war-peace problems.

70. Beliefs and attitudes regarding war-peace are transmitted through formal schooling, informal instruction, various social institutions, and the mass media.

71. New, credible information often has the capability of changing attitudes.

72. *Homines pacifici* seek to be as rational as possible by understanding the outside forces affecting their judgments.

73. Most persons tend to avoid reality, including what they can perceive in the mass media, when it is unpleasant and affects them directly.

74. In democratic countries a reciprocal relation exists between the mass media and public opinion.

75. Knowledge concerning the effective ways to influence individuals progressively increases without being adequately utilized in behalf of peace.

76. Communication about peace in the contemporary world is inadequate.

77. Culture contacts in the interest of establishing or reinforcing friendly relations between peoples of different countries can have negative as well as positive consequences.

Whither? How?

78. Basic reform to achieve peace requires changing human beings into *homines pacifici* and creating the societal conditions that facilitate the emergence of such persons.

79. In seeking basic reforms, the milieu must be changed in order to change parents, and parents must be changed in order to change the milieu.

2   VARIABILITY-UNIQUENESS

Person-to-Person

1. Susceptibility to aggression
2. Goals achieved or protected by war
3. Aggression- and war-proneness
4. Learning of beliefs and attitudes
5. Skill of leaders
6. Personality traits
7. Ability to kill
8. Correlates of attitudes
9. Patriotism
10. Relation of leaders and followers
11. Personality of leaders
12. Leaders' reasons for selecting ways to resolve conflicts
13. Deviation from modal personalities
14. Attributes of existing *homines pacifici*
15. Origins of *homines pacifici*
16. Individual differences in utopia
17. Simulation
18. Components of every negotiation
19. Personality factors in negotiations
20. Techniques of negotiations
21. Operating procedures of a United Nations Peacekeeping Force Commander
22. Qualifications of mediators and intervenors
23. Role of violence in the mass media
24. Effects of culture contacts

Group-to-Group

25. Salience of war-peace
26. Patriotism
27. Predisposing causes of war-peace
28. Controls to produce nonviolence
29. Hospitality of physical environments
30. Formal warfare in traditional societies
31. Precipitating causes of war
32. Effects of science fiction on wars
33. Relations of leaders and followers
34. Values in various religions
35. Proposed reforms to attain peace
36. Details concerning human rights
37. Desirable attributes of leaders
38. Equivalence of societies for research purposes
39. Significance of past events
40. Massacres in the past
41. Conditions favoring nonviolence
42. Fruitful international cooperation on specific issues
43. Prominence of information promoting peace

3   EXTRAPOLATION

Inferences

1. From neurotic patients to participants in war
2. From animal to human aggressiveness
3. From attitudes to behavior

From the Past or Present to the Future

4. Persistence of war
5. Nature of war
6. Correlates of war
7. Failures of deterrence
8. Causes of war
9. Decisions of leaders
10. Declarations concerning human rights
11. Vigilance of leaders
12. Successful or unsuccessful resolution of conflicts
13. Course of conflicts
14. Appeasement in the past
15. Devices to increase bargaining power
16. Successes of limited nonviolence
17. Inevitability of patriotism
18. Relation of war-peace and international organizations
19. Assessment and behavior of peacekeepers

4   IGNORANCE

1. Precise nature of human nature
2. Differences between apparent and real aggressiveness
3. Detailed relation between socialization practices and adult personality
4. Exact reasons for changes in attitudes, beliefs, and actions
5. Components of leaders' skills
6. Measurement of attitudes
7. Persons responsible for crucial decisions in conflict situations
8. Feasibility of generalizations concerning war-peace conditions
9. Interpretation of correlation between military expenditures and wars
10. Conditions in childhood promoting gratification
11. Determination of values placed upon violence in a society
12. Influence of poverty upon unrest and war-peace
13. Factors affecting socialization practices
14. Identifying some leaders
15. Motives of leaders
16. Consequences of leaders' decisions
17. Leaders' reasons for selecting ways to resolve conflicts
18. Forecasting war-peace
19. Leaders' decisions concerning escalation
20. Halting infinite regress concerning perfect people and perfect societies
21. Sources for postulating human perfection
22. Sources for postulating human rights
23. Happiness of slaves
24. Effects of equality of opportunity
25. Evaluating values
26. Origins of nonaggressive behavior

27. Desirable traits of *homines pacifici*
28. Details of events affecting behavior
29. Cultivating peace-prone leaders
30. Methods for testing "Moral Equivalent of War"
31. Optimal contents of a modern credo
32. Selection of optimum nonviolent attributes
33. Enemy's military potential
34. Achieving a balance of power
35. Consequences of nondeterrence
36. Guides to disarmament and deterrence
37. Optimal conditions for negotiations
38. Long-term effects of intervention
39. Effects of mediation
40. Anticipated consequences of conflicts
41. Qualifications of peacekeepers
42. Assessing attributes of peacekeepers
43. Effectiveness of "hot lines" between leaders
44. Optimal amount of anxiety to avoid war
45. Effects of international propaganda
46. Effects of science fiction on war-peace
47. Value of culture contacts
48. Ways to improve the economic and political structures of societies
49. Problem of the just war

5   MULTIVARIANCE

1. Reductionist explanations of war-peace
2. Motives tapped by war
3. Variables characterizing personality
4. Relation between attitudes and action
5. Generalizations concerning modern warfare
6. Causal factors in war-peace
7. Theories concerning war-peace
8. Decisions of leaders
9. Interactions of groups
10. Events affecting behavior
11. Interchangeability of goals
12. Selection of nonviolent techniques
13. Historical events in general
14. Realization of peace
15. Simulation of solutions to the problem of multivariance
16. Adoption of national policies
17. Success or failure of nonviolence
18. Factors affecting negotiations
19. Techniques of negotiation

Extremely Eclectic Bibliography

Aiken, William and Hugh LaFollette (eds.). *World Hunger and Moral Obligation* (Englewood Cliffs: Prentice-Hall, 1977).

Akindele, R. A. *The Organization and Promotion of World Peace* (Toronto: University of Toronto Press, 1976).

Berman, Maureen R. and Joseph E. Johnson (eds.). *Unofficial Diplomats* (New York: Columbia University Press, 1977).

Brook, David (ed.). *Search for Peace* (New York: Dodd, Mead, 1970).

Burton, John W. *Peace Theory* (New York: Knopf, 1962).

Campbell, John C. *Successful Negotiation* (Princeton: Princeton University Press, 1976).

Cantril, Hadley (ed.). *Tensions that Cause Wars* (Urbana: University of Illinois Press, 1950.

Centre de Sociologie de la Guerre (ed.). *La Paix par la Recherche Scientifique*. (Brussels: Éditions de l'Institut de Sociologie, 1970).

Choucri, Nazli and Robert C. North. *Nations in Conflict* (San Francisco: W. H. Freeman, 1975).

Christ, Franz. *Gestalt und Geschichte des europäischen Friedengedankens* (Ronco-Ascona, Tessin: Verlag des Andragogiums, 1968).

Clutterbuck, Richard. *Living with Terrorism* (London: Faber and Faber, 1975).

Coste, R. *Dynamique de la Paix* (Paris: Desclée, 1965).

Curle, Adam. *Making Peace* (London: Tavistock Publications, 1971).

Dedring, Jeurgen. *Recent Advances in Peace and Conflict Research* (Beverly Hills: Sage Publications, 1976).

Doob, Leonard W. *Patriotism and Nationalism* (Westport, Conn.: Greenwood Press, 1976).

Doob, Leonard W. (ed.). *Resolving Conflict in Africa* (New Haven: Yale University Press, 1970).

Druckman, Daniel. *Human Factors in International Negotiations* (New York: Academy for Educational Development, 1971).

Erasmus, Desiderius. *The Education of a Christian Prince* (New York: Columbia University Press, 1936).

Falk, Richard A. *A Study of Future Worlds* (New York: Free Press, 1975).

Fein, Helen. *Accounting for Genocide* (New York: Free Press, 1979).

Fisher, Roger (ed.). International Conflict and Behavioral Science (New York: Basic Books, 1964).

Fisher, Roger and William Ury. *International Mediation* (New York: International Peace Academy, 1978).

Frank, Jerome D. *Sanity and Survival* (New York: Random House, 1968).

Frei, Daniel. *Kriegsverhütung und Friedenssicherung* (Frauenfeld: Verlag Huber, 1970).

Galtung, John. Peace, *International Encylopedia of the Social Sciences* 11 (1968): 487-96.

Haas, Ernst B. *Human Rights and International Action* (Stanford: Stanford University Press, 1970).

Iklé, Fred Charles. *Every War Must End* (New York: Columbia University Press, 1971).

International Peace Academy. *Peacekeeper's Handbook* (New York: International Peace Academy, 1978).

Jervis, Robert. *Perception and Misperception in International Problems* (Princeton: Princeton University Press, 1976).

Kabel, Rainer. *Mobilmachung zum Frieden* (Tübingen: Katzmann, 1971).

Kateb, George. *Utopia and its Enemies* (Glencoe: Free Press, 1973).

Kelman, Herbert C. (ed.). *International Behavior* (New York: Holt, Rinehart and Winston, 1965).

Larson, Arthur (ed.). *A Warless World* (New York: McGraw-Hill, 1963).

McDougal, Myres S. and Florentino P. Feliciano. *Law and Minimum World Public Order* (New Haven: Yale University Press, 1961).

Mannheim, Karl. *Man and Society in an Age of Reconstruction* (New York: Harcourt, Brace and World, 1940).

May, Mark A. *A Social Psychology of War and Peace* (New Haven: Yale University Press, 1943).

Melko, Matthew. *52 Peaceful Societies* (Oakville, Ontario: CPRI Press, 1973).

Montagu, Ashley. *Learning Non-Aggression* (New York: Oxford University Press, 1978).

Moskos, Charles C., Jr. *Peace Soldiers* (Chicago: University of Chicago Press, 1976).

Mumford, Lewis. The Story of Utopias (New York: Boni and Liveright, 1922).

Naroll, Raoul, Vern L. Bullough, and Frada Naroll. *Military Deterrence in History* (Albany: State University of New York Press, 1974).

Nelson, Keith L. and Spencer C. Olin, Jr. *Why War?* (Berkeley: University of California Press, 1979).

Ornauer, H., H. Wiberg, A. Siciński, and J. Galtung (eds.). *Images of the World in the Year 2000* (Mouton, The Hague: Humanities Press, 1974).

Osgood, Charles E. *An Alternative to War or Surrender* (Urbana: University of Illinois Press, 1962).

Otterbein, Keith F. *The Evolution of War* (New Haven: HRAF Press, 1970).

Pire, Dominique. *Vivre ou Mourir Ensemble* (Brussels: Presses Académiques Européennes, 1969).

Pruitt, Dean G. and Richard C. Snyder (eds.). *Theory and Research on the Causes of War* (Englewood Cliffs: Prentice-Hall, 1969).

Rikhye, Indar Jit, Michael Harbottle, and Bjørn Egge. *The Thin Blue Line* (New Haven: Yale University Press, 1974).

Röling, Bert V. A. *Einführung in die Wissenschaft von Krieg und Frieden* (Neukirchen-Vluyn: Neukirchener Verlag, 1970).

Russett, Bruce M. (ed.). *Peace, War, and Numbers* (Beverly Hills: Sage Publications, 1972).

Sharp, Gene. *Exploring Nonviolent Alternatives* (Boston: Porter Sargent, 1970).

Singer, J. David and Melvin Small. *The Wages of War, 1816-1965* (New York: Wiley, 1972).

Smith, Valene L. (ed.). *Hosts and Guests* (Philadelphia: University of Pennsylvania Press, 1977).

Somerville, John. *The Peace Revolution* (Westport, Conn.: Greenwood Press, 1975).

Tolstoy, Leo. *War and Peace* (New York: Penguin Books, 1957).

Waltz, Kenneth N. *Man, the State and War* (New York: Columbia University Press, 1954).

Walzer, Michael. *Just and Unjust Wars* (New York: Basic Books, 1977).

Watson, Peter, *War on the Mind* (New York: Basic Books, 1978).

Wright, Quincy. *A Study of War* (Chicago: University of Chicago Press, 1965).

Wright, Quincy, William E. Evan, and Morton Deutsch (eds.). *Preventing World War III* (New York: Simon and Schuster, 1962).

Yarrow, C. H. Mike. *Quaker Experiences in International Conciliation* (New Haven: Yale University Press, 1978).

Young, Oran R. *The Politics of Force* (Princeton: Princeton University Press, 1968).

Index

The page numbers in *italics* indicate the text pages on which a note reference is made without mentioning the author's name; full citations appear at the end of the chapter.

ABOUT THE AUTHOR

LEONARD W. DOOB is Sterling Professor Emeritus of Psychology and Senior Research Scholar at the Institution for Social and Policy Studies at Yale University. He has conducted seminars for military and diplomatic personnel for the International Peace Academy, and has organized workshops for groups in the Horn of Africa, Northern Ireland, and other conflict areas. He is editor of the *Journal of Social Psychology*. His many books include *Panorama of Evil* (Greenwood Press, 1978) and *Ezra Pound Speaking* (Greenwood Press, 1978).